Newtonian Studies

ALEXANDRE KOYRÉ

Newtonian Studies

PHOENIX BOOKS

The University of Chicago Press

The University of Chicago Press, Chicago 60637

Contents

CONTENTS

Preface

The following collection of Newtonian Studies comprises essays written during the last dozen years, each illustrating a different aspect of Newton's scientific thought. Although each one was written separately and is to be considered independent of all the others, the ensemble is, nevertheless, unified by more than the mere fact that each essay deals with an aspect of the thought of the same man. The central theme is the illustration by means of conceptual analysis of the way in which fundamental scientific ideas are at the same time related to the main currents of philosophical thought and yet determined by empirical controls.

All of these essays save one ("Newton and Descartes") have been previously published, but each is here presented with some additional material. This may consist of slight revisions, additions to bring certain discussions up to date in the light of current research, or in some cases merely the citation of recent studies which may add new dimensions to several of the points discussed.

Three of the essays, "Newton, Galileo, and Plato," "Newton's 'Regulae Philosophandi,' " and "Concept and Experience in Newton's Scientific Thought" (originally "L'Hypothèse et l'expérience chez Newton"), first printed in French, are given here in English translation. "Newton and Descartes," hitherto unpublished, is based on the third Horblit Lecture on the History of Science at Harvard University. I should like to express my thanks to Mr. Mark M. Horblit, founder of these lectures, and the Committee on History of Science at Harvard University for the privilege of having been invited to participate in this series. For publication I have greatly expanded the text of the lecture and have added a considerable number of notes and appendices. This study explores but a small part, although a most significant one, of the relations between these two great men. It does not go into any details concerning a number of obvious contacts between Newton and Descartes. For instance, I do not study the relations between the geometry of Descartes and the geometrical methods of Newton which were conceived on the Greek model.

Finally, I should like to express my gratitude to those who have helped to prepare the manuscript for book publication, Professor I. B. Cohen of Harvard University, Mrs. Helen R. Kessler and Mr. Edward J. Collins of Cambridge, Massachusetts and Mme. Mimica Cranaki Belaval of Paris.

A. KOYRÉ

Paris, 20 January 1964

Professor Koyré died in Paris on 28 April 1964. Prior to his death, he had carefully gone over each chapter, revising the typescript of "Newton and Descartes," checking the translations of the French articles, and expanding and rewriting considerable portions of the articles printed in English. Thus the versions published here represent his final wishes.

Newtonian Studies

I

The Significance
of the Newtonian Synthesis

It is obviously utterly impossible to give in a brief space a detailed history of the birth, growth, and decay of the Newtonian world view. It is just as impossible even to give a reasonably complete account of the work performed by Newton himself.[1] Thus, by necessity, I am obliged to restrict myself to the very essentials and to give the barest outline of the subject. Moreover, in doing so I will assume a certain amount of previous knowledge. It is, I believe, a legitimate assumption, because, as a matter of fact, we all know something about Newton, much more, doubtless, than we know about any of the other great scientists and philosophers whose common effort fills the seventeenth century – the century of genius, as Whitehead has called it.

We know, for instance, that it is to Newton's insight and experimental genius – not *skill*: others, for instance, Robert Hooke, were just as skilled, or even more so than he – that we owe the idea of decomposition of light and the first scientific theory of spectral colors;[2] that it is to his deep philosophical mind that we owe the

[1] The best general account of Newton's scientific work is still F. Rosenberger, *I. Newton und seine physikalischen Principien* (Leipzig, 1895). See, however, H. W. Turnbull, *The Mathematical Discoveries of Newton* (London: Blackie, 1945); S. I. Vavilov, *Isaac Newton* (Moscow: Akademiia Nauk, 1943), German translation (Berlin: Akademie-Verlag, 1951); and I. B. Cohen, *Franklin and Newton* (Philadelphia: The American Philosophical Society, 1956). The best biography is L. T. More's *Isaac Newton* (New York and London: Scribner, 1934).

[2] The production of spectral colors by crystals and drops of water, and the concomitant theory of the rainbow, has a long history and even prehistory behind it extending through the Middle Ages to antiquity. In the seventeenth century it had been studied chiefly by Marcus Antonius de Dominis, *De radiis visus et lucis in vitris perspectivis et iride tractatus* (Venice, 1611); by Descartes in "Dioptrique" and "Météores," essays appended to his *Discours de la méthode* (Leiden, 1637); by Marcus Marci, *Thaumanthias, liber de arcu coelesti deque colorum apparentium natura* (Prague, 1648); by F. M. Grimaldi, *Physico-mathesis de lumine, coloribus et iride* (Bologna, 1665); and especially by Robert Boyle, *Experiments and Considerations Upon Colours* (London, 1664), and Robert Hooke, *Micrographia: or some Physiological Descriptions of Minute Bodies made by Magnifying Glasses* (London, 1665). To Newton belongs not the discovery of the phenomenon, but (1) the application of exact measurements to its study and (2) its

3

formulation – though not the discovery – of the fundamental laws of motion[1] and of action, together with the clear understanding of the method and meaning of scientific inquiry; that it was his invention of the calculus that enabled him to demonstrate the identity of terrestrial and celestial gravitation and to find out the fundamental law of attraction that binds – or at least until recently bound – together the smallest and the largest bodies – stars and atoms – of the infinite Universe. We know too, of course, that it is not to him, but to his great rival Leibniz,[2] that we owe *de facto* the actual spread and development of the infinitesimal calculus, without which the gradual extension and perfection of the Newtonian *systema mundi* would be impossible.

Besides, all of us, or if not all still most of us, have been born and bred – or better and more exactly, not *born* (as this is impossible) but only *bred* – in the Newtonian or, at least, a semi-Newtonian world, and we have all, or nearly all, accepted the idea of the Newtonian world machine as the expression of the true picture of the universe and the embodiment of scientific truth – this because for more than two hundred years such has been the common creed, the *communis opinio*, of modern science and of enlightened mankind.

Thus it seems to me that I have the right to assume that when we are speaking about Newton and Newtonianism we know more or less what we are speaking of. More or less! Somehow this very expression used in connection with Newton strikes me as improper, because it is possible that the deepest meaning and aim of Newtonianism, or rather, of the whole scientific revolution of the seven-

---

explanation as a decomposition (and recomposition) of white light into its colored components by the prism, in contradistinction to the pre-Newtonian conception that explained the appearance of the spectral colors by a process of qualitative change suffered by white light in its passage through a prism. On the history of that question see Vasco Ronchi, *Storia della luce* (Bologna: Zanichelli, 1939; 2nd ed., 1952), and Roberto Savelli, "Grimaldi e la rifrazione," *Cesalpina*, 1951.

[1] The laws of motion owe their discovery to Galileo and Descartes. See my *Études galiléennes* (Paris: Hermann, 1939); also R. Dugas, *Histoire de la mécanique* (Paris: Éditions Dunod, 1950), and *La Mécanique au XVIIᵉ siècle* (Paris: Éditions Dunod, 1954), and A. R. Hall, *The Scientific Revolution* (London: Longmans, Green, 1954).

[2] Nobody doubts today the complete independence of Leibniz's invention of the differential calculus; nobody has ever doubted the superiority of the Leibnizian symbolism. See H. G. Zeuthen, *Die Geschichte der Mathematik im XVI. and XVII. Jahrhundert* (Leipzig: Teubner, 1903); C. B. Boyer, *The Concepts of the Calculus* (New York: Columbia University Press, 1939; 2nd ed., New York: Hafner, 1949). Therefore it is very interesting to note that Professor Hadamard believes it to be just as inferior to the Newtonian one as the conception of the "differential" is to that of the "fluxion." See Jacques S. Hadamard, "Newton and the Infinitesimal Calculus," in the Royal Society of London, *Newton Tercentenary Celebration* (Cambridge, England: University Press, 1947), pp. 35–42.

teenth century, of which Newton is the heir and the highest expression, is just to abolish the world of the "more or less," the world of qualities and sense perception, the world of appreciation of our daily life, and to replace it by the (Archimedean) universe of precision, of exact measures, of strict determination.

Let us dwell for a moment upon this revolution, one of the deepest, if not the deepest, mutations and transformations accomplished – or suffered – by the human mind since the invention of the cosmos by the Greeks, two thousand years before.[1] This revolution has been described and explained – much more explained than described – in quite a number of ways. Some people stress the role of experience and experiment in the new science, the fight against bookish learning, the new belief of modern man in himself, in his ability to discover truth by his own powers, by exercising his senses and his intelligence, so forcefully expressed by Bacon and by Descartes, in contradistinction to the formerly prevailing belief in the supreme and overwhelming value of tradition and consecrated authority.

Some others stress the practical attitude of modern man, who turns away from the *vita contemplativa*, in which the medieval and antique mind allegedly saw the very acme of human life, to the *vita activa;* who therefore is no longer able to content himself with pure speculation and theory; and who wants a knowledge that can be put to use: a *scientia activa, operativa*, as Bacon called it, or, as Descartes has said, a science that would make man master and possessor of nature.[2]

The new science, we are told sometimes, is the science of the craftsman and the engineer, of the working, enterprising, and calculating tradesman, in fact, the science of the rising bourgeois classes of modern society.[3]

There is certainly some truth in these descriptions and explana-

[1] See my "Galileo and the Scientific Revolution of the Seventeenth Century," *Philosophical Review 52* (1943), 333–348.

[2] Philosophers are often inclined to misjudge the situation of contemporary philosophical positions and – when dealing with the past – to forget that, as often as not and even more often than not, philosophical (and religious) teachings are not so much *expressing* as *opposing* the prevailing trends of their time.

[3] The psychosociological explanations of the rise of modern science present us usually with a mixture of two by no means equivalent theories: (1) modern science is the offshoot of the technical development of the sixteenth and seventeenth centuries; it was made by technicians, civil and especially military engineers (Leonardo, Stevinus), by the *proti* of the Arsenal of Venice, and so on; and (2) modern science is made by scientists who, because of the increasing importance of technics and the growing significance of the bourgeoisie in the sixteenth and seventeenth centuries, started thinking about problems of industry that they had persistently neglected since Archimedes' time. Both these theories seem to me to miss (1) the role of purely theoretical interest in mathematics which led to – and was maintained by – the rediscovery of Greek science,

tions: it is clear that the growth of modern science presupposes that of the cities, it is obvious that the development of firearms, especially of artillery, drew attention to problems of ballistics; that navigation, especially that to America and India, furthered the building of clocks, and so forth – yet I must confess that I am not satisfied with them. I do not see what the *scientia activa* has ever had to do with the development of the calculus, nor the rise of the bourgeoisie with that of the Copernican, or the Keplerian, astronomy. And as for experience and experiment – two things which we must not only distinguish but even oppose to each other – I am convinced that the rise and growth of experimental science is not the source but, on the contrary, the result of the new *theoretical,* that is, the new *metaphysical* approach to nature that forms the content of the scientific revolution of the seventeenth century, a content which we have to understand before we can attempt an explanation (whatever this may be) of its historical occurrence.

I shall therefore characterize this revolution by two closely connected and even complementary features: (*a*) the destruction of the cosmos, and therefore the disappearence from science – at least in principle, if not always in fact – of all considerations based on this concept,[1] and (*b*) the geometrization of space, that is, the substitution

---

and (2) the overwhelming importance of the study, and the autonomous evolution, of astronomy, promoted much less by practical needs, such as the determination of longitude at sea, than by theoretical interest in the structure of the universe. Besides, they forget that mathematicians and astronomers (not to speak of experimental physicists) need money as much as (or even more than) theologians and jurists and are therefore likely to stress the practical value of their work in order to "sell" their science to wealthy and ignorant patrons. This kind of propaganda is by no means a feature of the twentieth century: it had already begun in the sixteenth. It is chiefly to his skill and value as propagandist (*buccinator*) that Bacon owed his popularity among the seventeenth- and eighteenth-century scientists. The psychosociological (Marxist and semi-Marxist) theory is to be found at its best in F. Borkenau, *Der Uebergang vom feudalen zum bürgerlichen Weltbild* (Paris: Alcan, 1934); B. Hessen, "The Social and Economic Roots of Newton's *Principia*," in *Science at the Cross-roads: Papers Presented to the International Congress of the History of Science and Technology Held in London, 1931*, by the delegates of the U.S.S.R. (London: Kniga, 1931); and E. Zilsel, "The Sociological Roots of Science," *American Journal of Sociology 47* (1942), 544–562. For criticism see G. N. Clark, *Science and Social Welfare in the Age of Newton* (London: Oxford University Press, 2nd ed., 1949); H. Grossmann, 'Die gesellschaftlichen Grundlagen der mechanistischen Philosophie und die Manufaktur," *Zeitschrift für Sozialforschung*, 1935, pp. 161 sq. See equally P. M. Schuhl, *Machinisme et philosophie* (Paris: Presses Universitaires de France, 1938; 2nd ed., 1947), and my papers "Les Philosophes et la machine," *Critique 23* (1948), 324–333 and 27: 610–629; and "Du monde de l'à peu près à l'univers de la précision," *Critique 28* (1948), 806–823, reprinted in *Études d'histoire de la pensée philosophique* (Paris: Armond Colin, 1961).

[1] As we shall see, Newtonian science, or at least the Newtonian world view, asserted the purposeful character of the world (solar system). It *did not* explain its features by deducing them from a purpose. Kepler still used this pattern of explanation.

of the homogeneous and abstract – however now considered as real – dimension space of the Euclidean geometry for the concrete and differentiated place-continuum of pre-Galilean physics and astromony.

As a matter of fact, this characterization is very nearly equivalent to the mathematization (geometrization) of nature and therefore the mathematization (geometrization) of science.

The disappearance – or destruction – of the cosmos means that the world of science, the real world, is no more seen, or conceived, as a finite and hierarchically ordered, therefore qualitatively and onto-logically differentiated, whole, but as an open, indefinite, and even infinite universe, united not by its immanent structure but only by the identity of its fundamental contents and laws;[1] a universe in which, in contradistinction to the traditional conception with its separation and opposition of the two worlds of becoming and being, that is, of the heavens and the earth, all its components appear as placed on the same ontological level; a universe in which the *physica coelestis* and *physica terrestris* are identified and unified, in which astronomy and physics become interdependent and united because of their common subjection to geometry.[2]

This, in turn, implies the disappearance – or the violent expulsion – from scientific thought of all considerations based on value, per-fection, harmony, meaning, and aim, because these concepts, from now on *merely subjective*, cannot have a place in the new ontology. Or, to put it in different words: all formal and final causes as modes of explanation disappear from – or are rejected by – the new science and are replaced by efficient and even material ones.[3] Only these

[1] Geometrization of space implies necessarily its infinitization: we cannot assign limits to Euclidean space. Accordingly, the destruction of the cosmos can be charac-terized – as by Miss M. Nicolson – as "the breaking of the circle," or – as by myself – as "the bursting of the sphere."

[2] See my *Études galiléennes* and "Galileo and Plato," *Journal of the History of Ideas 4* (1943), 400–428, reprinted in Philip Wiener and Aaron Noland, eds., *Roots of Scientific Thought* (New York: Basic Books, 1957).

[3] It has often been said that modern science is characterized by the renunciation of the search for causes and restriction to that of laws. Yet, as has been shown by P. Duhem, *ΣΩZEIN TA ΦAINOMENA, Essai sur la notion de la théorie physique de Platon à Galilée* (Paris: Hermann, 1908), *La Théorie physique: Son object, sa structure* (Paris: Chevalier and Rivière, 1906), this "positivistic" attitude is by no means modern but was widely represented in Greek and also medieval astronomy and philo-sophy, which, as often as not, considered the circles, eccentrics, and epicycles of Pto-lemy as pure mathematical devices and not as physical realities. The chief advocate of that view in the Middle Ages was Averroes; as for Ptolemy himself, he seems to adopt it in his *Almagestum (Mathematical Syntax)*, though not in his *Hypotheses of the Planets*. On the other hand, as was conclusively shown by E. Meyerson, *Identité et réalité* (Paris: Vrin, 5th ed., 1951), trans. Kate Loewenberg as *Identity and Reality*

latter have right of way and are admitted to existence in the new universe of hypostatized geometry and it is only in this abstract-real (Archimedean) world, where abstract bodies move in an abstract space, that the laws of being and of motion of the new – the classical – science are valid and true.

It is easy now to understand why classical science – as has been said so often – has substituted a world of quantity for that of quality: just because, as Aristotle already knew quite well, there are no qualities in the world of numbers, or in that of geometrical figures. There is no place for them in the realm of mathematical ontology.

And even more. It is easy now to understand why classical science – as has been seen so seldom – has substituted a world of being for the world of becoming and change: just because, as Aristotle has said too, there is no change and no becoming in numbers and in figures.[1] But, in doing so, it was obliged to reframe and to reformulate or rediscover its fundamental concepts, such as those of matter, motion, and so on.

If we take into account the tremendous scope and bearing of this so deep and so radical revolution, we shall have to admit that, on the whole, it has been surprisingly quick.

It was in 1543 – one hundred years before the birth of Newton – that Copernicus wrested the earth from its foundations and hurled it into the skies.[2] It was in the beginning of the century (1609 and 1619) that Kepler formulated his laws of celestial motions and thus destroyed the orbs and spheres that encompassed the world and held it together;[3] and did it at the same time that Galileo, creating the first scientific instruments and showing to mankind things that no human

---

(New York: Dover, 1962), and *De l'explication dans les sciences* (Paris: Payot, 1921), this renunciation has always been temporary, and scientific thought has always attempted to penetrate behind the laws and to find out the "mécanisme de production" of the phenomena. I could add that on one hand it was just the search for causal laws of the celestial motions which led Kepler to his "New Astronomy" conceived as *Celestial Physics*, and on the other hand, that the absence of any theory of gravity led Galileo to the erroneous conception of gravitation as constant force.

[1] Thus Newton's *Opticks* denies the existence of any qualitative change in the light passing through a prism: the prism acts only as a sieve; it disentangles a mixture and sorts out the different rays which compose the white light, already present as such, in the mixture in which it consists. According to Newton, the prism experiment, like every good experiment, reveals something which is already there; it does not produce anything new.

[2] *De revolutionibus orbium coelestium* (Nuremberg, 1543).

[3] The first two in the *Astronomia nova ΑΙΤΙΟΛΟΓΗΤΟΣ sive physica coelestis tradita commentariis de motibus stellae martis* (1609); the third one in the *Harmonices mundi* (Lincii, 1619).

eye had ever seen before,[1] opened to scientific investigation the two connected worlds of the infinitely great and the infinitely small.

Moreover, it was by his "subjecting motion to number" that Galileo cleared the way for the formulation of the new concepts of matter and motion I have just mentioned, which formed the basis of the new science and cosmology;[2] concepts with the aid of which – identifying matter and space – Descartes, in 1637,[3] tried, and failed, to reconstruct the world; concepts that – redistinguishing between matter and space – Newton so brilliantly, and so successfully, used in his own reconstruction.

The new concept of motion which so victoriously asserts itself in the classical science is quite a simple one, so simple that, although very easy to use – once one is accustomed to it, as we all are – it is very difficult to grasp and fully to understand. Even for us, I cannot analyze it here,[4] yet I would like to point out that, as Descartes quite clearly tells us, it substitutes a purely mathematical notion for a physical one and that, in opposition to the pre-Galilean and pre-Cartesian conception, which understood motion as a species of becoming, as a kind of process of change that affected the bodies subjected to it, in contradistinction to rest, which did not, the new – or classical – conception interprets motion as a kind of being, that is, not as a process, but as a *status*, a *status* that is just as permanent and indestructible as rest[5] and that no more than this latter affects the bodies that are in motion. Being thus placed on the same ontological level, being deprived of their qualitative distinction, motion and rest become indistinguishable.[6] Motion and rest are still – and even

---

[1] *Sidereus nuncius* (Venice, 1610).

[2] *Dialogo . . . sopra i due massimi sistemi del mondo* (Florence, 1632) and *Discorsi e dimostrazioni intorno à due nuove scienze* (Leiden, 1638).

[3] *Discours de la méthode pour bien conduire sa raison et chercher la verité dans es sciences* (Leiden, 1637) and *Principia philosophiae* (Amsterdam, 1644); but already in 1629 and 1630 in his unpublished "Monde ou traité de la lumière."

[4] See my *Études galiléennes*.

[5] Motion, therefore, persists *sua sponte* – just like rest – not needing for its persistence either an external or an internal motor, or cause. Accordingly, it persists changeless – as change implies a cause – that is, with the same speed, and in the same direction; it is to this kind of motion – rectilinear and uniform – that Newton applied the term "inertial"; see Chapter III, "Newton and Descartes." The term "inertia" originated with Kepler, who gave it the meaning of "resistance to change." Accordingly, motion for Kepler being a change, *inertia* is resistance to motion; for Newton, for whom motion is no longer change, *inertia* is the force of resistance to (positive or negative) acceleration and change of direction.

[6] The equivalence of rectilinear motion and rest is asserted by Descartes *expressis verbis*. In the Newtonian physics *relative* motion and rest are equivalent; *absolute* motion and rest, of course, are not. Unfortunately, they remain indistinguishable, at least for us, if not for God.

more than ever – opposed to each other, but their opposition becomes a pure correlation. Motion and rest no longer exist in the
bodies themselves; bodies are only in rest or in motion in respect to
each other, or to the space in which they exist, rest, and move; motion and rest are relations, though, at the same time, they are considered as *states*. It is this conception (of the inner difficulties of which
Newton was doubtless quite aware) that carries – and perhaps under-
mines – the magnificent structure of classical science and it is about
this motion that in his famous first law or axiom Newton tells us that
*corpus omne perseverare in statu suo quiescendi vel movendi uniform-
iter in directum nisi quatenus a viribus impressis cogitur statum illum
mutare.*[1]

The motion dealt with in this law is not the motion of the bodies
of our experience; we do not encounter it in our daily lives. It is the
motion of geometrical (Archimedean) bodies in abstract space. That
is the reason why it has nothing to do with change. The "motion"
of geometrical bodies in geometrical space changes nothing at all;
the "places" in such a space are equivalent and even identical. It is
a changeless change, if I may say so, a strange and paradoxical blend-
ing together of the same and the other that Plato tried – and failed
– to effect in his *Parmenides*.

The transformation of the concept of motion by substituting for
the empirical concept the hypostatized mathematical one is inevitable if we have to subject motion to number in order to deal with
it mathematically, to build up a mathematical physics. But this is
not enough. Conversely, mathematics itself has to be transformed
(and to have achieved this transformation is the undying merit of
Newton). Mathematical entities have to be, in some sense, brought
nearer to physics, subjected to motion, and viewed not in their
"being" but in their "becoming" or in their "flux."[2]

The curves and figures of geometry have to be seen, and understood, not as built up of other geometrical elements, not as cut out
in space by the intersection of geometrical bodies and planes, nor

[1] "Every body perseveres in its state of rest, or of uniform motion in a right line, unless it is compelled to change that state by forces impressed upon it" (Isaac Newton,
Philosophiae naturalis principia mathematica, axiomata sive leges motus, Lex I). According to this law, whereas *motion* is a state, *acceleration* is a change. Circular motion,
being an accelerated one because it implies a continuous change of direction, is, therefore, easily recognizable and distinguishable from rest. E. Mach in his famous criticism
of Newton seems to have overlooked this simple fact; see *The Science of Mechanics*,
trans. T. J. McCormack (La Salle, Illinois: Open Court, 1942), pp. 276–285.

[2] See Hadamard, "Newton and the Infinitesimal Calculus," and Boyer, *The Concepts of the Calculus*.

even as presenting a spatial image of the structural relations expressed in themselves by algebraic formulas, but as engendered or described by the motion of points and lines in space. It is a timeless motion, of course, that we are here dealing with, or, even stranger, a motion in a timeless time – a notion as paradoxical as that of changeless change. Yet it is only by making changeless change proceed in timeless time that we can deal – effectively as well as intellectually – with such realities as speed, acceleration, or direction of a moving body in any point of its trajectory, or, *vice versa*, at any moment of the motion describing that trajectory.

It is a thrilling story, the story of the successful and unsuccessful efforts of the human mind to formulate these new and strange ideas, to build up, or, as Spinoza so pregnantly has said, to *forge*, the new tools and patterns of thinking and of understanding. It fills the fifty years that separate the *Discours de la méthode* from the *Philosophiae naturalis principia mathematica*. A series of great thinkers – to mention only Cavalieri and Fermat, Pascal and Wallis, Barrow and Huygens – had made their contributions to the final success, and without them the *Principia* would not have been written; the task would have been too arduous, even for Newton, *qui genus humanum ingenio superavit*.[1]

Thus, modifying somewhat the celebrated statement of Newton, made in his famous letter to Robert Hooke, we could, with truth, say that if Newton saw as far as he did, and so much farther than anybody had seen before him, it was because he was a giant standing on the shoulders of other giants.[2]

The physicomathematical current I have just been sketching is certainly the most original and most important trend of seventeenth-century scientific thought. Yet, parallel to it there runs another one, less mathematical, less deductive, more empirical and experimental. Being less pretentious (or more diffident), it does not attempt the sweeping generalizations of the mathematicians. It views them with misgiving and even with hostility and it restricts itself to the discovery of new facts and to the building up of partial theories explaining them.

This current is inspired not by the Platonic idea of the mathe-

[1] Zeuthen, *Die Geschichte der Mathematik im XVI. und XVII. Jahrhundert*; L. Brunschvicg, *Les Étapes de la philosophie mathématique* (Paris: Alcan, 1912).
[2] This famous phrase is not Newton's invention, but originates in the Middle Ages with Bernard of Chartres and was used also in the sixteenth and seventeenth centuries; see Chapter V, p. 227, n. 3.

matical structure and determination of being, but by the Lucretian, Epicurean, Democritean conception of its atomic composition (strange as it may seem, most modern ideas lead back to some old Greek fancy). Gassendi, Roberval, Boyle (the best representative of their group), Hooke – they all oppose the more timid, more cautious, and more secure *corpuscular philosophy* to the panmathematism of Galileo and Descartes.[1]

Thus when Galileo tells us that the book of nature – that book in which the medieval mind perceived the *vestigia* and the *imagines Dei* and read the glory of God expressed in sensible symbols of beauty and splendor revealing the hidden meaning and aim of the creation – was, in truth, written in geometrical characters, in circles, triangles, and squares, and only told us the intellectually marvelous story of rational connection and order, Boyle protests: the book of nature, said he, was certainly "a well-contrived romance" of which every part, "written in the stenography of God's omniscient hand," stood in relation to every other; but it was written not in geometrical but in *corpuscular* characters.

Not mathematical structure but corpuscular texture formed for him the inner reality of being. In the explanation of the universe we have to start with – or stop at – matter, not homogeneous Cartesian matter, but matter already formed by God into various, diversely determined corpuscles. These are the letters which motion forms into the words of the divine romance.

Looking at things from this perspective we see quite clearly that Newton presents us with a synthesis of both trends, of both views. For him, just as for Boyle, the book of nature is written in corpuscular characters and words. But, just as for Galileo and Descartes, it is a purely mathematical syntax that binds them together and gives its meaning to the text of the book.

Thus, in contradistinction to the world of Descartes, the world of Newton is conceived as composed not of two (extension and motion) but of three elements: (1) *matter*, that is, an infinite number of mutually separated and isolated, hard and unchangeable – but not identical – particles; (2) *motion*, that strange and paradoxical relation-state that does not affect the particles in their being, but only trans-

[1] See K. Lasswitz, *Geschichte der Atomistik* (Leipzig, 1890), vol. II; R. Lenoble, *Mersenne et la naissance du mécanisme* (Paris: Vrin, 1943); Marie Boas, "The Establishment of the Mechanical Philosophy," *Osiris 10* (1952), 412–541; and E. J. Dijksterhuis, *Die Mechanisierung des Weltbildes* (Berlin: Springer, 1956), trans. C. Dikshoorn as *The Mechanization of the World Picture* (Oxford: Clarendon Press, 1961).

ports them hither and thither in the infinite, homogeneous void; and (3) *space*, that is, this very infinite and homogeneous void in which, unopposed, the corpuscles (and the bodies built of them) perform their motions.[1]

There is, of course, a fourth component in that Newtonian world, namely, attraction which binds and holds it together.[2] Yet this is not an *element* of its construction; it is either a hyperphysical power – God's action – or a mathematical stricture that lays down the rule of syntax in God's book of nature.[3]

The introduction of the void – with its correlative, attraction – into the world view of Newton, in spite of the tremendous physical and metaphysical difficulties involved by this conception (action at a distance; existence of the nothing), was a stroke of genius and a step of decisive importance. It is this step that enabled Newton to oppose and unite at the same time – and to do it *really*, and not *seemingly*, like Descartes – the discontinuity of matter and the continuity of space. The corpuscular structure of matter, emphatically asserted, formed a firm basis for the application of mathematical dynamics to nature.[4] It yielded the *fundamenta* for the relations expressed by space. The cautious corpuscular philosophy did not really know what it was doing. But, as a matter of fact, it had been only showing the way to the Newtonian synthesis of mathematics and experiment.

[1] On Newton's conception of space, see Léon Bloch, *La Philosophie de Newton* (Paris: Alcan, 1908); E. A. Burtt, *The Metaphysical Foundations of Modern Physical Science* (London: Kegan Paul, 1925; 2nd ed., 1932); Hélène Metzger, *Attraction universelle et religion naturelle chez quelques commentateurs anglais de Newton* (Paris: Hermann, 1938); also Max Jammer, *Concepts of Space* (Cambridge, Mass.: Harvard University Press, 1954); Markus Fierz, "Ueber den Ursprung und die Bedeutung der Lehre Isaac Newtons vom absoluten Raum," *Gesnerus 11* (1954), 62–120; and my *From the Closed World to the Infinite Universe* (Baltimore: Johns Hopkins Press, 1957). See also A. J. Snow, *Matter and Gravity in Newton's Physical Philosophy* (New York: Oxford University Press, 1926), and Stephen E. Toulmin, "Criticism in the History of Science: Newton on Absolute Space, Time and Motion," *The Philosophical Review* (1959). Space for Newton (as for Henry More or Thomas Bradwardine) is the eternal realm of God's presence and action – not only his *sensorium* but also, if one may say so, his *actorium*.

[2] To be quite correct, I should mention also the repulsive forces that hold the corpuscles apart and prevent them from gathering together in a cluster. However, these repulsive forces are short-range forces, and, though very important in physics, they play no role in the building of the universe so long as they are not used for the formulation of a theory of aether whose action on the bodies "explains" gravitation; see Chapter III, Apps. A and B.

[3] As a matter of fact, it is both: a hyperphysical power acting according to a strict mathematical law.

[4] The physics of central forces necessarily involves an atomic structure of matter, even if the matter is reduced to mere points, as by Boscovich.

The void... action through the void... action at a distance (attraction) – it was against these features and implications of the Newtonian world view that the opposition of the great Continental contemporaries of Newton – Huygens, Leibniz, Bernoulli – well trained in the Cartesian rejection of unclear and unintelligible ideas, was directed.[1]

In his famous, brilliant *Lettres anglaises*, or, to give them their official title, *Lettres philosophiques*[2] – readable even today – Voltaire very wittily sums up the situation: a Frenchman who arrives in London finds himself in a completely changed world. He left the world *full;* he finds it *empty.* In Paris the universe is composed of vortices of subtle matter; in London there is nothing of that kind. In Paris everything is explained by pressure which nobody understands; in London by attraction which nobody understands either.[3]

Voltaire is perfectly right: the Newtonian world is chiefly composed of void.[4] It is an infinite void, and only a very small part of it – an infinitesimal part – is filled up, or occupied, by matter, by bodies which, indifferent and unattached, move freely and perfectly unhampered in – and through – that boundless and bottomless abyss. And yet it is a world and not a chaotic congeries of isolated and

[1] The criticism of the conception of attraction was made by Descartes in his attack on Roberval, who asserted universal attraction in his *Aristarchi Sami De mundi systemate partibus et motibus eiusdem libellus cum notis. Addictae sunt Æ. P. de Roberval notae in eundem libellum* (Paris, 1644), reissued by Mersenne in his *Novarum observationum physico-mathematicarum* (Paris, 1644), vol. III. Descartes points out (see his letter to Mersenne of 20 April 1646, *Oeuvres,* ed. C. Adam and P. Tannery (Paris, 1897–1913), IV, 401) that, in order to be able to attract body B, body A should know where to find it. Attraction, in other words (as W. Gilbert and also Roberval recognized without considering it an objection), involves animism. (See Chapter III, p. 59, n. 2.)

[2] The *Lettres philosophiques* were published first in English, under the title *Letters Concerning the English Nation* (London, 1733); then in French under the title *Lettres philosophiques par M. de Voltaire* (Amsterdam [in fact Rouen, by Jore], 1734) and *Lettres écrites de Londres sur les anglais par M. de Voltaire* (Basel [in fact London], 1734). Numerous other editions, more or less modified by Voltaire, followed. See the introduction of G. Lanson to his critical edition of these letters: *Lettres philosophiques,* 2 vols. (Paris: Cornely, 1909; 3rd ed., 1924). On Voltaire and Newton see Bloch *La Philosophie de Newton;* Pierre Brunet, *L'Introduction des théories de Newton en France* (Paris: Blanchard, 1931), vol. I; and R. Dugas, *Histoire de la mécanique au XVII siècle* (Paris: Dunod Éditeur, 1954).

It is well known that Voltaire had been converted to Newtonianism by Maupertuis who, as Huygens did for Locke, assured him that the Newtonian philosophy of attraction was true. Maupertuis even agreed to read through the letters (XIV and XV) dealing with Descartes and Newton. On Maupertuis see Pierre Brunet, *Maupertuis* (Paris: Blanchard, 1929).

[3] See letter XIV, Lanson edition, II, 1.

[4] Not only are the heavenly spaces empty and void, but even the so-called "solid bodies" are full of void. The particles that compose them are by no means closely packed together, but are separated from one another by void space. The Newtonians, from Bentley on, took an enormous pride and pleasure in pointing out that "matter" proper occupies a practically infinitesimal part of space.

14

mutually alien particles. This, because all of these are bound together by a very simple mathematical law of connection and integration – the law of attraction – according to which *every one of them is related to and united with every other*.[1] Thus each one takes its part and plays its role in the building of the *systema mundi*.

The universal application of the law of attraction restores the physical unity of the Newtonian universe and, at the same time, gives it its intellectual unity. Identical relations hold together identical contents. In other words, it is the same set of laws which governs all the motions in the infinite universe: that of an apple which falls to the ground[2] and that of the planets which move round the sun. Moreover, the very same laws explain not only the identical pattern (discovered by Kepler) of the celestial motions but even their individual differences, not only the regularities, but also the irregularities (inequalities). All the phenomena which for centuries baffled the sagacity of astronomers and physicists (such, for instance, as tides) appear as a result of the concatenation and combination of the same fundamental laws.

The Newtonian law of attraction according to which its force *diminishes* in proportion to the square of the distance is not only the only law of that kind that explains the facts but, besides, is the only one that can be uniformly and universally applied to large and small bodies, to apples and to the moon. It is the only one, therefore, that it was reasonable for God to have adopted as a law of creation.[3]

Yet, in spite of all this, in spite of the rational plausibility and

[1] According to Newton, only these corpuscular attractions, whatever they may be, are real. Their resultants are by no means real forces, but only "mathematical" ones. Thus, it is not the earth that attracts the moon, but each and every particle of the earth attracts each and every particle of the moon. The resultant global attraction has no other than mathematical existence.

[2] The famous story according to which Newton's thinking on gravitation had been aroused by the sight of an apple falling to the ground, which has been treated as legend by generations of historians, appears to be perfectly true, as has been convincingly demonstrated by J. Pelseneer in "La Pomme de Newton," *Ciel et terre 53* (1937), 190–193; see also *Lychnos* (1938), 366–371. See also I. B. Cohen, "Authenticity of Scientific Anecdotes," *Nature 157* (1946), 196–197, and D. McKie and G. R. de Beer, "Newton's Apple," *Notes and Records of the Royal Society 9* (1951–52), 46–54, 333–335.

[3] The inverse-square law of the diminishing of attraction with distance is the only one which makes possible a direct comparison between the earth's attraction of an apple and the earth's attraction of the moon, because it is the only one according to which the earth, or, generally, a spherical body, attracts all external bodies, irrespective of their distance from it, as if all its mass were concentrated in its center. It is true that it shares this mathematical property with another law, namely the one according to which the force of attraction increases proportionally to the distance. But as in this case all celestial bodies would accomplish their circuits in the same time, it is obviously not the law of our world.

mathematical simplicity of the Newtonian law (the inverse-square law is simply the law of extension of spherical surfaces identical with that of the propagation of light), there was in it something that baffled the mind. Bodies attract each other, act upon each other (or, at least, behave as if they did). But how do they manage to perform this action, to overcome the chasm of the void that so radically separates and isolates them from each other? We must confess that nobody, not even Newton, could (or can) explain, or understand, this *how*.

Newton himself, as we well know, never admitted attraction as a "physical" force. Time and again he said, and repeated, that it was only a "mathematical force," that it was perfectly impossible – not only for matter but even for God – to act at a distance, that is, to exert action where the agent was not present; that the attractive force, therefore – and this gives us a singular insight into the limits of the so-called Newtonian empiricism – was not to be considered as one of the essential and fundamental properties of bodies (or matter), one of these properties such as extension, mobility, impenetrability, and mass, which could neither be diminished nor increased;[1] that it was a property to be explained; that he could not do it,[2] and that, as he did not want to give a fanciful explanation when lacking a good theory, and as science (mathematical philosophy of nature) could perfectly well proceed without one, he preferred to give none (this is one meaning of his celebrated *Hypotheses non fingo*), and leave the question open.[3] Yet, strange, or natural, as it may seem, nobody – with the single exception of Colin Maclaurin – followed him in that point. The very first generation of his pupils (Cotes, Keill, Pemberton) accepted the force of attraction as a real, physical, and even primary property of matter and it was their doctrine which swept over Europe and which was so strongly and persistently opposed by Newton's Continental contemporaries.

[1] A property which can be neither increased nor diminished belongs to the essence of the thing.

[2] As a matter of fact he tried – three times – to do it, that is, to explain attraction by aetherical pressure. See Philip E. B. Jourdain, "Newton's Hypotheses of Ether and Gravitation," *The Monist 25* (1915).

[3] The famous *Hypotheses non fingo* of the General Scholium of his second edition of the *Principia* does not mean a condemnation of all hypotheses in science but only of those that cannot be proved or disproved by mathematically treated experiment, specifically, of global qualitative explanations such as were attempted by Descartes. This pejorative meaning of the term coexists in Newton with a nonpejorative one (in the first edition of the *Principia* the axioms or laws of motion are called *hypotheses*) and is certainly inherited by him from Barrow and Wallis, or even from Galileo.

Newton did not admit action at a distance. Yet, as Maupertuis and Voltaire very reasonably pointed out, from the point of view of purely empirical knowledge (which seemed to be the point of view of Newton), the ontological distinction between the attraction and the other properties of bodies could not be' justified. We do not, of course, understand attraction. But do we understand the other properties? Not understanding is not a reason to deny a fact.[1] Now attraction is a fact. Thus we have to admit it just as we are admitting other facts or properties of bodies. Who knows, besides, what unknown properties we may discover as pertaining to them? Who knows with what sort of properties God has endowed matter?

The opposition to Newtonianism – understood as *physics* – was in the beginning deep and strong. But gradually it crumbled away.[2] The system worked and proved its worth. And as for attraction, progressively it lost its strangeness. As Mach has very finely expressed it, "the uncommon incomprehensibility became a common incomprehensibility." Once used to it, people – with very few exceptions – did not speculate about it any more. Thus fifty years after the publication, in 1687, of the *Philosophiae naturalis principia mathematica* – a title just as daring and just as consciously challenging as the *Physica coelestis* of Kepler eighty years earlier or the *Évolution créatrice* of Bergson two hundred years later – the leading physicists and mathematicians of Europe – Maupertuis, Clairaut, D'Alembert, Euler, Lagrange, and Laplace – diligently began the work of perfecting the structure of the Newtonian world, of developing the tools and methods of mathematical and experimental investigation (Desaguliers, s'Gravesande, and Musschenbroek),[3] and of leading it from success to success, till, by the end of the eighteenth century, in the *Mécanique analytique* of Lagrange and the *Mécanique céleste* of Laplace, the Newtonian science seemed to reach its final and definitive perfection – such a perfection that

---

[1] For Malebranche as well as for Locke, all action of a body upon another – communication of motion – was understandable.

[2] See Brunet, *L'Introduction des théories de Newton en France*, vol. I.

[3] J. T. Desaguliers, *Physicomechanical Lectures* (London, 1717), in French translation (Paris, 1717); *A System of Experimental Philosophy* (London, 1719); *A Course of Experimental Philosophy* (London, 1725; 2nd ed. in 2 vols., London, 1744–1745); W. J. s'Gravesande, *Physices elementa mathematica experimentis confirmata, sive introductio ad philosophiam Newtonianam*, 2 vols. (Leiden, 1720–1721); *Philosophiae Newtonianae institutiones* (Leiden, 1728); *Éléments de physique ou introduction à la philosophie de Newton* (Paris, 1747); Petrus Musschenbroek, *Epitome elementorum physicomathematicorum* (Leiden, 1726); *Elementa physices* (Leiden, 1734). See Pierre Brunet, *Les Physiciens hollandais et la méthode expérimentale en France au XVIII siècle* (Paris: Blanchard, 1926).

Laplace could proudly assert that his *System of the World* left no astronomical problem unsolved.

So much for the mathematicians and scientists. As for the others, for those who could not understand the difficult intricacies of geometrical and infinitesimal reasoning and who, like Locke (reassured by Huygens), took them for granted, there came forth a series of books – and very good ones – such as Pemberton's *View of Sir Isaac Newton's Philosophy* (London, 1728; French translation, Paris, 1755), Voltaire's *Lettres philosophiques* (1734) and *Éléments de la philosophie de Newton* (Amsterdam, 1738), Algarotti's *Il Newtonianismo per le dame* (Naples [Milan], 1737; 2nd ed., 1739; French translation, Paris, 1738), Colin Maclaurin's *Account of Sir Isaac Newton's Philosophical Discoveries* (London, 1746; French translation, Paris, 1749),[1] Euler's *Lettres à une princesse d'Allemagne* (St. Petersburg, 1768–1772), and finally Laplace's *Système du monde* (1796), which in a clear and accessible language preached to the *honnête homme*, and even to the *honnête femme*, the Newtonian gospel of mathematicophysical and experimental science.

No wonder that (in a curious mingling with Locke's philosophy) Newtonianism became the scientific creed of the eighteenth century,[2] and that already for his younger contemporaries, but especially for posterity, Newton appeared as a superhuman being[3] who, once and for ever, solved the riddle of the universe.

Thus it was by no means in a spirit of flattery but in that of deep and honest conviction that Edmund Halley wrote, *nec fas est propius Mortali attingere Divos*.[4] Did not, a hundred years later, Laplace, somewhat regretfully, assign to the *Principia* the pre-eminence above all other productions of the human mind? Indeed, as Lagrange somewhat wistfully put it, there being only one universe to be explained, nobody could repeat the act of Newton, the luckiest of mortals.

Small wonder that, at the end of the eighteenth century, the century that witnessed the unfettered progress of Newtonian science, Pope could exclaim:

[1] All these books, when not written in French, were immediately translated into it and thus made accessible to all educated people throughout Europe.

[2] For Voltaire, as well as for Condorcet, Locke and Newton represent the summits of science and philosophy.

[3] It is well known that the Marquis de L'Hôpital asked – quite seriously – if Newton ate and slept like other mortals.

[4] "Nearer the gods no mortal may approach"; "Isaac Newton, an Ode," trans. Leon J. Richardson in *Sir Isaac Newton's Mathematical Principles of Natural Philosophy*, trans. Andrew Motte, ed. Florian Cajori (Berkeley: University of California Press, 1947), p. xv.

> Nature and nature's laws lay hid in night:
> God said, Let Newton be! and all was light.

Pope could not know indeed that

> 'T was not for long: for Devil, howling, "Ho,
> Let Einstein be!" restored the *status quo*.

But let us now come back to Newton. It has often been said that the unique greatness of Newton's mind and work consists in the combination of a supreme experimental with a supreme mathematical genius. It has often been said, too, that the distinctive feature of the Newtonian science consists precisely in the linking together of mathematics and experiment, in the mathematical treatment of the phenomena, that is, of the experimental or (as in astronomy, where we cannot perform experiments) observational data. Yet, though doubtless correct, this description does not seem to me to be a complete one: thus there is certainly much more in the mind of Newton than mathematics and experiment; there is, for instance – besides religion and mysticism – a deep intuition for the limits of the purely mechanical interpretation of nature.[1] And as for Newtonian science, built, as I have already mentioned, on the firm basis of corpuscular philosophy, it follows, or, better, develops and brings to its utmost perfection, the very particular logical pattern (by no means identical with mathematical treatment in general) of atomic analysis of global events and actions, that is, the pattern of reducing the given data to the sum total of the atomic, elementary components (into which they are in the first place dissolved).[2]

The overwhelming success of Newtonian physics made it practically inevitable that its particular features became thought of as essential for the building of science – of any kind of science – as such, and that all the new sciences that emerged in the eighteenth century – sciences of man and of society – tried to conform to the Newtonian pattern of empirico-deductive knowledge, and to abide by the rules laid down by Newton in his famous *Regulae philosophandi*, so often quoted and so often misunderstood.[3] The results of

---

[1] It seems to me quite certain that Newton arrived at the conclusion that a purely mechanical explanation of attraction was perfectly impossible because, in order to do so, he had to postulate another – less awkward, yet still nonmechanical – power, namely, that of repulsion.

[2] Thus (see p. 15, n. 1) the global effect of a body acting upon another body is the sum total of atomic actions.

[3] On the *Regulae philosophandi*, see Chapter VI.

this infatuation with Newtonian logic, that is, the results of the un-critical endeavor mechanically to apply Newtonian (or rather *pseudo* Newtonian) methods to fields quite different from that of their original application, have been by no means very happy, as we shall presently see. Yet, before turning our attention to these, in a certain sense illegitimate, offshoots of Newtonianism, we have to dwell for a moment upon the more general and more diffuse consequences of the universal adoption of the Newtonian synthesis, of which the most important seems to have been the tremendous reinforcement of the old dogmatic belief in the so-called "simplicity" of nature, and the reintroducing through science into this very nature of very impor-tant and very far-reaching elements of not only *factual* but even *struc-tural* irrationality.

In other words, not only did Newton's physics use *de facto* such obscure ideas as power and attraction (ideas suggesting scholasti-cism and magic, protested the Continentals), not only did he give up the very idea of a rational deduction of the actual composition and formation of the choir of heaven and furniture of earth, but even its fundamental dynamic law (the inverse-square law), though plausible and reasonable, was by no means necessary, and, as Newton had carefully shown, could be quite different.[1] Thus, the law of attraction itself was nothing more than a mere fact.

And yet the harmonious insertion of all these facts into the rational frame of spatiomathematical order, the marvelous *compages* of the world, seemed clearly to exclude the subrationality of chance, but rather to imply the suprarationality of motive; it seemed perfectly clear that it had to be explained not by the necessity of cause, but by the freedom of choice.

The intricate and subtle machinery of the world seemed obviously to require a purposeful action, as Newton did not fail to assert. Or, to put it in Voltaire's words: the clockwork implies a clockmaker (*l'horloge implique l'horloger*).

Thus the Newtonian science, though as *mathematical philosophy of nature* it expressedly renounced the search for causes (both physi-cal and metaphysical), appears in history as based on a dynamic conception of physical causality and as linked together with theistic or deistic metaphysics. This metaphysical system does not, of course, present itself as a constitutive or integrating part of the New-

---

[1] Newton, *Mathematical Principles of Natural Philosophy*, Book I, Theorem IV, Corr. 3–7.

tonian science; it does not penetrate into its formal structure. Yet it is by no means an accident that not only for Newton himself, but also for all the Newtonians – with the exception only of Laplace – this science implied a reasonable belief in God.[1]

Once more the book of nature seemed to reveal God, an engineering God this time, who not only had made the world clock, but who continuously had to supervise and tend it in order to mend its mechanism when needed (a rather bad clockmaker, this Newtonian God, objected Leibniz), thus manifesting his active presence and interest in his creation. Alas, the very development of the Newtonian science which gradually disclosed the consummate skill of the Divine Artifex and the infinite perfections of his work left less and less place for divine intervention. The world clock more and more appeared as needing neither rewinding nor repair. Once put in motion it ran for ever. The work of creation once executed, the God of Newton – like the Cartesian God after the first (and last) *chiquenaude* given to matter – could rest. Like the God of Descartes and of Leibniz – so bitterly opposed by the Newtonians – he had nothing more to do in the world.

Yet it was only at the end of the eighteenth century with Laplace's *Mécanique céleste* that the Newtonian God reached the exalted position of a *Dieu fainéant* which practically banished him from the world ("I do not need that hypothesis," answered Laplace when Napoleon inquired about the place of God in his system), whereas for the first generation of Newtonians, as well as for Newton himself, God had been, quite on the contrary, an eminently active and present being, who not only supplied the dynamic power of the world machine but positively "ran" the universe according to his own, freely established, laws.[2]

It was just this conception of God's presence and action in the world which forms the intellectual basis of the eighteenth century's world feeling and explains its particular emotional structure: its optimism, its divinization of nature, and so forth. Nature and nature's laws were known and felt to be the embodiment of God's will and reason. Could they, therefore, be anything but good? To follow

[1] See Metzger, *Attraction universelle*, and John H. Randall, *The Making of the Modern Mind* (Boston: Houghton Mifflin, 2nd ed., 1940).

[2] In a world made up of absolutely hard particles there is necessarily a constant loss of energy; the Newtonian God, therefore, had not only to supply the initial amount but constantly to replace the loss. Later, of course, he became a mere tinker and repairman.

nature and to accept as highest norm the law of nature, was just the same as to conform oneself to the will, and the law, of God.[1]

Now if order and harmony so obviously prevailed in the world of nature, why was it that, as obviously, they were lacking in the world of man? The answer seemed clear: disorder and disharmony were man-made, produced by man's stupid and ignorant attempt to tamper with the laws of nature or even to suppress them and to replace them by man-made rules. The remedy seemed clear too: let us go back to nature, to our own nature, and live and act according to its laws.

But what is human nature? How are we to determine it? Not, of course, by borrowing a definition from Greek or Scholastic philosophers. Not even from modern ones such as Descartes or Hobbes. We have to proceed according to pattern, and to apply the rules which Newton has given us. That is, we have to find out, by observation, experience, and even experiment, the fundamental and permanent faculties, the properties of man's being and character that can be neither increased nor diminished; we have to find out the patterns of action or laws of behavior which relate to each other and link human atoms together. From these laws we have to deduce everything else.

A magnificent program! Alas, its application did not yield the expected result. To define "man" proved to be a much more difficult task than to define "matter," and human nature continued to be determined in a great number of different, and even conflicting, ways. Yet so strong was the belief in "nature," so overwhelming the prestige of the Newtonian (or pseudo-Newtonian) pattern of order arising automatically from interaction of isolated and self-contained atoms, that nobody dared to doubt that order and harmony would in some way be produced by human atoms acting according to their nature, whatever this might be – instinct for play and pleasure (Diderot) or pursuit of selfish gain (A. Smith). Thus return to nature could mean free passion as well as free competition. Needless to say, it was the last interpretation that prevailed.

The enthusiastic imitation (or pseudo-imitation) of the Newtonian (or pseudo-Newtonian) pattern of atomic analysis and recon-

---

[1] The eighteenth-century optimism had its philosophical source not only in the Newtonian world view but just as well in the rival world conception of Leibniz. More importantly, it was based simply on the feeling of a social, economic, and scientific progress. Life was rather pleasant in the eighteenth century and became increasingly so, at least in the first half of it.

struction that up to our times proved to be so successful in physics,[1] in chemistry,[2] and even in biology, led elsewhere to rather bad results. Thus the unholy alliance of Newton and Locke produced an atomic psychology, which explained (or explained away) mind as a mosaic of "sensations" and "ideas" linked together by laws of association (attraction); we have had, too, atomic sociology, which reduced society to a cluster of human atoms, complete and self-contained each in itself and only mutually attracting and repelling each other.

Newton, of course, is by no means responsible for these, and other, *monstra* engendered by the overextension – or aping – of his method. Nor is he responsible for the more general, and not less disastrous, consequence of the widespread adoption of the atomic pattern of analysis of global events and actions according to which these latter appeared to be not *real*, but only *mathematical* results and summings up of the underlying elementary factors. This type of analysis led to the nominalistic misconception of the relation between a *totum* and its parts, a misconception which, as a matter of fact, amounted to a complete negation of *tota* (a *totum* reduced to a mere sum of its parts is not a *totum*) and which nineteenth- and twentieth-century thought has had such difficulty in overcoming. No man can ever be made responsible for the misuse of his work or the misinterpretation of his thought, even if such a misuse or misinterpretation appears to be – or to have been – historically inevitable.

Yet there is something for which Newton – or better to say not Newton alone, but modern science in general – can still be made responsible: it is the splitting of our world in two. I have been saying that modern science broke down the barriers that separated the heavens and the earth, and that it united and unified the universe. And that is true. But, as I have said, too, it did this by substituting for our world of quality and sense perception, the world in which we live, and love, and die, another world – the world of quantity, of reified geometry, a world in which, though there is place for everything, there is no place for man. Thus the world of science – the real world – became estranged and utterly divorced from the world of life, which science has been unable to explain – not even to explain away by calling it "subjective."

[1] Contemporary physics has been obliged to transcend the atomic pattern of explanation: the whole is no longer identical to the sum of its parts, particles cannot be isolated from their surroundings, and so forth.
[2] On Newton's influence on chemistry, see Hélène Metzger, *Newton, Stahl, Boerhaave et la doctrine chimique* (Paris: Alcan, 1930).

True, these worlds are every day – and even more and more – connected by the *praxis*. Yet for *theory* they are divided by an abyss.

Two worlds: this means two truths. Or no truth at all.

This is the tragedy of modern mind which "solved the riddle of the universe," but only to replace it by another riddle: the riddle of itself.[1]

[1] See Alfred North Whitehead, *Science and the Modern World* (New York: Macmillan, 1925); Burtt, *The Metaphysical Foundations of Modern Physical Science*.

II

Concept and Experience
in Newton's Scientific Thought

Newton's hostility to hypotheses is a matter of common knowledge. Everybody knows the famous first paragraph of the *Opticks* in which Newton announces: "My design in this Book is not to explain the Properties of Light by Hypotheses, but to propose and prove them by reason and experiments."[1] And everybody knows, too, the even more famous *Hypotheses non fingo* of the final General Scholium of the *Principia*, where Newton tells us – I quote the translation of Andrew Motte about which I will say more later – "Hitherto I have not been able to discover the cause of those properties of gravity from phenomena and I frame no hypotheses. For whatever is not deduced from the phenomena is to be called a hypothesis; and hypotheses, whether metaphysical or physical, whether of occult qualities or mechanical, have no place in experimental philosophy."[2]

It would be rather easy to supplement these quotations – which form the basis for the current positivistic interpretation of Newton's thought – by others which are very similar. It is much more difficult, at least in my opinion, to find out exactly what Newton meant by these pronouncements. The difficulties I have in mind are twofold: availability of materials on the one hand, and semantic or historical problems on the other. The latter difficulties are obvious.

[1] *Opticks or a Treatise of the Reflexions, Refractions, Inflexions and Colours of Light. Also Two Treatises on the Species and Magnitudes of Curvilinear Figures* (London, 1704); a Latin translation (without the mathematical treatises) appeared in 1706, followed by a second English edition in 1717. The first (English) edition contains, at the end, 16 queries; the Latin one increases the number to 23; the second English edition adds 8 more. The most recent edition, with an introduction by I. B. Cohen and an analytical table of contents prepared by Duane H. D. Roller, was published in New York by Dover Publications in 1952. For the study of the queries see F. Rosenberger, *Isaac Newton und seine physikalischen Principien* (Leipzig, 1895), pp. 302 sq., Professor Cohen's preface to the above-mentioned edition, and my paper, "Les Quéries de L'Optique," *Archives Internationales d'Histoire des Sciences 13* (1960), 15–29.

[2] Andrew Motte's translation was published in two volumes in 1729. A revised edition, prepared by Florian Cajori, was first published by the University of California Press in 1934, and has been reprinted several times since then.

Let us, therefore, begin looking at the material difficulties. First of all, we do not yet have a good modern edition of Newton, as we have for instance, of Descartes, Galileo, and Huygens. The *Opera omnia*, edited by Horsley from 1779 to 1785, can bear this title only by courtesy.[1] England, which nearly divinized Newton, treated him as we treat sacred things: we touch them as little as possible.[2]

We do not even have a good – I mean critical – edition of the *Principia*. It is well known that the texts of the three editions – 1687, 1713, 1726 – are not identical and that among the differences there are some, notably those between the first and the second editions, that are rather important. Curiously enough, although the differences between the second and third editions were noted – though not in a complete and definitive way – in 1855 by the astronomer John Couch Adams,[3] he did not make a study of their significance. Apparently nobody has had the idea of making a systematic comparison of the first and second editions – other than to note that the final General Scholium appeared for the first time in the second edition – and hence we do not have in print a complete list of the alterations of the first edition, which are more numerous and more important than those introduced in the preparation of the third edition. So far as we know, neither S. P. Rigaud nor J. Edleston very carefully collated the first two editions, though Rigaud wrote a very important essay on the publication of the *Principia*[4] and Edleston edited Newton's correspondence with Roger Cotes, the very correspondence dealing with the preparation of the second edition of the *Principia*.[5] Such a comparison was alleged to have been made by W. W. Rouse Ball,

[1] *Isaaci Newtoni Opera quae extant omnia*, ed. Samuel Horsley, 5 vols. (London, 1779–1785).

[2] Since this article was written, three volumes of the Royal Society's edition of *The Correspondence of Isaac Newton* have been issued by the Cambridge University Press (1959, 1960, 1961), and an edition of Newton's mathematical works has been undertaken by Dr. Derek Thomas Whiteside. There has appeared under the editorship of I. B. Cohen, assisted by Robert E. Schofield (with explanatory prefaces by Marie Boas, Charles C. Gillispie, Thomas S. Kuhn, and Perry Miller), a volume of *Isaac Newton's Papers and Letters on Natural Philosophy, and Related Documents* (Cambridge: Harvard University Press, 1958). A. Rupert Hall and Marie Boas Hall have edited *Unpublished Scientific Papers of Isaac Newton* (Cambridge, England: University Press, 1962). Although a critical edition of the *Principia* by A. Koyré and I. B. Cohen is being completed, there is no prospect yet of a truly complete edition of all of Newton's writings, published and unpublished.

[3] This list has been published as appendix XXXIV to volume II of Sir David Brewster, *Memoirs of the Life, Writings, and Discoveries of Sir Isaac Newton* (Edinburgh, 1855).

[4] Stephen Peter Rigaud, *Historical Essay on the First Publication of Sir Isaac Newton's Principia* (Oxford, 1838).

[5] J. Edleston, *Correspondence of Sir Isaac Newton and Prof. Cotes* (London, 1850).

author of an excellent essay on the *Principia*, but this work was never published and no one has ever seen it.[1] As to later historians, it would seem that not one of them – not even F. Rosenberger,[2] who is ordinarily so precise, nor Florian Cajori,[3] who gives a comparison of the relevant texts of the first, second, and third editions and of those of the *Tractatus de quadratura curvarum* published by Newton in 1704 as an addition to his *Opticks* and to whom we owe the re-edition (in modernized form) of Andrew Motte's translation of the *Principia* – ever made such a comparison.[4]

One must admit, however – and it is surely a mitigating circumstance – that such a comparison has not been very easy to make, for purely material reasons. Actually, the *Principia* – I speak of the first edition, of which there were only 250 to 300 copies printed[5] – is an extremely rare and valuable book. It is generally to be found only in the very large libraries. Those libraries which happen to possess this treasure usually keep it under lock and key in order to preserve it from degrading contact with readers. As to private collectors, very few in number, they take good care that their copies are not spoiled by being read. The publication by Messrs. William Dawson & Son of a facsimile reproduction of the first edition of the *Principia*

---

[1] W. W. Rouse Ball, *An Essay on Newton's "Principia"* (London, 1893), p. 74: "I possess in manuscript a list of the additions and variations made in the second edition." Presumably, he was referring to a curious copy of the first edition in his personal library; into it some early eighteenth-century owner had transferred practically all of the alterations introduced into the second edition (including the index). This copy is now in the Trinity College Library. On p. 106 Rouse Ball makes an allusion to the first edition, stating that the *Regulae philosophandi* of the third edition are much clearer than the *Hypotheses* of the first edition that they replace.

[2] See p. 25, n. 1.

[3] Florian Cajori, *A History of the Conceptions of Limits and Fluxions in Great Britain from Newton to Woodhouse* (Chicago and London: Open Court, 1919).

[4] *Sir Isaac Newton's Mathematical Principles of Natural Philosophy and His System of the World*. Translated into English by Andrew Motte in 1729. The translation revised and supplied with a historical and explanatory appendix by Florian Cajori (Berkeley: University of California Press, 1934; 2nd ed., 1946). In the appendix Cajori, however, quotes (p. 634) "three additions" of the second edition of the *Principia* in which Newton "made his position [concerning gravity and attraction] clearer," and (pp. 653 sq.) Augustus de Morgan's article, "On the Early History of Infinitesimals in England," *Philosophical Magazine* [4] *4* (1852), 321–330, on the difference between the first and the second editions in the treatment of infinitely small quantities and fluxions.

[5] See A. N. L. Munby, "The Distribution of the First Edition of Newton's *Principia*. The Keynes Collection of the Works of Sir Isaac Newton at King's College, Cambridge," *Notes and Records of the Royal Society of London 10* (1952), 28–39, 40–50, and Henry P. Macomber, *A Descriptive Catalogue of the Grace K. Babson Collection of the Works of Sir Isaac Newton* (New York: Herbert Reichner, 1950), p. 9. Macomber estimates that about 250 copies were printed; Munby (p. 37) thinks there were at least 300 copies, and possibly 400.

(1687)[1] at last makes it less difficult for a comparison to be made of the first and second editions and will facilitate the preparation of a critical edition, or at least a list of variants, the need of which in scholarly investigations is becoming more and more apparent.[2] The text of the third edition, prepared by H. Pemberton and published in 1726,[3] was many times reprinted during the eighteenth and nineteenth centuries, and is readily available. But it should be added that, with the exception of the Geneva edition of 1739–1742[4] (and its reprints), none of the editions of the *Principia* possesses a table of contents worthy of the name, a table that is particularly necessary for a volume that is rather bulky and so poorly put together.[5]

[1] *Philosophiae naturalis principia mathematica* (London, 1687; reproduced in facsimile by Wm. Dawson & Sons, Ltd., London, 1954).

[2] A critical edition of Newton's *Principia* has been undertaken by A. Koyré and I. B. Cohen, of which the text is based on a *verbatim et litteratim* collation of the three printed editions, the original manuscript, the annotated and interleaved copies of the first and second editions from Newton's own library, and certain other copies annotated and corrected by Newton, such as the copy of the first edition which Newton presented to John Locke.

[3] George J. Gray, *A Bibliography of the Works of Sir Isaac Newton, Together with a List of Books Illustrating His Works* (Cambridge: Macmillan and Bowes, 1888; 2nd ed., revised and enlarged, Cambridge: Bowes and Bowes, 1907), and Macomber, *A Descriptive Catalogue of the Babson Collection*.

[4] *Philosophiae naturalis principia mathematica auctore Isaaco Newtone*, 3 vols. (Geneva, 1739, 1740, 1742); this edition has very careful and still interesting comments on the works of David Gregory, Pierre Varignon, Jacob Hermann, John Keill, and J. L. Calandrin, who also supervised the printing. The third volume also contains the *Traité sur le flux and le reflux de la mer* by Daniel Bernoulli (pp. 132–246), the *De causa physica fluxus et refluxus maris* by Maclaurin (pp. 247–282), and the *Inquisitio physica in causam fluxus et refluxus maris* by Euler (pp. 283–374). The edition is dedicated to the Royal Society!

[5] The first edition has none whatever, the second and third only a list (prepared by Cotes) of the *sections* of each book. This "table of contents" is reproduced in all the subsequent reprints of the *Principia* up to that of Sir William Thomson and Hugh Blackburn (Glasgow, 1871) and its translations, from Motte and Mme. du Châtelet to Cajori. The Geneva edition contains at the end of Book III (pp. 678–703) an "Index propositionum totius operis," where there are listed first the axioms or laws of motion from Book I, followed by the statement of all the propositions of Book I, then the propositions of Book II, and finally the propositions of Book III. It must be observed, however, that this index, while listing the propositions, that is, the theorems and problems, of the *Principia*, does not mention either the *scholia* or the *hypotheses* occurring in the book. Thus even this "table of contents" cannot be considered as complete and satisfactory.

The Geneva edition, reprinted in 1760 in Cologne and in 1833 in Glasgow, is often – but erroneously – called the "Jesuits' edition," although the title page explicitly says: "Perpetuis commentariis illustrata, communi studio PP. Thomae Le Seur & Francisci Jacquier ex Gallicanâ Minimorum Familiâ." Any good dictionary, for instance, the Merriam-Webster or *Petit Larousse*, would inform the reader that the Minims are a type of Franciscans. The explanation of this transformation of the Minims into Jesuits may be found in the fact that the editors of the last, Glasgow, edition (where, by the way, the tables of contents are put at the end of each book of the *Principia* and not at the end of the whole), though giving on the title page to Le Seur and Jacquier their

Most editions of the *Principia* have an index (prepared by Cotes for the second edition),[1] but it is an index which, to put it mildly, is not very helpful. Thus, for instance, if you look for the word "hypothesis," you will find in the index of Motte's translation of the third Latin edition an entry, "rejects all hypotheses," and a reference to the passage of the General Scholium that I have quoted at the beginning of this article. Yet if we do not confine ourselves to the index and instead make a search of Newton's work itself (starting with the third edition), we will find, in the second book of the *Principia* (Book II, "The Motion of Bodies," Section IX, "The circular motion of fluids"), a *Hypothesis* stating that "the resistance arising from the want of lubricity in the parts of a fluid, is, other things being equal, proportional to the velocity with which the parts of the fluid are separated from one another."[2] And in the third book of the *Principia*, the book that bears the title "The System of the World," we find two more propositions that are expressly called *Hypotheses*. This is rather interesting and worthy to be studied more closely. These hypotheses are:

Hypothesis I. The centre of the system of the world is immovable.[3] This is acknowledged by all, while some contend that it is the Earth, others that the Sun, is fixed in the Centre.[4]

Hypothesis II. If the bulk of the Earth were taken away, and the remaining ring was carried alone about the Sun in the orbit of the Earth by the annual motion, while by the diurnal motion it was in the meantime revolved about its own axis, inclined to the plane of the ecliptic by an angle of $23\frac{1}{2}$ degrees, the motion of the equinoctial points would be the same, whether the ring were fluid, or whether it consisted of a hard and rigid matter.[5]

Now if, encouraged by finding these two hypotheses in a place where there should not be any, we start looking through the second

---

rightful title of Minims of the Gallican province, announce in their own preface to the reader that, *Newtoni illustrissimi opus* having become a rarity, "cujus exemplaria . . . immenso pretio parantur," they decided to republish it; and that they thought that they could do no better than to reprint (under the supervision of John M. Wright) an improved edition of the work of "Le Seur et Jacquier, Societatis Jesu Sociorum."

[1] It is lacking, however, in the Geneva edition and also in Motte-Cajori.

[2] First edition, Book II, Sec. IX, *De motu circulari fluidorum*, p. 373; Cajori, p. 385. *Hypothesis*: "Resistentiam, quae oritur ex defectu lubricitatis partium fluidi caeteris paribus, proportionalem esse velocitati, qua partes fluidi separantur ab invicem." This hypothesis is found in the same place in all three editions of the *Principia*. I shall not study it here, as it is too technical. Neither this hypothesis nor the following two are mentioned in the "Index" of the Minims' edition.

[3] Hypothesis I follows Proposition X in the third edition.

[4] The elaboration of this hypothesis shows that the immovable center of the world – that is to say, of the solar system – is found to be the center of gravity of the system, and not the sun or the earth, both of which are in motion.

[5] Hypothesis II follows Lemma III to Proposition XXXVIII in the third edition.

(Latin) edition of the *Principia*, we will find the same hypotheses in the same place. But if in pursuing our inquiry we proceed to the first (Latin) edition, we will find that Hypothesis II of the third edition is there called Lemma IV of Proposition XXXVIII. As for Hypothesis I, it bears the number IV, and is surrounded by eight other hypotheses. Indeed, at the very beginning of Book III of the first edition, we find a title, *Hypotheses*, and a series of propositions, nine in all, expressly designated by that name. This is rather curious; perhaps even more than curious.

These *hypotheses*, to tell the truth, form a rather unwieldy group. Let me quote the first three.

Hyp. I: We are to admit no more causes of natural things, than such as are both true and sufficient to explain their appearances.

Hyp. II: Therefore [of natural effects of the same kind] the causes are the same.

Hyp. III: Every body can be transformed into another, of whatever kind, and all the intermediary degrees of qualities can be successively induced in it.

Hypotheses V to IX introduce astronomical data, such as: "the circumjovial planets" (that is, the satellites of Jupiter) in their motion about Jupiter obey Kepler's second law; "the five primary planets" revolve around the sun; the periodic times of these planets and of the earth around the sun (or of the sun around the earth) are related to their mean distances from the sun according to Kepler's third law, which would not hold if the "primary planets" all revolved around the earth (although it does hold for the moon).

What does this mean? It means that Newton's *Principia* is, *inter alia*, devoted to proving the truth of the Copernican hypothesis or the Copernican–Keplerian astronomical system. (Indeed, at a meeting of the Royal Society on 28 April 1686, Newton's book was said to contain "a mathematical demonstration of the Copernican hypothesis as proposed by Kepler."[1]) Newton, accordingly, uses the word "hypothesis," though rather loosely, in the accepted and normal meaning in astronomy: a premise or basic proposition of the theory that he intends to develop.

Let us now return to the second edition. The title *Hypotheses* has disappeared and has been replaced by *Regulae philosophandi*.[2] The

[1] Quoted in Rouse Ball, *Essay*, p. 62.

[2] Motte translates *Regulae philosophandi* by "Rules of Reasoning in Philosophy." Mme. du Châtelet, in the French translation, writes, "Règles qu'il faut suivre dans l'étude de la physique."

first two hypotheses are now called *Rules*.[1] The third, which tells us of the transformation of one body into another,[2] disappears completely, at least from the *Principia*[3] (although it comes back again in the later *Quaeries* of the *Opticks*).[4] Hypotheses V to IX become *Phaenomena*. Hypothesis IV remains a hypothesis, and, as I have already said, Lemma IV of Proposition XXXVIII – stating that the motions of a rotating sphere and a rotating ring are equivalent – becomes a hypothesis.[5] Whereupon Newton declares that he does *not* "frame hypotheses," and that hypotheses "have no place in natural philosophy."

One may well understand that, confronted by these terminological – and even more than terminological – changes which accompanied Newton's violent attack upon all hypotheses in the final *Scholium Generale*, Roger Cotes, who was preparing the second edition, was disconcerted and made certain objections.[6] After all, is not the work of Newton in fact filled with hypotheses? And is not universal gravitation itself a hypothesis? Most certainly – at least as long as one takes this term in its traditional and classical sense, which is the way Newton takes it in the first edition of his *Principia*. "Hypothesis" means then an assumption or a fundamental supposition of the theory. Thus Copernicus spoke of *principia et assumptiones quas Graeci hypotheses vocant* ("principles and assumptions which the Greeks call hypotheses") in the introduction to his *De revolutionibus orbium coelestium* (published in 1543); and in his *Commentariolus de*

---

[1] For these transformations see Chapter VI, "Newton's 'Regulae Philosophandi.'"

[2] In his "Hypothesis explaining the Properties of Light, discoursed of in my several Papers" (1675), Newton insists rather strongly on the unity and universal transformability into each other of all things, all of which may be nothing else than diversely condensed aether. See Thomas Birch, *The History of the Royal Society of London* (London, 1757), III, 250; reproduced in Cohen, *Newton's Papers and Letters*, p. 180.

[3] We may find a trace of it in Newton's discussion of the "vapori" forming the tails of the comets, which, spreading through space, "may be at last dissipated and scattered through the whole heavens, little by little be attracted towards the planets by its gravity, and mixed with their atmosphere," renewing and restoring this latter. "I suspect moreover," adds Newton, "that it is chiefly from the comets that spirit comes which is indeed the smallest but the most subtle part of our air and so much required to sustain the life of all things in it." See *Principia* (first edition), Book III, Prop. XLI, Prob. XX, example, pp. 505–506; Cajori trans., Book III, Prop. XLI, Prob. XXI, example, pp. 529–530.

[4] See Query 22 of the Latin edition (Query 30 of the second English edition), where Newton asserts the convertibility into one another of light and gross bodies; Cohen and Roller edition, p. 374.

[5] Lemma IV of Proposition XXXVIII of the first edition becomes Hypothesis II in the second edition.

[6] Cotes to Newton, 18 February 1712/13, in Edleston, *Correspondence*, pp. 151–154, especially p. 153. See Chapter VII, "Attraction, Newton, and Cotes."

hypothesibus motuum coelestium a se constitutis[1] he presented these "hypotheses" as *petitiones, quas axiomata vocant* ("assumptions which are called axioms"). Newton, in his turn, listed at the beginning of *De systemate mundi* (or Book III of the *Principia*) the "hypotheses," that is to say, the fundamental presuppositions, of his own astronomy.[2]

We must not forget, furthermore, that the term "hypothesis" is never a term with a univocal meaning and that it covers a whole gamut of meanings which, moreover, slide very easily one into the other. All the meanings have this in common, that they attenuate (or suppress) provisionally (or definitively) the affirmative character and the relation to truth (or reality) of the "hypothetical" proposition. A hypothesis then is not a judgment, properly speaking, but an assumption or a conjecture that one examines in its consequences and implications, which should either "verify" or "falsify" it. These consequences and implications can be internal ones, as in the case of the "hypotheses" of the *Parmenides* of Plato and the *petitiones* of Euclid and Archimedes, or they may be external ones, like those of the natural sciences.

The term "hypothesis" can designate also a proposition, or a group of propositions, that one poses purely and simply in order to deduce the logical consequences. This is what the mathematicians do when they say: let us suppose or admit that in a right triangle the angle A has a given value ... or, while a right line turns in a uniform manner about one of its terminal points, a point moves along it with a given uniform speed, or with a given uniformly accelerated motion ... or yet again, as Newton does himself, let us suppose or admit that bodies attract each other not with a force that is inversely proportional to the square, but with a force that is directly proportional or inversely proportional to the cube, of the distance between them. What then will be the result of these assumptions? It may be pointed out, however, that when Newton analyzes the consequences of just such different possible laws of attraction, in Book I of the *Principia*, he does not actually use the term "hypothesis," nor does he use it when he studies the movements of bodies in

---

[1] See Edward Rosen, trans. and ed., *Three Copernican Treatises* (2nd ed., New York: Dover, 1959), p. 58.

[2] Newton's early tract *De motu* begins with a set of "Definitiones," followed by four "Hypotheses" which lead to the lemmas, theorems, and problems. See Rouse Ball, *Essay*, pp. 33, 36; also Hall and Hall, *Unpublished Scientific Papers*, pp. 243, 267, 293.

various types of hypothetical resistant media. But the good Newtonian Clairaut, by contrast, uses this term expressly.

One can also, as all astronomers since the time of Ptolemy have
done, call by the name "hypothesis" a proposition, or a group of
propositions, which permit one to order and to deduce therefrom –
and thus to predict – the celestial phenomena (hence, to "save the
phenomena"), without affirming that the "verification" of these
propositions by observed data implies the ontological or material
"truth" of the hypothesis to the slightest degree. It is in this sense
that Osiander, in his (anonymous) preface to the *De revolutionibus
orbium coelestium* of Copernicus,[1] presents the Copernican astronomical system as a mere hypothesis, a mathematical artifice pure
and simple, which in no sense implies the assertion of the truth of the
system, that is to say, the assertion of a real and actual motion of
the earth around the sun; this "hypothesis" as a computing device
is even perfectly compatible with a belief in the earth's immobility.[2]
This is the very same meaning of "hypothesis" that was used by
Galileo to present the Copernican system in his *Dialogue on the
Two Principal Systems of the World*,[3] and also by the Holy Office,
which later reproached Galileo for having only simulated the presentation of the condemned opinion *quamvis hypothetice*.

Nevertheless, it is clear that the same conclusions can be deduced
from very different premises, and that phenomena do not determine
a unique set of hypotheses which must "save" them. Indeed, as
Kepler put it in a famous letter to Maestlin (12/22 December 1616):
*Astronomica hypothesis est quicquid se praebet ad computanda loca
planetarum* ("an astronomical hypothesis is whatever lends itself to
the comparison [computation] of planetary positions").

It is thus possible that there can be several different methods of
effecting these "comparisons" or computations, and that they may
even be equivalent. An example is given by the "hypotheses" of the
epicycles and of the eccentrics of Ptolemaic astronomy, as Kepler

---

[1] Rosen, *Three Copernican Treatises*, pp. 57–90. For Osiander *all* astronomical
"hypotheses" are only mathematical devices, the obvious "falsity" of which, for instance, that of the Ptolemaic theory of Venus, does not affect their practical value.
This "positivistic" conception goes back to the Greeks and, during the Middle Ages,
was adopted by Averroes and his followers.

[2] See A. Koyré, *La Révolution astronomique* (Paris: Hermann, 1961), chap. 3. This
topic is discussed by Rosen in the introduction to *Three Copernican Treatises*, pp. 22–33.

[3] In the preface, Galileo wrote: "I have personified the Çopernican in this discourse,
proceeding upon an hypothesis purely mathematical"; see the Salusbury translation,
revised and annotated by Giorgio de Santillana (Chicago: University of Chicago Press,
1953).

explains to us at the very beginning of his *Astronomia nova*, the "First Part" of which is specifically entitled *De comparatione hypothesium* ("Of the comparison of hypotheses").

It could be, then, that of two, or even three, hypotheses in conflict – those of Ptolemy and Copernicus, or those of Ptolemy, Copernicus, and Tycho Brahe – each one could be capable of "saving" the phenomena and that as a result, at least from the strictly astronomical point of view, there is no reason to make any choice among them. Each of them could be true and they could all be false. We know that this is the point of view adopted, at least officially, by a number of Catholic (and also Protestant) astronomers of the seventeenth century; this enabled them to teach, or at least expound, the conflicting systems, though maintaining the geocentric one for religious reasons.[1]

One can stress even more strongly the fictitious character of a hypothesis, as in the famous declaration made by Descartes in his *Principia philosophiae* (III, Sec. 44), where he tells us: "I desire that what I have written be only taken as a hypothesis, something that is perhaps far removed from the truth; but however that may be, I will believe myself to have really accomplished something if all the things which are deduced from it are entirely in conformity with experience." Descartes, furthermore, maliciously and wickedly, insists upon the divorce between truth and the "hypothetical" premises advanced by him, announcing, "I will suppose here several [hypotheses] which I believe to be false," though "their falsity does not at all prevent what may be deduced from them from being true."[2]

[1] We may doubt, of course, whether this acceptance of the traditional geocentric world view was always sincere – for instance, in the cases of Gassendi or Borelli; but we can only smile when we see Le Seur and Jacquier announce in a *declaratio* published at the beginning of volume III of their edition (the volume containing Book III of the *Principia*, "De mundi systemata") that, as Newton in this book assumes the hypothesis of the motion of the earth, they could not explain his propositions except on the basis of this hypothesis "caeterum latis a summis Pontificibus contra – Telluris motum Decretis nos obsequi profitemur." Kepler himself, in his *Astronomia nova*, though rejecting the "positivistic" point of view and insisting that astronomy has to discover the true structure of the cosmos, studies the astronomical data (the "phenomena") according to the three fundamental hypotheses (Ptolemaic, Copernican, Tychonic) and finally comes to total rejection of the hypotheses of Ptolemy and Tycho and to partial rejection of that of Copernicus. He keeps the heliostatic feature of the Copernican hypothesis, but abandons the mechanism of circles common to both Copernicus and Ptolemy, in order to replace it by a celestial dynamics founded upon the motive power of the sun, which produces elliptical rather than circular orbits for the planets. It remains nevertheless true that from the strictly kinematic point of view the three "hypotheses" – and above all, the last two – are perfectly equivalent.

[2] *Principia philosophiae*, III, 44, 45, 47; *Oeuvres*, ed. Adam and Tannery, VIII, 99–101. It may be doubted, however, whether Descartes was entirely sincere in his statements; see Chapter III.

One may well understand that Petrus Ramus – in the face of epistemologies of this kind, which led science to posit falsity in order to deduce truth, epistemologies current already in his time, that is, long before Descartes had given to the divorce of theory (hypothesis) and truth the perfect formulation that I have just quoted – voiced a vehement protest, holding that it was *absurdum naturalium rerum reveritatem per falsas causas demonstrare* ("absurd to demonstrate by false reasons the truth of natural things")[1] and asked for an astronomy without hypotheses, even offering his chair at the Collège Royal (today the Collège de France) to anyone who could do this,[2] and that Kepler, rejecting the "positivistic" interpretation of astronomy, claimed for science the pursuit of truth. One can also understand why, some hundred years later, Newton so strongly rejected as not scientific the procedure of "feigning hypotheses," and proudly asserted that he, in any case, did not indulge in any such procedures. *Hypotheses non fingo*, "I do not feign hypotheses," thus means for Newton: I do not make use of fictions, I do not use false propositions as premises or explanations.

The reader will have noticed that I have translated *Hypotheses non fingo* by "I do not feign hypotheses," and not "I do not frame hypotheses," as is usually done. My reason for doing so is quite simple: "feign" and "frame" do not have the same meaning. "Feign" – *feindre* – implies falsehood, and "frame" does not, or at least does not necessarily. To "feign" a hypothesis is thus by no means the same thing as to "frame" one. Now, as a matter of fact, *fingo* means "feign" and not "frame," and Newton, who knew his Latin as well as his English, nowhere used the word "frame," which is employed by Motte in his translation of the *Principia*.[3] When Newton said *non*

---

[1] *Scholarum mathematicarum libri XXXI* (Basel, 1569), lib. II, p. 50. Ramus was particularly affected by the above-mentioned preface of Osiander to the *De revolutionibus* of Copernicus, all the more so as he thought it was written by Rheticus. See E. Rosen, "The Ramus-Rheticus Correspondence," *Roots of Scientific Thought* (New York: Basic Books, 1957), pp. 287 sq. On Petrus Ramus see Charles Waddington, *P. Ramus, sa vie, ses écrits, et ses opinions* (Paris, 1855), and R. Hooykaas, "Humanisme, science et réforme," *Free University Quarterly*, August 1958.

[2] In a letter to his master Maestlin (October 1597; *Gesammelte Werke*, XIII, 140), Kepler jestingly announces to him that by his *Mysterium cosmographicum* he has acquired the chair (of Ramus) in the Collège Royal de France. It is rather amusing to note that on the back of the title page of his *Astronomia nova* he repeats the claim that he had accomplished the wish of Ramus and that therefore he had the right to the recompense promised by the latter, that is to say, his chair at the Collège Royal. Kepler, alas, was a little late. Furthermore, the absence of all hypotheses in his *Astronomia nova* is more than questionable.

[3] In a parallel passage of the *Opticks* Newton writes: "without feigning hypotheses"; Query 28, Cohen-Roller edition, p. 369. The usage of "feign" by Newtonians is dis-

fingo he meant "I do not feign," but so great a hold was gained by the false interpretation of Andrew Motte that Mme. du Châtelet followed suit, writing "Je n'imagine pas d'hypothèses" rather than "Je ne feins pas d'hypothèses." Did Andrew Motte and Mme. du Châtelet merely err? Perhaps. As the Italian proverb has it, *traduttore-traditore*[1] (translators are traitors). For my part, I hold that they did something far worse. They did not limit themselves to translating; they made an "interpretation" and in doing so they gave to Newton's assertion a sense which was not exactly Newton's sense.

For Newton himself, the word "hypothesis" had two (or more) meanings in addition to the classical sense of the word which is to be found in the first edition.[2] First of all, there was the good, or at least acceptable, meaning, according to which a hypothesis was a plausible though not provable conception. Newton himself was willing to use this kind of hypothesis. Opposed to this meaning was the bad sense in which the term – and the train of thought corresponding to it – was employed by Descartes, Hooke, Leibniz, and others, and which for Newton was simply identical with fiction, and even a gratuitous and necessarily false fiction. The use of hypotheses in this latter and bad sense implies, therefore, a divorce between science and reality or truth. It means either complete skepticism, if the fiction is conceived and presented as divorced from reality, or, as is generally the case, it means the substitution of a fictitious reality for the given one, or at least of a reality in itself inaccessible to perception and knowledge, a pseudo reality endowed with properties imagined or fancied in an arbitrary manner for that very purpose.

Newton, from his very first publication on optics, objected to this manner of using hypotheses in the construction of theories, as he also objected to using explanations *per causas* which are false or which are at least incapable of being either "demonstrated" or "deduced" from experience – causes that we give ourselves the liberty to imagine, or more exactly to *feign*, as we wish.[3] "Hypothesis," from that time

---

cussed in I. B. Cohen, "The First English Version of Newton's *Hypotheses non fingo*," *Isis 53* (1962), 379–388.

[1] See A. Koyré, "Traduttore-traditore. À propos de Copernic et de Galileo," *Isis 34* (1943), 209–210.

[2] An inventory of the various senses in which Newton used the word "hypothesis" may be found in I. B. Cohen, *Franklin and Newton* (Philadelphia: American Philosophical Society, 1956), app. 1, "Newton's Use of the Word *Hypothesis.*"

[3] Undoubtedly Newton was to some degree inspired by Bacon and by Boyle. A comparative study of Boyle and Newton would be extremely interesting, but would

on, means for Newton something that cannot be proved. Accordingly, following a pattern of thought closely resembling that of Pascal in his *Expériences nouvelles touchant la vide*,[1] he always presents his experiments in a pure or "brute" form, or – to use the term introduced by Samuel Clarke in his Latin translation of the *Opticks*, but not to be found in Newton's original English version – in a "naked" form. Thus he does not intermingle with the account of the experiments, as others such as Hooke and Grimaldi did, any hypotheses which transcend the data and the demonstrable.

The bad sense of the term "hypothesis" seems to have been predominant in Newton's mind in his old age. If you take the term in this bad sense, or even in the sense of something that cannot be proved, it becomes awkward to call the factual data of astronomy, which Newton considers to have been demonstrated, *hypotheses*. You will have to use some other term, for instance the old name *phenomena*, though, as a matter of fact, that old name meant something a little different.[2] Nor can you continue to call hypotheses the fundamental and *true* bases of your theory. You will thus need for them some new designation and will call them rules, laws, or axioms.[3]

That is precisely what Newton does in the second edition of the *Principia*, establishing a distinction between general, logicometaphysical *rules* of reasoning in philosophy, *axioms* and *laws* of motion, and experimental or observational data which, together with their immediate implications, he calls *phenomena*. That is precisely what Newton explains to Cotes, telling him that "as in Geometry the word Hypothesis is not taken in so large a sense as to include the Axiomes & Postulates, so in Experimental Philosophy it is not to be taken in so large a sense as to include the first Principles or Axiomes wch I call the laws of motion. These Principles are deduced from Phaenomena & made general by Induction: wch is highest evidence that a Proposition can have in this Philosophy. And the word Hypothesis is here

take us too far afield. For a notable essay on this topic, see Marie Boas, "The Establishment of the Mechanical Philosophy," *Osiris 10* (1952), 412–541.

[1] See A. Koyré, "Pascal savant," *Cahiers de Royaumont*, Philosophie No. 1, pp. 259–285 (Paris: Éditions de Minuit, 1957).

[2] Newton actually includes under the designation "phenomena" not only the data of observation, but also the Keplerian laws of planetary motion.

[3] Thus, in the *Principia* Newton uses the expression "axioms or laws of motion" (*axiomata sive leges motus*), whereas in his tract *De motu* of 1684–85 (see Rouse Ball, *Essay*, pp. 35 sq.) he calls these "propositions" *hypotheses*. According to J. W. Herivel, "On the Date of Composition of the First Version of Newton's Tract *De motu*," *Archives Internationales d'Histoire des Sciences 13* (1960), 68, n. 7, this change of terminology had already occurred in Newton's University Lectures *De motu* of 1684–85.

used by me to signify only such a Proposition as is not a Phaenomenon nor deduced from any Phaenomena but assumed or supposed without any experimental proof."[1] Thus, in order to make his meaning perfectly clear, Newton enjoins Cotes to add to the paragraph which they are discussing the famous pronouncement: "For whatever is not deduced from the phenomena is to be called a hypothesis and hypotheses, whether metaphysical or physical, whether of occult qualities or mechanical, have no place in experimental philosophy. In this philosophy particular propositions are inferred from the phenomena, and afterwards rendered general by induction. Thus it was that impenetrability, the mobility, and the impulsive forces of bodies and the laws of motion and gravitation, were discovered. And to us it is enough that gravity does really exist, and act according to the laws which we have explained, and abundantly serves to account for all the motions of the celestial bodies, and of our sea."[2] Hypotheses "metaphysical or physical, of occult qualities or mechanical . . ." I must confess that I have not been able to determine exactly what Newton means by "metaphysical hypotheses." These could be the "hypotheses" of the Aristotelian cosmology or those of the Keplerian one; but they could also, and more probably, be the Cartesian assertions which deduce the conservation of motion from God's immutability.[3] Newton certainly did not mean by "metaphysical hypothesis" the existence of God and his action in the world.[4] Laplace may have called God a hypothesis – and a hypothesis which he did not need – but for Newton the existence of God was a certainty, and a certainty by which the phenomena, all the phenomena, had ultimately to be explained.

The "occult qualities" are, probably, the occult qualities of alchemy, in which, as we know, Newton was deeply interested and which, with his friend Boyle, he tried to transform into chemistry. A passage in the *Opticks* (in the *Quaeries*) suggests this interpretation,[5] that is, that the occult qualities are not, once again, merely the Cartesian preconceptions, as Cotes insinuates in his preface to the second

---

[1] Newton to Cotes, 28 March 1713, in Edleston, *Correspondence*, p. 155.

[2] Motte-Cajori, p. 547.

[3] See A. Koyré, *Études galiléennes* (Paris: Hermann, 1939), part III, "Galilée et la loi d'inertie."

[4] As has been suggested by E. W. Strong, "Newton and God," *Journal of the History of Ideas 13* (1952), 147–167.

[5] Query 31. This subject has been explored in A. Rupert Hall and Marie Boas Hall, "Newton's Chemical Experiments," *Archives Internationales d'Histoire des Sciences 11* (1958), 113–152; "Newton's Theory of Matter," *Isis 51* (1960), 131–144.

edition of the *Principia* when he writes: "Those rather have recourse to occult causes, who set imaginary vortices of a matter entirely fictitious and imperceptible by our senses, to direct those motions."[1]

"Mechanical hypotheses" could be those of Bacon, but more probably are those of Descartes and the Cartesians, which Newton rejected for more than one reason. First of all, they were unable to explain the astronomical phenomena, that is, Kepler's laws.[2] Moreover – and this is perhaps just as important – mechanical hypotheses were impious and led, according to Newton,[3] to the exclusion of God from the universe.

As to "physical hypotheses," in my opinion Newton here has in mind the frequent misinterpretations of his theory of universal attraction by those who, like Bentley and Cheyne,[4] Huygens and Leibniz,[5] transformed gravitation into a physical force and made it an essential or at least a primary property of bodies – the first pair in order to accept, the others in order to reject, this "hypothesis." Mechanical and physical explanations taken in this sense are rightly excluded from natural philosophy as false and unsubstantial fictions or, even worse, flagrant absurdities, just because gravitation is not a "mechanical" or even a "physical" force. Thus, "physical hypotheses" would be hypotheses in the very worst sense of the word, that is, false fictions which Newton quite properly refuses to *feign*.

This being so, it is all the more interesting to see Newton continuing to designate as hypotheses the immobility of the center of the world, as well as the equivalence between a liquid or a rigid shell and a solid earth. He takes the term here, of course, in a good or at least intermediate sense. Still there seems to be some implication that for Newton these two propositions – though plausible – were somewhat doubtful. He could not demonstrate either of them and for that reason with perfect honesty he called them "hypotheses." Prob-

[1] Motte-Cajori, p. xxvii.

[2] Let us not forget that a criticism of the hypothesis of vortices is to be found at the very beginning of the famous *Scholium Generale*, of which the opening sentence is: "The hypothesis of vortices is pressed with many difficulties." The Scholium at the end of Book II of the *Principia* begins: "Hence it is manifest that the planets are not carried round in corporeal vortices."

[3] This is also said by Roger Cotes in his preface to the second edition of the *Principia*. See Chapter III, "Newton and Descartes."

[4] On Dr. Cheyne see Hélène Metzger, *Attraction universelle et religion naturelle chez quelques commentateurs anglais de Newton* (Paris: Hermann, 1938).

[5] Leibniz even declared gravitation (attraction) to be an "occult quality"; see Chapter III; also M. Gueroult, *Dynamique et métaphysique Leibniziennes* (Paris: Les Belles Lettres, 1934). As a matter of fact, it was Roberval who first called attraction an "occult quality."

ably at the beginning he thought he could prove the second one. Thus in the first edition of the *Principia* he designated it a lemma. Then he found that he could not prove it (actually, it was Laplace who found the proof) and so in the second edition made this lemma a hypothesis, "Hypothesis II." As to "Hypothesis I" of the second and third editions, concerning the immobility of the center of the system of the world [solar system], Newton no doubt was well aware that it could, after all, be utterly false.

I think that we have now elucidated somewhat the meaning of the term "hypothesis" as understood and used by Newton. In the first edition of the *Principia*, this term is taken in its classical sense, as a fundamental proposition of a theory. In the second edition, on the contrary, a hypothesis is taken to be a fiction, and mostly a false one, or, at the very least, an unproved assertion. Newton's view is not the common one, as Roger Cotes's not understanding it at first sufficiently proves, yet one can interpret the Newtonian view as the end product of the English tradition of empiricism, that of Bacon and of Boyle. As I have already mentioned, the antihypothetical attitude is present – though in a much less rigid form – in the very first works of Newton. It is to them that we shall now turn our attention, because analysis of them will enlighten us somewhat about the role that Newton ascribed to experiments.

In December 1671 Newton sent to the Royal Society "for his Majesty's perusal" a reflecting telescope made by him in the autumn of that year. On 21 December he was proposed for membership by Seth Ward and on 11 January 1672 he was elected a Fellow of the Royal Society. On the 18th, in a letter to Oldenburg, he announced his intention of sending the Society an account of a philosophical discovery which, without false modesty, he describes as "being the oddest if not the most considerable detection which has hitherto been made in the operations of nature."[1]

In this account Newton turned upside down the most firmly established bases of optics. He demonstrated that colors did not belong to colored bodies but to the rays of light; that they were not modifications of light, but original and connate properties of the rays; and that white light, instead of being the fundamental and simple species out of which colored rays were produced by the prism, was on the contrary a confused mixture of variously colored rays pre-existing in it. His letter describing his discovery was received on the 8th of

[1] *Correspondence of Isaac Newton*, I, 82.

February and, on the 19th, was published in the Royal Society's *Philosophical Transactions* under the heading:

A letter of Mr. Isaac Newton, Mathematick Professor in the University of Cambridge; containing his New Theory about *Light* and *Colors:* Where *Light* is declared to be not Similar or Homogeneal, but consisting of difform rays, some of which are more refrangible than others: And *Colors* are affirm'd to be not Qualifications of Light, deriv'd from Refractions of Natural Bodies, (as 'tis generally believed;) but Original and Connate properties, which in divers rays are divers: Where several Observations and Experiments are alledged to prove the said Theory.[1]

In his letter to Oldenburg Newton gives him a historical account of his discovery:

In the beginning of the Year 1666 (at which time I applyed my self to the grinding of Optick glasses of other figures than *Spherical*,) I procured me a Triangular glass-Prisme, to try therewith the celebrated *Phaenomena* of *Colours*. . . . It was at first a very pleasing divertisement, to view the vivid and intense colours produced thereby; but after a while applying my self to consider them more circumspectly, I became surprised to see them in an *oblong* form; which, according to the received laws of Refraction, I expected should have been *circular*.[2]

It was this "surprise" that induced Newton to make the experiments and observations about which he reports to the Royal Society and which led him to establish his new theory of colors. I will not describe here the experiments presented by Newton – they are those that are still made in classrooms the world over;[3] it would be interesting, however, to compare them and their structure with the

[1] *Phil. Trans.*, No. 80, 19 February 1671/72, pp. 3075–3087; reprinted in facsimile in Cohen, *Newton's Papers and Letters*, pp. 47–59, with a study of "Newton's Optical Papers," by Thomas S. Kuhn. On Newton's theory of colors see M. Roberts and E. R. Thomas, *Newton and the Origin of Colours* (London: Bell, 1934), and R. S. Westfall, "The Development of Newton's Theory of Color," *Isis 53* (1962), 339–358.

[2] Cohen, *Newton's Papers and Letters*, p. 47; *Correspondence*, I, 92. It is rather surprising that Newton does not tell Oldenburg – or anybody else – that his new theory of colors is based not only on the experiments and observations made in 1666, but also on the investigations that he pursued in Cambridge and described in his *Lectiones opticae* for the years 1669, 1670, and 1671. These *Lectiones*, however, were not published by Newton; thus they remained practically unknown till 1728, when they were printed in an English translation under the title *Optical Lectures Read in the Public Schools of the University of Cambridge. Anno Domini 1669.* A Latin edition, *Lectiones opticae annis MDCLXIX, MDCLXX, MDCLXXI in scholis publicis habitae et nunc primum in ex. MS in lucem editae*, followed in 1729. Later these *Lectiones* were reprinted by J. Castillon in his edition of Newton's *Opuscula* (Lausanne and Geneva, 1744), and also by Horsley, *Opera omnia* (London, 1782), vol. III. The texts of those editions are not identical.

[3] An excellent analysis of these experiments has been given by E. Mach, *Principien der physikalischen Optik* (Leipzig: Barth, 1921); English translation, *The Principles of Physical Optics* (London: Methuen, 1926), reprinted by Dover Publications.

experiments of Boyle and Hooke,[1] who at nearly the same time as Newton (or somewhat earlier, to be precise), studied "the celebrated phaenomena of colours."

The difference, in short, can be boiled down to an extremely characteristic trait of Newton: the fact that he measures, whereas Boyle and Hooke do not. They describe, admire, and explain the lovely colors of birds' feathers, of metals, of mica – and, though Hooke's explanation of the appearance of colors in plates of mica, or (as they called it) "Muscovy glass," and soap bubbles is remarkably good, it is not based on measurements. Newton, on the other hand, finds it "a very pleasing divertisement, to view the vivid and intense colours" produced by the prism, but he does not stop at that; it is the elongation of the spectrum[2] and the different places occupied in it by different colors that seem to him to constitute the most important feature of the phenomenon. It is because of this quantitative approach – which transcends sensual perception – that he turns to precise measurements of the angles of refraction, and he thus discovers that "divers colours" are inseparably linked with "divers degrees of refrangibility," and that neither the colors nor the degrees of refrangibility can be modified by any means at his disposal, that is, neither by reflection nor by refraction. The meaning of his experiment, especially of the experiment in which rays of light of a determined pure spectral color are passed successively through prisms, and which Newton calls an *experimentum crucis*,[3] is perfectly clear to him. Let him draw his conclusion in his own words:

To the same degree of Refrangibility ever belongs the same colour, and to the same colour ever belongs the same degree of Refrangibility. The *least Refrangible* Rays are all disposed to exhibit a *Red* colour, and contrarily those Rays, which are disposed to exhibit a *Red* colour, are all the least refrangible: So the *most refrangible* Rays are all disposed to exhibit a deep *Violet Colour*, and contrarily those which are apt to exhibit such a violet colour, are all the most Refrangible. And so to all the intermediate

[1] R. Boyle, *Experiments and Considerations Upon Colours* (London, 1663), reprinted in Thomas Birch, ed., *The Works of the Hon. Robert Boyle* (London, 1744), I, 662 sq. R. Hooke, *Micrographia of some Physiological Descriptions of Minute Bodies made by magnifying glasses, with Observations and Inquiries thereupon* (London, 1665), reprinted by R. T. Gunther, *Early Science in Oxford* (Oxford: printed for the subscribers, 1938), vol. XIII.

[2] In his *Lectiones opticae* (pars II, sec. 1, § XX, p. 92 of the edition of Castillon; p. 267 of that of Horsley) he even tries the prism experiment on the light coming from Venus: the result is a *lineola*.

[3] Professor H. W. Turnbull (*Correspondence*, I, 104) points out that the expression *experimentum crucis* is a misquotation by Hooke (*Micrographia*, p. 54) of the Baconian *instantia crucis*. Thus, Newton in using it "is reminiscing from his reading of Hooke."

colours in a continued series belong intermediate degrees of refrangibility. And this Analogy 'twixt colours, and refrangibility, is very precise and strict; the Rays always either exactly agreeing in both, or proportionally disagreeing in both . . .

These things being so, it can be no longer disputed, whether there be colours in the dark, nor whether they be the qualities of the objects we see, no nor perhaps, whether Light be a Body. For, since Colours are the *qualities* of Light, having its Rays for their intire and immediate subject, how can we think those Rays *qualities* also, unless one quality may be the subject of and sustain another; which in effect is to call it *Substance*. We should not know Bodies for substances, were it not for their sensible qualities, and the Principal of those being now found due to something else, we have as good reason to believe that to be a Substance also.

Besides, whoever thought any quality to be a *heterogeneous* aggregate, such as Light is discovered to be. But, to determine more absolutely, what Light is, after what manner refracted, and by what modes or actions it produceth in our minds the Phantasms of Colours, is not so easie. And I shall not mingle conjectures with certainties.[1]

Thus the famous *questio disputata* – whether light is a *substance* or only an *attribute* – appears to Newton to be definitely settled: light is a substance. It may even be a body, though Newton, as we have seen – and this is something that Hooke and the others will fail to notice – does not assert this outright. He believes it, of course, but he thinks that he did not demonstrate it: "body" and "substance" are not identical concepts.

The results of the Newtonian experiments seem to me to throw a light on their very structure. They presuppose in an axiomatic fashion a mathematical structure of nature and their aim is to disentangle the confusion of the empirically given reality, to find out or to isolate its real and simple components. The Newtonian experiments do not have as their aim the establishing of numerical or functional relations between the phenomena, but the disclosing of their true and sufficient causes.

The publication of Newton's "Theory about Light and Colors" gave birth to an extremely interesting sequence of polemics that, alas, it would be too long to discuss here. Pardies, Linus, Huygens,[2]

---

[1] *Phil. Trans.*, No. 80, 19 February 1671/72, pp. 3081 and 3085; reprinted in facsimile in Cohen, *Newton's Papers and Letters*, pp. 53 and 57; *Correspondence*, I, 97, 100. It was the discovery of the unbreakable link between color and refrangibility that led Newton to the conviction that it was impossible to get rid of the chromatic aberration in refracting telescopes and that they had to be replaced by reflecting ones. Accordingly, he abandoned his efforts to perfect the former and made for himself, in 1668, a reflecting telescope, an improved copy of which he presented to the Royal Society.

[2] The documents of this polemic are now assembled in Cohen, *Newton's Papers and Letters*; the best account of it is still to be found in Rosenberger, *Isaac Newton und*

and, first and foremost, Hooke objected to Newton's new "hypothesis" that, if each ray of light was endowed with its own particular color, it implied a nearly infinite multiplication of these.[1] Hooke insinuated, moreover,[2] that there was nothing new (for him) in Newton's experiments, and that, in any case, all of them, even his *experimentum crucis*, did not demonstrate Newton's hypothesis that light is a body, and can be explained just as well, if not better, by his own hypothesis which he developed in his *Micrographia* and which interpreted light as an undulation, or pulse, propagated with an enormous speed in an aethereal medium, this pulse being straight, that is, perpendicular to the direction of propagation, in the case of white light and oblique in the case of colored.[3] Or there might even be "two or three other [hypotheses] very differing" from both Newton's and Hooke's that would explain the phenomena just as well.

Newton's reaction to Hooke's attack is rather curious.[4] He denies,

---

seine physikalischen Principien; see also L. Rosenfeld, "La Théorie des couleurs de Newton et ses adversaires," *Isis 9* (1927), 44–65; and R. S. Westfall, "Newton and His Critics on the Nature of Colors," *Archives Internationales d'Histoire des Sciences 15* (1962), 47–62, and "Newton's Reply to Hooke and the Theory of Colors," *Isis 54* (1963), 82–97.

[1] See Hooke's letter to Oldenburg, 15 February 1671/72, Cohen, *Newton's Papers and Letters*, pp. 110 sq; *Correspondence*, I, 110 sq.: "I have perused the Excellent Discourse of Mr. Newton about colours and Refractions, and I was not a little pleased with the niceness and curiosity of his observations. But though I wholy agree with him as to the truth of those he has alledged, as having, by many hundreds of tryalls found them soe, yet as to his Hypothesis of salving the phaenomena of Colours thereby, I confesse, I cannot see yet any undeniable argument to convince me of the certainty thereof."

[2] Cohen, *Newton's Papers and Letters*, p. 113; it is "wholly useless to multiply entities without necessity," says Hooke, who himself recognized only two fundamental colors, namely red and blue. Newton, on the other hand, though ascribing to each ray of light its particular color, admitted a certain number of original or primary ones. In the *Lectiones opticae* (pars II, sec. 1, p. 185 of the Castillon edition; vol. III, p. 352, of the Horsley one) he lists as such: *Rubrum, Flavum, Viridem, Caeruleum et Violaceum*; in the "New Theory about Light and Colors" (Cohen, *Newton's Papers and Letters*, p. 54), "*Red, Yellow, Green, Blew*, and a *Violet-purple*, together with Orange, Indico, and an indefinite variety of Intermediate gradations." In the "Hypothesis explaining the Properties of Light, discoursed of in my several Papers" of 1675 (*ibid.*, p. 192) he says that "possibly colour may be distinguished into its principal degrees, red, orange, yellow, green, blue, indigo, and deep violet, on the same ground, that sound within an eighth is graduated into tones."

[3] *Micrographia*, p. 64: "Blue is an impression on the Retina of an oblique and confus'd pulse of light whose weakest part precedes and whose strongest follows . . . Red is an impression on the Retina of an oblique and confus'd pulse of light, whose strongest part precedes and whose weakest follows."

[4] See Newton's reply to Hooke, *Phil. Trans.*, No. 88, 18 November 1672, pp. 5084–5103; reprinted in Cohen, *Newton's Papers and Letters*, pp. 116–135; *Correspondence*, I, 171 sq. The text published in the *Correspondence* reproduces the original letter of Newton and is somewhat different from the text printed by Oldenburg in the *Philosophical Transactions*. Oldenburg shortened it and made it impersonal, suppressing the name of Hooke and replacing it by expressions such as "opponent" or "animadversor."

of course, having advanced a hypothesis: what he presented was a theory. He reproaches Hooke (*a*) for having ascribed to him a hypothesis that he did not make, that of light being a body (did he not say "perhaps"?) and (*b*) for not understanding that his, Hooke's, hypothesis, besides being unable to explain the rectilinear propagation of light,[1] is just one of those hypotheses that had been disproved and refuted by Newton's crucial experiment.

Newton is obviously right and wrong at the same time, and even somewhat unfair – wrong and unfair because nobody, not even Hooke, ever presented a hypothesis without accompanying it, at least in his own mind, with a "perhaps" or a "maybe." It is just for this that Newton himself reproaches people who use hypotheses. One cannot therefore deny – and Hooke is quite right on this point – that in Newton's communication to the Royal Society he had in effect proposed a hypothesis, the materiality of light.[2] But Newton is right, too, in the sense that, though he suggested the materiality of light rays, he did not use that assumption as a base of his theory, in contradistinction both to Descartes, who built up his optics on preconceived and, moreover, incompatible hypotheses, and to Hooke himself, who founded his own optics on a false hypothesis and filled the *Micrographia* with all kinds of hypotheses to suit his needs as he went along.

Newton does not deny that his experiments might be explained by means of several mechanical hypotheses. This is why he has not proposed any hypotheses, but has limited himself to the elaboration of a *theory* which conforms strictly to what is demonstrable – and has been demonstrated – namely, the indestructible linkage between degree of refrangibility and color. That his theory suggests, and even makes likely, the corpuscular nature of light is quite true. But this is something perfectly legitimate: this hypothesis, if one wishes that it be a hypothesis, is formulated as a result of the data of experiment; it is not presented as demonstrated, and it does not form an integral part of his theory.

[1] According to Newton, if light was constituted by undulations or waves, it would bend around corners.

[2] Newton says, of course (Cohen, *Newton's Papers and Letters*, p. 119), that he "knew, that the *Properties* which [he] declar'd of *Light*, were in some measure capable of being explicated ... by many ... Mechanical *Hypotheses*. And therefore [he] chose to decline them all, and to speak of *Light* in *general* terms, considering it abstractly, as something or other propagated every way in streight lines from luminous bodies, without determining, what that Thing is." But did not Newton assert that light is a substance? And a substance endowed with sensible qualities cannot be anything else but a body.

As we know, Newton does not "deal in conjectures." Thus it is rather amusing to find him explaining that, if he were to propound a hypothesis, he would do it differently and in a much better way than his very esteemed friend Hooke, whose hostility toward the hypothesis of the corpuscular structure of light Newton does not understand. Newton himself has no such hostility toward the undulatory hypothesis, and, as a matter of fact, he needs both hypotheses. Thus if he were to construct a hypothesis, he would begin by establishing the facts, that is to say, the experimental data, thus to "ground" his hypothesis on phenomena and strict measurement. He would, then, begin by supposing that the rays of light are composed of exceedingly small corpuscles – an assumption, according to Newton, that is necessary in order to explain the rectilinear propagation of light. But Newton would join to this corpuscular hypothesis a further one, namely that of the existence of an aetheric medium in which these corpuscles of light excite vibrations or waves of different "bigness," these "bignesses" corresponding to the different colors of light, and use them both for a full explanation of refraction, reflection, and the appearance of colors in thin plates. He would thus make a synthesis of the two views, in a manner of which his answer to Hooke already gives a sketch.

In 1675, having observed that "the heads of some great virtuosos[1] . . . run much upon hypotheses,"[2] so much that they do not understand his discourses when he speaks about light "abstractedly," although they readily apprehend them when he supplements his theory by a hypothesis which makes it more concrete – "as if my discourses wanted an hypothesis to explain them by" – Newton sent to Oldenburg, that is, to the Royal Society, a very long paper containing "An hypothesis explaining the Properties of Light, discoursed of in my several Papers."[3] He specified, however, that he was propounding this hypothesis only as an "illustration" of his theory, and that he was not assuming it as true, even though speaking as if it were, which means that, although he believes his view to be true, he knows that he cannot demonstrate it. He tells us:

---

[1] The term "virtuosos" was, in the language of the day, neither prejorative nor ironic.

[2] Birch, *History of the Royal Society*, III, 249; reprinted in Cohen, *Newton's Papers and Letters*, p. 179.

[3] This *Hypothesis*, on Newton's request, was not published in the *Philosophical Transactions* and appeared in print only in Birch's *History of the Royal Society*, III, 247–305; see Cohen, *Newton's Papers and Letters*, pp. 178–235.

It is to be supposed [Newton likes the term "supposition"; a supposition is not a hypothesis, and of course we are entitled to make suppositions] ... that there is an aethereal medium[1] much of the same constitution with air, but far rarer, subtler, and more strongly elastic ...[2]

It is to be supposed, that the aether is a vibrating medium like air, only the vibrations far more swift and minute; those of air, made by a man's ordinary voice, succeeding one another at more than half a foot or a foot distance; but those of aether at a less distance than the hundred thousandth part of an inch. And, as in air the vibrations are some larger than others, but yet all equally swift ... so, I suppose, the aethereal vibrations differ in bigness, but not in swiftness.[3]

It is also to be supposed (Birch, p. 255) "that light and aether mutually act upon one another, aether in refracting light and light in warming aether; and that the densest aether acts more strongly." Indeed, since aether is not homogeneous but differs in density,[4] a ray of light is pressed or urged by a denser medium toward a rarer and is curved in toward the rarer one – a process that explains refraction, and also complete reflection if light is supposed to penetrate obliquely into succeeding layers of a denser and denser medium. And this process even explains simple reflection if we admit that the aethereal fluids, like fluids generally, "near their superficies are less

[1] Newton seems to have been influenced by Hooke's idea of luminiferous aether nearly as much as Hooke was influenced by Newton's suggestion of various "bignesses" of aethereal waves or pulses corresponding to different colors.

[2] Birch, *History of the Royal Society*, III, 249; Cohen, *Newton's Papers and Letters*, p. 179. Newton adds: "Of the existence of this medium the motion of a pendulum in a glass exhausted of air almost as quickly as in the open air, is no inconsiderable argument." It is interesting to note that in the *Scholium Generale* to Sec. VI of the second and third editions of the *Principia* (it is lacking in the first edition), Newton discusses the opinion (in the second edition, *Receptissima Philosophorum aetatis hujus opinio*, p. 292 of the Amsterdam ed. of 1714 and simply *nonnulorum opinio* in the third [Horsley, II, 379; Motte-Cajori, 325/607]), "that there is a certain etheral medium extremely rare and subtile which freely pervades the pores of all bodies; and from such a medium, so pervading the pores of the bodies, some resistance must needs arise." Newton then proceeds to relate (p. 326), "by memory, the paper being lost in which I had described it," the pendulum experiments which demonstrate that the resistance of the internal parts of a body really exists and that the greater resistance of the full box (compared to that of an empty one) "arises not from any other latent cause, but only from the action of some subtle fluid upon the included metal."

[3] Birch, *History of the Royal Society*, III, 251; Cohen, *Newton's Papers and Letters*, p. 181. The aethereal vibrations or waves of Newton – just like those of Hooke – are, of course, longitudinal "pulses" like vibrations or waves of air that produce sounds. The "bigness" of the vibrations is thus their wavelength. Newton assumes that as sounds of various tones correspond to air vibrations of various bignesses (p. 262, p. 192) so also to light rays of different color correspond aethereal vibrations of different bigness and "strength," the biggest and strongest being those that are produced in the aether by red rays, and the weakest and shortest those that are produced by violet ones. This explains why red light rays are less refracted than violet rays.

[4] Aether that is contained in the bodies is considered by Newton as being less dense than aether that is outside them.

pliant and yielding in their more inward parts," and that, therefore, a ray of light is sometimes unable to break through the "more stiff and tenacious" aethereal superficies of reflecting bodies.

We must further suppose (Birch, p. 263) that "though light be unimaginably swift, yet the aethereal vibrations excited by a ray, move faster than the ray itself,[1] and so overtake and outrun it one after another." This enables us to explain the phenomena of semi-reflection and the appearance of colors in thin plates: the rays that break through the first superficies are overtaken by the aethereal waves on their way toward the second surface and are "there reflected or refracted accordingly as the condensed or expanded part of the wave overtakes it there."

It is this synthetic, corpuscular, undulational hypothesis that Newton applies – and with great success – to the study of the rings that now bear his name[2] and also to the study of the diffraction of light which had been discovered by Grimaldi.[3]

As for himself, Newton writes:

I suppose light is neither aether, nor its vibrating motion, but something of a different kind propagated from lucid bodies.

Then he raises two possibilities. First, he says,

They, that will, may suppose it an aggregate of various peripatetic qualities.

Clearly, this is not Newton's own view. Next, he introduces those others (among whom we doubtless must include Newton himself) who

---

[1] At the time he wrote his *hypothesis*, Newton assumed that "light is not so swift as some are apt to think," and might spend "an hour or two, if not more, in moving from the sun to us" (p. 263, p. 193). Thirty years later in his *Opticks* (Book II, Part III, Prop. XII), when presenting a hypothetical explanation of the "fits" of easy transmission and easy reflection, Newton, though knowing the velocity of light, maintains that the vibrations of the refracting or reflecting medium excited in it by light rays move faster than these rays.

[2] Birch, *History of the Royal Society*, III, 263 sq.; Cohen, *Newton's Papers and Letters*, pp. 193 sq. The study of colors in thin plates by Hooke and Newton exemplifies once more the difference of which I have already spoken: Newton measures, whereas Hooke does not. Hooke, indeed, studies these colors in thin plates of mica, or soap bubbles, the thickness of which he does not, and cannot, measure. Newton uses large convex and planoconvex lenses pressed together, measures the diameters of the rings that appear, and thus is able to calculate the thickness of the air layer between them.

[3] *Ibid.*, pp. 269 sq., 199 sq. Strangely enough, Newton will never use the Grimaldian term "diffraction," but replaces it by that of "inflexion" used by Hooke, though in a different sense.

may suppose it multitudes of unimaginable small and swift corpuscles of various sizes, springing from shining bodies at great distances one after another; but yet without any sensible interval of time, and continually urged forward by a principle of motion, which in the beginning accelerates them.[1]

Furthermore, Newton states explicitly that any type of hypothesis may serve, as long as it provides a quantitative scale, and he illustrates his view by referring to both a type of particle (grains of sand) and a form of wave (water):

To avoid dispute, and make this hypothesis general, let every man here take his fancy: only, whatever light be, I suppose, it consists of rays differing from one another in contingent circumstances, as bigness, form, or vigour; like as the sands on the shore, the waves of the sea, the faces of men, and all other natural things of the same kind differ.[2]

In his *Opticks* of 1704 Newton seems to have abandoned the synthetic theory that he had developed in his *Hypotheses*. Then in order to explain refraction and reflection he does not make an appeal to the existence of aether, but to explain refraction he appeals to an (attractive) force that urges the body (light particle) toward the refracting surface;[3] and concerning reflection he only informs us that "the Reflexion of a Ray is effected . . . by some power of the [reflecting] Body which is evenly diffused all over its surface, and by which it acts upon the Ray without immediate contact."[4] Even when he comes to treat the phenomena of semitransparence and of rings, he carefully avoids any mention of aether and only tells us that "every Ray of light in its passage through any refracting surface is put into a certain transient condition or state which in the progress of the Ray returns at equal intervals," because in its progress through the glass plate the ray is "influenced by some action or disposition propagated from the first to the second" surface of the plate. The existence of these conditions or stages, which he calls "Fits of easy Reflexion" and "Fits of easy Transmission," is not a hypothesis. As usual, he tells us that he "does not inquire what kind of action or disposition" it is that puts the rays of light into these conditions."[5]

[1] *Ibid.*, p. 254, p. 184.

[2] *Ibid.*, p. 255, p. 185.

[3] The explanation of refraction and total reflection on the basis of the conception of attraction was developed by Newton in Book I, Sec. XIV, of the *Principia*.

[4] *Opticks*, Book II, Part III, Prop. VIII; Cohen-Roller edition, p. 268.

[5] *Ibid.*, Prop. XII; p. 278. The "fits" of the *Opticks* replace the aethereal vibrations of the *Hypotheses*, and play exactly the same role as these: they introduce periodicity into the light rays.

Those that are averse from assenting to any new Discoveries, but such as they can explain by an Hypothesis may for the present suppose that as Stones by falling upon Water put the water into an undulating Motion, and all Bodies by percussion excite vibrations in the Air; so the Rays of Light, by impinging on any refracting or reflecting Surface . . . excite vibration in the refracting or reflecting Medium or Substance . . . much after the manner that vibrations are propagated in the Air for causing Sound, and move faster than the Rays so as to overtake them [and thus produce the fits].[1]

But, adds Newton, "whether this Hypothesis be true or false, I do not here consider."[2]

Once more we see Newton faithful to his extremely rigorous distinction between things which can be demonstrated and those which cannot; faithful also to his aversion for what A. N. Whitehead has called "misplaced concreteness."

The Queries added by Newton at the end of the first English edition (1704) of the *Opticks* go still further. Newton there abandons any pretension to neutrality, or, if one prefers, to disinterestedness, with regard to the truth or falsity of the hypotheses which he proposes, allegedly only to be better understood by those that cannot do without. Nevertheless, he does not use the term "hypothesis."[3] Yet there is no doubt that he believes the suppositions which he advances to be true. Thus he uses the equivalent and convenient form of the rhetorical question: "Do not Bodies act upon Light at a distance . . . ?" and "Is not this action (*caeteris paribus*) strongest at the least distance?" (Query 1) or "Do not Bodies and Light act mutually upon one another . . . ?" (Query 5).[4]

In later years Newton adds further Queries to the Latin edition (1706) and the second English edition (1717) of the *Opticks*.[5] He

---

[1] *Optick*, Book II, Part III, Prop. XII, p. 280. Yet as Newton adds that "probably [light] is put into such fits at its first emission from luminous bodies and continues in them during all its progress" it is pretty clear that this medium cannot be anything else than the aether of the *Hypotheses*.

[2] Which is to say that Newton — and with good reason — finds himself incapable of demonstrating this conjecture.

[3] See A. Koyré, "Les Quéries de *L'Optique*."   [4] Cohen-Roller edition, p. 339.

[5] It should be noted that in the second English edition of the *Opticks* (and later editions), Query 17, which does not appear in the *Opticks* of 1704 or in the Latin one of 1706, presents exactly the same hypothesis which Newton had introduced in Book II, Part III, Prop. XII as necessary for those who without a hypothesis are "averse to assenting to any new discoveries." See a discussion of this point in Cohen, *Franklin and Newton*, pp. 162–163. Newtonians generally assumed that Newton believed the suppositions (hypotheses) of the Queries to be valid. Thus Stephen Hales, referring to Queries 18 and 21, mentioned the aethereal medium "by which (the great Sir Isaac Newton supposes) light is refracted and reflected." David Gregory, who in 1705 saw the new Queries in MS before they were printed, wrote that in them Newton "has by

still does not assert outright the truth of his views: he continues to use the convenient and equivalent form of rhetorical question. Thus he asks: "Is not the Heat of the warm room convey'd through the *Vacuum* by the Vibrations of a much subtler Medium than Air, which, after the Air was drawn out, remained in the *Vacuum*? And is not this Medium the same with that Medium by which Light is refracted and reflected . . . and is put into Fits of easy Reflexion and easy Transmission?"[1]

The Queries are full of these rhetorical questions. If we did not know that Newton does not ever make hypotheses, we could easily mistake them for a most exciting set of the boldest and even the most extravagant, and yet at the same time most fruitful and influential, hypotheses.[2] But of course we would be wrong. Hypotheses have no place in Newton's philosophy. Newton, one must remember, has told us this explicitly in the *Scholium Generale*. But, in fact, it is very well explained in Query 28, one of those first printed in the Latin edition of the *Opticks* (1706), and then again in the second English edition (1717), where Newton tells us that his own views are practically the same as those of the old Greek and Phoenician philosophers, who all admit the void, and also nonmechanical causes. Alas,

later Philosophers banish the Consideration of such a Cause out of natural Philosophy, feigning Hypotheses for explaining all things mechanically, and referring other Causes to Metaphysicks: Whereas the main Business of natural Philosophy is to argue from Phaenomena without feigning Hypotheses, and to deduce Causes from Effects, till we come to the very first Cause, which certainly is not mechanical.

The foregoing text projects a singular light on the end of the *Scholium Generale*, in which, after having announced that he has not yet been able to discover the cause of gravity, and that he does not feign hypotheses, Newton tells us:

And now we might add something concerning a certain most subtle spirit which pervades and lies hid in all gross bodies; by the force and action of which spirit the particles of bodies attract one another at near distances, and cohere, if contiguous; and electric bodies operate to greater distances, as well repelling as attracting the neighboring corpuscles; and light is emitted, reflected, refracted, inflected, and heats bodies; and all

---

way of quaere explained . . ." J. T. Desaguliers also held that the Queries contained an exposition of Newton's beliefs. See Cohen, *Franklin and Newton*, chap. 7.
[1] Query 18. In Queries 19 and 20 this medium is frankly called "aetherial."
[2] See Cohen, *Franklin and Newton*, chap. 7.

sensation is excited, and the members of animal bodies move at the command of the will, namely, by the vibrations of this spirit, mutually propagated along the solid filaments of the nerves, from the outward organs of sense to the brain, and from the brain into the muscles. But these are things that cannot be explained in few words, nor are we furnished with the sufficiency of experiments which is required to an accurate determination and demonstration of the laws by which this spirit operates.[1]

Apparently, then, to admit the existence of the void, of atoms, of aethereal spirit, and of nonmechanical forces is not to feign hypotheses; while to postulate the fullness of space, vortices, and the conservation of the quantity of motion in the universe is, on the contrary, to be guilty of using this method. The expression "hypothesis" thus seems to have become, for Newton, toward the end of his life, one of those curious terms, such as "heresy," that we never apply to ourselves, but only to others. As for us, *we* do not feign hypotheses, *we* are not heretics. It is *they*, the Baconians, the Cartesians, Leibniz, Hooke, Cheyne, and others—*they* feign hypotheses and *they* are the heretics.

---

[1] In Motte's version, reprinted by Cajori, the General Scholium concludes: "the laws by which this electric and elastic spirit operates." The words "electric and elastic" have been shown by A. R. Hall and M. B. Hall, "Newton's Electric Spirit: Four Oddities," *Isis 50* (1959), 473–476, to be additions by Motte which are not in the printed Latin text. Curiously enough these words are to be found in Newton's own annotated copy of the second edition of the *Principia*, but never found their way into the third edition; see A. Koyré and I. B. Cohen, "Newton's Electric and Elastic Spirit," *Isis 51* (1960), 337. It is to be noted that this "spirit" acts only at small distances and does not produce gravity or attraction. In the *Opticks* of 1717 these are, on the contrary, explained by the action of the same aethereal medium that produces reflection, refraction, and inflexion (diffraction) of light (Queries 17–22). Newton naturally adds that he does "not know what this aether is" (Query 21).

III
Newton and Descartes

The seventeenth century has been called, and rightly, the century of genius. Indeed, there is hardly another one that can pride itself on having produced such a galaxy of first-rate minds: Kepler and Galileo, Descartes and Pascal, Newton and Leibniz, not to mention Fermat and Huygens. Yet even in the skies, as we know, the stars are not all equal in glory. Thus it seems to me that in this galaxy there are two stars that outshine the others: Descartes, who conceived the ideal of modern science – or its dream? – the *somnium de reductione scientiae ad geometriam*, and Newton, who firmly put physics back on its own feet. I felt therefore that it would be interesting to examine, or re-examine, their relation, all the more so as the recent study of the Newtonian manuscripts has uncovered some hitherto unknown material that throws a new light upon this problem.

The comparison, or confrontation, of Newton and Descartes, somewhat on the Plutarchian pattern, was very often made in the eighteenth century.[1] It is no longer done. And we can understand

[1] See, for instance, Fontenelle's "Éloge de M. Newton," *Histoire de l'Academie Royale des Sciences*, année 1727 (Paris: De L'Imprimerie Royale, 1729), pp. 151–172; I quote the English translation, *The Elogium of Sir Isaac Newton* . . . (London, 1728), pp. 15 sq., reprinted with a very interesting introduction by C. C. Gillispie, "Fontenelle and Newton," in I. B. Cohen, ed., *Isaac Newton's Papers and Letters on Natural Philosophy* (Cambridge, Massachusetts: Harvard University Press, 1958), pp. 457 sq.: "These two great men, whose Systems are so opposite, resembled each other in several respects, they were both Genius's of the first rank, both born with superior understandings, and fitted for the founding of Empires in Knowledge. Being excellent Geometricians, they both saw the necessity of introducing Geometry into Physicks; For both founded their Physicks upon discoveries in Geometry, which may almost be said of none but themselves. But one of them taking a bold flight, thought at once to reach the Fountain of All things, and by clear and fundamental ideas to make himself master of the first principles; that he might have nothing more left to do, but to descend to the phenomena of Natures as to necessary consequences; the other more cautious, or rather more modest, began by taking hold of the known phenomena to climb to unknown principles; resolved to admit them only in such manner as they could be produced by a chain of consequences. The former sets out from what he clearly understands, to find out the causes of what he sees; the latter sets out from what he sees, in order to find out the cause, whether it be clear or obscure. The self-evident principles of the one do not always lead him to the causes of the phenomena as they are; and the

why: Cartesian science, for us, belongs entirely to the past, whereas Newtonian science, though superseded by Einstein's relativistic mechanics and contemporary quantum mechanics, is still alive. And very much so.[1] But it was different in the eighteenth century, at least in its first half. Then Cartesian philosophy, which in the later part of the seventeenth century inspired most of the scientific thinking of continental Europe,[2] was still an active force; Newton's influence was practically restricted to England.[3] It is well known that only after a long and protracted struggle against Cartesianism did Newtonian physics, or, to use the term by which it designated itself, Newtonian Natural Philosophy,[4] gain universal recognition in Europe.[5]

---

phenomena do not always lead the other to principles sufficiently evident. The boundaries which stop'd two such men in their pursuits through different roads, were not the boundaries of Their Understanding, but of Human understanding it self."

[1] Thus the "sputniks" constitute the first *experimental* proof of Newtonianism on a cosmic scale.

[2] Even those who, like Huygens and Leibniz, rejected some of the fundamental theses of Descartes, such as the identification of extension and matter and the conservation of momentum, and who therefore considered themselves as non-Cartesians (Huygens) or anti-Cartesians (Leibniz), were very deeply influenced by Descartes and accepted his ideal of a purely mechanical science; see P. Mouy, *Le Développement de la physique cartésienne, 1646–1712* (Paris: Vrin, 1934).

[3] Even in England the influence of Cartesianism was very great, owing to the excellent textbook of Jacques Rohault, *Traité de physique* (Paris, 1671; 12th ed., 1708) which was translated into Latin by Théophile Bonet, and published in Geneva as early as 1674 (*Jacobi Rohaulti Tractatus physicus*). Thus it was the masterstroke – a kind of Trojan-horse technique – of Samuel Clarke to use Rohault's textbook, of which he published a new and much better Latin translation in 1697 (*Jacobi Rohaulti Physica* [London, 1697; 4th ed., 1718; we shall cite this fourth Latin edition]), for the propagation of Newton's ideas by means of the *Annotationes* (from the third edition of 1710 they became footnotes) that flatly contradicted the text. The success of this rather unusual combination was so great that the book was reprinted several times (the last, sixth, edition appeared in 1739), and was even translated into English by Samuel Clarke's brother, John Clarke, in 1723 (reprinted in 1729 and 1735) under the significant title of *Rohault's System of Natural Philosophy, illustrated with Dr. Samuel Clarke's notes taken mostly out of Sir Isaac Newton's philosophy . . . done into English by John Clarke, D.D., Prebendary of Canterbury*, 2 vols. (London: James Knapton, 1723; we shall cite this edition). On the Continent, Rohault's *Physica* appeared, in Latin, *cum animadversionibus* Antonii Le Grand, in Amsterdam in 1700; and was reprinted in Cologne in 1713, *cum animadversionibus* of Legrand and of Clarke. See Michael A. Hoskin, " 'Mining All Within': Clarke's Notes to Rohault's *Traité de physique*," *The Thomist* 24 (1961), 353–363.

[4] Newton's *Opticks* gained recognition rather easily and quickly: it was translated into French by Coste in 1720 (*Traité d'optique*, Paris, 1720); a second edition "beaucoup plus correcte que la première" appeared in 1722.

[5] For the history of this struggle and the role played in it by the Dutch physicists P. Musschenbroeck and W. J. s'Gravesande on one side, and P. L. Maupertuis on the other, see P. Brunet, *Les Physiciens hollandais et la méthode expérimentale en France au XVIIIᵉ siècle* (Paris: Blanchard, 1926), and *L'Introduction des théories de Newton en France au XVIIIᵉ siècle* (Paris: Blanchard, 1931). See also D. W. Brewster, *Memoirs of the Life, Writings and Discoveries of Sir Isaac Newton* (Edinburgh, 1855), vol. I,

The result of this state of affairs was, on one hand, a complete divorce between British and Continental world views. As Voltaire in his famous *Lettres anglaises* wittily puts it,

A Frenchman who arrives in London finds a great change in philosophy, as in everything else. He left the world full, he finds it empty. In Paris one sees the Universe composed of vortices of subtle matter. In London one sees nothing of this. In Paris it is the pressure of the moon that causes the flux of the sea; in England it is the sea that gravitates toward the moon. With your Cartesians, everything is done by an impulsion that nobody understands; with Mr. Newton, it is by an attraction, the cause of which is not better known.[1]

On the other hand, the protracted struggle for and against Descartes and Newton transformed both of them into symbolic figures; the one, Newton, embodying the ideal of modern, progressive, and successful science, conscious of its limitations and firmly based upon

chap. XII; F. Rosenberger, *Isaac Newton und seine physikalischen Principien* (Leipzig, 1895), Buch I, Theil IV, Kap. 1: "Die erste Aufnahme der Principien der Naturlehre"; René Dugas, *La Mécanique au XVIIe siècle* (Paris: Dunod, 1954).

[1] *Lettres philosophiques*, édition critique par Gustave Lanson (Paris: Edouard Cornély, 1909, and later editions), letter 14, vol. 2, p. 1. Voltaire's *Lettres philosophiques* appeared first in English (anonymously) under the title *Letters Concerning the English Nation* (London, 1733); then in French under the titles *Lettres philosophiques par M. de V**** (Amsterdam, 1734; in fact they were printed by Jore in Rouen) and *Lettres écrites de Londres sur les anglais... par M. D. V**** (Basle, 1734; but in fact London, 1734). For the complete history of the *Lettres philosophiques*, see Gustave Lanson's "Introduction" to his above-mentioned edition. According to Descartes, the sun – and all other fixed stars – were surrounded by huge "liquid" vortices composed of luminous and luminiferous matter, the "first" and the "second" elements respectively (see p. 62, n. 2), in which the planets, endowed with their own, smaller, vortices, swam as specks of straw or bits of wood swim in a river, and were carried along by these vortices around the central body of the big vortex, in our case, around the sun. It is to the action or counteraction of these vortices, each restricted in its expansion by the surrounding vortices, that Descartes ascribed the centripetal forces that retained the planets in their orbits; and it is by an analogous action of the small, planetary vortices that he explained gravity. With his usual malevolence against Descartes, Leibniz accused him of having "borrowed" the vortex conception from Kepler, without acknowledging his debt, "as was his habit"; see *Tentamen de motuum coelestium causis*, in C. J. Gerhardt, ed., *Leibnizens mathematische Schriften* (Halle, 1860), VI, 148, and L. Prenant, "Sur les références de Leibniz contre Descartes," *Archives Internationales d'Histoire des Sciences 13* (1960), 95–97. See also E. J. Aiton, "The Vortex Theory of Planetary Motion," *Annals of Science 13* (1957), 249–264, *14* (1958), 132–147, 157–172; "The Cartesian Theory of Gravity," *ibid.*, *15* (1959), 24–49; and "The Celestial Mechanics of Leibniz," *ibid.*, *16* (1960), 65–82. Sir Edmund Whittaker, *A History of the Theories of Aether and Electricity* (London: Nelson, 2nd ed., 1951; New York: Harper, 1960), II, 9, n. 2, points out the relation of the Cartesian vortices to modern cosmological conceptions: "It is curious to speculate on the impression which would have been produced had the spirality of nebulae been discovered before the overthrow of the Cartesian theory of vortices." On the other hand there can hardly be any doubt about the analogy between the conceptions of Faraday, Helmholtz, and Maxwell, all based on the rejection of action at a distance (see Whittaker, I, 170 sq., 291 sq.), and the Cartesian conceptions, especially the "small vortices" of Malebranche. For the views of Huygens and Leibniz on gravitational attraction, see Appendix A.

experimental and experiential-observational data which it subjected to precise mathematical treatment; the other, Descartes, symbol of a belated, reactionary – and fallacious – attempt to subject science to metaphysics, disregarding experience, precision, and measurement, and replacing them by fantastic, unproved, and unprovable hypotheses about the structure and behavior of matter. Or, even more simply, the one, Newton, representing the truth, and the other, Descartes, a subjective error.[1]

This is, of course, the Newtonians' image. The Cartesians, needless to say, held a different view. They recognized, indeed, the great superiority of Newtonian precision as compared to the vagueness of the Cartesian cosmology, and the immense progress achieved by Newton in his reduction of Kepler's three descriptive laws of planetary motion to their dynamic foundation; they admitted the necessity of developing and improving Descartes's physics. Yet they rejected outright Newtonian attraction, in which they persisted in seeing immediate action at a distance, that is, an occult quality,[2]

---

[1] Voltaire, "Lettre à M. de Maupertuis sur les Éléments de la philosophie de Newton," *Oeuvres complètes* (Paris: Baudouin Frères, 1828), XLII, 31–32: "Descartes has hardly made any experiments . . . if he had made them he would not establish false laws of motion . . . if he had only deigned to read his contemporaries, he would not have made the blood of the Pacteous veins pass through the liver, fifteen years after the discovery of the true path by Azellius . . . Descartes has neither observed the laws of the fall of bodies and seen a new heaven, like Galileo, nor guessed the rules of the motion of the Stars, like Kepler, nor found the weight (heaviness) of air, like Torricelli, nor calculated the centrifugal forces and the laws of the pendulum, like Huygens, etc. On the other hand, Newton, with the aid of geometry and experience . . . has discovered the laws of gravitation between all bodies, the origin of colors, the properties of light, the laws of the resistance of fluids."

[2] Against this accusation of having introduced occult qualities into philosophy (which incidentally Newton resented all the more strongly since in the very first lines of the "Praefatio ad lectorem" of the first edition of the *Principia* he had already written: "Cum veteres *Mechanicam* in rerum Naturalium investigatione maximi fecerunt, et recentiores [by whom he obviously meant also himself], missis formis substantialibus et qualitatibus occultis, Phenomena Natura ad leges Mathematicas revocare agressi sunt: Visum est in hoc Tractatu *Mathesin* excolere quatenus ea ad *Philosophiam* spectat"), he defended himself in Query XXIII of the Latin *Opticks* (of 1706, p. 335; this is Query XXXI of the second English edition of 1717), attacking Cartesians on their own ground. Thus he writes (*Opticks*, ed. I. B. Cohen and D. H. D. Roller [New York: Dover, 1952], p. 388; I am quoting the English text): "The parts of all homogeneal hard bodies which fully touch another, stick together very strongly. And for explaining how this may be, some have invented hooked Atoms, which is begging the question; and others [Descartes] tell us that bodies are glued together by rest, that is, by an occult Quality or rather by nothing . . . I had rather infer from their cohesion that their Particles attract one another by some Force, which in immediate contact is exceeding strong, at small distances performs the chymical Operations . . . and reaches not far from the particles with any sensible effect." Somewhat later (pp. 344 sq. of the Latin edition; p. 401 of the English edition) he says: "It seems to me further that these particles [the Latin text has *primigeniae*] have not only a *Vis inertiae* accompanied with such passive Laws of Motion as naturally result from that force, but also that they

or, even worse, magic or a miracle,[1] and this in spite of Newton's repeated declarations that he did not take the term "attraction" in its literal meaning and did not ascribe gravity to bodies as their own inner and essential property.[2] Nor could they, with the exception of Huygens, admit the existence of a perfectly void space, that is, the existence of *nothing*,[3] through which that attraction was supposed to act.

Thus Fontenelle, in his famous *Elogium* of Sir Isaac Newton, voiced their and his own misgivings; having presented and duly praised the Newtonian system of universal gravitation and having mentioned Sir Isaac's unwillingness to explain its true nature, he continues:

It is not known in what Gravity consists. Sir Isaac Newton himself was ignorant of it. If Gravity acts only by impulse, we may conceive that a block of marble falling, may be pushed towards the Earth, without the Earth being in any manner pushed towards it; and in a word all the centers to which the motions caused by Gravity have relation, may be immoveable. But if it acts by Attraction the Earth cannot draw the block of marble, unless the block of marble likewise draw the Earth, why should then that attractive power be in some bodies rather than others? Sir Isaac always supposes the action of Gravity in all bodies to be reciprocal and in proportion only to their bulk; and by that seems to determine Gravity to be really an attraction. He all along makes use of this word to express the active power of bodies, a power indeed unknown, and which he does not take upon him to explain; but if it can likewise act by Impulse, why should not that clearer term have the preference? for it must be agreed that it is by no means possible to make use of them both indifferently, since they are so

are moved by certain active Principles such as that of Gravity, and that which causes Fermentation, and the Cohesion of Bodies. These Principles I consider not as occult qualities supposed to result from the specific Forms of Things [Latin: *oriri fingantur*] but as general Laws of Nature, by which the things themselves are formed. Their truth appearing to us by Phenomena, though their causes be not yet discovered [Latin: *licet ipsorum Causae quae sint, nondum fuerit explicatum*]. To tell us that every species of things is endowed with an occult specific Quality by which it acts and produces manifest effects [Latin: *per quas eae Vim certam in Agendo habeant*], is to tell us nothing. But to derive two or three general Principles of Motion from Phaenomena and afterwards to tell us how these Properties and Actions of all corporeal Things follow from those Principles, would be a very great step in Philosophy though the Causes of those Principles were not yet discovered. And therefore I scruple not to propose the Principles of motion above-mention'd, they being of a very general extent, and leave their causes to be found out."

[1] For further discussion of the controversy about Newtonian attraction as a miracle or an occult quality, see Appendix B.

[2] For a further discussion of the controversy about whether gravity is an essential property of matter, see Appendix C.

[3] As is well known, Descartes and many of the Cartesians denied the existence of a void or vacuum, and held instead that extension and matter were identical. For a further discussion of this topic, see Appendix D.

opposite. The continual use of the word Attraction supported by great authority, and perhaps too by the inclination which Sir Isaac is thought to have for the thing itself, at least makes the Reader familiar with a notion exploded by the Cartesians, and whose condemnation had been ratified by the rest of the Philosophers; and we must now be upon our guard, lest we imagine that there is any reality in it, and so expose our selves to the danger of believing that we comprehend it . . .

We must be upon our guard . . . but most people are not:

Thus attraction and vacuum banished from Physicks by Des Cartes, and in all appearance for ever, are now brought back again by Sir Isaac Newton, armed with a power entirely new, of which they were thought incapable, and only perhaps a little disguised.[1]

Fontenelle was right, of course. Words are not neutral. They have, and convey, meanings. They also have a history. Thus the term "attraction," even if mutual attraction be meant, implies, or suggests – as Fontenelle rightly points out – a certain active relation between the attracting and the attracted body: the former is active, the latter is not. Thus the magnet "attracts" iron by the means of a "force" or "virtue" that has its seat within the magnet; it acts upon a piece of iron *ab extra*: the piece of iron is "pulled" toward the magnet by the magnet; it does not "tend" toward the magnet by itself; nor is it "pushed" toward it by the surrounding medium. William Gilbert, for example, who made the earth an immense magnet, when dealing with the mutual "attraction" of two magnets, characteristically does not use this term; he speaks instead of their "coitio."[2] So much for the meaning. As for the history, "attraction" was, of course, widely used by writers on magnetism; and – much more important – it was borrowed from them by Kepler, who explained gravity as the effect of a magnetic or, more exactly, magnetiform force, a *vis attractiva*, or *vis tractoria*, inherent in bodies, by which they drag, or pull, *trahunt*, each other when they are similar; the *vis* by which the earth drags toward itself stones, and also the moon; the force by which the moon attracts our sea. Indeed, Kepler chose the terms "attraction" and "traction" in order to oppose his theory

---

[1] Fontenelle, *Elogium*, pp. 11 sq.; Cohen, *Newton's Papers and Letters*, pp. 453 sq. On Fontenelle, see J. R. Carré, *La Philosophie de Fontenelle ou le sourire de la raison* (Paris: Alcan, 1932). For a discussion of the controversy about attraction as it is found in the *Physica* of the Cartesian Rohault and in the notes added to it by the Newtonian Samuel Clarke, see Appendix E.

[2] See William Gilbert, *De magnete, magnetisque corporibus et de magno magnete tellure physiologia nova* (London, 1600), pp. 65 sq.

to that of Copernicus, according to whom similar bodies – earthen, lunar, and so forth – were endowed (or animated) by an inner tendency to come together and build a whole;[1] "attraction" was also used by Roberval[2] – as Leibniz did not fail to point out – whose

[1] The views held by Copernicus and Kepler on gravity are discussed in Appendix F.

[2] The explanation of gravity by attraction was formulated by Roberval, as a hypothesis, as early as 1636. Thus in a "Letter of Étienne Pascal and Roberval to Fermat," 16 August 1636, in Leon Brunschvicg and Pierre Boutroux, ed., *Oeuvres de Blaise Pascal* (Paris: Hachette, 1923), I, 178 sq., or Paul Tannery and Charles Henry, ed., *Oeuvres de Fermat* (Paris, 1894), II, 36 sq., we find:

"3. It may be that gravity is a quality that resides in the very body that falls itself; it may be that it is in another, that attracts the one which descends, as in the earth. It may also be, and it is very probable, that it is a mutual attraction, or a natural desire of bodies to unite together as is obvious in the case of iron and magnet, which are such that, if the magnet is arrested, the iron, being not hindered, will move toward it. If the iron is arrested, the magnet will move toward it, and if they are both free, they will approach each other reciprocally. Thus, however, that the stronger of the two will traverse a lesser distance . . .

"9. We do not know which of these three causes of gravity is the true one, and we are not even assured that it is one of these, it being possible that it is a different one . . .

"As for us, we call all those bodies equally or unequally heavy that have an equal or unequal power to tend to the common center of heavy things; and the same body is said to have the same weight when it has always the same power: but if this power increases or diminishes, then, though it be the same body, we do not consider it as [having] the same weight. Whether it happens to bodies that move farther away from this center, or approach it, that is what we would like to know, but having found nothing concerning this question that would give us satisfaction, we leave it undecided."

Some years later, Roberval published his *System of the World*. In order to avoid the censure of the Church, he published it as the work of Aristarchus of Samos, claiming, moreover, that he had only corrected the style of a poor Latin version of an Arabic translation of the Greek astronomer's original book; Roberval thus could not be held responsible for the views of the author, although he did acknowledge that the system of Aristarchus seemed to him the simplest. *Aristarchi Samii de mundi systemate partibus et motibus ejusdem libellus* (Paris, 1644); reprinted by Mersenne in his *Novarum observationum physico-mathematicarum . . . tomus III. Quibus accessit Aristarchus Samius* (Paris, 1647).

In his *System of the World*, Roberval asserts that each part of the (fluid) matter which fills the universe is endowed with a certain property, or accident, that makes all parts draw together (*nisus*) and attract each other reciprocally (*sese reciproce attrahant*, p. 39). At the same time he admits that in addition to this universal attraction there are other, similar, forces proper to each of the planets (something that Copernicus and Kepler also admitted) which hold them together and explain their spherical shapes.

Twenty-five years later, on the occasion of a debate in the French Academy of Sciences on the causes of gravity ("Débat de 1669 sur les causes de la pesanteur," in C. Huygens, *Oeuvres complètes* [The Hague: Martinus Nijhoff, 1937], XIX, 628–645), Roberval read a memoir on 7 August 1669 (pp. 628–630) in which he practically reproduced the contents of his letter to Fermat, asserting that there are three possible explanations of gravity, and further that the explanation by mutual attraction, or the tendency of the different parts of matter to unite, was the simplest one. Curiously enough, in this memoir he called attraction an "occult quality."

Roberval's cosmology, as it is presented in his *System of the World*, is extremely vague and even full of confusion. It is understandable that it was heartily condemned by Descartes and that Newton was deeply angered by Leibniz's identification of Newton's views with those of Roberval (see Appendix B). Yet, historically, Roberval's work is interesting not only because it was the first attempt to develop a "system of the world" on the basis of universal attraction, but also because it presented some charac-

cosmology was subjected by Descartes to scathing criticism, and by Gassendi, who tried to combine the Keplerian conception with that of Copernicus and both of them with his own atomism, and finally by Hooke, in his *Attempt to prove the motion of the Earth by Observations* (London, 1674).[1]

Fontenelle did not mention, of course, the historical precedents I am quoting; but he was perfectly aware of them. Thus we can well understand him: was not Sir Isaac reviving all these obsolete, mythical, irrational conceptions from which Descartes had freed us? By no means, answers Voltaire:

Nearly all Frenchmen, learned and others, have repeated this reproach. One hears everywhere: why did Newton not use the word impulsion which we understand so well, instead of attraction which we do not understand? – Newton could have replied to his critics: first, you no more understand the word impulsion than attraction . . . Secondly, I could not accept impulsion, because it would be necessary, in that case, that I should know that celestial matter effectively pushes the planets; but not only do I not know of this matter, I have proved that it does not exist . . . Thirdly, I use the word attraction only to express an effect that I have discovered in nature, a certain and indisputable effect of an unknown principle, a quality inherent in matter, the cause of which someone other than myself will, perhaps, find. It is the vortices that one can call an occult quality, because their existence has never been proved. Attraction, on the contrary, is something real because we demonstrate its effects and calculate its pro-

---

teristic features, or patterns of explanation, which, or at least the analogies of which, we shall find discussed later by Hooke and advocated by Newton and Leibniz.

Thus, according to Roberval, the fluid and diaphanous matter which fills or constitutes the "great system of the world" (*magnum systema mundi*) forms a huge – but finite – sphere in the center of which is the sun. The sun, a hot and rotating body, exerts a double influence on this fluid matter: (*a*) It heats and thus rarefies it; it is this rarefaction and the ensuing expansion of the world-matter that counterbalances the force of the mutual attraction of its various parts and prevents them from falling upon the sun. This rarefaction also confers on the world-sphere a particular structure; the density of its matter increases with the distance from the sun. (*b*) The sun's rotating motion spreads through the whole world-sphere, the matter of which turns around the sun with speeds diminishing with its distance from the sun. The planets are considered as small systems, analogous to the great one, which swim or place themselves at distances from the sun corresponding to their densities, that is, in regions the density of which is equal to their own; thus they are carried around the sun by the circular motion of the celestial matter, as is the case with bodies swimming in a rotating vessel. Strangely enough, Roberval – who never takes any account of centrifugal forces – believes that these bodies will describe circular trajectories!

Roberval has never been studied as he deserves: most of his works remain unpublished; see, however, the excellent *Study of the "Traité des indivisibles" of Gilles Persone de Roberval* . . . by Evelyn Walker (New York: Bureau of Publications, Teacher's College, Columbia University, 1932) and the semipopular book by Léon Auger, *Un Savant méconnu: Gilles Personne de Roberval* . . . (Paris: Blanchard, 1962).

[1] Gassendi's views on attraction and gravity are further discussed in Appendix G, and Hooke's in Appendix H.

portions. The cause of this is in the bosom of God. *Procedes huc, et non ibis amplius.*[1]

Thus, it is not Newton, it is Descartes who made the error of believing that he understood something that he did not, namely matter, than which there is nothing more alien to our minds. This is the reason why he conceived it as filling universal space, whereas, as Newton has shown, it is not certain that there is a cubic inch of solid matter in the whole universe. Newton, on the contrary, has taught us to admit that there are things that we do not understand, and to accept the obvious and palpable qualities of things – of which the force of attraction is one – without trying to get behind them and explain them by fancies.[2]

Geometry, which Descartes had, in a sense, created, was a good guide and would have shown him a safe path in physics. But at the end he abandoned this guide and delivered himself to the spirit of system. From then on his philosophy became nothing more than a ingenious romance . . .[3] He erred [in what he said] about the nature of the soul, the laws of motion, the nature of light; he admitted innate ideas, invented new elements, created a world

that existed only in his imagination and filled it with vortices of subtle matter, the speed of which some people – a nice jibe at Huygens – even calculated, alleging it to be seventeen times that of the earth's rotation without bothering to ascertain whether these vortices existed *in rerum natura.*[4]

For Voltaire, Descartes is another Aristotle, more dangerous even than the old one, because he seems to be more rational. Indeed, Voltaire says,

---

[1] Voltaire, *Lettres philosophiques*, letter XV (vol. 2, p. 27 of Lanson's edition). The scriptural text, which is from the Book of Job, chap. 38, v. 11, should read: "*Usque huc venies, et non procedes amplius.*" In dealing with Newton's philosophy (letters XV and XVI), Voltaire drew his inspiration chiefly from Fontenelle, *Éloge* (see p. 53, n. 1), Pemberton, *A View of Sir Isaac Newton's Philosophy* (London, 1728), and Maupertuis, *Discours sur les différentes figures des astres . . . avec une exposition abbrégée des systèmes de M. Descartes & de M. Newton* (Paris: 1732). Indeed, it was under Maupertuis's influence that Voltaire became converted to Newtonianism; accordingly he asked Maupertuis to read his *Lettres philosophiques* in manuscript at the end of 1732; see Lanson's edition of the *Lettres philosophiques*, vol. 2, pp. 8 and 29. On Maupertuis, see P. Brunet, *Maupertuis* (Paris: Blanchard, 1929).

[2] *Lettres philosophiques*, letter XVI, vol. 2, p. 46. See Pemberton, *A View of Sir Isaac Newton's Philosophy*, p. 291. All Newtonians – Bentley, Keill, Desaguliers, Pemberton – seem to have felt a great satisfaction in proving that there was in the world infinitely more void than solid matter, and that even solid matter was chiefly composed of void.

[3] *Lettres philosophiques*, letter XIV, vol. 2, p. 7.

[4] *Ibid.*, letter XV, vol. 2, pp. 17 sq.

the system of Descartes seems to give a plausible reason for the phenomena, and that reason appeared all the more true as it seemed simple and intelligible to everyone. But in philosophy we have to defend ourselves against things that we believe we understand too easily as well as against things that we do not understand.[1]

The Cartesians believed that philosophy could never renounce the ideal of perfect intelligibility, which was so forcefully enhanced by Descartes, and that science could never accept as its basis nonunderstandable facts. Yet the victorious Newtonian science with its nonunderstandable forces of attraction and repulsion was doing precisely that. And with what success! But the victors not only make history, they also write it. And they are seldom lenient toward those they have vanquished. Thus Voltaire – I am quoting Voltaire because he is the most brilliant and the most influential of all the promoters of Newton – in his famous preface to the French translation of the *Principia*, that of Mme. du Châtelet (and Clairaut), which announced to the world the definitive victory of Newtonian science, pronounced the judgment:

Everything that is given here as principle is indeed worthy of that name; they are the first springs [*ressorts*] of nature, unknown before him; and it is no longer possible to call oneself a physicist without knowing them.

If there were still somebody absurd enough to defend subtle and twisted (screwformed) matter, to assert that the Earth is an encrusted Sun, that the Moon has been drawn into the vortex of the Earth, that subtle matter produces gravity, and all those other romantic opinions that replaced the ignorance of the Ancients, one would say: this man is a Cartesian; if he should believe in monads, one would say he is a Leibnizian. But there are no Newtonians, as there are no Euclideans. It is the privilege of error to give its name to a sect.[2]

[1] *Lettres philosophiques*, letter XV, vol. 2, pp. 16 sq.

[2] *Principes mathématiques de la philosophie naturelle* par feue Madame la Marquise du Chastelet (Paris, 1759), p. vii. In the Cartesian world matter is primitively divided by God into cubes – the simplest geometric figure into which it can be divided – and put in motion or "agitation," in pursuance of which the angles of the cubes are scraped away and the cubes themselves become little spheres. These scraps form the first element, the "agitation" of which constitutes light which is transmitted by the small spheres of the "second" element. Besides the luminous and the luminiferous (first and second) elements, there is also a third one, constituted by the reunion of the "scraps" into twisted, screwformed or "channeled" (*cannelés, striatae*) particles that, on one hand, could "twist" through the intervals or interstices of the closely packed round particles of the "second" element, and, on the other hand, could combine with one another and thus form the larger chunks of gross matter that constitute the surface of the earth and the planets. See Descartes's *Principia philosophiae*, pars 3, art. 52; and Whittaker, *History of the Theories of Aether and Electricity*, I, 8 sq. In his youthful *Monde*, Descartes associated his three elements with the traditional elements of fire, air, and earth (*Oeuvres*, ed. C. Adam and P. Tannery [Paris: 1897–1913], XI, 24). According to Descartes, all heavenly bodies started their existence as luminous and

A harsh judgment. And Sir Isaac, in spite of his aversion to Descartes, and the Cartesians, would probably have made it less harsh. Yet we have to admit that there is in it some measure – and even a great measure – of truth. But it is not the whole truth. Of course it is true that Descartes, who started with a program of a purely rational physics – "There is nothing in my Physics that is not in geometry," he wrote to Mersenne – ended by building a purely imaginary physics, a philosophical romance, as Huygens and Leibniz have called it. It is true that there are in the world neither subtle matter nor twisted (screwformed) particles nor even round ones of the second element that for Descartes constitutes light; it is also true that there are no vortices, and that, if there were any, they would not explain attraction and gravity; last, but not least, it is also true that matter and space are not identical and that, therefore, physics cannot be reduced to geometry,[1] and that, paradoxically, it is the very attempt to do so – something that I have called *géométrisation à outrance* – that led Descartes into a quandary.

One could argue that, in spite of its falseness, the idea of cosmic vortices was not so ridiculous as Voltaire suggests; after all, quite a number of people, among them such unromantic minds as Huygens and Varignon, not to speak of Leibniz, accepted it, though with certain improvements, and Newton himself did not reject it outright, but subjected it to a careful and serious criticism and analysis.[2]

---

fiery stars, and only later became "encrusted" by the accumulation of gross matter on their surfaces; thus they are all "extinguished Suns," a conception by no means as absurd as Voltaire believes it to be. On Descartes's physics, see J. F. Scott, *The Scientific Work of René Descartes* (London: Taylor and Francis, 1952), and G. Milhaud, *Descartes savant* (Paris: Alcan, 1921).

[1] Physics cannot be reduced to geometry – but attempts to so reduce it belong to its nature. Is not Einstein's theory of relativity an attempt to merge together matter and space, or, better, to reduce matter to space?

[2] See *infra*, pp. 97 sq. It may be that he even accepted them in his youth. Whiston, indeed, in his autobiography, says so; see *Memoirs of the Life of Mr. William Whiston by Himself* (London, 1749), pp. 8 sq.: "I proceed now in my own history. After I had taken Holy Orders, I returned to the College, and went on with my own Studies there, particularly the Mathematicks and the *Cartesian* Philosophy; which was alone in Vogue with us at that Time. But it was not long before I, with immense Pains, but no Assistance, set myself with the utmost Zeal to the Study of *Sir Isaac Newton's* wonderful Discoveries in his *Philosophiae Naturalis Principia Mathematica*, one or two of which Lectures I had heared him read in the Publick Schools, though I understood them not all at that Time. . . . We at *Cambridge*, poor Wretches, were ignominiously studying the fictitious Hypotheses of the *Cartesian*, which *Sir Isaac Newton* had also himself done formerly, as I have heared him say. What the Occasion of *Sir Isaac Newton's* leaving the *Cartesian* Philosophy, and of discovering his amazing Theory of Gravity was, I have heared him long ago, soon after my first *Acquaintance* with him, which was 1694, thus relate, and of which Dr. *Pemberton* gives the like Account, and somewhat more fully, in the Preface to his Explication of his Philosophy: It was this. An In-

One could argue, indeed, that it was rather natural to extend to the skies the mode of action that, on this earth, pulled or pushed things toward the center of a rotating fluid and thus seemed to present a model of a mechanism able to engender centripetal forces; and that the need of such a mechanism was so strongly felt that Newton himself, not once but three times, tried to provide it by postulating motion in, or the pressure of, an aethereal medium, the existence of which was just as uncertain as that of the subtle matter from which it descends. And finally one could argue that, somewhat later, the idea of cosmic vortices served as a model for Kant and Laplace; one could also argue that, though there are always limits to our understanding of nature, and that, therefore, we are always obliged to admit things as mere facts without being able to understand and explain them, we, that is, human thought, have never accepted these limits as final, and have always attempted to get beyond them, Comte and Mach notwithstanding. But we cannot dwell on these points. Let us rather remind ourselves that there are other things in Cartesian physics which are of a more lasting value than the vortices and the three elements. Thus, for instance, we find there the first consistent,

---

clination came into *Sir Isaac's* mind to try, whether the same Power did not keep the Moon in her Orbit, notwithstanding her projectile Velocity, which he knew always tended to go along a strait Line the Tangent of that Orbit, which makes Stones and all heavy Bodies with us fall downward, and which we call *Gravity*? Taking this Postulatum, which had been thought of before, that such Power might decrease in a duplicate Proportion of the Distances from the Earth's center. Upon *Sir Isaac's* first Trial, when he took a Degree of a great Circle on the Earth's Surface, whence a Degree at the Distance of the Moon was to be determined also, to be 60 measured miles only, according to the gross Measures then in Use. He was, in some Degree, disappointed, and the Power that restrained the Moon in her Orbit, measured by the versed Sines of that Orbit, appeared not to be quite the same that was to be expected, had it been the Power of Gravity alone, by which the Moon was there influenc'd. Upon this Disappointment, which made Sir *Isaac* suspect that this Power was partly that of Gravity, and partly that of *Cartesius's* Vortices, he threw aside the Paper of his Calculation, and went to other Studies. However, some time afterward, when Monsieur *Picart* had much more exactly measured the Earth, and found that a Degree of a great Circle was 69½ such miles, Sir *Isaac*, in turning over some of his former Papers, light[ed] upon this old imperfect Calculation; and, correcting his former Error, discover'd that this Power, at the true correct Distance of the Moon from the Earth, not only tended to the Earth's center, as did the common Power of Gravity with us, but was exactly of the right Quantity; and that if a Stone was carried up to the Moon, or to 60 Semid[i]-ameters of the Earth, and let fall downward by its Gravity, and the Moon's own menstrual Motion was stopt, and she was let fall by that Power which before retained her in her Orbit, they would exactly fall towards the same Point, and with the same Velocity; which was therefore no other Power than that of Gravity. And since that Power appear'd to extend as far as the Moon, at the Distance of 240000 Miles, it was natural, or rather necessary, to suppose it might reach twice, thrice, four Times, etc., the same Distance, with the same Diminution, according to the Squares of such Distances perpetually. Which noble Discovery proved the happy Occasion of the Invention of the wonderful *Newtonian* Philosophy."

though of course unsuccessful, attempt at a rational cosmology, an identification of celestial and terrestrial physics, and therefore the first appearance in the skies of centrifugal forces; neither Kepler nor even Galileo dared to attribute such forces to the motion of celestial bodies and, accordingly, did not need centripetal forces to counteract them.[1] That is not a mean merit. Voltaire could ignore it; Newton, however, could not. Yet he did not mention it, as he did not mention the Cartesian origin of the concept *quantity of motion* (mv), which he stubbornly maintained as a measure of force against the Huygenian and Leibnizian *vis viva* (mv^2), even while he rejected the Cartesian assertion of the conservation of motion in our world.[2] Nor did he mention that it was Descartes's formulation of the principle of inertia, which placed motion and rest on the same ontological level, that inspired his own.

We shall not judge the Newtonians, nor even Newton, for being unfair to Descartes. Human thought is polemic; it thrives on negation. New truths are foes of the ancient ones which they must turn into falsehoods. It is difficult to acknowledge one's debts to one's enemies. Now Newton's thought, nearly *ab ovo*, had been formed and developed in opposition to that of Descartes. Accordingly, we cannot expect to find praise, or even historical justice, for Descartes in a book whose title, *Mathematical Principles of Natural Philosophy*, contains an obvious reference to, and a rejection of, his *Principles of Philosophy*. We, however, have to try to be more impartial.

[1] For Kepler, circular motion is still the natural motion; his planets, therefore, being pushed by the *species motrix* of the sun, would naturally move in circles without developing any tendency to run away; in other words, their circular motion does not give rise to centrifugal forces, and if in the case of the moon (see p. 174) he needs a force preventing its "fall" upon the earth, it is to an animal or vital force that he recurs, and not to a centrifugal force. It is nearly the same for Galileo; his planets, of course, no longer need moving forces, motors, that would push them around the sun: motion is naturally conserved by itself – but no more than for Kepler do the planets develop centrifugal forces, and thus they do not have to be retained in their orbits by centripetal forces.

[2] The quantity of motion (momentum), in the Cartesian sense, that is, taken as an absolute, positive value, is of course not conserved, either in the world, or even in impact where it has to be taken algebraically, as was discovered by Wren and Huygens, whereas the *vis viva* (kinetic energy) is. It is, however, Descartes's great merit to have posited that some kind of energy is, or must be, conserved; the subsequent development of scientific thought fully maintained this fundamental principle, though substituting progressively for particular kinds of energy the general concept of it. On the history of the struggle between the Cartesians (and Newtonians) with the Leibnizians about the measurement of forces by mv or mv^2, see Erich Adickes, *Kant als Naturforscher* (Berlin, 1924–1925); J. Vuillemin, *Physique et métaphysique kantiennes* (Paris: Presses Universitaires de France, 1955); and Erwin N. Hiebert, *Historical Roots of the Principle of Conservation of Energy* (Madison, Wisconsin: State Historical Society of Wisconsin, 1962).

I shall not develop here a full historical examination of the three Axioms or Laws of Motion (and the corresponding Definitions) that open Newton's *Principia*, though I am convinced that all of them, even the third law, that of equality of action and reaction, are connected with the Cartesian conception of the transmission of motion from one body to another in such a manner that a body cannot give or "communicate" to another more or less than it loses. I shall concentrate on the first law, the law of inertia, which Newton ascribes to Galileo.

This celebrated law tells us that "every body continues in its state of rest or of uniform motion in a right line, unless it is compelled to change that state by forces impressed upon it," or in Latin, which expresses Sir Isaac's thought much better than the modern English translation: *corpus omne perseverare in statu suo quiescendi vel movendi uniformiter in directum, nisi quatenus a viribus impressis cogitur statum ille mutare.*[1] Every word of this formulation is important, both *in se* and for Newton who, as we now know, was an extremely careful writer, who wrote and rewrote the same passage, sometimes five or six times, until it gave him complete satisfaction. Moreover, this was not the first time that he had endeavored to formulate these axioms, or laws, which, by the way, started by being called "hypotheses."[2] Each and every word is important, for instance, the *perseverare*, which is rather badly rendered as "continues." Yet among these words there are two or three that seem to me to be more important than the others; key words, so to speak. Such are, in my opinion, *status* and *in directum*.

Status of motion: by using this expression Newton implies or asserts that motion is not, as had been believed for about two thousand years – since Aristotle – a process of change, in contradistinction to *rest*, which is truly a *status*,[3] but is also a *state*, that is, something that no more implies change than does rest. Motion and rest are, as I have just said, placed by this word on the same level of being, and no longer on different ones, as they were still for Kepler, who

---

[1] *Philosophiae naturalis principia mathematica* (London, 1687), "Axiomata sive Leges Motus," lex I, p. 12; *Sir Isaac Newton's Mathematical Principles of Natural Philosophy*, translated by Andrew Motte, the translation revised by Florian Cajori (Berkeley: University of California Press, 1934), p. 13. The original Motte translation (London, 1729), p. 19, renders the Latin of Newton much better than the Motte-Cajori translation: "Every body perseveres in its state of rest, or uniform motion in a right line, unless it is compelled to change that state by forces impressed thereon."

[2] See p. 32, n. 2.

[3] *Status* comes from *sto, stare,* "to stay," and means station, position, condition. *Status movendi* is just as paradoxical as *statical dynamics*.

66

compared them to darkness and light, *tenebrae et lux*. Now it is precisely and only because it is a *state* – just like rest – that motion is able to conserve itself and that bodies can persevere in motion without needing any force or cause that would move them, exactly as they persist at rest. It is obvious that bodies could not do so as long as motion was considered a process of change. Nothing changes without a cause – at least before quantum physics – as Newton expressly states. Thus, so long as motion was a process, it could not continue without a mover. It is only motion as *state* that does not need a cause or mover. Now, not all motion is such a *state*, but only that which proceeds uniformly and in a right line, *in directum*, that is, in the same direction and with the same speed. No other motion, and particularly no circular or rotational motion, even if it be uniform, is such a state, even though rotation seems able to conserve itself just as well as or perhaps better than rectilinear motion, which, in our experience at least, always comes to a rather quick end.[1] As a matter of fact, as the Greeks observed long ago, the only perpetual motion that we encounter in this world is the circular motion of the skies. The Greeks even thought that circular motion was the only one that was truly uniform and unchanging and could conceive of no other as perpetual. They were wrong, of course. Yet not as wrong as would seem at first – our first – glance. One could even maintain that, for their world, a finite world, they were right: the law of inertia implies an infinite world. We must bear this in mind in order not to be too harsh on those who could not liberate themselves from the spell of circularity and who could not replace the circle by the straight line.

Alas, Galileo was one of them. His great merit was to destroy the scholastic, Aristotelian conception of motion as process, and to assert its perpetual conservation, that is, to assert that a body, once put in motion, will forever continue to move by itself and will never slow down and revert to rest, provided, of course, it does not encounter an outside resistance. But he also assumed such conservation for

[1] Thus the best example of conservation of motion, according to Rohault, is given by a rotating sphere (see *Physica*, pars I, cap. XI, p. 50; *System*, vol. I, p. 53: "11. *Thirdly, if a body moves almost wholly within itself*, so as to transfer very little of its Motion to the Bodies that surround it, *it ought to continue moving longest of all*: Thus we find by Experience, that a smooth well polished Brass Ball, of half a Foot Diameter, supported by two Pivots, will, with a small Stroke, continue to run around for three or four Hours.") This does not imply that Rohault misunderstands the principle of inertia: Newton, indeed, gives the same example; see Lex I: "Trochus . . . non cessat rotari. Majora autem Planetarum & Cometarum corpora motus suos & progressivos et circulares . . . conservant diutius."

circular motion, the eternal motion of the heavenly bodies, and of the earth. And as for rectilinear motion, he, as a matter of fact, never speaks about it as motion in a straight line; he speaks about horizontal motion or motion on a horizontal plane.[1] But at least once he does speak about motion as being a *state*, although this conception, indeed, is implied in all his discussions of motion.[2]

This conception is lacking in Gassendi, who rightly is credited with having been one of the first to publish a formulation of the principle of inertia in his *De motu impresso a motore translato* (1642). Gassendi, indeed, asserted[3] that "stones and other bodies that we qualify as heavy do not have that resistance to motion that is commonly (*vulgo*) thought of" and that in the void space, the imaginary space outside the world where bodies would be neither resisted by other bodies nor attracted by them, all bodies, once put in motion, would move eternally and uniformly in the same direction (*parte*) *in whatever direction* (*in quacumque partem*) *they be impelled;* wherefrom he concludes that all motion, of its own nature, is of such a kind, and that if, *de facto*, in our world, bodies do not move in this way, that is, neither perpetually, nor uniformly, nor in the same direction, it is because they are prevented from doing so and diverted from their path by the attraction of the earth which pulls them "down."[4] We have to recognize the advance made by Gassendi; we have to recognize also that he did not use the term *straight*

---

[1] See Galileo Galilei, *Opere* (Edizione Nazionale; Florence, 1897), VIII, 268, 269, 272, 285. For an English translation, see *Dialogues Concerning Two New Sciences*, trans. by Henry Crew and Alfonso De Salvio (New York: Dover, n.d.), pp. 244, 245, 248, 262.

[2] In Galileo's "Letters on Sunspots," in Stillman Drake, trans., *Discoveries and Opinions of Galileo* (Garden City, New York: Doubleday Anchor Books, 1957), we find: "And therefore, all external impediments removed, a heavy body ... will maintain itself in that state in which it has once been placed; that is, if placed in a state of rest, it will conserve that; and if placed in movement toward the west (for example), it will maintain itself in that movement." But this is an example of motion "on a spherical surface concentric with the earth," and so illustrates circular rather than linear inertia.

[3] One could claim for Bonaventura Cavalieri the distinction of having been the first, in his *Lo specchio ustorio, overo tratato delle settioni coniche et Alcuin loro mirabili effetti intorno al lume, caldo, freddo, suono et moto ancora* . . . (Bologna, 1632), cap. XXXIX, pp. 153 sq., to assert that a body, thrown in any direction whatever, would – if it were not deflected by gravity – continue to move uniformly in that direction by the virtue impressed in it, and, if gravity were added, it would describe a parabola. See my *Études galiléennes* (Paris: Hermann, 1939), part III, p. 133. J. B. Baliani, for whom this distinction has also been claimed, in fact asserted the equivalence of directions only in the second edition of his *De motu gravium solidorum et liquidorum* (Geneva, 1646).

[4] Petri Gassendi, *De motu impresso a motore translato, epistolae duae* (Paris, 1642), cap. XV, p. 60. Also see my *Études galiléennes*, part III, p. 144, and *infra*, Appendix I.

line when asserting that motion will be *in the same part*; that he did not equate motion and rest, and did not treat them as *states*, though asserting conservation of motion as such and stating that "nothing but motion is impressed on the moved [body] by the moving one," the same "motion which the moving [body] has as long as the moved one is conjoined with it," and "that would be continued, and would be eternal, if it were not weakened by a contrary one."[1]

It is only in Descartes, and this already in his unfinished and unpublished *Monde*[2] (1630), that is, long before Gassendi, and also before Cavalieri and Baliani, that we find not only the clear assertion of the uniformity and rectilinearity of "inertial" motion,[3] but also the explicit definition of motion as a *status*. It is precisely the institution of the concept of *status* of motion for actual motion that enables Descartes – and will enable Newton – to assert the validity of his first law or rule of motion, though postulating a world in which pure inertial motion, uniform and rectilinear, is utterly impossible. Actual motion, indeed, is essentially temporal; a body takes a certain time to move from a certain place, *A*, to another place, *B*, and during that time, be it as short as we want, the body is necessarily subjected to the action of forces *qui cogent* it *statum suum mutare*. The *status* as such, however, is connected with time in a different way: it can either endure, or last only an instant. Accordingly, a body in curvilinear, or accelerated, motion changes its *status* every instant, as every instant it changes either its direction or its speed; it is nevertheless every instant *in statu movendi uniformiter in directum*. Descartes expresses this clearly by telling us that it is not the actual motion of a body but its inclination, *conatus*, that is

---

[1] Gassendi, *De motu* . . . , cap. XIX, p. 75; *Études galiléennes*, part III, p. 144; and *infra*, Appendix I.

[2] *Le Monde ou traité de la lumière*; written in or about 1630, published for the first time in 1662, in Leiden; Descartes, *Oeuvres*, vol. XI.

[3] Descartes, of course, does not use this Keplerian term, which means resistance to motion (since Newton, of course, "inertia" means resistance to acceleration); on the contrary, Descartes expressly denies that there is in bodies any kind of *inertia*. See "Lettre à Mersenne," December 1630, *Oeuvres*, II, 466 sq: "I do not recognize any inertia or natural tardity in bodies, any more than M. Mydorge . . . But I concede to M. de Beaune that larger bodies, pushed by the same force, such as larger boats by the same wind, always move more slowly than the others, and this, perhaps, may be sufficient for his reasons, without having recourse to a natural inertia that cannot at all be proved . . . I hold that there is a certain Quantity of Motion in all the created matter that never increases nor diminishes; so that when a body moves another, it loses as much of its motion as it gives to it . . . Now, if two unequal bodies receive as much motion, the one as the other, this same quantity of motion does not give as much speed to the larger as to the smaller, and because of that we can say, in this sense, that the more matter a body contains the more *Natural Inertia* it has."

rectilinear. Newton puts it more cryptically, using only the Cartesian formula *quantum in se est*.

It is, of course, in quite different ways that Descartes and Newton explain that bodies persevere in their *states*. Newton does it by ascribing to matter a certain *vis insita*, "a certain power of resisting by which every body as much as in it lies perseveres in its present state whether it be rest or moving uniformly in a right line" – *potentia resistendi qua corpus unumquodque, quantum in se est, perseverat in statu suo vel quiescendi vel movendi uniformiter in directum*. This power, or force, borrowing a Keplerian term and enlarging its meaning (for Kepler it meant, as we know, resistance *to motion*), Newton calls *vis inertiae*.[1]

Now Descartes did not believe in endowing bodies with powers, not even the power of self-conservation. He believed in continuous creation, the continuous action of God on the world without which, abandoned, so to speak, to itself, the world would immediately revert to the *nihil* out of which it had been created. Thus it is not a *vis insita*, it is God that he entrusts with the task of conserving the bodies in their *states* of motion and rest. It is clear that, being immutable, God can only conserve them in their rectilinear (right) motions, *mouvements droits*,[2] and not in the curved ones, just as it is because of this immutability that he conserves in the world the quantity of motion he has put into it.

In his *Monde*, Descartes tells us that he will not describe *our* world, but another one, a world that God has, or could have, created somewhere, far from ours, in the imaginary spaces beyond our world. It is a trick, of course. Descartes wants to avoid criticism; he wants also, and even in the first line, to show that this new *monde*, where there is nothing but extension and motion, will turn out to be absolutely indistinguishable from ours[3] and thus to suggest – without incurring the danger of being accused of impiety – that the laws of

---

[1] Newton is perfectly aware of the origin of the term and of the new meaning that he gives to it. Thus, as Professor I. B. Cohen of Harvard informed me, Newton, in his own annotated and interleaved copy of the second edition of his *Principia*, made the following note, which he probably planned to insert in a later edition: "Non intelligo vim inertiae Kepleri qua corpora ad quietem tendunt, sed vim manendi in eodem seu quiescendi seu movendi statu." This and similar annotations will appear in our critical edition of the *Principia*. On the difference between the two concepts of inertia, see E. Meyerson, *Identité et réalité* (Paris: Alcan, 1908), app. III, pp. 528 sq.

[2] Descartes makes a word play: *droit* = right and *droit* = straight. See *Oeuvres*, XI, 46; see also *infra*, p. 74.

[3] Newton will do the same in his youthful *De gravitatione et aequipondio fluidorum* (see Newton's *Unpublished Scientific Papers*; cited below in note 2, p. 82).

nature suffice to bring order out of chaos and to build up a world – like ours – without any special act of God giving it its present shape.[1]

The supreme law of the *monde* is the law of constancy, or conservation. What God has created, he maintains in being; thus we do not need to inquire about the first cause of the motion of things, *primum movens* and *mobile*; we can simply admit that things started to move at the same time the *monde* was created; and, this being so, it follows therefrom that this motion will never cease, but only pass from subject to subject.

Yet, what is this motion and what are the laws relevant to it? It is not at all the motion of the philosophers, *actus entis in potentia prout est in potentia*, a congeries of words that Descartes declares to be so obscure that he fails to understand them,[2] nor even the motion that the philosophers call *local motion*. Indeed, they tell us on the one hand that the nature of motion is difficult to understand, and on the other that motion has a much greater degree of reality than rest, which they assert to be a privation. For Descartes, on the contrary, motion is something about which we have a perfect and complete understanding. In any case, he says that he will deal with that motion which is easier to understand than the lines of geometers[3] and that makes bodies pass from one place to another and occupy successively all the spaces that are between them. "This motion has not a higher degree of reality than rest; quite the contrary, I conceive that rest is just as much a quality that has to be attributed to matter when it remains in a place as motion is one that has to be

---

[1] See *Le Monde, Oeuvres,* **XI,** 37. In his *Principia philosophiae* (pars 3, art. 43), Descartes says that, although it is hardly possible that causes from which all phenomena can be clearly deduced should be false, he nevertheless (art. 44) will hold those causes that he will write about only as hypotheses (the French translation says that he will not assert that those hypotheses which he proposes are true); and he says further (art. 45) that he will even assume some causes that are clearly false (the French translation says that he will suppose some causes that he believes to be false); for example, those cosmological hypotheses from which one deduces that the world evolved from chaos to cosmos are certainly false; they must be false because Decartes does not doubt that the world was created by God with all the perfections which it now has, as the Christian religion teaches.

[2] *Ibid.,* p. 39.

[3] *Ibid.:* "Geometers . . . explain the line by the motion of a point and the surface by that of a line"; Descartes adds: "Philosophers suppose also several motions that, as they think, can be performed without the body changing its place, as those that they call: *motus ad formam, motus ad calorem, motus ad quantitatem* and a thousand others. As for myself, I do not know any which is easier to conceive than the lines of geometers: which allows bodies to pass from one place to another, and occupy successively all the spaces that are between."

attributed to matter when it changes place."[1] Moreover, the motion of the philosophers is of such a strange nature that it tends toward its own destruction in rest, whereas the Cartesian motion, like everything else, tends to its self-preservation.

The rules or laws of nature which Cartesian motion obeys, that is, the rules according to which God makes nature act, are derived herefrom very easily.[2] The first is that every particular part of matter continues always in the same state (*état*) as long as the encounter of other parts of matter does not force it to change. That is, if it has a certain bulk it will never become smaller, if not divided by others; if it is round or square, it will never change that shape without being compelled to do so by others; if it is at rest somewhere, it will never depart therefrom, if not driven by others; and if it has once begun to move, it will continue forever, with the same force, and in the same direction until others stop or retard it.

There is nobody who believes that this rule is not observed in the ancient [our] world concerning bulk, figure, rest, and similar things; but the Philosophers have made an exception for motion, which, however, is what I want most expressly to be comprised under this rule. However, do not think, therefore, that I wish to contradict them: the motion they are speaking about is so much different from the one that I conceive, that it is quite possible that what is true concerning one is not true concerning the other.[3]

The second rule concerns the conservation of motion in the action of one body upon another.

When one body pushes another, it cannot impart any motion to the other, unless it loses at the same time as much of its own; nor take away [motion] from the other unless its own increases as much. This Rule, together with the preceding one, tallies very well with all those experiences in which we see that a body begins or ceases to move because it is pushed or stopped by another. For, having supposed the preceding Rule, we are

[1] *Le Monde, Oeuvres*, XI, 40.

[2] *Ibid.*, p. 38. See Rohault, *Physica*, pars I, cap. XI, p. 51; *System*, vol. 1, p. 53: "13. Because the World is full, a Body moving in a straight Line, must of Necessity push another, and that a Third, but it ought not to go on thus infinitely; for some of those which are thus pushed, will be forced to turn out of the Way, in order to take the Place of that which was first moved, that being the only Place where they can go, and which is free for them, Wherefore when any Body is moved, a certain Quantity of Matter must always necessarily be moved in the Form of a Ring or a Circle, or some way equivalent thereto." See Newton, *Principia* (1687), Book II, Prop. XLIII, Th. XXXIII, pp. 359–360; (1713), Book II, Prop. XLIII, Th. XXXIV, Cor. 2, p. 334; Motte-Cajori, Prop. XLIII, Th. XXXIV, p. 372.

[3] Descartes is perfectly right, even more than he is aware: indeed his motion – *status* – is quite different from the motion – *process* – of the "philosophers"; accordingly what is true concerning one is not true concerning the other.

exempt from the trouble in which the *Docti* find themselves when they want to give a reason why a stone continues to move for some time after having left the hand of the one who threw it: for one should rather ask why it does not continue to move forever? But the reason is easy to give. For who can deny that the air in which it moves opposes to it some resistance?[1]

However, it is not the resistance as such that has to be taken into account, but only that part of it that the moving body succeeds in overcoming; that is, the moving body slows down in direct proportion to the motion it imparts to the resisting body. In spite of his appeal to experience – resistance of air – Descartes is fully conscious that the rules that he is formulating – not to mention those that he will formulate later (the rules of impact) – do not agree very well with the common-sense experience of everyday life. So much the worse for this latter! Indeed,

though everything that our senses have ever experienced in the Old World, would seem manifestly contrary to what is contained in these two Rules, the reason which taught them to me seems so strong that I feel myself obliged to suppose them in the new world that I am describing to you. For what more firm and solid foundation could be found on which to establish a truth, even if one could choose according to one's wish, than the constancy and immutability of God?[2]

Yet not only the two preceding rules follow manifestly from the immutability of God, but also a third one. "I shall add," continues Descartes,

that when a body moves, though its motion is most frequently performed in a curved line . . . nevertheless each of its particular parts tends always to continue its own [motion] in a right line. Thus their action, or the inclination that they have to move, is different from their [actual] motion.

[1] *Le Monde, Oeuvres*, XI, 41; see Rohault, *Physica*, pars I, cap. XI, p. 44; *System*, vol. 1, p. 47: "How it comes to pass that a Body in Motion, should continue to be moved, is one of the most considerable Questions relating to Motion, and has very much perplexed the Skill of Philosophers; but upon our Principles, it is not difficult to account for it: For, as was before observed, nothing tends to the Destruction of itself, and it is one of the Laws of Nature, *that all Things will continue in the State they once are*, unless any external Cause interposes; thus that which exists to Day, will endeavour, as far as it can, to exist always; and on the contrary, that which has no Existence, will endeavour, if I may so speak, never to exist; for it never will exist of itself, if it be not produced by some external Cause: So also that which is now a Square, will, as far as is in its Power, always continue a Square. And as that which is at Rest, will never of it self begin to move, unless something move it; so that which is once in Motion, will never of itself cease to move, unless it meets with something that retards or stops its Motion. And this is the true Reason why a Stone continues to move after it is out of the Hand of him that throws it."

[2] *Le Monde, Oeuvres*, XI, 43.

[Thus for instance, if one turns a wheel on its axis,] its parts, though moving circularly, have an inclination to move in a straight line. [Thus, also,] when a stone is whirled in a sling, it not only moves [in a] straight [line] as soon as it leaves the sling, but, moreover, all the time that it is in the sling, it [the stone] presses the center of the sling [showing thereby that it follows the circular path by compulsion.] This Rule – the rule of rectilinear motion – is based on the same foundation as the other two, namely on the principle that God conserves everything by one continuous action, and consequently, does not conserve it as it may have been some time previously, but precisely as it is at the very instant in which He conserves it. But of all movements, it is only right-line motion that is entirely simple, and whose whole nature is comprised in an instant. For,[1] in order to conceive right-line motion, it is sufficient to think that a body is in action to move toward a certain side, which is something that is found in each of the instants that can be determined during the time that it moves. Whereas, in order to conceive circular motion, or any other that may occur, one needs to consider at least two of its instants, and the relation that there is between them.[2]

As we see, rectilinear – right – motion is endowed with very particular ontological properties, or perfections; it is literally the "right" motion. Descartes thus concludes with a jest:

According to this Rule, we have to say that God alone is the Author of all motions that there are in the world in so far as they are, and in so far as they are right; but that it is the diverse dispositions of matter that makes them irregular and curved, just as the Theologians teach us that God is also the Author of all our actions in so far as they are, and in so far as they have any goodness, but that it is the diverse dispositions of our will that may render them vicious.[3]

Descartes's *Principles of Philosophy*, the Latin edition of which appeared in 1644 and the French translation in 1647,[4] changes the order of the rules of nature that govern motion (now consistently called laws) – thus the third becomes the second, and the second, the third – as well as the manner in which they are presented: the *Principles* was – or was intended to be – a textbook, whereas the *Monde* was not. But Descartes does not change their derivations, nor their contents, at least for the rules or laws of motion *proprio sensu*. The rule concerning the action of bodies on one another (the second rule of the *Monde*, the third law of the *Principles*) and asserting the conservation of (the quantity of) motion in percussion is

---

[1] *Le Monde, Oeuvres*, XI, pp. 43, 49.
[2] *Ibid.*, p. 45.
[3] *Ibid.*, pp. 46, 69.
[4] The text of the French translation, due to the Abbé Petit, who made it under Descartes's supervision, is sometimes more explicit than the Latin original. It is, therefore, indispensable to use both.

not changed, but enriched and developed in the *Principles* so as to enable Descartes to derive from it the rules of impact – something that he neglected to do in the *Monde*.

As he did in the *Monde*, Descartes here introduces the fundamental law of nature, the law of conservation, by an appeal to divine immutability according to which God acts always in the same manner, maintaining in the world the same quantity of motion and rest that he put in the world when he created it:[1]

Indeed, though this motion is only a mode of the moved matter, it has nevertheless a certain and determined quantity, which, as we can easily understand, is always the same in the whole universe, though it can change in its singular parts. Thus, for instance, we have to think, that when a part of matter moves twice as quickly as another, and this other is twice as large as the first, there is as much motion in the small as in the large part; and that every time the motion of one part becomes slower, the motion of the other becomes proportionally quicker. We understand also that it is a perfection in God that not only is He immutable in Himself, but also that He acts in a most constant and immutable manner[2] . . . Wherefrom it follows that it is in the highest degree conformable to reason to think . . . that He maintains in matter the same quantity of motion with which He created it.[3]

From divine immutability we can also derive the knowledge of certain rules, or laws or nature,

of which the first is that every thing, considered as simple and undivided, perseveres, as far as it can, in the same state and never changes [its state] but for external causes. Thus, if a certain part of matter is square, we are convinced very easily that it will perpetually remain square . . . If it is at rest, we do not believe that it will ever begin to move if not compelled by some cause. Nor is there any reason to think that, if it moves . . . and is not impeded by anything, it should ever by itself cease to move with the same force. It is therefore to be concluded that a thing which moves, will move forever as far as it can [and will not tend to rest because] rest is contrary to motion, and nothing by its own nature can tend toward its contrary, that is toward its own destruction; [therefrom comes] the first law of nature, that everything, as much as in it lies, perseveres always in the same state; thus that which once started to move will continue to move forever.[4]

[1] *Principia philosophiae*, pars 2, art. 36: "Deum esse primariam motus causam, et eandem semper motus quantitatem in universo conservare."

[2] Descartes makes an exception for the "mutatio" about which we are informed by divine Revelation.

[3] *Principia philosophiae*, pars 2, art. 37.

[4] *Ibid.*: "Prima lex naturae: quod unaquaeque res, quantum in se est, semper in eodem statu perseveret: sicque quod semel movetur, semper moveri pergat." The Latin expression *quantum in se est* is not easy to render in a modern language.

As in the *Monde*, Descartes tells us that the rectilinearity of the *status* of motion in which bodies persevere *quantum in se sunt* follows equally from the immutability of God, wherefore the second law of nature asserts *quod omnis motus ex se ipso sit rectus* though, as a matter of fact, no actual motion is such *in rerum natura*, where, indeed, all motions proceed in a kind of circle.[1] As in the *Monde*, centrifugal forces that arise in the circular motion are cited as proof.[2] As in the *Monde*, nay, much more strongly than in the *Monde*, Descartes insists that it is a vulgar error to put motion and rest on different levels of being and to think that one needs more power in order to put in motion a body that is at rest than, conversely, to put at rest a body that is in motion. He is right, of course: the ontological equivalence or equiperfection of motion and rest is the very center of the new conception of motion, as Newton will tacitly recognize by using the Cartesian term *status*.[3] It is, moreover, something that the contemporaries not only of Descartes but also of Newton found very difficult to admit, or even to understand; thus neither Malebranche nor Leibniz was ever able to grasp it.[4]

The French translation of Descartes's *Principia philosophiae* has "autant qu'il se peut"; John Clarke, in his translation of Rohault (see p. 54, n. 3), says "as far as it can"; the Motte–Cajori translation of Newton's *Principia* says "as much as in it lies" (Definition III, p. 2). I am using the text of the French translation of Descartes, since it is more explicit than the Latin text.

[1] *Principia philosophiae*, pars 2, art. 33: "Quomodo in omni motu integer circulus corporum simul moveatur." See p. 72, n. 2.

[2] *Ibid.*, art. 39: "Altera lex naturae: quod omnis motus ex se ipso sit rectus; et ideo quae circulariter moventur, tendere semper ut recedant a centro circuli quem describunt." It is interesting to note that Descartes, still fully conscious that the conservation of motion does not immediately imply its rectilinearity, asserts conservation and rectilinearity in *two* different laws, whereas Newton reunites them in *one*.

[3] For a further discussion of motion and rest as states, see Appendix J.

[4] Clarke will not fail to point this out. Thus he mentions Malebranche's *De la recherche de la vérité* (Paris, 1674–1675; 6th ed., Paris, 1712), which had been translated into English in 1694–1695 and 1700. See Rohault, *Physica*, pars I, cap. X, p. 39; *System*, vol. 1, p. 41, note 1: "As to the Definition of *Rest*, all are very well agreed in it: But whether Rest be a mere *privation* of Motion, or *any Thing positive*, this is sharply disputed. Cartes and some others contend, that That which is at Rest, has some kind of Force by which it continues at Rest, and whereby it resists every thing that would change its State; and that Motion may as well be called a Cessation of Rest as Rest a Cessation of Motion. *Malebranch in his Enquiry after Truth, Book 6 Chap. 9* and others, contend to the contrary, that Rest is a mere privation of Motion; their Arguments may be seen briefly exposed in M. Le Clerc's Physics Book 5, Chap. 5. One thing only I would observe by the way, relating to this Matter, and that is, that *Malebranch* and *M. Le Clerc*, who follows his opinion, in the following Argument, beg the Question. Suppose, say they, a Ball at Rest; suppose that God should cease to Will any Thing concerning it; what would be the consequence? It would be at rest still. Suppose it be in Motion; and that God should cease to will that it should be in Motion, what would follow then? It would not be in Motion any longer. Why not? Because the Force, whereby the Body in Motion continued in the State it was, is the *positive* Will of God, but that whereby it is at Rest is only privative: This is a manifest beg-

We have to admit, however, that this complete equivalence of motion and rest led Descartes to his unfortunate conception of rest as resistance (a kind of antimotion) and to attribute to the body at rest a force of resistance (a quantity of rest) opposed and parallel to the moving force (quantity of motion) of a body in motion, and it is from this conception that, with perfect logic, he deduces his utterly wrong rules of impact, according to which a smaller body, with whatever speed it might move, will never be able to put in motion a larger one, because it will not be able to overcome the force of resistance of the larger and "stronger" one.[1] It will, therefore (pro-

---

ging of the Question. In reality the *Force* or *Tendency* by which Bodies, whether in *Motion* or at *Rest* continue in the State in which they once are, is the mere *Inertia* of Matter; and therefore, if it could be that God should forbear willing at all; a Body that is once in Motion, would move on for ever, as well as a Body at Rest, continue at Rest for ever."

And as for Leibniz, Clarke adds to the edition of his polemics with the "learned M. Leibniz" (see *The Leibniz–Clarke Correspondence*, ed. by H. G. Alexander [Manchester: Manchester University Press, 1956], p. 135) a long choice of quotations from the works of the latter that demonstrate rather clearly that Leibniz has never understood the principle of inertia. Which, by the way, was a blessing . . . how could he, otherwise, have conceived the principle of least action?

Malebranche's *De la recherche de la vérité où l'on traite de la nature de l'esprit de l'homme et de l'usage qu'il en doit pour éviter l'erreur dans les sciences* was first published in Paris in 1674–1675 by A. Pralard, but without the name of the author; only in the fifth edition, published in Paris by M. David in 1700, was the author identified as "Nicholas Malebranche, Prêtre de l'Oratoire de Jésus." English translations appeared in 1694–1695 and in 1700. The best modern critical edition of the *Recherche de la vérité* is that of Mlle. Geneviève Lewis in 3 volumes (Paris: Vrin, 1946). The discussion on motion and rest is to be found in Book 6 ("De la méthode"), part 2, ch. 9 (vol. 2, pp. 279 sq. of the Lewis edition).

Le Clerc, *Opera philosophica*, tomus IV, *Physica sive de rebus corporeis libri quinque* (Amsterdam, 1698, fifth ed., 1728; also Leipzig, 1710; and Nordlusae, 1726), lib. V, cap. V, *De motu et quiete*, sec. 13, "Regulae sive leges motus," says that a body once put in motion *in eodem statu manet*; he raises the question (sec. 14), however, whether rest, *quae est motui opposita sit aliquid positivum an vero privatio dum taxat motus*, and concludes that it is only a privation – an opinion accepted by all philosophers but Descartes. Le Clerc does not quote Malebranche, but he does follow his reasoning closely: "Fingamus Deum nunc globo motum induere, qui opus est ab eo fieri ut motus sistantur? Nihil profecto, nisi ut desinat velle globum moveri."

[1] See Descartes's fourth rule, *Principia philosophiae*, pars 2, art. 49. The Latin text is rather short and simply says, "If body C were at rest, and were somewhat larger than B, then, with whatever speed B should move toward C, it would never move this C; but would rebound from it in the opposite direction; this because the body at rest resists the greater speed more than the lesser, and that in proportion to the excess of the one over the other; and therefore the force of C to resist B will always be greater than that of B to impel." The French translation adds an explanation: "As B would not be able to push C without making it move as quickly as it would move thereafter itself, it is certain that C must resist as much more in proportion to the speed with which B approaches it as B comes toward it more quickly, and that this resistance must prevail over the action of B, because it is larger than it. Thus, for instance, if C is double B, and if B has three degrees of motion, it cannot push C, which is at rest, if it does not transfer to it two degrees, that is one for each half of it, and retains for itself only the third; this is because it [B] is not larger than each of the halves of C, and cannot move

vided both bodies are *hard*), rebound and return with the same speed:

Third law: that a body that encounters another, stronger [than itself], loses none of its own motion [wherefore the stronger gains nothing]; and, when it encounters a weaker one, it loses as much as it gives [transfers] to this latter.[1]

Of course this is not so in common experience, and Descartes has to admit it, as he did in the *Monde*. This time, however, he does not reject common experience; he explains that his law, valid in itself, presupposes conditions that are not realized – and cannot be realized – in *rerum natura*, namely, that the bodies in question are completely separated not only from each other, but also from the rest of the world, that they are absolutely rigid, and so on. *De facto* they are immersed in a more or less liquid medium, that is, they are in the midst of other matter that moves in all possible directions and presses and pushes the rigid bodies from all sides. Accordingly, a body that pushes another *in a fluid* has the "help" of all the particles of the fluid that move in the same direction, and therefore "the

---

thereafter more quickly than they. In the same way, if B has thirty degrees of speed, it would be necessary for it to transfer twenty of these to C; and if it has three hundred, it must transfer two hundred and so on conferring always the double of what it would retain for itself. But as C is at rest, it resists ten times more the reception of twenty degrees than that of two, and a hundred times more the reception of two hundred; thus, in proportion as C has more speed, it finds in B more resistance, And because each half of C has as much force to remain in its rest as B has to push it, and as they resist it both at the same time, it is obvious that they must prevail and compel it to rebound. Accordingly, with whatever speed B should move toward C, at rest and larger than it, it can never have the force to move it."

The reasoning of Descartes appears, at first glance, utterly absurd. As a matter of fact, it is perfectly correct, provided, of course, we accept his premises, that is, the absolute rigidity of C and B; in this case, indeed, the transmission of motion, that is, its acceleration, should be instantaneous and, accordingly, a body would resist ten times as strongly its jumping from rest to twenty degrees of speed as it would resist its jumping to two.

[1] *Principia philosophiae*, pars 2, art. 40. It is usually admitted that of the Cartesian rules of impact the first one, according to which two equal (hard) bodies, moving toward each other in a straight line and with equal speed, rebound after impact with the same speed but in opposite directions, is correct, in contradistinction to the others that are false. As a matter of fact, as Montucla has already noticed (*Histoire des mathématiques* [nouvelle ed.; Paris, 1799], II, 212), the first law is just as false as the rest: perfectly hard bodies (not "infinitely elastic," but rigid) will not rebound, and if Descartes asserts that they will it is only because he cannot admit the loss of motion that would result if they did not.

The Cartesian rules of impact are so false, and appear even so utterly absurd (for instance, rule IV, dealt with in the preceding note), that they are usually dismissed with a shrug by historians who do not recognize the perfect logic with which they are deduced by Descartes from his premises, that is, conservation of motion and absolute rigidity of the bodies that hit each other.

least force suffices to move hard bodies surrounded by a fluid," that is, all bodies that exist in the world.[1]

It is not my intention to discuss here the Cartesian laws of impact, in spite of the inherent interest of such a study. As I have already mentioned, they are all wrong, as Newton could not fail to recognize, and their perusal could only strengthen his aversion to Descartes's physics – mathematical physics without mathematics – and justify the famous "error, error" that he allegedly wrote upon the margins of his copy of the *Principia philosophiae*.[2] Yet, be that as it may. Here we are dealing only with Newton's first law of motion, that of inertia, and it is enough for us to have shown that, in its conception as well as in its formulation in the *Philosophiae naturalis principia mathematica*, Newton was directly influenced by Descartes.

As we have seen, the rules or laws of motion of Descartes's *Principia* are in full agreement with those that he established in the *Monde*. There is, however, in his later work something that, in respect to the former, constitutes an important change, namely, a semirelativistic conception and a purely relativistic definition of motion together with the identification of his notions in the *Monde* with the common, or vulgar, conception. Thus he explains first that

the words place [locus] and space do not signify anything really different from the body which we say is in a certain place, and designate only the dimension, the figure of the body, and the way in which it is situated among other bodies. For it is necessary, in order to determine this situation, to take into account some other [bodies] that we consider to be at rest; but as

[1] *Principia philosophiae*, pars 2, art. 56. It is because he did not take into account the "abstract" (Descartes does not use this term) character of the laws of impact that Rohault raised objections against this law; see Rohault, *Physica*, pars I, cap. XI, p. 50; *System*, vol. 1, p. 53: "But because a Body cannot so transfer its Motion to another as not to partake with that Body to which it is transferred, but will retain some to itself, though it be never so little; therefore it should seem that a Body once in Motion should never afterwards be entirely at rest, which is contrary to Experience. But we ought to consider, that two Bodies which have but very little Motion, may be so connected and adjusted to each other, as to be *in a manner* at Rest, which is all that Experience shows us."

[2] See Voltaire, *Lettres philosophiques*, letter XV (Amsterdam [=Rouen], 1734), p. 123: "M. Conduitt, nephew of Newton, assured me that his uncle had read Descartes when he was 20 years of age, that he put pencil notes on the margins of the first pages, and that it was always the same note that he repeated: *error*; but that, tired of having to write *error* everywhere, he threw the book away and never re-read it." In the subsequent editions of the *Lettres philosophiques*, Voltaire suppressed this passage (see Lanson's edition, vol. 2, p. 19). According to Sir David Brewster, *Memoirs of the Life, Writings and Discoveries of Sir Isaac Newton* (Edinburgh, 1855), I, 22, n. 1, it was in the margins of Descartes's *Geometry* and not in the margins of his *Principia philosophiae* that Newton wrote *error, error*: "Newton's copy of Descartes's *Geometry* I have seen among the family papers. It is marked in many places in his own hand: *Error, Error, non est Geom.*"

those which we so consider can be different, we can say that the same thing, at the same time, changes its place and does not change it. For instance, if we consider a man sitting at the stern of a boat which the wind drives away from the harbor, and take into account only this vessel, it will seem to us that this man does not change his place, because we see that he remains always in the same situation with respect to the parts of the vessel on which he is; and if we refer to the neighboring lands, it will seem to us that this man changes incessantly his place because he goes away from them; if, besides that, we suppose that the Earth turns on its axis and that it makes as much way from sunset to sunrise as the vessel makes from sunrise to sunset, it will, once more, seem to us that the man who is sitting at the stern, does not change his place, because we determine this place by reference to some immobile points that we imagine to be in the Heaven.[1]

Having thus explained the relativity of "place," Descartes continues:

Motion (that is, *local* motion – I find no other in my thought, and therefore think there is no other to be feigned in *rerum natura*), as it is commonly understood, is nothing else than the *action by which a body passes from one place to another*. And therefore, in the same way that, as we have previously mentioned, the same thing can at the same time be said to change and not to change its place, it can be said to move and not to move. For example, someone who sits in a boat while it departs from the harbor thinks that he is moving if he refers himself to the shore and considers it unmoved; but not if [he refers himself] to the very boat in the midst of the parts of which he maintains his position. And since we commonly [*vulgo*] think that there is action in every motion, but in rest a cessation of action, he is more properly said to be at rest than to move, as he does not feel in himself any action.

But if we consider what must be understood as motion, not according to the vulgar use [of the term] but according to the truth [*ex rei veritate*], in order to attribute to it a determinate nature, we shall say that it is a translation of a part of matter, or of a body, from the vicinity of those bodies that immediately touch it, and that are considered at rest, to the vicinity of others.[2]

Descartes explains that he said "from the vicinity of those that touch it to the vicinity of others"[3] and not "from one place to

---

[1] *Principia philosophiae*, pars 2, art. 13.

[2] *Ibid.*, art. 25: ["Motum esse" translationem unius partis materiae, sive unius corporis ex vicinia eorum corporum quae illud immediate contingunt et tanquam quiescentia spectantur, in viciniam aliorum." Descartes insists upon referring moving bodies to bodies *considered* as *being at rest*, something to which Newton will object (see *infra*, pp. 105 sq).

[3] *Ibid.*, art. 28. It is rather curious to see Descartes oppose to the concept of "place" (*locus*) his concept of the "vicinity of bodies that immediately touch it," since this is nothing else than an adaptation of the Aristotelian definition of place: surface surrounding a body.

another" only because "place" is a relative concept, and that, accordingly, all kinds of motion can be attributed to a given body; whereas, if we take his definition of motion, there will be only one motion that we will attribute to a body as being its own and proper motion. He adds, moreover, that his definition implies reciprocity of motion, and that

we cannot conceive that a body AB could be transported from the vicinity of a body CD without knowing also that the body CD is transported from the vicinity of the body AB, and that there is needed, obviously, as much force and action for the one as for the other. Thus, if we should want to attribute to motion a proper nature, not related to anything else, we would say that, when two reciprocally contiguous bodies become mutually separated, and transported one to one side and the other to the other, there will be as much motion in the one as in the other.[1]

The insertion of a semi-Aristotelian conception of place into a world in which everything is in motion and in which there is no fixed point to which motion could be referred enabled Descartes to "save" the relativistic conception of motion with its full choice of the point of reference, the value of which is sufficiently obvious, and to give a precise meaning to the concept of the "proper" motion of a body, which was rather important.[2] Also, which was even more important, it gave him the means to circumvent the condemnation of the Copernican system by the Church; this condemnation – the trial of Galileo – frightened Descartes and made him decide not to publish his *Monde*. Ten years later he found, or at least believed he found, a way out: his new definition of motion enabled him to maintain that, *secundum veritatem*, the earth, though carried in and by its vortex around the sun, did not move. Accordingly, Descartes claimed, the condemnation did not touch him: indeed he did not ascribe motion to the earth; quite the contrary, he asserted that it was at rest.[3] It is hardly surprising that this attempt, so subtle and at the

[1] *Ibid.*, art. 29. This statement is obviously incompatible with Descartes's "third" law of motion.
[2] After all, we move with respect to the earth, houses, and so forth, and we participate in a number of motions, as does a sailor on a ship, or the watch in his pocket.
[3] Having explained that the hypotheses of Copernicus and Tycho are not different *in quantum hypotheses* (*Principia philosophiae*, pars 3, art. 17), Descartes continues: "That I deny the motion of the earth with more care than Copernicus, and more truth than Tycho" [art. 19]; "that the earth is at rest in its heaven, being nevertheless transported by it" [art. 26]; "the earth, properly speaking, does not move, nor the planets, though they are transported by the heavens" [art. 28]; "even if motion were taken improperly and according to the vulgar usage, no motion should be attributed to the earth; in this case, however, it would be proper to say that the other planets move" [art. 29]. See Rohault's *Physica*, pars II, cap. 24, pp. 303 sq.; *System*, vol. 2, p. 62.

same time so naïve, of the "trop précautionneux philosophe," as Bossuet has called him, to dissociate himself from Copernicus and Galileo did not deceive anyone, except some modern historians. Yet it worked.[1]

On the other hand, it was this relativistic definition of motion – a definition which indeed became official in the Cartesian school – that first aroused Newton's opposition to Cartesian physics, and not the theory of vortices, which later became the main focus of his attack on Descartes in the *Principia mathematica*. This definition, or conception, together with some of Descartes's most fundamental philosophical theses, such as the identification of extension and matter and the concomitant rejection of the void and the independent reality of space, the radical distinction of thinking and extended substances, and, curiously enough, Descartes's assertion that the world is only "indefinite" but not "infinite" – these are subjected by Newton to a long and searching criticism in one of his hitherto unknown papers to which I have already referred.

This paper, a long manuscript of 40 pages, the transcript of which Dr. John Herivel and Professor Rupert Hall have kindly put at my disposal, is only a fragment.[2] Newton's aim, as he tells us at the very beginning, was to treat the problems of the equilibrium of fluids and of bodies in fluids, and to treat them in two different ways: "insofar as this matter pertains to mathematics . . . in the manner of geometers, deriving particular propositions from abstract, self-evident principles"; and, insofar as it is a part of natural philosophy, to illustrate the propositions thus arrived at "by numerous experiments" in a series of *scholia et lemmata*.[3] As a matter of fact he did neither: instead of writing a hydrostatic paper, he wrote a philosophic one. I, at least, do not regret it. I think, indeed, that it is for us of exceptional value, as it enables us to get some insight into the formation of Newton's thought, and to recognize that preoccupation with philosophical problems was not an external *additamentum*

[1] It was only in 1664 that the *Principia philosophiae* was put on the *Index librorum prohibitorum*, and even then not because of the obvious Copernicanism of Descartes, but because of the incompatibility of his conception of matter with the dogma of transubstantiation.

[2] *MS. Add.* 4003, "De gravitatione et aequipondio fluidorum." It is now included in A. Rupert Hall and Marie Boas Hall, *Unpublished Scientific Papers of Isaac Newton, A Selection from the Portsmouth Collection in the University Library, Cambridge* (Cambridge, England: Cambridge University Press, 1962), pp. 89 sq. I shall give references to this publication.

[3] *Unpublished Scientific Papers*, p. 90. It is interesting to note that this is exactly the manner in which he will write his *Principia*.

but an integral element of his thinking.[1] Unfortunately, we cannot assign a precise date to this manuscript; it is some time around 1670.[2]

Newton, as he will always do, starts with Definitions and informs us that the terms *quantity*, *duration*, and *space* do not need definitions and, moreover, cannot be defined, as they are better known than all the terms by which we may try to define them. But he defines

I. *Place* as *the part of space which a thing fills adequately;*
II. *Body* as *that which fills a place;*
III. *Rest* as *continuation in the same place;*
IV. *Movement* as *change of place*, or, if one prefers, *transition, translation, or migration of a body from place to place*, the term *body* being taken not in a philosophical manner as a physical substance endowed with sensible qualities, but, abstracting from these much in the same way as geometers, only as something extended, mobile, and *impenetrable*.[3]

Newton's definitions, especially the listing of impenetrability as a fundamental characteristic of body – for Descartes it was a derivative one – imply clearly the rejection of the Cartesian identification of extension and matter, as well as Descartes's relativistic definition of motion. Newton, of course, is perfectly conscious of this. Thus, he writes:

Since in these definitions I have supposed that there is space apart from bodies, and [have defined] motion with respect to the parts of this space itself and not with respect to the position of neighboring bodies . . . lest this should be thought to have been assumed gratuitously against the Cartesians, I shall now try to demolish his fictions.[4]

One of the worst, if not the worst, of these "fictions" is the relativistic view of motion, insofar as it is considered to be the true view – or, in Newton's terminology, the "philosophical" view – and opposed to the common view, which Newton identifies with his own, and which Descartes considered as "vulgar" and false. Newton therefore tries to "demolish" it by a series of arguments, good, bad, and even sophistic, of which the most important – it appears in the *Principia mathematica* – makes an appeal to the effects

[1] It shows also that Newton had very thoroughly studied the *Principia* of Descartes.
[2] The Halls (*Unpublished Scientific Papers*, p. 90) think that it was "an essay written by a young student . . . between, say, 1664 and 1668," or, if later, in any case before 1672.
[3] *Ibid.*, p. 91.
[4] *Ibid.*

engendered, or not engendered, for the definition of true and real motion and, conversely, of false and only apparent motion. Thus, in particular, it is clear that it is not the "philosophical" rest of the earth and the planets, but their "vulgar" motion around the sun that gives rise to centrifugal forces. It is also clear that a purely relative "philosophical" motion will never produce such forces. It is clear, therefore, which of the two should be treated as real.

Descartes, moreover, seems to admit it,

in contradicting himself. For he says that the Earth and the other planets, properly speaking and in the philosophical sense, do not move and that he who says they are moved because of their translation in respect to the fixed stars speaks without reason, in the vulgar sense.[1] Yet later he posits in the Earth and Planets an endeavor [*conatus*] to recede from the Sun as from a centre about which they are moved, by which [*conatus*, and] through a similar *conatus* of the revolving vortex, they are librated in their distances from the Sun. What then? Does this *conatus* result from the, according to Descartes, true and philosophical rest, or from the vulgar and non-philosophical motion?[2]

The conclusion is obvious: it is the motion that has true and real effects – and not that which has none – that is the true and real motion: that is, *absolute and physical* motion is not change of position with respect to other bodies – this is only an external denomination – but change of place in, or with respect to, the unmoved and unmovable space that exists apart from bodies and that, later, will be called absolute space. And it is only in such a space that "the velocity of a body whose motion is unimpeded could . . . be said to be uniform, and the line of its motion straight."[3]

It is interesting to note that in his opposition to the relativistic conception of motion Newton goes so far as to reject the contention that, if two bodies move with respect to each other, motion can be ascribed, *ad libitum*, to the one or to the other, and to object to Descartes, that, if one accepted the Cartesian theory, it would be impossible, even for God, to determine exactly the place that celestial bodies had occupied, or will occupy, in some previous or future moment – this because there are, in the Cartesian world, no stable landmarks with respect to which these places could be calculated:

It is necessary therefore that the determination of place, and conse-

---

[1] *Principia philosophiae*, pars 3, arts. 26, 27, 28, 29.
[2] *Unpublished Scientific Papers*, pp. 92 sq.; see *supra*, p. 81, n. 3.
[3] *Ibid.*, p. 97. Newton is perfectly right: the law of inertia implies absolute space.

quently of local motion, be referred to some immovable entity, such as extension or space alone, as it is regarded as something actually distinct from bodies (*quale est sola extensio vel spatium quatenus ut quid a corporibus revera distinctum spectatur*).[1]

Still, a doubt remains. Did not Descartes demonstrate that there is no space distinct from bodies, that extension, matter, and space are identical? This he did, on one hand, by showing "that body in no wise differs from extension," that is, if we abstract from body all the sensible and dispensable qualities, such as "hardness, color, weight, cold, heat, etc. . . . only one remains, its extension in length, breadth, and depth," and, on the other hand, by pointing out that void space is nothing and cannot therefore have any determinations, all of which, such as distance, dimension, and so on require a subject, or a substance, in which to inhere.[2]

We have thus "to respond to these arguments by showing, in turn, what is extension and body and how they differ from one another."[3] We must go even further and, "since the distinction of substances into thinking and extended . . . is the main foundation of the Cartesian philosophy," we have to attempt its utter destruction. According to Newton, the great mistake made by Descartes was to try to apply to extension the old division of being into substance and accident, whereas, as a matter of fact, it is neither.[4] It is not a sub-

---

[1] *Unpublished Scientific Papers*, p. 98.

[2] *Ibid.*, pp. 98 sq.

[3] *Ibid.*, p. 98.

[4] *Ibid.*, p. 99: "[Extensio] habet quendam sibi proprium existendi modum qui neque substantiis, neque accidentibus competit." It is interesting to note that the traditional division of being into substance and accident is inapplicable to space (and time), they being neither, as was asserted by Pascal, in 1648, in his letter to M. Le Pailleur (see Pascal, *Oeuvres complètes* [Paris: Bibliothèque de la Pléiade, 1954], p. 382): "*Ni substance ni accident.* Cela est vrai, l'on entend par le mot substance, ce qui est ou corps ou esprit; car en ce sens, l'espace ne sera ni substance, ni accident; mais il sera espace, comme, en ce même sens, le temps n'est ni substance, ni accident, mais il est temps, parce que pour être, il n'est pas nécessaire d'être substance ou accident." It is also asserted by Gassendi, who may have been the source for both Pascal and Newton; see *Syntagma philosophicum, Physica*, pars I, sec. I, lib. II, cap. I, p. 182, col. 1 (*Opera philosophica* [Lyons, 1658]), t. I: "Being (*ens*) in the general acceptance of this term, is not adequately divided into substance and accident; but place and time must be added as two (supplementary) members of the division, as if we said: all being (*ens*) is substance, or accident, or place in which are all substances and all accidents, or time in which all substances and all accidents perdure." *Ibid.*, p. 183: "Besides it is clear that by the name of space and spatial dimensions we do not understand anything else but the spaces commonly called imaginary, which the greatest part of the Holy Doctors admit to exist outside of the world"; *ibid.*, lib. IV, cap. IV, p. 307: "It seems that place is nothing else than space which, if it is occupied by a body is called full (*plenum*), if unoccupied is called empty (*inane*)"; see also his earlier *animadversiones* against the tenth book of Diogenes Laertius (dealing with the philosophy of Epicurus) of 1649 (Petri Gassendi, *Animadversiones in decimum librum Diogenis Laertii . . .*

stance because it does not, as substances do, sustain or support (*substat*) affections, and also because it does not subsist absolutely by itself. In truth, extension is a certain effect of God, *effectus emanativus*,[1] and also, or thus, a certain affection of every entity, that is, of everything that is. But it is also not an accident,

since we are able clearly to conceive extension as existing alone without any subject as when we imagine spaces beyond the world or spaces void of bodies; since we believe it to exist wherever we imagine bodies to be absent, and are unable to believe that it would perish with a given body if God were to destroy that [body]; it follows [therefrom] that it [extension] does not exist in the manner of an accident inhering in a subject. It is, therefore, not an accident.[2]

As for the negation of the reality of void space, Descartes is also in error, an error of which he can be convicted by his own principles. It is true, of course, that there is no clear idea of nothing, since it has no properties; but we have a most clear idea of space unlimited in length, breadth, and depth. And there are many properties of space that we conceive quite as clearly. Space, therefore, is by no means nothing.[3] It is, as we have just said, an *effectus emanativus Dei*.

Space, of course, is conceived by Newton as being infinite, which is neither surprising nor very original.[4] But it is interesting to note (*a*) that Newton feels himself to be in opposition to Descartes, who, indeed, asserted space – or, more exactly, the world – to be only indefinite, in contradistinction to God, whom alone he conceived to be infinite;[5] (*b*) that Newtonian demonstrations, in their spirit,

---

[Lyons, 1649]. I, 613): "Enim vero videtur [Peripatetici] primum in generali illa seu Entis, seu Rei distributione peccari; quoniam illis duobus divisionis membris, Substantiae nempe, et Accidenti, adjicienda alia duo sunt, ipsis etiam generaliora, videlicet Locus et Tempus, res exclusissimae a Substantia, Accidentisque categoriis"; *ibid.*, p. 614: "Hoc igitur modo tam Locus, quam Tempus, neque Substantia, neque Accidens sunt; et res tamen sunt, seu nihil non sunt; Sunt enim omnium Substantiarum, Accidentarumque Locus et Tempus" (in this way neither place nor time is either substance or accident; and nevertheless they are entities, that is, they are not nothing; they are, indeed, the place and time of all substances and accidents. On Gassendi's possible influence on Newton, see R. S. Westfall, "The Foundations of Newton's Philosophy of Nature," *British Journal for the History of Science 1* (1962), 171–182.

[1] The expression *effectus emanativus* gives us to understand that space, though not independent of God (*independens et improductum*; see Gassendi, *Syntagma*, p. 182) is not, *proprie loquendo*, a creature produced in being by God's will; it is an *effectus* (and not an attribute), but a necessary one.

[2] Hall and Hall, *Unpublished Scientific Papers*, p. 99.

[3] *Ibid.*, pp. 98 sq. Newton turns Descartes's reasoning (see *supra*, p. 85) upside down.

[4] *Ibid.*, p. 101.

[5] Descartes, in the *Principia philosophiae*, asserted the indefinite extension of space, stating that we cannot feign a limit without imagining at the same time that it extends beyond that limit (pars 1, art. 26). "We shall recognize, moreover, that this world, or

are deeply Cartesian; and finally (c) that, to a certain extent at least, his objections parallel those that Henry More raised against the Cartesian distinction.[1]

Space, indeed, is extended in all directions to infinity. For we are unable to imagine any limit [of it] without, at the same time, *understanding* (*intelligendo*) that there is space beyond it. And hence all lines, straight, parabolic, hyperbolic, and all cones and cylinders, and all other figures [that we may conceive inscribed in it] extend to infinity and are nowhere limited though [they may be] intercepted here and there by lines and surfaces of all kinds proceeding transversely to them.[2]

The infinity we are dealing with here is an actual one; and the demonstration of this actuality that Newton gives us is rather interesting: he asks us to consider a triangle in which we increase one of the angles at the base. The apex then will continually recede from this base until, when the angles become supplementary, that is, when the sides of the triangle become parallel, the distance of this apex, or point of intersection,

will be greater than any assignable value . . . nor can anyone say that it is infinite in imagination only and not actually so, [as] the point where the produced lines [sides of the triangle] meet will always be actual, even if it is imagined to be beyond the limits of the world.

If, on the other hand,

someone objects that we are unable to imagine an infinite distance, this I concede; contending nevertheless that we are able to *understand* it . . .

---

the totality of corporeal substance, has no limits of its extension. Indeed, wherever we should feign such limits to be, we shall not only imagine that there are beyond them some indefinitely extended spaces, but we shall also perceive that they are truly imaginable and real; and, for that reason, they contain also an infinitely extended corporeal substance" (pars 2, art. 21). We shall, however, not call it infinite but only indefinite: "Of all the things in which, under certain considerations, we cannot find a limit, we shall, however, not assert that they are infinite, but shall consider them as indefinite. Thus, as we cannot imagine so large an extension that we would not understand that it can be still larger, we shall say that the multiplicity of possible things is indefinite" (pars 1, art. 26). Thus also the number of parts into which matter can be divided, the number of stars, and so on: "All these we shall call indefinite rather than infinite, in order to reserve the term infinite to God alone, because in Him alone in all respects we not only do not recognize any limits, but also understand positively that there are none; and also because concerning other things we do not understand in the same positive way that (in certain respects) they lack limits, but only, in a negative way, we confess that their limits, if they had them, cannot be found by us" (pars 1, art. 27).

[1] See my *From the Closed World to the Infinite Universe* (Baltimore: Johns Hopkins Press, 1957).

[2] Newton (*Unpublished Scientific Papers*, p. 100) conceives space as the *locus* of all kinds of figures (spheres, cubes, triangles, straight lines, and so forth) inscribed in it *ab aeternitate*, and only revealed by "material delineation": "we firmly believe that space was spherical before the sphere occupied it." This space is all figures in mathematical actuality, but in physical potentiality it is the "receptacle," the platonic *chōra*.

We are able to *understand* that a greater extension exists than we can ever imagine. Which faculty of *understanding* has to be clearly distinguished from imagination.[1]

Which is undoubtedly true. But it is also purely Cartesian, as purely Cartesian as the following passage in which Newton asserts the positive nature of the concept of infinity:

If one says further that we do not conceive what is infinite except by the negation of the limits of what is finite, and that it is a negative and therefore worthless concept, I deny it. Quite the contrary. It is the concept of limit that contains a negation, and so "infinitude", since it is the negation of a negation (that is, of finitude), will be a word which, with respect to both its meaning and our conception, is most positive, even though grammatically it seems negative.[2]

Yet, if this is so, why does Descartes assert that "extension" is not infinite but indefinite? An assertion which is not only false but even wrong with respect to grammar:[3] *indefinite*, indeed, always denotes something future, that is, not yet determined, whereas the world, which may have been indefinite before it was created, is certainly not indefinite now. And if Descartes maintains that we do not know, positively, that the world has no limits, but are only ignorant whether it has them, this has nothing to do with the matter, since God knows positively that there are no such limits; furthermore, we ourselves very certainly understand that extension, or space, transcends all limits.

As a matter of fact, Newton knows very well why Descartes denies the infinity of space and ascribes it only to God. For Descartes, infinity means perfection of being.[4] Thus he "fears" [*metuit*] that if he asserts space to be infinite he would have to identify it with God because of the perfection of infinity. Yet he cannot do this, because for him space or extension is identical with material substance, which is utterly and absolutely opposed to thinking, or spiritual, substance. But for Newton all of this is erroneous: space is not the same thing as body; infinity, as such, is not a perfection; and extension and mind belong close together.

---

[1] *Unpublished Scientific Papers*, p. 101.
[2] *Ibid.*, pp. 101 sq. Descartes's views on the infinite and the indefinite are discussed in Appendix K.
[3] Newton says: "a Grammaticis corrigendus est," *Unpublished Scientific Papers*, p. 102.
[4] *Ibid.* For a brief history of ideas about God and the infinite until the time of Descartes, see Appendix L.

Indeed, space is connected not with matter but with being, *spatium est entis quatenus ens affectio.*

No being exists, or can exist, which is not related to space in some way. God is everywhere, created minds are somewhere, and body is in the space that it occupies; and whatever is neither everywhere nor anywhere [*nec ubique, nec ullibi*] does not exist. And hence it follows that space is an emanative effect of the primary existing being [that is, of God: *spatium sit entis primario existentis effectus emanativus*] because, if an entity is being posited, space is posited also. And the same can be said about duration; namely, both are affects, or attributes, according to which is denominated the quantity of existence of any individual [entity] with respect to the amplitude of its presence and of its perseverance in being. Thus, the quantity of existence of God with respect to duration is eternal and with respect to the space in which he is [present], infinite. And the quantity of existence of a created thing with respect to duration is as great as its duration since the beginning of its existence, and with respect to the amplitude of presence, as great as the space in which it is.[1]

Rather curious, this complete parallelism of time and space which leads Newton to frame the concept of quantity (or magnitude) of presence that supplements the Cartesian conception of duration as quantity (or magnitude) of being. Curious, and important. Indeed, it seems to me that we can perceive its echo in the famous texts of the *Principia* in which Newton insists so strongly on God's being always (*semper*) and everywhere (*ubique*), not only by his action but also by his substance.[2] Where does the idea come from? Probably from Henry More, who criticized Descartes's contention that the world is only "indefinite" and not infinite; who opposed Descartes's negation of void and his identification of extension and matter, asserting that the essence of matter was different from mere extension and included impenetrability and solidity, and that, *vice versa*, extension, or space, was different from matter and existed quite independently of it – whence the possibility and even the necessity of space void of matter; and who rejected the Cartesian radical separation of extended and thinking substances, asserting that every thing, not only matter but also minds and even God, was extended – space for More being just God's "extension" as opposed to the Cartesian conception which would exclude minds and God from the world by making them unable to be in it, neither somewhere (*alicubi*) nor

---

[1] *Unpublished Scientific Papers*, p. 103.
[2] *Philosophiae naturalis principia mathematica* (2nd ed., Cambridge, England, 1713); *Scholium Generale*, p. 485; Motte–Cajori, p. 545.

everywhere (*ubique*), thereby compelling them to be nowhere (*nullibi*). More, therefore, called Cartesians *nullibistae*.[1]

Let us dwell for a moment on young Newton's conception of space in its being and in its relation to God and time. The connection between Newton's earlier view and the view which he develops, or hints at, in the Queries and in the *Principia* is rather striking. Thus from the young Newton we learn that space is necessary, eternal, immutable, and unmovable, that though we can imagine there is nothing in space we cannot think that space is not (More had said that we

[1] In his first letter to Descartes, 11 December 1648, More writes (*Oeuvres*, V, 238): "*First*, you establish a definition of matter, or of body, which is much too wide. It seems, indeed, that God is an extended thing (*res*), as well as the Angel; and in general everything that subsists by itself, so that it appears that extension is enclosed by the same limits as the absolute essence of things, which however can vary according to the variety of these very essences. As for myself, I believe it to be clear that God is extended in His manner just because He is omnipresent and occupies intimately the whole machine of the world as well as its singular particles. How indeed could He communicate motion to matter, which He did once, and which, according to you, He does even now, if He did not touch the matter of the universe in practically the closest manner, or at least had not touched it at a certain time? Which certainly He would never be able to do if He were not present everywhere and did not occupy all the spaces. God, therefore, extends and expands in this manner; and is, therefore, an extended thing (*res*) . . .

"*Fourth*, I do not understand your indefinite extension of the world. Indeed this indefinite extension is either *simpliciter* infinite, or only in respect to us. If you understand extension to be infinite *simpliciter*, why do you obscure your thought by too low and too modest words? If it is infinite only in respect to us, extension, in reality, will be finite; for our mind is the measure neither of the things nor of truth. And therefore, as there is another *simpliciter* infinite expansion, that of the divine essence, the matter of your vortices will recede from their centers and the whole fabric of the world will be dissipated into atoms and grains of dust."

This is not quite correct, as in the Cartesian world there is no "expansion" into which the vortices could recede; they are bound and limited by other vortices, and so on *ad infinitum*, or, to speak with Descartes, *ad indefinitum*. It is different, of course, for Henry More, who believes in infinite space, which he considers to be an attribute of God, and in finite matter, utterly different from space. Yet he understands that Descartes, who identifies space (extension) and matter, can hardly admit the infinity of such (material) extension. Thus he tells him (*ibid.*): "I admire all the more your modesty and your fear of admitting the infinity of matter as you recognize, on the other hand, that matter is divided into an actually infinite number of particles. And if you did not, you could be compelled to do so."

Descartes answers, of course, that, though he does not want to dispute about words, and thus will not object if someone wants to say that God is extended because he is everywhere, he has to deny that there is any real extension in a spiritual substance, such as God, or an angel; he adds (letter of 5 February 1649 to Henry More, *Oeuvres*, V, 267 sq.) that it is not as "an affectation of modesty, but as a precaution, and, in my opinion, a necessary one, that I call certain things indefinite rather than infinite. For it is God alone whom I understand positively to be infinite; as for the others, such as the extension of the world, the number of parts into which matter is divisible, and so on, whether they are *simpliciter* infinite or not, I confess not to know. I only know that I do not discern in them any end, and therefore, in respect to me, I say they are indefinite. And though our mind is not the measure of things or of truth, it must, assuredly, be the measure of things that we affirm or deny. What indeed is more absurd or more inconsiderate than to wish to make a judgment about things which we confess to be unable to perceive with our mind?"

cannot disimagine space), and that if there were no space God would be nowhere. We learn also that all points of space are simultaneous; we learn finally that space is not divisible and that, therefore, the divine omnipresence does not introduce composition in God, any more than our presence to, or in, our body introduces divisibility or partition in our soul. Nay, "in the same way as we conceive one moment of duration to spread throughout universal space without having parts, so is it not contradictory that mind should be diffused throughout space without being divided in parts."[1]

There is, of course, nothing more traditional – and anti-Cartesian – than the idea of the mind, or soul, being present in the body *tota in toto et tota in omnibus partibus*; still, in spite of the traditional assertion of God's omnipresence, this idea had seldom been applied to the relation of God and the world.[2] Yet, for Newton, it is just this presence that explains how God is able to move bodies in space by his will – just as we move our body by the command of our will – and that even explains how he could have created bodies out of pure space, or at least – and here Newton follows the Cartesian pattern of presenting his idea as a mere "hypothesis" – how he could have created something that, without being body, would nevertheless be able to exhibit all the phenomena that are actually produced by bodies.[3]

As a matter of fact, all God had to do was to endow some determined parts of space with impenetrability with respect to each other, with the ability to reflect light, and also with mobility and perceptibility. There was no need to create matter, because in order to obtain the "phenomena" of bodies it is not necessary to postulate the existence of an incomprehensible material substance: the impenetrable and mobile parts or particles of space explain the "phenomena" perfectly; thus, they would impede each other's motion, and reflect one another, as well as light, and, generally speaking, behave exactly like, or at least in a manner very similar to, material bodies.

And if they were bodies, then we should be able to define bodies as being

---

[1] *Unpublished Scientific Papers*, p. 104; see *infra*, pp. 112. sq. On Newton's view of time (and its relation to that of Barrow), see E. A. Burtt, *The Metaphysical Foundations of Modern Physical Science* (Garden City, New York: Doubleday Anchor Books, 1954), pp. 155 sq.

[2] Newton's God is not the soul of the world and the world is not his body. See Newton's *Opticks* (New York: Dover, 1952), Query 31, p. 403; and the "General Scholium" at the end of Book III of the 1713 and later editions of Newton's *Principia* (p. 544 of the Motte–Cajori edition).

[3] *Unpublished Scientific Papers*, p. 105.

determinate quantities of extension that God, present everywhere, endows with certain conditions, which are (1) that they be movable and therefore I have not said [that they are] numerical parts of space that are absolutely immobile, but only definite quantities that can be transferred from space to space; (2) that two [particles] of this kind be not able to coincide in whatever part, that is, that they be impenetrable and therefore when they meet by mutual motion, they stop and are reflected according to certain laws; (3) that they be able to excite in created minds different perceptions of the senses and phantasy and conversely be moved by them [the created minds]... They would be no less real than bodies, and no less entitled to be called substances.[1]

Nay, they would *be* substances. And even intelligible ones.

Thus, as we see, all that God had to do was to make *some* parts of the Cartesian extension impervious to each other – some, but not all: the persistence of void spaces between these impervious parts is

[1] *Unpublished Scientific Papers* p. 106. See the Halls' comment in the introduction to Part II (Mechanics) of *Ibid.*, (p. 81): "Berkeley ... invoked God ... in order that matter should exist. Newton, on the other hand, denied matter in order that God should exist. The scientist was more a theologian than a philosopher." I shall not discuss here the Halls' interpretation of Berkeley's philosophy, but, as for Newton, it is interesting to note that, according to Pierre Coste – Coste translated Newton's *Opticks* into French (Amsterdam, 1720; 2nd ed., Paris, 1722) and knew Newton rather well – Newton did not abandon his view of "immaterial matter" and its creation by God, even in his old age. Indeed, in a footnote to the third edition of his translation of Locke's *Essay Concerning Human Understanding*, which was published in Amsterdam in 1735 (the first edition of Coste's translation of the fourth English edition of Locke's *Essay*, *Essai philosophique concernant l'entendement humain* . . . was published in Amsterdam by Henri Schelte in 1700), Coste reports a conversation that he had with Newton a long time after Locke's death about a particularly obscure passage of the *Essay*. In this passage (Book IV, ch. X, par. 18; see A. C. Fraser's critical edition of the *Essay* [Oxford: Clarendon Press, 1894], II, 321) Locke tells us that if we made an effort we could, though very imperfectly, conceive the creation of matter by God. As Locke, however, does not say anything about the manner of this creation, Coste could not make any sense out of the passage until he was enlightened by Newton; see p. 521, note, of the above-mentioned Amsterdam, 1735, third edition, which is partially quoted by Hélène Metzger, *Attraction universelle et religion naturelle* (Paris: Hermann, 1938), p. 32, and partially translated by Fraser in note 2, p. 321, of his previously cited edition of Locke's *Essay*: "Enfin, longtemps après sa mort, M. le Chevalier Newton, à qui je parlais, par hazard, de cet endroit du Livre de M. Locke me découvrit tout le mystère. Souriant il me dit d'abord que c'était lui même qui avait imaginé cette manière d'expliquer la création de la matière, que la pensée lui en étoit venue dans l'esprit un jour qu'il vint à tomber sur cette question avec M. Locke et un Seigneur Anglois (le feu comte de Pembroke, mort au mois de Fevrier de la présente année 1733). Et voici comment il expliqua sa pensée: *On pourrait*, dit-il, *se former en quelque manière une idée de la création de la matière en supposant que Dieu eût empêché par sa puissance que rien ne pût entrer dans une certaine portion de l'espace pur, qui de sa nature est pénétrable, éternel, nécessaire, infini, car dès la cette portion d'espace aurait l'impénétrabilité, l'une des qualités essentielles à la matière; et comme l'espace pur est absolument uniforme, on n'a qu'à supposer que Dieu aurait communiqué cette espèce d'impénétrabilité à autre pareille portion de l'espace, et cela nous donnerait en quelque sorte une idée de la mobilité de la matière, autre qualité qui lui est aussi très essentielle.*" It is difficult to understand why Newton told Coste that this view occurred to him during a conversation with Locke and Pembroke and did not tell him that he had developed it in his youth – but we cannot doubt Coste's report.

essential and it was the great error of Descartes to fail to recognize this, and thus fail to recognize that impenetrability is something that does not belong to extension as such, but that God has to confer impenetrability on some parts of extension by a special act of his will, which, of course, being present in all extension, or space, he could easily do.

Newton's insistence on God's "presence" in the world and on the analogy between his action upon it and the way in which we move our own bodies is rather amazing. It leads him to certain assertions that one does not expect to find from his pen. Thus he tells us that, if we knew how we move our limbs, we would be able to understand how God causes a given space to become impenetrable and to put on the form of a body. "It is clear that God created the world by no other action than that of willing in the same way as we also by the sole action of willing move our bodies." Wherefrom it follows that "that analogy between our faculties and the divine faculties is greater than Philosophers have . . . supposed it to be: it is stated in the Scripture that we have been created in the image of God."[1] Accordingly even the creative power of God is somehow adumbrated in us.

This creation of matter out of pure space invincibly reminds us of the manner in which, in the *Timaeus*, bodies are formed out of the chaos – the Cartesian extension, incidentally, is only a modernized re-edition of Plato's chaos; yet it is not to Plato but to Aristotle that Newton refers his conception, telling us that "between extension and the form imprinted on it there is nearly the same relation that the Aristotelians posit between primary matter and substantial form, insofar as they say that matter is able to assume all forms."[2] A rather curious statement, which shows that Newton's knowledge of the history of philosophy was just as bad as Descartes's. But let us go back to Newton's comments on Descartes. According to Newton, his own conception of the relation of God to space and of mind to body has a great advantage over Descartes's, as it clearly involves the most important truths of metaphysics and best confirms and explains them. Indeed,

we are not able to posit bodies without at the same time positing that God exists and that he has created bodies in empty space out of nothing . . . But if with Descartes we say that extension is body, are we not opening the way to atheism? . . . Extension is not created but was from eternity and since we have an absolute conception of it without having to relate

---

[1] *Unpublished Scientific Papers*, pp. 107–108.   [2] *Ibid.*, p. 107.

it to God, we are able to conceive that it exists though imagining at the same time that God is not. [This all the more so since] if the division of substance into extended and thinking is legitimate and perfect, then God would not contain in himself extension even in a preeminent manner and would therefore be unable to create it; God and extension would be complete and absolute entities and the term substance would be applicable to each of them in the same sense [*univoce*].[1]

It may seem rather unfair to raise an accusation of opening the way to atheism against a philosophy which asserts that God's existence is known *per se* and is the first and most certain truth in our possession, on which everything else is based; which so far rejects the autonomy and the autarchy of the world that it denies to it the very faculty of existing and maintaining itself in being – even with God's "habitual" concourse – and requires instead a continuous creation; and which, conversely, so far magnifies the creative power of God that it makes not only the existence of the world but also the "eternal truth" of mathematics dependent on his will.[2] Yet, as we know, such an accusation was made by More,[3] and was repeated by Newton and Cotes,[4] who thought the Cartesian world was too complete and too self-sufficient to need, or even admit, any intervention of God. According to Newton, Descartes had confused created bodies with the "eternal, infinite, and uncreated" extension – that is, with void space – a confusion which leads to metaphysical errors as it leads to physical ones, rendering the motion of planets and even projectiles impossible. "For it is impossible that a corporeal fluid should not oppose the motions of projectiles" . . . And "if aether were a corporeal fluid without any pores, it would, however subtilised by division, be as dense as any other such fluid and would yield with no less inertia to the motion of projectiles."[5] This is an argument which Newton will use in the *Principia*, and in the *Opticks*.[6] As for the

---

[1] *Unpublished Scientific Papers*, p. 109.

[2] According to Descartes, even the "eternal ideas and truths" of mathematics are created by God, who could have made twice two be equal to five, etc., etc., etc. Could have – but did not; for if twice two was *really* five and not *four*, God would be deceiving us and that is something that he cannot do.

[3] See *supra*, pp. 89 sq. See also p. 271, n. 4.

[4] See *infra*, p. 95; though primarily directed against Leibniz's conception of God as *intelligentia supra mundana*, the insistence of the *Scholium Generale* that God is *Dominus* and not *Ens perfectissimum* aims certainly also at Descartes; see *infra*, p. 112, n. 1, and p. 271, n. 4. [5] *Unpublished Scientific Papers*, p. 113.

[6] See *Philosophiae naturalis principia mathematica* (1687), Book III, Prop. VI, Th. VI, Cor. 3, p. 411; Motte–Cajori, p. 414; *Optice* (London, 1706), Qu. 20, pp. 310 sq.; *Opticks* (second English edition of 1717 and later editions), Qu. 28. The first edition of the *Opticks* appeared in English in 1704; a Latin edition appeared in 1706; a second English edition appeared in 1717; a third in 1721; a fourth in 1730, reprinted 1952 (New York, Dover).

Principia, I have already said that it is, in my opinion, anti-Cartesian to the core; its aim is to oppose to the Cartesian philosophy, with its apriorism and its attempt at global deduction, another and rather different "philosophy," a philosophy more empirical and at the same time more mathematical than that of Descartes, a philosophy which restricts itself to the knowledge of "la surface des choses," to use the expression of Jean Perrin, and which sees its goal in the study of the mathematical framework of nature, and the mathematical laws of the forces acting in nature. Or, to quote Newton himself, "from the phenomena of motion to investigate the forces of nature, and from these forces to demonstrate other phenomena."

Yet, in spite of this radical opposition, we do not find in the *Principia* an open criticism of the philosophy of Descartes; what we find is a detailed and decisive criticism of his purely scientific theories, or hypotheses. There are, of course, good reasons for this, the best one being the very structure of the *Principia*: it is essentially a book on rational mechanics, which provides principles for physics and for astronomy. In such a book there is a normal place for the discussion of Cartesian optics, or of the vortices, but not of his conception of the relations of mind and body, and other such things. The criticism, however, is not absent but only hidden behind, or in, the carefully worded definitions of the fundamental concepts of Newton's own physics, or of Newton's own world: space, time, motion, and matter. Moreover, such criticism becomes more apparent in the Latin *Opticks* of 1706, and in the second edition of the *Principia*. It is even quite explicit in Cotes's "Preface."

We shall come back to this philosophical criticism of, and opposition to, Descartes. Let us now turn our attention to Newton's treatment of his more concrete scientific hypotheses.

We could, as a matter of fact, consider the whole second book of the *Principia*, which deals with the motion of bodies in *resisting media*, as a criticism, a positive criticism, of Cartesian conceptions, and as the execution of the program that the young Newton set for himself. Descartes, indeed, denied the existence of vacuum; all space – in Newtonian terminology – was for him filled with matter, or even – in his own – identical with matter. Accordingly, bodies moving in that space-matter had to encounter resistance. But what was this resistance? Descartes did not ask this question, and it is very characteristic of Newton and his way of thinking that it was precisely this question that he asked in his very first attempt to criticize Descartes. He did not then work out an answer to the question in any great detail. But in the *Principia* he treats the problem in all generality; this, too, is characteristic of Newton: not to attach himself to particular problems but to deal with them as cases of a more general nature. Thus, it is only after having analyzed all possible, and even impossible, cases of motion, and of propagation of motion, in elastic and inelastic media, in media whose resistance grows in proportion to speed or to the square of speed, media that pulsate like air or undulate like water, that he comes down to the specific problems of optics and cosmology. Even then he treats them as "cases," as problems; he reconstructs them and gives the solution, mentioning neither the name of Descartes nor even, in his criticism of Cartesian optics, that he is dealing with Descartes's hypothesis on the nature and structure of light.

Of course, he is right. Descartes's conception of a luminiferous element (second element) made up of hard, round particles closely packed together, and of light as pressure transmitted by and through this medium, is only a case of a more general problem, that of the propagation of pressure, or motion, through fluids (Book II, Sec. VIII). Thus the results arrived at are general too: pressure will not be propagated in straight lines; moreover, it will "turn around corners." Or, to quote Newton himself:

A pressure is not propagated through a fluid in rectilinear directions except where the particles of the fluid lie in a right line.
If the particles *a*, *b*, *c*, *d*, *e* lie in a right line, the pressure may be indeed directly propagated from *a* to *e*; but then the particle *e* will urge the obliquely posited particles *f* and *g* obliquely and those particles *f* and *g* will not sustain this pressure unless they be supported by the particles *h* and *k* lying beyond them; but the particles that support them are also pressed by them; and those particles cannot sustain that pressure without being supported by, and pressing upon, those particles that lie still farther, as *l* and *m* and so on *in infinitum*. Therefore the pressure, as soon as it is propagated to particles that lie out of right lines, begins to deflect towards one hand and the other, and will be propagated obliquely *in infinitum*; and after it has begun to be propagated obliquely if it reaches more distant particles lying out of the right line, it will deflect again on each hand; and this it will do as often as it lights on particles that do not lie exactly on a right line. Q.E.D. *Cor.* If any part of a pressure, propagated through a fluid from a given point, be intercepted by any obstacle, the remaining part, which is not intercepted, will deflect into the spaces behind the obstacle.[1]

[1] *Principia* (1687), Book I, Prop. XLI, Th. XXXI, p. 354; (1713), Book II, Prop. XLI, Th. XXXII, p. 329; Motte–Cajori, p. 367. See also *Optice* (1706), Qu. 20, pp. 310 sq.; *Opticks*, Qu. 28, p. 362.

Yet it is not only to pressure that these results apply, but to all kinds of motion:

All motion propagated through a fluid diverges from a rectilinear progress into the unmoved spaces.[1]

The conclusion, which Newton does not draw himself, but leaves to the reader, is clear: the hypotheses of Descartes, of Huygens, and of Hooke[2] are all false; they are all cases of the general mechanism that has just been studied and therefore incompatible with the rectilinearity of light rays. This negative conclusion, however – and I should like to stress this point – is not arrived at directly; it is only a counterpart, or a *sous-produit*, of a positive result.

It is nearly in the same way – enlarging and generalizing the problem, studying its different cases, calculating the effects of such or such disposition – that Newton deals with the Cartesian vortices. Here, however, he tells us what he aims at, though here, too, he does not mention names. But just as in the case of optics, the rejection of the vortices is a by-product of a positive investigation that yields results incompatible with the firmly established – astronomical – data. Thus the problem of the vortices becomes the general problem (Book II, Sec. IX) of "the circular motion of fluids," which circular motion can be considered as taking place either in an infinite fluid or in a fluid enclosed in a vessel, as occurring in only one place, or simultaneously in different places, and so on and on. What is aimed at in each case is a mathematical, numerical determination of the structure of the corresponding motion.

Thus we learn:

If a solid cylinder, infinitely long, in an uniform and infinite fluid, revolves with an uniform motion about an axis given in position, and the fluid be forced round by only this impulse of the cylinder, and every part of the fluid continues uniformly in its motion: I say that the periodic times of the parts of the fluid are as their distances from the axis of the cylinder.[3]

On the other hand:

If a solid sphere, in an uniform and infinite fluid, revolves about an axis

---

[1] *Principia* (1687), Book II, Prop. XLII, Th. XXXII, p. 356; (1713), Book II, Prop. XLII, Th. XXXIII, p. 331; Motte–Cajori, p. 369.

[2] Newton is wrong, of course: waves, if they are small enough in comparison to the opening through which they pass, do not "turn around the corner." But we cannot blame Newton for not having anticipated the development of the wave theory of light, or even for not having appreciated at its just value Huygens's explanation of this fact.

[3] *Principia* (1687), Book II, Prop. LI, Th. XXXVIII, p. 373; (1713), Book II, Prop. LI, Th. XXXIX, p. 345; Motte–Cajori, p. 385.

given in position with an uniform motion, and the fluid be forced round by only this impulse of the sphere; and every part of the fluid continues uniformly in its motion; I say that the periodic times of the parts of the fluid are as the squares of their distances from the centre of the sphere . . . [because the rotation of the sphere] will communicate a whirling motion to the fluid, like that of a vortex, and that motion will by degrees be propagated onwards *in infinitum*; and this motion will be increased continually in every part of the fluid, till the periodical times of the several parts become as the squares of the distances from the centre of the globe.[1]

A very important conclusion, as we shall see in a moment.

Now, what would happen if the whirling sphere, that is, the central body (the sun or the earth), influenced another sphere, that is, a planet or a satellite? A corollary enlightens us:

If another globe should be swimming in the same vortex at a certain distance from its centre, and in the meantime by some force revolve constantly about an axis of a given inclination, the motion of this globe will drive the fluid round after the manner of a vortex; and at first this new and small vortex will revolve with its globe about the centre of the other; and in the meantime its motion will creep on farther and farther, and by degrees be propagated *in infinitum*, after the manner of the first vortex. And for the same reason that the globe of the new vortex was carried about before by the motion of the other vortex, the globe of this other will be carried about by the motion of this new vortex, so that the two globes will revolve about some intermediate point, and by reason of that circular motion mutually fly from each other, unless some force restrains them.[2]

But in the solar system there are not one but several "globes" swimming in the vortex of the sun and turning on their axes. In such a case:

If several globes in given places should constantly revolve with determined velocities about axes given in position, there would arise from them as many vortices going on *in infinitum*. For upon the same account that any one globe propagates its motion *in infinitum* each globe apart will propagate its motion *in infinitum* also; so that every part of the infinite fluid will be agitated with a motion resulting from the actions of all the globes. Therefore the vortices will not be confined by any certain limits, but by degrees run into each other; and by the actions of the vortices on each other, the globes will be continually moved from their places . . . Neither can they possibly keep any certain position among themselves, unless some force restrains them.[3]

[1] *Principia* (1687), Book II, Prop. LII, Th. XXXIX, p. 375, Cor. 2, p. 378; (1713), Book II, Prop. LII, Th. XL, p. 347, Cor. 2, p. 349; Motte–Cajori, pp. 387, 389–390.
[2] *Ibid.* (1687), Cor. 5, pp. 378–379; (1713), p. 350; Motte–Cajori, p. 390.
[3] *Ibid.* (1687), Cor. 6, p. 379; (1713), p. 350; Motte–Cajori, p. 391.

Applied to the cosmic, or astronomical, reality, this conclusion means that *in the vortex hypothesis* a system such as the solar system would lack stability and persistence. It would disintegrate if some force – a force not accounted for by the vortex mechanism – did not "restrain" it. Even a smaller system, with only one planet, or satellite, would not be stable without such a force. Moreover, as motion is continuously transferred from the rotating globes to the matter of the fluid that surrounds them, and as they cannot impart motion without surrendering motion in the same amount, this imparted motion (1) would be "swallowed up and lost in the boundless" space; and, (2) if the globes were not constantly receiving new motion from some "active principle," their motion would "languish by degrees" and they, and also the vortices, "at last would quite stand still." A most important result, as it shows that the vortex conception is incompatible with the principle of conservation of motion, in which the Cartesians believed, but Newton did not. Further, Newton's result shows that the vortex theory implies a continuous replacement of the "loss" by an "active principle," that is, it implies something in which Newton believed, but the Cartesians did not.

Until now Newton had only investigated the case of a single vortex system in infinite space. But in the Cartesian world conception there is not one but an infinite – or indefinite – number of such systems (each star is one) which, so to say, surround each other and thus mutually prevent each other's expansion. It is *in se* a false conception: the boundaries of the vortex systems would not remain stable, the vortices would not remain separated but would merge into one another. This notwithstanding, the case of a finite vortex, that is, of a "whirling motion" that takes place in a limited and closed space, is different from that of a vortex that can freely expand *in infinitum*. Newton therefore proceeds to the study of it; he does not, however, as I did, make any reference to the impossible Cartesian conception, namely, that of the vortices "limiting" each other; on the contrary, he substitutes the quite possible and even empirically realizable motion of a fluid in a circular vessel. The result is rather surprising: the "enclosure" does not change the behavior of the fluid and the "periodical times will be as the squares of the distances from the centre of the vortex. No constitution of a vortex can be permanent but this."[1]

[1] *Principia* (1687), Cor. 7, p. 379; (1713), p. 351; Motte–Cajori, p. 391.

But

if the vessel be not spherical [as a matter of fact, the shape of the Cartesian vortices is not spherical] the particles will move in lines not circular but answering to the figure of the vessel; and the periodic times will be nearly as the squares of the mean distances from the centre [and] in the spaces between the centre and the circumference the motions will be slower where the spaces are wide and swifter when narrow.[1]

This for the motion of the vortices themselves; as for the motion of bodies swimming in or carried round by them, we have to distinguish the case of bodies having the same density as the "whirling fluid" from the case of bodies whose densities are different – either greater or smaller – from the density of the "whirling fluid." As a matter of fact, it is only in the former case (same densities) that bodies will move in closed orbits: "a solid if it be of the same density with the matter of the vortex, will move with the same motion as the parts thereof, being relatively at rest in the matter that surrounds it."[2]

Conversely, if a body "carried about in a vortex" returns in the same orbit, it must be of the same density as the vortex. In that case, indeed, "it would revolve according to the same law with those parts of the fluid that are at the same or equal distances from the centre of the vortex." It would, therefore, be relatively quiescent in the fluid that carries it. "And if the vortex be of a uniform density, the same body may revolve at any distance from the centre." However,

if [the body in question] be more dense, it will endeavour more than before to recede from the centre: and therefore, overcoming that force of the vortex by which, being as it were, kept in equilibrium, it was retained in its orbit, it will recede from the centre, and in its revolution describe a spiral returning no longer into the same orbit. And, by the same argument, if it be more rare, it will approach to the centre. Therefore it can never continually go round in the same orbit unless it be of the same density with the fluid.[3]

That is, if we translate these conclusions into cosmological terms, only if the earth and the planets are of the same density as the matter of interplanetary spaces could they be moved around the sun by its vortex.

[1] *Principia* (1687), *Scholium*, p. 381; (1713), p. 352; Motte–Cajori, p. 393.
[2] *Ibid.* (1687), Book II, Prop. LIII, Th. XL, p. 383; (1713), Book II, Prop. LIII, Th. XLI, p. 354; Motte–Cajori, pp. 394–395.
[3] *Ibid.*

This seems to be rather a strong objection against the vortex hypothesis. Newton, however, does not use it. Possibly because difference in density (as he explains and later develops in Book III of the *Principia*, and as he had pointed out in CUL 4003) is impossible in the Cartesian world; indeed, it is this impossibility that will form the basis of his general criticism of Descartes's identification of extension and matter. Yet, be this as it may, it remains that for his rejection of the vortex hypothesis Newton puts forward a purely astronomical reason: it is incompatible with Kepler's laws. Newton, indeed tells us:

I have endeavoured . . . to investigate the properties of vortices that I might find whether the celestial phenomena can be explained by them; for the phenomenon is this, that the periodic times of the planets revolving about Jupiter are as the $\frac{3}{2}$ power of their distances from Jupiter's centre; and the same rule obtains also among the planets that revolve about the Sun . . . Therefore if those planets are carried round in vortices revolving about Jupiter and the Sun, the vortices must revolve according to that law. But here we found the periodic times of the parts of the vortex to be as the square of the distances from the centre of motion; and this ratio cannot be diminished and reduced to the $\frac{3}{2}$ power . . . If, as some think, the vortices move more swiftly near the centre, then slower to a certain limit, then again swifter near the circumference, certainly neither the $\frac{3}{2}$ power nor any other certain and determinate power can obtain in them.[1]

Having dealt this blow to Descartes – the theory ascribed to "some" is exactly that of Descartes – Newton concludes: "Let philosophers [Cartesians] then see how that phenomenon of the $\frac{3}{2}$ power can be accounted for by vortices."

As a matter of fact, not only the periodic times of the planets but also the speeds with which they move in their orbits would be quite different in the vortex hypothesis from those that they must have according to Kepler, and that they have in fact:

Scholium. Hence it is manifest that the planets are not carried round in corporeal vortices; for, according to the Copernican hypothesis, the planets going round the sun revolve in ellipses having the sun in their common focus; and by radii drawn to the sun describe areas proportional to the times.[2] But the parts of a vortex can never revolve with such a

---

[1] *Principia* (1687), Book II, Prop. LII, Th. XXXIX, *Scholium*, pp. 381–382; (1713), Book II, Prop. LII, Th. XL, *Scholium*, pp. 352–353; Motte–Cajori, p. 393. An excellent résumé of Newton's criticism of the vortex hypothesis is given by Cotes in his "Preface" to the second edition (1713) of the *Principia*.

[2] Newton, of course, knew perfectly well that Copernicus never taught anything of the kind, and that it was not Copernicus but Kepler who formulated the two laws of planetary motion which he referred to (the first and the second of Kepler's laws).

motion. For let AD, BE, CF [Fig. 1] represent three orbits described about the sun S, of which let the outmost circle CF be concentric to the sun; let the aphelions of the two innermost be A, B, and their perihelions D, E. Hence a body revolving in the orb CF, describing by a radius drawn to the sun, areas proportional to the times, will move with an uniform motion.

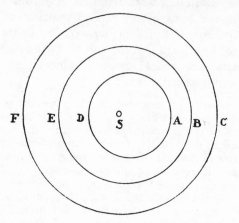

FIG. 1.

Why did he speak instead of the "Copernican hypothesis," thus attributing these laws to Copernicus and not to their rightful owner? Was it because – like Galileo before him – he felt an aversion for Kepler, for his continuous mixture of "metaphysical hypotheses" with "natural philosophy"? This may have been the case, and would explain why he did not name Kepler among his predecessors, even though he borrowed from him the term, and the concept, of *inertia*, though modifying its contents (see *supra*, p. 70, n. 1); nor mention that the sesquialterate proportion of the periodic times which, according to Book I of the *Principia*, implies the inverse-square law of attraction ("If the periodic times are as the sesquialterate powers of the radii, and therefore the velocities inversely as the square roots of the radii, the centripetal forces will be inversely as the squares of the radii"), is nothing else than Kepler's third law, from which not only Sir Christopher Wren, Dr. Hooke, and Dr. Halley, but also he himself deduced it. *Ibid*. (1687), Book I, Prop. IV, Th. IV, Cor. 6, and *Scholium*, p. 42; (1713), Book I, Prop. IV, Cor. 6, and *Scholium*, p. 39; Motte–Cajori, p. 46. In the same way, in Book III he does not mention Kepler, either in connection with his second law ("areas which planets describe by radii drawn to the Sun are proportional to the times of Description"; *ibid*. [1687], Book III, Hypothesis VIII, p. 404; [1713], Book III, Phaenomenon V, p. 361; Motte–Cajori, p. 405) or with the first ("the planets move in ellipses which have their common focus in the center of the Sun"; *ibid*. [1687], Book III, Prop. XIII, Th. XIII, p. 419; [1713], Book III, Prop. XIII, Th. XIII, p. 375; Motte-Cajori, p. 420). On the other hand, he does mention Kepler as the discoverer of the third law (*ibid*. [1687], Book III, Hypothesis VII, p. 403; [1713], Book III, Phaenomenon IV, p. 360; Motte–Cajori, p. 404). We must, however, take into account that through the whole of the seventeenth century heliocentric astronomy was called "Copernican," as Kepler himself did in calling *Epitome astronomiae Copernicanae* a book in which, besides heliocentrism, there was nothing Copernican; and as for the term "hypothesis," it, too, was a common and standing expression. Indeed, Newton's *Principia* was announced at the Royal Society as a work designed to demonstrate the "Copernican hypothesis." See *supra*, p. 30.

And, according to the laws of astronomy, the body revolving in the orbit
BE will move slower in its aphelion B, and swifter in its perihelion E;
whereas according to the laws of mechanics the matter of the vortex ought
to move more swiftly in the narrow space between A and C than in the
wide space between D and F, that is more swiftly in the aphelion than in
the perihelion. Now these two conclusions contradict each other . . . So
that the hypothesis of vortices is utterly irreconcilable with astronomical
phenomena and rather serves to perplex than to explain the heavenly
motions. How these motions are performed in free spaces without vortices
may be understood by the first Book; and I shall now more fully treat of it
in the following Book.[1]

Without vortices . . . in free spaces . . . Indeed, both the third book,
which describes the "System of the World," and the first book,
which develops the fundamental theories of rational mechanics,
postulate the existence of free, or void, spaces. The third book does
it explicitly, the first implicitly, by studying the motion of bodies
without taking any account of the medium in which such motions
are performed. And it is by implication also that the rejection of
vortices is hinted at in the definitions that assert the reality of absolute time, absolute space, and absolute motion, as distinguished
from and opposed to relative time, relative space, and relative
motion. The implication here was, of course, perfectly clear to Newton's contemporaries. I think that the texts of the manuscript that
I have quoted make it also quite clear to us. Everyone knows, of
course, these celebrated definitions. I would like, nevertheless, to
repeat them:

Absolute true and mathematical time, of itself, and from its own
nature, flows equably without relation to anything external, and by another name is called *duration*; relative apparent and common time is some
sensible and external (whether accurate or unequable) measure of duration
by the means of motion which is commonly used instead of true time.[2]

That is, time is not the measure (number) of motion, as the
school tradition defined it; nor is it the duration of things, their
amount of being, as Descartes defined it. Time has its own nature,
independent of everything "external," that is, independent of the
existence or nonexistence of the world.[3] If there were no world,

---

[1] *Principia* (1687), Book II, Prop. LIII, Th. XL, *Scholium*, pp. 383–384; (1713), Book
II, Prop. LIII, Th. XLI, *Scholium*, pp. 354–355; Motte–Cajori, pp. 395–396.
[2] *Ibid.* (1687), *Scholium* to *Definitiones*, p. 5; (1713), *Scholium* to *Definitiones*, p. 5;
Motte–Cajori, p. 6.
[3] See *The Geometric Lectures of Isaac Barrow*, ed. J. M. Child (Chicago: Open Court,
1916), Lecture I, pp. 35 sq.

there would still be time, and duration.[1] The duration of what? Newton does not tell us, but we know the answer: the duration of God. Yet this time, this duration – Newton has lost something of his youthful enthusiasm and confidence – is not *our* duration or *our* time. *Our* time and *our* duration are only sensible, relative, and imperfect measures of the steady and equable flow of "absolute true and mathematical time." Even astronomical time, by which we correct our common time measures, is no more than an approximation. Time, indeed, is measured by motion. But

it may be that there is no such thing as an equable motion, whereby time may be accurately measured. All motions may be accelerated and retarded, but the flowing of absolute time is not liable to any change. The duration or perseverance of the existence of things remains the same, whether the motions are swift or slow, or none at all; and therefore this [absolute] duration ought to be distinguished from what are only sensible measures thereof.[2]

Space, like time, is not directly and essentially connected with the world, or with matter. The world, of course, is *in space* as it is *in time;* but if there were no world there would still be space. In the manuscript from which I have been quoting Newton told us outright what it was: God's space. He still thinks so; but he does not *say* so; he calls it instead absolute space. It is true that absolute space is not directly given to us; in perception we perceive only bodies, and it is in relation to bodies, to movable bodies, that we determine *our* space, or *our* spaces. Still it is an error not to recognize that *our* relative, movable "spaces" are possible only in an unmovable space. Newton writes therefore:

[1] For Descartes – as for Aristotle – if there were no world, there would be also no time. Henry More, following the Neoplatonic tradition, objects that time has nothing to do with the world (see "Second Letter to Descartes," 5 March 1649, Descartes, *Oeuvres*, ed. C. Adam and P. Tannery, V, 302): "for, if God annihilated this universe and then, after a certain time, created from nothing another one, this *intermundium* or this absence of the world would have its duration which would be measured by a certain number of days, years or centuries. There is thus a duration of something that does not exist, which duration is a kind of extension. Consequently, the amplitude of nothing, that is of void, can be measured by ells or leagues, just as the duration of what does not exist can be measured in its inexistence by hours, days and months." Descartes, however, maintains his position (see "Second Letter to Henry More," 15 April 1649, *Oeuvres*, V, 343): "I believe that it implies a contradiction to conceive a duration between the destruction of the first world and the creation of the second one; for, if we refer this duration or something similar to the succession of God's ideas, this will be an error of our intellect and not a true perception of something."

[2] *Principia* (1687), *Scholium* to *Definitiones*, p. 7; (1713), *Scholium* to *Definitiones*, p. 7; Motte–Cajori, p. 8. Newton tells us that we determine, or try to determine, the absolute time from the phenomena by means of astronomical equations. Alas, we cannot do it for space.

Absolute space, in its own nature without relation to anything external, remains always similar and immovable. Relative space is some movable dimension or measure of the absolute spaces; which our senses determine by its position to bodies.[1]

One step further: bodies are in space, that is, they have places, or they are in places, which they fill, or occupy. But:

Place is a part of space which a body takes up, and is, according to the space, either absolute or relative. I say, a part of space; not the situation, nor the external surface of the body,[2]

as it is defined by Descartes or the scholastics. Bodies are in places; but they do not stay there; they move, that is, they change places – places, not their situation among, or with respect to, other bodies, as Descartes had put it. Thus, because there are two kinds of places, there are also, and consequently, two kinds of motion:

Absolute motion is the translation of a body from one absolute place into another; and relative motion, the translation from one relative place into another. Thus in a ship under sail, the relative place of a body is that part of the ship which the body possesses or that part of the cavity which the body fills and which therefore moves together with the ship; and relative rest is the continuance of the body in the same part of the ship or of its cavity. But real, absolute rest is the continuance of the body in the same part of that immovable space in which the ship itself, its cavity, and all that it contains, is moved . . .

As the order of the parts of time is immutable, so also is the order of the parts of space. Suppose those parts to be moved out of their places and they will be moved (if the expression may be allowed) out of themselves. For times and spaces are, as it were, the places as well of themselves as of all other things. All things are placed in time as to order of succession; and in space as to order of situation . . . [3] And that the primary places of things should be movable is absurd. These are therefore the absolute places; and translations out of those places are the only absolute motions.[4]

We remember how strongly Newton reproached Descartes for making all motion relative, thereby precluding the determination of the true places and true motions of the heavenly bodies; since then Newton had recognized that he was too severe; such a determination *is* nearly impossible – at least for us: we cannot refer motion directly to absolute places.

---

[1] *Principia* (1687), p. 5; (1713), p. 6; Motte–Cajori, p. 6.

[2] *Ibid.* See also Rohault, *Physica*, pars I, cap. X, note 1, p. 36; *System*, I, 39 sq.; and *infra*, Appendix M.

[3] For Leibniz, it is these orders that constitute time and space.

[4] *Principia* (1687), *Scholium* to *Definitiones*, p. 6; (1713), *Scholium* to *Definitiones*, p. 6; Motte–Cajori, pp. 7–8. See also Clarke's comments in Rohault's *Physica*, pars I, cap. X, note 1, p. 36; *System*, I, 39 sq.; and *infra*, Appendix M.

But because the parts of space cannot be seen or distinguished from one another by our senses, therefore in their stead we use sensible measures of them. For from the positions and distances of things from any body considered as immovable, we define all places; and then with respect to such places, we estimate all motions . . . And so, instead of absolute places and motions, we use relative ones.[1]

This causes no inconveniences in common affairs. "Yet" – Newton has not abandoned his old ideal – "in philosophical disquisitions we ought to abstract from our senses, and consider things themselves, distinct from what are only sensible measures of them." But we cannot do this by referring all motions to a body at absolute rest. "For it may be that there is no body really at rest, to which places and motions of others may be referred." And even if there were "in the region of the fixed stars, or perhaps far beyond them such a body,"[2] it would be impossible to know it from the positions of bodies in our region.

Thus we cannot determine absolute motion as a motion relative to a body at absolute rest; and yet we cannot, as does Descartes, abandon the idea of absolute motion. Accordingly we have to maintain that

entire and absolute motions cannot be otherwise determined than by immovable places; and for that reason I did before refer those absolute motions to immovable places, but relative ones to movable places. Now no other places are immovable but those that from infinity to infinity do all retain the same given position one to another; and upon this account must ever remain unmoved and do thereby constitute immovable space.[3]

From infinity to infinity. . . . It is obvious that Newton does not mean spatial infinity; he means temporal infinity. From infinity to infinity means from eternity to eternity, from the infinite past to the infinite future, through the whole infinite flow of absolute time. Once more we are reminded of the nature of space as described in the manuscript.

And again: how can we determine motion with respect to the unmovable places? As a matter of fact, we already know the answer: by its effects, or causes: "The causes by which true and relative motions are distinguished, one from the other, are the forces impressed upon bodies to generate motion." We have to impress

---

[1] *Principia* (1687), p. 7; (1713), p. 7; Motte–Cajori, p. 8. "Considered immovable . . .," see *supra*, p. 80.

[2] The body *a* of C. Neumann.

[3] *Principia* (1687), pp. 8–9; (1713), p. 8; Motte–Cajori, p. 9.

force on a body in order to generate or to change its absolute motion; we need not do so in order to produce relative motion; we can instead impress a force on other bodies. Conversely, absolute motion does produce effects that relative motion does not have, at least in the one case of circular motion.

The effects which distinguish absolute from relative motion are the forces of receding from the axis of circular motion. For there are no such forces in a circular motion purely relative, but in a true and absolute circular motion, they are greater, or less, according to the quantity of motion.[1]

Thus in the famous Newtonian experiment of a rotating vessel "hung by a long cord" in which "water forms itself in a concave figure," it is the absolute motion of that water, and not its relative motion with respect to the sides of the vessel nor with respect to the ambient bodies (Descartes's definition of the true or "philosophical" motion), that produces this effect. We can even, by measuring these forces, determine both the direction and the absolute speed of the circular motion, for

there is only one real circular motion of any one revolving body, corresponding to only one power of endeavouring to recede from the axis of its motion, as its proper and adequate effect; but relative motions in one and the same body are innumerable, according to the various relations it bears to external bodies, and like other relations, are altogether destitute of any real effect . . . And therefore in their system who suppose that our heavens, revolving below the sphere of the fixed stars, carry the planets along with them; the several parts of those heavens, and the planets, which are indeed relatively at rest in their heavens, do yet really move. For they change their position one to another . . . and as parts of revolving wholes, endeavour to recede from the axis of their motions.[2]

Thus, absolute motion emerges victorious from the contest, and with it absolute space, which, as such, having no essential relation to things that it contains, can be *free*. But is it? The third book of the *Principia* gives us the answer.

In this book, in which Newton describes the "System of the World," that is, the system of the planetary motions that "demonstrate" the action of a gravitational force and, conversely, are explained by it, Newton reinforces the argument that he had already

---

[1] *Principia* (1687), p. 9; (1713), p. 8; Motte–Cajori, p. 10.
[2] *Ibid.* (1687), p. 10; (1713), p. 9; Motte–Cajori, p. 11; see *infra*, pp. 119, sq., on Huygens's experiment. Huygens, having enclosed his vessel by a glass plate, did not notice the phenomenon observed by Newton.

used in his manuscript, telling us that if all spaces were equally full, as they should be according to Descartes, all bodies would be equally dense, which is absurd.[1] It is clear that the quantity of matter in a given space can be rarefied, and even extremely so; if it could not, the motion of the planets would encounter strong resistance, but, in fact, the planets encounter hardly any resistance, the comets none at all. "But if the quantity of matter can by rarefaction be diminished, what hinders its diminishing to infinity?" *Itaque vacuum necessario datur.*

Ten years later, in one of the Queries appended to the Latin edition of his *Opticks*, Newton becomes more explicit:

Against filling the heavens with fluid mediums, unless they be exceeding rare, a great objection arises from the regular and very lasting motion of the planets and comets in all manner of courses through the heavens. For thence it is manifest that the heavens are void of all sensible resistance, and by consequence, of all sensible matter . . .

[Indeed,] if the Heavens were as dense as water, they would not have much less resistance than water; if as dense as quick-silver, they would not have much less resistance than quick-silver; if absolutely dense, or full of matter without any *Vacuum*, let the matter be never so subtle and fluid, they would have a greater resistance than quick-silver.[2]

Thus there cannot be any continuous matter in the skies; there might be very thin "vapours," perhaps, or an exceedingly rare aethereal medium, but no dense, Cartesian fluid. Such a fluid

can be of no use for explaining the phenomena of nature; the motion of the planets and comets being better explained without it. It serves only to disturb and retard the motions of those great bodies and make the Frame of Nature languish . . . And as it is of no use . . . so there is no evidence for its existence and therefore it ought to be rejected.

This, however, is not all. There are deeper, philosophical reasons for rejecting this medium. For doing so

we have the authority of those the oldest and most celebrated philosophers of Greece and Phoenicia, who made a Vacuum and Atoms, and the gravity of Atoms the first principles of their philosophy; tacitly attributing gravity to some other cause than dense matter. Later philosophers banished the consideration of such a cause out of natural philosophy, feigning hypotheses for explaining all things mechanically and referring other causes to metaphysics.[3]

[1] *Principia* (1687), Book II, Prop. VI, Th. VI, Cor. 3, p. 411; (1713), Book III, Prop. VI, Th. VI, Cor. 3, p. 368; Motte–Cajori, pp. 414.
[2] *Optice* (1706), Qu. 20, pp. 310, 313; *Opticks* (1952), Qu. 28, pp. 364–365, 368.
[3] *Ibid.*, p. 314; p. 368–369.

Thus we see that Newton's anti-Cartesianism is not purely scientific; it is also religious; Cartesianism is materialism that banishes from natural philosophy all teleological questions, that reduces everything to blind necessity,[1] which obviously cannot explain the variety and the purposeful structure of the universe, "whereas the main business of Natural Philosophy is just to ask these questions and, without feigning hypotheses, deduce causes from effect till we come to the very first Cause which is certainly nonmechanical." It is therefore "unphilosophical to pretend that it might arise out of Chaos by the mere laws of nature."

Cartesians banish from nature all nonmaterial forces, whereas, in fact, there are "active principles" operating that cannot be entirely reduced to material forces;[2] chief of these is the force of gravity, as the ancient philosophers of Chaldea and Greece had already seen. These active principles derive directly from the

powerful ever-living agent Who being in all places is more able by His will to move the bodies within His boundless uniform *Sensorium* [that is, within absolute space] and thereby to form and reform the parts of the Universe, than we are by our will to move the parts of our own bodies.[3]

[1] See *supra*, p. 94. As we see, Cotes in his condemnation of Cartesianism and Leibnizianism faithfully expresses the views of Newton himself.

[2] *Optice* (1706), Qu. 23, pp. 322, 341, 343, 344–345, 346; *Opticks* (1952), Qu. 31, pp. 375–376, 397, 399, 401, 403.

[3] *Ibid.* (1706), Qu. 23 and 20, pp. 346 and 315; *Opticks* (1952), Qu. 31 and Qu. 28, pp. 403 and 370. The attribution of a *sensorium* to God and the identification of space with this *sensorium* was one of the main objections raised by Leibniz against Newton and his philosophy ("Letter to the Abbé Conti," see *infra*, p. 144, n. 1; "Letter to the Princess of Wales," in *The Leibniz–Clarke Correspondence*, ed. H. G. Alexander [Manchester, England: Manchester University Press, 1956], p. 11). In his answer to Leibniz, Clarke protested: "Sir Isaac has never said that space was the *sensorium Dei*; he only compared it with the *sensoria* of living beings and said that God perceived things in Space *tanquam in sensorio suo*." In order to prove his assertion, Clarke quoted a passage from the *Optice* ([1706], Qu. 20, p. 315; *Opticks* [1952], Qu. 28, p. 370), which said indeed: "*annon ex phaenomenis constat, esse Entem incorporeum, viventem, intelligentem, omnipraesentem qui in spatio infinito tanquam Sensorio suo res ipsas intime cernat penitusque perspiciat.*" As a matter of fact, Newton used the very term *sensorium* on the same page (*Optice* [1706], Qu. 20, p. 315; *Opticks* [1952], Qu. 28, p. 370; see also *Optice* [1706], Qu. 23, p. 346; *Opticks* [1952], Qu. 31, p. 403); as for the passage quoted by Clarke, Newton first wrote, "*Annon Spatium Universum Sensorium est Entis Incorporei, Viventis et Intelligentis . . .*," then, the volume having been already printed, decided to change his text, introducing into it a face-saving "tanquam," probably because Dr. Cheyne, with whom Newton did not want to be associated (see *infra*, p. 156, n. 1), expressed the same view in his *Philosophical Principles of Natural Religion* (London, 1705), P. II, Def. IV, p. 4, "A Spirit is an extended, penetrable, active indivisible, intelligent Substance"; Cor. IV, p. 53, "*Universal* Space, is the Image and Representation in Nature of the Divine Infinitude"; Cor. V, p. 53, "Hence Universal Space may be very aptly called the *Sensorium Divinitatis* since it is the Place where the natural Things, or the whole System of material and compounded Beings is presented to the *Divine Omniscience*." It is rather amusing to find Addison, ten years later, praising this conception as "the noblest and most exalted way of considering

Some years later Newton became even more explicit, no doubt angered by the persistent opposition of the Cartesians, with whom Leibniz, forgetting for a moment his own hostility toward Descartes, had joined forces in the war against the common foe. Thus in the third of his *Regulae philosophandi*, which in the second edition of the *Principia* he added to the two *Hypotheses* of the first, which he also now called *Regulae* (the other "Hypotheses" of the first edition he now calls *Phaenomena*), he insisted on the "experimental," empirical character of natural philosophy and in the General Scholium pronounced his celebrated condemnation of hypotheses – *Hypotheses non fingo*[1] – that have no place in experimental philosophy: "We are certainly not to relinquish the evidence of experiments for the sake of dreams and vain fictions of our own devising,"[2] and he listed "hardness, impenetrability, mobility, and inertia" together with extension as essential properties of matter, which in whole bodies result from these same properties which are possessed by the least particles of bodies. And, though denying that gravity is essential to bodies, he asserts nevertheless that their mutual universal gravitation is more certain even than their extension, because gravitation is inductively derived from phenomena, and *argumentum inductionis* must not be abandoned for the sake of *hypotheses*. Whose hypotheses? The Cartesians', of course, with their insistence on clear and distinct innate ideas. Indeed, in a fifth "Rule," which, however, he did not publish, he says quite clearly:

Everything that is not derived from things themselves, either through the external senses or by the sensation of the *cogitationes*, must be considered as hypotheses. Thus I feel that I think, which could not be if I did not feel at the same time that I am. But I do not feel that any idea is innate.[3]

And in the famous General Scholium, a curious conglomerate of what we would call today purely scientific and purely metaphysical

infinite Space"; see *Spectator*, no. 565 (July 1714), quoted by H. G. Alexander, *Correspondence . . .* , p. xvi. For a further discussion of Newton's views on the *Sensorium Dei*, see E. A. Burtt, *The Metaphysical Foundations of Modern Physical Science* (2nd ed.; London: Kegan Paul, 1932), pp. 128, 233, 258 sq.; (Garden City, New York: Doubleday Anchor Books, 1954), pp. 135, 236 sq., 259 sq. See also A. Koyré and I. B. Cohen, "Newton and the Leibniz–Clarke Correspondence," *Archives Internationales d'Histoire des Sciences 15* (1962), 63–126.

[1] On "hypotheses," see I. B. Cohen, *Franklin and Newton: An Inquiry into Speculative Newtonian Experimental Science and Franklin's Work in Electricity as an Example Thereof* (Philadelphia: American Philosophical Society, 1956), Appendix One, pp. 575–589; and A. Koyré, "Concept and Experience in Newton's Scientific Thought," *supra*, Chapter II.

[2] *Principia* (1713), Book III, Regula III, p. 357; Motte–Cajori, p. 398.

[3] See A. Koyré, "Newton's *Regulae Philosophandi*," *infra*, Chapter VI.

considerations – Newtonian science is after all still Natural Philosophy – he starts by an attack on the hypothesis of vortices which "is pressed by many difficulties,"[1] most notably that the periodic times of the planets cannot on the vortex hypothesis obey Kepler's law. Nor would the motion of their satellites. As for the comets, the motion of which is "exceedingly regular" and "governed by the same laws as the motion of the planets," their motions can by no means be accounted for by the hypothesis of vortices, "for the comets are carried with eccentric motions through all parts of the heavens indifferently, with a freedom that is incompatible with the motion of a vortex."

This for the vortices. As for the identification of extension with matter and the denial of the vacuum:

Bodies projected in our air suffer no resistance but from the air. Withdraw the air, as is done in Mr. Boyle's vacuum and the resistance ceases; for in this void a bit of fine down and a piece of solid gold descend with equal velocity. And the same argument must apply to the celestial spaces above the earth's atmosphere.[2]

These spaces do not resist the motion of planets and must, therefore, be void. Besides, the Cartesian idea that the well-ordered system of the world could be the result of mere mechanical causes is absurd.

This most beautiful system of the sun, planets, and comets, could only proceed from the counsel and dominion of an intelligent and powerful Being.

Not only this system, but the whole of the infinite universe in which

lest the systems of the fixed stars should by their gravity fall on each other, He hath placed those systems at immense distances from one another.

This Being governs all things, not as the soul of the world but as Lord over all and on account of his dominion he is wont to be called Lord God παντοκράτωρ, or *Universal Ruler* . . . The supreme God is a Being eternal, infinite, absolutely perfect.

But not only that: an *ens infinitum et perfectissimum* is not *God*. Newton writes therefore: "He [the true God] is a living, intelligent, and powerful Being . . . He is eternal and infinite, omnipotent and omniscient."

This, of course, is purely traditional. Newton adds, however: "His duration reaches from eternity to eternity; His presence from

---

[1] *Principia* (1713), Book III, *Scholium Generale*, p. 481; Motte–Cajori, p. 543.
[2] *Ibid.*

infinity to infinity." It is impossible – at least so it seems to me – not to connect this addition with the texts that express the convictions of the young Newton, and not to see in it the rejection of Descartes's God,[1] who for Newton is absent from the world, and now also the God of Leibniz.[2] And this especially when we read that God "is not eternity and infinity, but eternal and infinite." As a matter of fact, for Newton he is not eternal in the traditional sense of the word, but *sempiternal*,[3] that is, he is not above time but "extended" in time and in space.

He is not duration, or space, but He endures and is present. He endures forever, and is everywhere present, and by existing always and everywhere [*semper et ubique*] He constitutes duration and space. Since every particle of space is *always*, and every indivisible moment of duration is *everywhere*, certainly the Maker and Lord of all things cannot be *never* and *nowhere* [*nullibi*].

We remember the insistence of the young Newton on God's *presence* in the world; he does not seem to have changed his mind since then. Thus he tells us that God

is omnipresent not *virtually* only [as for Descartes], but also *substantially*, for virtue cannot subsist without substance.[4] In Him are all things contained and moved; yet neither affects the other: God suffers nothing from the motion of bodies; bodies find no resistance from the omnipresence of God.

A rather curious assertion, since assuredly Newton knew as well as we do ourselves that nobody had ever thought God's omnipresence could constitute a hindrance to the motion of bodies. Yet it is there.

[1] In the drafts of the *Scholium Generale* (see Hall and Hall, *Unpublished Scientific Papers*, p. 357), Newton writes: "Aeternus est & Infinitus, seu durat in aeternum & adest ab infinito in infinitum. Duratio ejus non est nunc stans sine duratione neque praesentia ejus est nusquam"; and (p. 359): "Qui Ens perfectum dari demonstraverit, & Dominum seu παντοκράτορα universorum dari nondum demonstraverit, Deum dari nondum demonstraverit. Ens aeternum, infinitum, sapientissimum, summe perfectum sine dominio non est Deus sed natura solum. Haec nonnullis aeterna, infinita, sapientissima, et potentissima est, & rerum omnium author necessario existens. Dei autem dominium seu Deitas non ex ideis abstractis sed ex phaenomenis et eorum causis finalibus optime demonstratur." It seems that for Newton, as for Pascal, the "God of the philosophers" was not the God of faith.

[2] Leibniz's God, an *Intelligentia supramundana*, is a "Dieu fainéant." See Clarke's criticism of Leibniz in his *Correspondence* with him, and my *From the Closed World*.

[3] According to the classical definition of Boethius, who was inspired by Plato's idea of time as a mobile image of an unmovable eternity, "aeternitas est innumerabilis vitae simul tota et perfecta possessio," that is, an everlasting present, without past or future, nor any kind of succession; it is a *nunc*. Newton, however, explicitly rejects this conception in his above-mentioned drafts; see p. 112, n. 1.

[4] Traditionally, and also for Descartes, God is present in the world by his power.

Thus perhaps it is more than curious: it reveals the way in which Newton thought about God's *substantial* presence in this world.

It is allowed by all that the Supreme God exists necessarily; and by the same necessity He exists *always* and *everywhere*.

Always and *everywhere* – that is, in infinite time and eternal space, the existence of which is therefore as necessary as that of God; nay, necessary even for the existence of God who cannot be if not *semper* and *ubique*; it is in this space, the absolute space, that God – and not "blind metaphysical necessity, which is certainly the same always and everywhere" and could not produce "a variety of things" – creates the world, that is, hard, impenetrable, passive, inert particles, upon which he acts by an "electric and elastic spirit,"[1] which seems now to be entrusted with the production of all short-range phenomena such as the attraction and repulsion of particles and the reflection and refraction of light,[2] and by the power of gravity, which propagates its virtue to immense distances.[3]

"Metaphysical hypotheses," so Newton told us, "have no place in experimental philosophy." Yet it seems quite clear that metaphysical convictions play, or at least have played, an important part in the philosophy of Sir Isaac Newton. It is his acceptance of two absolutes – space and time – that enabled him to formulate his fundamental three laws of motion, as it was his belief in an omnipresent and omniactive God that enabled him to transcend both the shallow empiricism of Boyle and Hooke and the narrow rationalism of

[1] The Latin text of the *Principia* does not mention the elastic and electric nature of this spirit; it says only *spiritus subtilissimus*. But Motte, in his translation, writes "electric and elastic" and Newton himself adds these terms in his own copy of the *Principia*; see A. R. Hall and M. Boas Hall, "Newton's Electric Spirit: Four Oddities," *Isis 50* (1959), 473–476; I. B. Cohen and A. Koyré, "Newton's Electric and Elastic Spirit," *Isis 51* (1960), 337; and Henry Guerlac, "Francis Hauksbee: expérimentateur au profit de Newton," *Archives Internationales d'Histoire des Sciences 16* (1963), 113–128.

[2] On Newton's conception of short-range attractive forces, both inter- and extra-molecular, and their reduction of electrical forces, see Hall and Hall, *Unpublished Scientific Papers*, pp. 349–355. According to Professor H. Guerlac, "Francis Hauksbee," Newton was influenced by Hauksbee's experiments.

[3] It is interesting to note that Newton does *not* ascribe the production of gravity to the action of "electric and elastic" spirits, but maintains the distinction of gravitational and electric forces. To use today's language, he maintains the distinction between the gravitational and electromagnetic fields. Thus, even in the Queries of the *Opticks*, where he presents an explanation of gravity by aethereal pressure (*Opticks* [1952], Qu. 21, 22, pp. 350–353), he nevertheless repeats that "Nature will be very conformable to herself and very simple, performing all the great motions of the heavenly bodies by the attraction of gravity which intercedes those bodies, and almost all the small ones of their particles by some other attractive and repelling powers which intercede the particles" (*Optice* [1706], Qu. 23, p. 340–341; *Opticks* [1952], Qu. 31, p. 397).

Descartes, to renounce mechanical explanations, and, in spite of his own rejection of all action at a distance, to build up his world as an interplay of forces, the mathematical laws of which natural philosophy had to establish. By induction, not by pure speculation. This because our world was created by the pure will of God; we have not, therefore, to prescribe his action for him; we have only to find out what he has done.

The belief in creation as the background of empiricomathematical science – that seems strange. Yet the ways of thought, human thought, in its search for truth are, indeed, very strange. *Itinerarium mentis in veritatem* is not a *right* line. That is why the history of this search is so interesting, so passionate; or, to quote Kepler, who knew something about it: "*Non minus admirandae videntur occasiones quibus homines in cognitionem rerum coelestium deveniunt, quam ipsa natura rerum coelestium.*"

Huygens and Leibniz on Universal Attraction

It was Newton's conception of universal attraction, or gravitation – his greatest triumph – understood or misunderstood as meaning an action at a distance, that formed the strongest obstacle to the acceptance of Newtonianism. Thus the very first review of the *Principia* that appeared in France,[1] having praised to the skies its value as "mechanics," rather harshly condemns its "physics":

> The work of M. Newton is a mechanics, the most perfect that one could imagine, as it is not possible to make demonstrations more precise or more exact than those that he gives in the first two books on lightness, on springiness, on the resistance of fluid bodies, and on the attractive and repulsive forces that are the principal basis of Physics. But one has to confess that one cannot regard these demonstrations otherwise than as only mechanical; indeed, the author recognizes himself at the end of page four and the beginning of page five that he has not considered their Principles as a Physicist, but as a mere Geometer.
>
> He confesses the same thing at the beginning of the third book, where he endeavors nevertheless to explain the System of the World. But it is [done] only by hypotheses that are, most of them, arbitrary, and that, consequently, can serve as foundation only to a treatise of pure mechanics. He bases the explanation of the inequality of the tides on the principle that all the planets gravitate reciprocally toward each other . . . But this supposition is arbitrary as it has not been proved; the demonstration that depends on it can therefore only be mechanics.
>
> In order to make an *opus* as perfect as possible, M. Newton has only to give us a Physics as exact as his Mechanics. He will give it when he substitutes true motions for those that he has supposed.

The author of this review – according to Mouy he may have been Régis – was a Cartesian of rather strict observance; moreover, he probably was not able to appreciate at its just value the immense mathematical progress achieved by Newton in the *Principia*. Much more interesting, from these points of view, are the reactions of Huygens and Leibniz. Huygens, who some twenty years earlier

---

[1] *Journal des Sçavans* (2 August 1688), pp. 153 sq., quoted in part by P. Mouy, *Le Développement de la physique cartésienne* (Paris, 1934), p. 256.

had devised and (in 1669) even presented to the Académie Royale des Sciences a rather elaborate theory of terrestrial gravity in which he replaced the Cartesian vortex by an ensemble of circular motions of small particles turning around the earth on spherical surfaces in all possible directions, voiced his misgivings. He wrote to Fatio de Dullier (11 July 1687): "I have nothing against his not being a Cartesian, provided he does not give us suppositions like that of attraction."[1]

But the persual of the *Principia* seems to have overwhelmed him. Thus, on 14 December 1688, he makes a note:

> The famous M. Newton has brushed aside all the difficulties [concerning the Keplerian laws] together with the Cartesian vortices; he has shown that the planets are retained in their orbits by their gravitation toward the Sun. And that the excentrics necessarily become elliptical.[2]

This means that Newton had achieved something that Huygens, having discovered the law of centrifugal force, could have done . . . but did not: (1) from his inverse-square law of universal gravitation he was able to demonstrate the ellipticity of the planetary orbits about which Huygens, being unable to reconstruct them by purely mechanical means (that is, by means of circular motions) had doubts; and (2) he decided this law of universal gravitation by extending the Keplerian attraction between the earth and the moon to the whole solar system (something that Huygens, who did not admit such an "attraction," did not and could not do), and he determined the centripetal force that retained the planets in their orbits by means of the theorem about centrifugal force (which Huygens established before Newton, but failed to apply to celestial motions). Huygens paid a tremendous price for his fidelity to the Cartesian rationalism *à outrance.*

It must have been hard for Huygens to recognize, and to admit, that he missed the great discovery. Yet he did so with good grace, as we shall see in a moment.[3] But he did not become converted to Newtonian views; nor did he abandon his firm convictions concerning the necessity of a mechanical explanation of gravity and the impossibility of dispensing with some kind of vortices: without them planets would not remain in their orbits, but would run away from the

---

[1] *Oeuvres complètes* (The Hague: Martinus Nijhoff, 1888-1950), IX, 190.
[2] *Ibid.*, XXI, 143.
[3] In the "Additions" to the *Discours de la cause de la pesanteur* that he published in 1690 as an appendix to his *Traité de la lumière* (Leiden, 1690), *Oeuvres complètes*, XXI, 443 sq.

sun. Thus, in his *Pensées privées* (1686), he wrote: "Planets swim in matter. For, if they did not, what would prevent the planets from fleeing, what would move them? Kepler wants, but wrongly, that it should be the sun,"[1] and in 1688 he still wrote:

Vortices destroyed by Newton. Vortices of spherical motion in their place.
To rectify the idea of vortices.
Vortices necessary; [without them] the earth would run away from the sun; but very distant the one from the other, and not, like those of M. Des Cartes, touching each other.[2]

It may seem rather strange to see Huygens trying to replace by a set of smaller vortices the huge Cartesian vortices that Newton had destroyed and swept from the skies. Yet what could he do? He could no more admit Newtonian attraction than Keplerian attraction; thus he had to retain the vortices that prevented the planets from moving away from the sun. As for gravity, he felt that his own theory could still hold its own, especially if he proved it somewhat by extending as far as the moon the sphere of motion of his weight-producing particles. He even felt that he could and should oppose his theory of gravity to Newton's. Thus, in 1689, during his visit to London, where he met Newton and was received by the Royal Society, he gave a lecture on the cause of gravity.[3] We do not know exactly what he said in his lecture; but we cannot doubt that its contents were not different from those of his *Discourse on the Cause of Gravity* of 1690, which comprises a somewhat corrected version of his *Discourse* of 1669 plus a discussion of the shape of the earth written, as he tells us, some years later, plus "Additions" in which, "having read the very learned work of M. Newton," he discusses some of Newton's conceptions, among them universal gravity or attraction, understood as a direct, or at least nonmechanical, action of one body upon another. About this he says in a letter to Leibniz of 18 November 1690:

Concerning the Cause of the flux given by M. Newton, I am by no means satisfied [by it], nor by all the other Theories that he builds upon his Principle of Attraction, which to me seems absurd, as I have already mentioned in the addition to the *Discourse on Gravity*. And I have often wondered how he could have given himself all the trouble of making such a

[1] *Oeuvres complètes*, XXI, 366.
[2] *Varia astronomica, ibid.*, XXI, 437–439.
[3] *Ibid.*, IX, 333, n. 1; XXI, 435, n. 31, 443, n. 34, 466.

number of investigations and difficult calculations that have no other foundation than this very principle.[1]

As a matter of fact, Huygens, a polite and well-mannered gentleman, does not tell the readers of his *Discourse on the Cause of Gravity* that he considers Newtonian attraction an "absurdity." He only informs them (*a*) that he does not accept it because such an attraction would be unexplainable by mechanical means, (*b*) that it seems to him superfluous for the explanation of gravity, and (*c*) that he has nothing against the Newtonian *vis centripeta*, provided, of course, that he can explain it away and that he need not admit gravity as an inherent quality of bodies, which is something, he adds, that Newton himself certainly does not admit. Thus he writes:

> I do not agree with a Principle according to which all the small parts that we can imagine in two or several different bodies mutually attract each other or tend to approach each other.
> That is something I would not be able to admit because I believe that I see clearly that the cause of such an attraction is not explainable by any of the principles of Mechanics, or of the rules of motion. Nor am I convinced of the necessity of the mutual attraction of whole bodies, since I have shown that, even if there were no Earth, bodies would not cease to tend toward a center by that which we call gravity.[2]

Yet, what is it that we call gravity? Or even: what *is* gravity?

For Huygens, who, in this respect, is a good Cartesian, gravity is not, of course, as it is for the Aristotelians, a constitutive property of some bodies (the heavy ones), as levity is a property of some others (the light ones); nor is gravity, as for Archimedes and his sixteenth- and seventeenth-century followers, an essential property of *all* bodies; nor is it, as for Copernicus and possibly even for Galileo, the expression of an inner tendency of homogeneous parts to reunite and build up a whole; nor is it, as for Kepler and Roberval, the effect of the mutual attraction of these parts and the whole. Instead, gravity is for Huygens, as for Descartes, the effect of an extraneous action: bodies are heavy because, and insofar as, they are pressed and pushed toward the earth by some other bodies – more precisely by a whirlwind of subtle or liquid matter that, with immense speeds, turns around the earth. Thus:

> If we look at bodies simply, without [taking into account] that quality

---

[1] *Oeuvres complètes*, XXI, 538; C. J. Gerhardt, ed., *Leibnizens philosophische Schriften* (Berlin, 1882), Abt. I, Bd. II, p. 57.

[2] Huygens, *Discours sur le cause de la pesanteur*, p. 159; *Oeuvres complètes*, XXI, 471.

which is called gravity, their motion is naturally straight or circular; the first one pertaining to them when they move without hindrance, the other when they are retained around some center, or when they turn on this very center. We know sufficiently the nature of straight motion and the laws that bodies, when they meet, observe in the communication of their motions. But as long as one considers only this kind of motion and the reflections that are produced by it among the parts of matter, one does not find anything that [would] determine them to tend toward a center. We have, thus, necessarily to turn to the properties of circular motion and to see whether there are some that could serve us.

I know that M. Des Cartes has also endeavored in his *Physics* to explain gravity by the motion of a certain matter that turns around the Earth; and it is a great merit to have been the first to have that idea. But we shall see by the remarks that I shall make in the sequel to this *Discourse*, that his manner is different from the one that I shall propose, and also in what respect it seems to me to be defective.[1]

Having reminded the reader of the properties of centrifugal force, Huygens continues:

The effort to move away from the center is, thus, a constant effect of circular motion and though this effect seems to be directly opposed to that of gravity, and though it was accordingly objected to Copernicus that by the rotation of the Earth in 24 hours houses and men would be thrown in the air, I will show nonetheless that the same effort which bodies turning round are making in order to move away from the center, is the cause that other bodies concur toward that same center.[2]

In order to explain, or better to show, this rather paradoxical effect, Huygens reminds us of an experiment that he had made "especially for that purpose, which is worthy of being noticed as it makes accessible to the eye an image of gravity." In this experiment, which he performed in 1668 and which became very famous – Rohault describes it in his *System of Natural Philosophy*[3] – Huygens took a cylindrical vessel 8 or 10 inches in diameter, put it on a turntable so that it could be rotated around its axis, filled it with water, to which he added pieces of Spanish wax, and closed it in the top by a glass plate. When he started to turn it, he noticed that the pieces of Spanish wax–a substance heavier than water – received the circular motion more quickly and easily than the water and moved toward the sides of the vessel. Yet if he turned the vessel long

[1] *Discours* (Leiden, 1690), p. 135; *Oeuvres complètes*, XXI, 455; see *Discours* of 1669, *Oeuvres complètes*, XIX, 634.
[2] *Discours*, p. 131; *Oeuvres complètes*, XXI, 452.
[3] *Physica*, pars II, cap. XXVIII, sec. 8, p. 326; *Rohault's System of Natural Philosophy*, trans. John Clarke (London, 1723), II, 94.

enough, so that the water fully participated in the circular (rotational) motion of the vessel, and then suddenly stopped it, he observed that

> Instantly all the Spanish wax flew in a heap toward the center [and that] represented to me the effect of gravity. And the reason of it was that water, the rest (immobility) of the vessel notwithstanding, continued its circular motion, whereas the Spanish wax had lost it, or nearly so, because it touched the bottom of the vessel that was stopped. I noticed also that this powder, in going to the center, followed spiral lines because water dragged it somewhat along.
>
> But [Rohault did not describe this phase of the experiment] if, in that vessel, we place a body in such a manner that it should not at all be able to follow the [circular] movement of the water but only move toward the center, it will then be pushed directly there. Thus if L is a small ball that can freely roll on the bottom between the threads AA, BB and a third one, placed somewhat higher, KK, stretched horizontally through the middle of the vessel, we shall see that when the motion of the vessel is stopped, this ball will at once move toward the center D.[1]

Having thus presented to us a case where centrifugal force produces centripetal motion – in fact an excellent model of a Cartesian vortex – Huygens uses the same dynamical scheme for the explanation of gravity, improving it, however, in order to avoid the difficulties implied in Descartes' conception. Indeed, Cartesian vortices, (a) just like the water in the Huygens vessel, turn around the axis, wherefore the centripetal motion resulting from their rotation is also directed toward an axis, and not toward a center, as is the case with gravity, and, (b) since all matter constituting them moves in one direction – once more like water in the vessel – drag along bodies immersed in them and make such bodies describe spirals and not straight lines.

Huygens postulates, therefore, that the particles of the "vortex" turn not in the same direction and in parallel planes, but in *all* directions and in *all* planes that pass through the center of the earth:

> I shall suppose that in the spherical space which comprises the Earth and the bodies that are around it up to a very great distance, there is a fluid matter that consists of very small particles and that is diversely agitated in all directions, with a very great speed. I say that the motion of this matter, being unable to leave this space, which is surrounded by other bodies, must become partially circular around the center; not in such a manner however that its particles should turn all in the same way, but in the manner that most of its movements should be made on spherical

[1] Huygens, *Discours*, p. 133; *Oeuvres complètes*, XXI, 453.

surfaces around the center of this space which becomes, so to say, the center of the Earth.[1]

This being admitted, Huygens goes on:

> It is not difficult to explain how, by this motion, gravity is produced. For, if among the fluid matter that turns in space as we have supposed there happen to be parts that are much bigger than those that compose the fluid matter, or else bodies made up of bundles of small particles linked together, and [if] these bodies do not follow the rapid motion of the said [fluid] matter, they will necessarily be pushed toward the center of the movement, and will form there the terrestrial globe, if we suppose that the Earth should not yet be [in existence]. And the reason is the same as that which, in the above-mentioned experiment, makes the Spanish wax congregate at the center of the vessel. Thus it is in this [effect] that, probably, the gravity of bodies consists, and we can say that it [that is, gravity] is the effort that the fluid matter makes to move away from the center and to push into its place bodies that do not follow its movement. Now the reason why heavy bodies that we see descending in the air do not follow the spherical movement of the fluid matter is rather clear; for, as there is motion toward all sides, the impulses that a body receives from them follow each other so quickly that it [is acted upon during] less time than it would need in order to acquire a sensible movement.[2]

Having thus solved the problem of gravity to his own satisfaction, Huygens proceeds to the determination of the speed with which the fluid matter should move around the earth in order to overcome the centrifugal force of the earth's rotation and to give to falling bodies the acceleration that they actually have. The result of these calculations is rather striking: the fluid matter has to move 17 times more quickly than a point on the equator. "I know," admits Huygens,

> that this speed may seem strange to those who would want to compare it with the motions that are seen here among us. But this should not make any difficulty; and even in respect to the sphere, or to the dimensions of the Earth, it will not appear extraordinary. For if, for instance, looking at a terrestrial globe from outside, we imagine on this globe a point which advances only one degree in 14 seconds, or pulse-strokes, we will find this motion very moderate, and it could even seem slow.[3]

Having thus discovered the *causa gravitatis* to be motion, and not the mechanically unexplainable force of attraction, Huygens concludes:

> Thus I have nothing against the *Vis Centripeta*, as M. Newton calls it, by which he makes planets gravitate toward the Sun and the Moon toward

[1] *Discours*, p. 135; *Oeuvres complètes*, p. 455. [2] *Ibid.*, p. 137; p. 456.
[3] *Ibid.*, p. 143; p. 460.

the Earth, but am in agreement [with him] without [feeling] any difficulty: because not only is it known by experience that there is in nature such a manner of attraction or impulsion, but also that it is explainable by the laws of motion as one has seen in what I have written *supra* concerning gravity. Indeed, nothing prohibits that the cause of this *Vis Centripeta* toward the Sun be similar to that which makes the bodies that we call heavy descend toward the Earth. It was long ago that it was imagined that the spherical figure of the Sun could be produced by the same [cause] that, according to me, produced the sphericity of the Earth; but I had not extended the action of gravity to such great distances as those between the Sun and the Planets, or between the Moon and the Earth; this because the vortices of M. Descartes which formerly seemed to me rather likely, and that I still had in mind, crossed them. I did not think, either, about this regular diminishing of gravity, namely, that it was in reciprocal proportion to the squares of the distances from the centers: which is a new and remarkable property of gravity, which it is, indeed, worth while to investigate. But seeing now by the demonstrations of M. Newton that, supposing such a gravity toward the Sun, and that it diminishes according to the said proportion, it counterbalances so well the centrifugal forces of the planets and produces precisely the effect of the elliptical motion that Kepler had guessed and proved by observation, I cannot doubt the truth either of these hypotheses concerning gravity or of the System of M. Newton, in so far as it is based upon it . . .

It would be different, of course, if one should suppose that gravity is a quality inherent in corporeal matter. But that is something which I do not believe that M. Newton would admit because such a hypothesis would remove us far away from Mathematical or Mechanical Principles.[1]

There was, moreover, something else in Newton's conception of the world that Huygens could not accept, namely, the perfect, or nearly perfect, vacuity of the celestial spaces. Not that Huygens wanted them to be full: as we know, he did not accept the Cartesian identification of extension and matter, and he had no objection (metaphysical) against a void; nay, being an atomist, he had to postulate its existence. But, to use traditional terms, he accepted only the *vacuum interspersum*, or *disseminatum*, and not the *vacuum separatum*. This for a very good reason: he believed – in opposition to Newton – that light was constituted not of particles, but of waves or the pulses of particles, and as he did not believe – also in opposition to Newton – in the existence of a luminiferous aether distinct from matter, he had to conclude that a perfect vacuum, or even a vacuum not quite perfect but nearly perfect like Newton's, would not transmit light. And, of course, such a rare medium would not be able to

---

[1] *Discours*, pp. 160, 162; *Oeuvres complètes*, pp. 472, 474.

provide a mechanical basis for "gravitational" action. Accordingly he concluded his criticism of Newton by saying:

There is only this difficulty, that M. Newton, rejecting the vortices of Descartes, wants the celestial spaces to contain [nothing] but a very rare matter in order that the Planets and the Comets encounter a minimum of resistance in their course. Which rareness being posited, it seems not possible to explain the action of Gravity, or that of Light, at least by the ways which I used. In order to examine this point, I say, that the aethereal matter can be considered rare in two manners, namely that its particles are distant one from the other leaving a large void between them; or that they touch each other, but that their tissue is rare and interspersed with a great number of small void spaces. Concerning the void, I admit it without difficulty and even believe it to be necessary for the motion of the little corpuscles among themselves, as I am not of the opinion of M. Des Cartes, who wants extension alone to constitute the essence of body; I add to it [extension] also the perfect hardness that makes it impenetrable and unable to be broken or dented. However, if one considered rareness in the first manner, I do not see how one could account for gravity; and, concerning light, it seems to me utterly impossible, admitting such voids, to explain its prodigious velocity which, according to the demonstration of M. Roemer which I have reported in the *Traité de lumière*, must be six hundred thousand times greater than that of Sound. That is [the reason] why I hold that such a rareness cannot be suitable for celestial spaces.[1]

Thus Huygens. He never changed his mind, and never accepted Newtonian attraction. He also – wisely – never made a serious attempt to revive the medieval conception of celestial orbs by substituting for the huge sun vortex of Descartes a series of separate planetary vortices: his *Cosmotheoros* of 1698 is just as vague about them as his notes of 1688:

I think that every Sun [that is, every star] is surrounded by a certain vortex of matter in quick movement, but that these vortices are very different from the Cartesian vortices as well in respect to the space that they occupy as in respect to the manner in which their matter is moving.[2]

Huygens then reminds us that it is gravity which retains the planets in their orbits, as Alphonse Borelli and especially Isaac Newton have shown, and continues:

Now according to our opinion about the nature of gravity by which the planets tend toward the Sun by their own weight, it is necessary that the vortex of the celestial matter turn around it not in one direction only, but in such a manner that it moves in different, very quick, movements, in all

[1] *Discours*, p. 161; *Oeuvres complètes*, p. 473.
[2] Huygens, *Cosmotheoros* (The Hague, 1698); *Oeuvres complètes*, XXI, 819–821.

possible directions . . . It is by a vortex of this kind that we have endeavoured, in our *Discourse*, to explain the gravity of bodies toward the Earth and all its effects. For the nature of the gravity of planets toward the Sun is the same according to our opinion.

Another difference between Huygens's and Descartes's theories consists in the dimensions attributed to vortices: "As I have said, I make the spaces occupied by these vortices much smaller than he does and separate them by vast distances wherefore they do not interfere one with the other."

Curiously enough, it was Leibniz who, in his *Tentamen de motuum coelestium causis*,[1] did what Huygens failed to do. And it is rather significant that Huygens did not approve. The *Tentamen* does not take issue with the Newtonian conceptions. Leibniz tells us, moreover, that when he wrote it he was in Rome and had not read – or even seen – Newton's *Principia*, having learned about it only from the review published in 1688 in the *Acta eruditorum* (see *infra*, p. 133). In the *Illustratio tentaminis de motuum coelestium causis*,[2] defending himself against D. Gregory,[3] who expressed his astonishment at the publication of the *Tentamen* two years after Newton's *Principia*, Leibniz repeats (quoting Sec. 20 of the *Tentamen*) that he did not read the *Principia* but only the report of it in the *Acta*: "But this report incited me to publish my thoughts, not seen nor heard by others, and till then not published." Leibniz adds that the difference between his approach and derivation of the inverse-square law and Newton's, and the interconnection of the propositions of the *Tentamen*, are a sufficient proof of his having had these thoughts before having read the report in the *Acta*.

We have no reason to doubt Leibniz's assertion, all the more so as the study of the *Principia* would have prevented him from making the glaring mistakes about celestial motions and their causes that we find in his paper. And yet the *Tentamen* is certainly an attempt made by Leibniz – doubtless prompted by the appearance of the above-mentioned review – to oppose Newton's celestial mechanics with a sketch of his own, and to try to "save" the *plenum* against Newton's onslaught.

The *Tentamen* exists in two versions: the one that was printed in

---

[1] *Acta eruditorum* (1689); see C. J. Gerhardt, ed., *Leibnizens mathematische Schriften* (Halle, 1860), VI, 144 sq., 161 sq.

[2] *Mathematische Schriften*, VI, 255.

[3] *Astronomiae physicae et geometricae elementa* (London, 1702), lib. I, prop. LXXVII, p. 99.

the *Acta eruditorum* and another that was found among Leibniz's papers (published by Gerhardt as the "second version").[1] The "second version" is very similar to the published one, but it contains a rather important addition dealing with the nature and structure of gravity. As this addition was obviously written by Leibniz some time after the publication of his paper in the *Acta*, I shall deal with the two versions in the same order, that is, first with the published version, and only thereafter with the additions. It must be mentioned also that for his published paper Leibniz projected, and even wrote, an introductory preface intended to show the authorities of the Catholic Church that, if they recognized, as they should, that *motion* was a relative concept, they would also recognize that the systems of Copernicus, Tycho Brahe, and Ptolemy were equivalent, and that therefore the condemnation of Copernicus was meaningless and should be lifted. He did not, however, publish it: he learned from his Catholic friends that it was better for him to keep quiet.

The *Tentamen* is based on Keplerian astronomy, which Leibniz considers to be true in all its descriptive laws of celestial motion; it can be interpreted as an investigation of the possibility of their validity in a world full of matter, that is, a world where motion, in general, encounters resistance, and where, therefore, planets would also encounter resistance (a possibility that Kepler has never considered) unless either – this is the Leibnizian solution – this matter itself moves with the planets or, conversely, the planets move together with the matter that surrounds them. In other words, the *Tentamen* is an investigation of planetary motion in which the planets are thought to be transported through the skies by fluid orbs in the midst of which they remain at rest, the orbs and the planets all the while obeying in their motion the fundamental – Keplerian – law, which Leibniz calls "harmonic." Accordingly, Leibniz starts with overwhelming praise of Kepler, to whom, in order to belittle Descartes and not to acknowledge his indebtedness to him, he even ascribes discoveries that he did not make (for instance, that the planetary motions engender centrifugal forces) and whom he presents as the true author of the vortex conception that Descartes had stolen from him.[2]

Thus Leibniz writes:

Kepler has found that each primary planet describes an elliptical orbit

---

[1] *Mathematische Schriften*, VI, 161 sq.
[2] L. Prenant, "Sur les références de Leibniz contre Descartes," *Archives Internationales d'Histoire des Sciences 13* (1960), 95.

in one of the foci of which is the sun, their motion being [performed according] to the law that by the radii drawn toward the sun are always determined areas proportional to times. He also discovered that the periodic times of the several planets of the same system are in a sesquialteral proportion to the mean distances to the sun; he would, indeed, be exceedingly triumphant if he knew that (as stated by the illustrious Cassini) even the satellites of Jupiter and Saturn observe, in respect to their primary planet, the same laws as these in respect to the sun. But he could not assign the causes of these so numerous and so constant truths, either because he had a mind hampered by [the belief in] intelligences and sympathetic radiations, or because in his time geometry and the science of motion were inferior to what they are now.

Yet it is to him that we owe the first disclosure of the true cause of gravity, and of the law of nature, on which gravity depends, namely that bodies moving circularly [around a center] tend to recede from this center by the tangent; thus, if a stalk or a straw swim in water, and if by the rotation of the vessel [this water] is moved in a vortex, the water being more dense than the stalks and being therefore driven out from the center more strongly than the stalks, then forces will push the stalks toward the center, as he has himself clearly explained in two and more places in his *Epitome of the Astronomy*.[1]

As a matter of fact Kepler, as I have already mentioned, never admitted that planets tend to recede by the tangent from their circular orbits; and if in the *Astronomia nova*[2] he had actually presented the *exemplum* of a vortex, he used this vortex not for counteracting the centrifugal force by a centripetal force produced by this vortex, but in order to explain (on the pattern of a ferry moving forward and back across a river) the periodic variations of the distances (access and recess) of the planets from the sun. Moreover, in the *Epitome astronomiae Copernicanae*[3] he did not reassert a vortex but on the contrary rejected it and replaced it by the theory of magnetic attraction and repulsion of the planets by the sun.[4] It is difficult to tell whether Leibniz was aware of all this or not. In any case he continues, stating that Kepler

remained somewhat in doubt about [his vortex conception], ignorant of his own riches [Leibniz applies to Kepler what Kepler said about Copernicus], and insufficiently conscious how many things follow therefrom both in Physics and, especially, in Astronomy. But of these Descartes has later

[1] *Mathematische Schriften*, VI, 148 sq., 162 sq.
[2] Cap. XXXVIII; see Kepler, *Opera omnia*, ed. Frisch (Frankfurt, 1858–1891), III, 313 sq.; *Gesammelte Werke*, ed. M. Caspar (Munich, 1938–1959), III, 254 sq.
[3] *Opera omnia*, VI, 345 sq.; *Gesammelte Werke*, VII, 300 sq.
[4] See A. Koyré, *La Révolution astronomique* (Paris: Hermann, 1961), part III, "Kepler et l'astronomie nouvelle," chap. 1.

made ample use though, according to his habit, he hid their author. And I have often wondered that, as far as we know, Descartes has never attempted to give the reasons of the celestial laws discovered by Kepler, be it that he could not sufficiently reconcile them with his own principles, or that he ignored the fruitfulness of the discovery, and did not believe it to be so faithfully observed by nature.

Now, as it seems hardly to conform to physics and even unworthy of the admirable workmanship of God to assign to the stars particular intelligences, as if God lacked the means to achieve the same [result] by corporeal laws; and as the solid orbs have since been destroyed [Leibniz, once more, uses Kepler's expressions], whereas sympathies and magnetic and other abstruse qualities of the same sort are either not understandable, or, where they are understood, are judged to be effects of a corporeal impression; I think that there remains nothing else but to admit that the celestial motions are caused by the motions of the aether, or, to speak astronomically, by [the motions of] the deferent orbs [which are, however, not solid] but fluid.

This opinion is very old, though it has been neglected: for Leucippus already before Epicurus expressed it, so that in forming the system [of the world] he attributed to it the name of δίνη (vortex) and we have seen how Kepler vaguely represented [*adumbravit*] gravity by the motion of water moved in a vortex. And from the itinerary of Monconys,[1] M. de Monconys tells, indeed, that during his "voiage" XX in Italy he paid a visit to Torricelli (November 1646, pp. 130 sq.) and that:

"Le dit Torricelle m'expliqua aussi, comme les corps se tournent sur leur centre, côme le ☀ [soleil] la terre et Jup. font tourner tout l'Eter, qui les environne, mais plus viste les parties prochaines que les éloignées, aussi que l'expérience le montre à une eau où l'on tourne un baton dans le centre, et le mesme en arrive aux planettes, au respect du ☀ [soleil], et à la ☽ [lune], au respect de la terre; aux Médicées au respect de Jup. et me dit aussi que Galilei a observé que la tache de la Lune qu'on nomme Mare Caspium est par fois plus proche de la circonférence, et quelquefois plus éloignée, qui fait reconnoistre quelque petit mouvement de trépidation en son corps."

We learn that it was also the opinion of Toricelli (and, as I suspect, even of Galileo of whom he was a disciple) that the aether, together with the planets turned around the sun, moved by the motion of the sun around its center, as water [is moved] by a stick rotated around its axis in the middle of a quiescent vessel; and just like straw or stalks swimming in water, the stars [planets] nearer to the center turn around more quickly. But these more general [considerations] come rather easily to mind. Our intention, however, is to explain the laws of nature more clearly . . . And as in this matter we have gained some light and as the investigation seems to proceed easily

---

[1] *Journal des voyages de Monsieur de Monconys, conseiller du roy en ses conseils d'estat et privé, et lieutenant criminel au siège présidial de Lyon,* publié par le Sieur de Liergves son Fils (Lyon: Chez Horace Boissat et George Remeurs, 1665), Première Partie, "Voyage de Portugal, Provence, Holiè, Égypte, Syrie, Constantinople et Natolie."

and naturally, and with success, I do hope that we have approached [the knowledge of] the true causes of celestial motions."

Leibniz then says:

First of all it can be demonstrated that, according to the laws of nature, *all bodies which, in a fluid, describe a curved line, are carried along by the motion of this fluid.* For indeed all [bodies] describing a curve tend to recede from it by the tangent (because of the nature of motion); there must therefore be something that forces [them not to do it]. But there is nothing contiguous but the fluid (by hypothesis), and no *conatus* is restrained unless by (something) contiguous and moving (because of the nature of body); it is therefore necessary that the fluid itself be in motion . . .

It follows therefrom that planets are moved by their aether, that is to say, that they have deferent or moving fluid orbs. For it is generally admitted that they describe curved lines, and it is not possible to explain the phenomena by supposing only rectilinear motions. Accordingly (by what precedes) they are moved by the ambient fluid. The same thing can be demonstrated from the fact that the motion of a planet is not uniform, that is, it describes equal spaces in equal times. Wherefrom it follows that they must be moved by the motion of the ambient.[1]

Thus far we are on purely Cartesian or Huygenian ground: a planet is swimming in an aethereal vortex, or orb, and is carried along by it. This motion, however, is somewhat different from that of Cartesian or Huygenian vortices: it is a "harmonic" motion.

Yet what is a "harmonic" motion or "circulation"? As a matter of fact, it is the motion, or circulation, in which, according to Kepler (who, by the way, does not call it "harmonic"), planets are actually moving around the sun; that is, as Kepler erroneously deduced from the area law of planetary motion,[2] the planets move in such a way that their speeds are always inversely proportional to their distances from the sun. Leibniz, however, who did not recognize the error committed by Kepler, does not tell us anything about the astronomical origin of his concept (nor that it is Keplerian); quite the contrary, he gives an abstract definition of the "harmonic circulation," wherefrom, triumphantly (but also erroneously), he deduces Kepler's second law (historically, the first), that is, the law of areas. Thus he writes:

I call a circulation *harmonic*, if the velocities of the circulation of a certain body are reciprocally proportional to the radii or distances from the center of circulation; or (what is the same) if the velocities of circulation

[1] *Mathematische Schriften*, VI, 149, 166.
[2] Koyré, *La Révolution astronomique*.

around the center decrease in the same proportion in which the distances from the center increase, or, in short, if the velocities of circulation increase in proportion to the nearness [to the center]. Thus, indeed, if the radii or distances increase uniformly or in arithmetical proportion, the velocities will decrease in a harmonic progression. In this way the harmonic circulation can take place not only in the arcs of a circle, but also in all kinds of curves described [by one body]. Let us posit that the moved

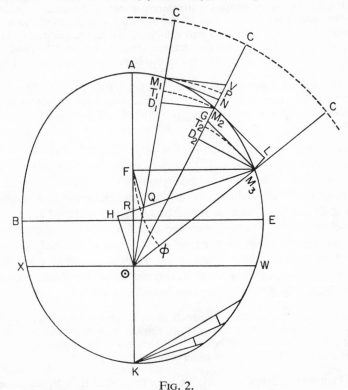

FIG. 2.

[body] M moves in a certain curve $M_3 M_2 M_1$ (or $M_1 M_2 M_3$) and in equal elements of time describes the elements $M_3 M_2$, $M_2 M_1$, of the curve [Fig. 2]; [this motion] can be understood as composed of circular motion around some center, e.g., ⊙ [the sun] (such as $M_3 T_2$, $M_3 T_1$) and a rectilinear [one] such as $T_2 M_2$, $T_1 M_1$ (assuming ⊙ T_2 to be equal to ⊙ M_3, and ⊙ T_1 equal to ⊙ M_2); which motion can furthermore be understood from one assumption that a rule or an indefinite rigid straight [line] ⊙ C [passing through the planet] moves around the center ⊙ and at the same time the mobile moves on this straight [line] ⊙ C [toward ⊙].[1]

[1] *Mathematische Schriften*, VI, 150 sq., 167 sq. Fig. taken from E. J. Aiton, *Annals of Science 16* (1960), 69.

According to Leibniz, the "harmonic" character of the curvilinear "circulation" is not affected by the fact

that the motion by which [the mobile] approaches the center or recedes from it, is rectilinear (I call it *paracentric* motion), as long as the circulation of the mobile M, such as $M_3 T_2$, is [in the same proportion] to another circulation of the same mobile, $M_2 T_1$, as $\odot M_1$ is to $\odot M_2$; that is, as long as the circulations performed in the same elements of time are reciprocally as the radii. For, as these arcs of the elementary circulations are in the composite ratios of the times and velocities, and as the elementary times are assumed to be equal, the circulations will be as the velocities, and thus the velocities inversely as the radii; therefore the circulation will be a harmonic one. . . .

If the mobile moves in a harmonic circulation (whatever the paracentric motion), the areas swept out by the radii drawn from the center of the circulation to the mobile will be proportional to the assumed times and vice versa.

Alas, it is not so. Retracing backward Kepler's analysis of the planetary motions – the only new elements in Leibniz's presentation are the terms "harmonic" and "paracentric" which he gives to motions that Kepler called *solipetes* (and Newton, *centripetes*) – Leibniz commits the same error as Kepler: as a matter of fact, "harmonic" circulation, elliptic orbits, and the area law are incompatible and planets do not move on their orbits with speeds inversely proportional to their distances from the sun. Leibniz, fortunately or unfortunately, did not notice this (Newton did, however; Hooke did not, nor did Wren or Halley); he concludes therefore:

It follows herefrom that the planets move in a harmonic circulation, the primary around the sun, the satellites around their primaries as centers. For the radii drawn from the center of circulation describe areas proportional to times (according to observation).[1]

Having established the fact, we have to explain it. Why do planets move in this way? According to Leibniz, they do so because they are carried along by a harmonically circulating aether:

It is therefore necessary that *the aether, or the fluid orb of each planet should move in a harmonic circulation;* for it has been shown *supra* that no body [can] by itself move in a fluid in a curved line; there will therefore be a circulation in the aether, and it conforms to reason to believe that it will be in agreement with the circulation of the planet, and that the circulation of the aether of each planet will also be harmonic; so that if the fluid orb of the planet were divided by thought into innumerable circular concentric

[1] *Mathematische Schriften*, VI, 151, 168.

orbs of inconsiderable thickness, the circulation of each of them would be proportionally much quicker as each [of them] is nearer to the sun.[1]

Leibniz is right, of course: if we assume that planets move in the aether and that their motion is not hampered by this aether, we have to assume that this aether moves in exactly the same way as the planets. But why should the aether move in this particular manner? Leibniz does not raise this rather natural question. Moreover, his aether, formed into fluid planetary orbs, not only accompanies the planets in their motion, but also determines it:

We posit thus that *the planet moves in a double or composite motion [resulting] from the harmonic circulation of its deferent fluid orb and the paracentric motion*, as [is produced] by a certain gravity or attraction, that is, by *impulse towards the sun, or the primary planet*. Indeed the circulation of the aether makes the planet circulate harmonically, and not its own motion, by which it is only *quasi* quietly swimming in the deferent fluid, the motion of which it follows; wherefore it does not retain the quicker impetus of circulation which it had in an orb inferior or nearer [to the sun] when it is transported to a superior [orb] (which resists a velocity greater than its own), but it accommodates itself insensibly to the orb to which it accedes, continuously abandoning the quicker impetus for a feebler one. *Vice versa*, when it [the planet] tends from a superior to an inferior [orb], it takes its impetus.

The "paracentric" motion, at first glance, seems superfluous: do not the planets swim quietly in the fluid orbs that carry them along in a harmonic motion? By no means: they only *quasi* do so, and without this paracentric *quasi*-attractive or *quasi*-gravitational motion they would run away along the tangent; Leibniz therefore continues:

The harmonic circulation having been explained, we must consider the *paracentric motion of the planets, which originates from the extruding [excussorius] impression of the circulation* [centrifugal force] *and the solar attraction combined together*. We may call it attraction, though in truth it should be impulse; indeed the sun can, with some reason, be regarded as a magnet; however, its magnetic actions derive, doubtless, from the impulses of fluids. Therefore we shall call it also *Solicitation of Gravity*, considering the planet as a heavy body tending towards the center, that is, the sun. But the shape of the orb depends on a special law of attraction. Let us see therefore which law of attraction produces the elliptic line.[1]

Once more Leibniz is right: different laws of attraction determine different orbits. And yet one is somewhat astonished to see him use terms and concepts that one would expect him to avoid, or even reject. One is, moreover, somewhat puzzled: it is, indeed, not quite clear whether the law of attraction determines the form of the fluid orb and thus the orbit of the planet, or, on the contrary, whether it determines the orbit of the planet to which the fluid orb must be adapted. Or does this "law of attraction" only express the particular structure of the fluid orbs? Yet, be this as it may, it is obvious that Leibniz – though, after all, Newton did the same thing – wants to use the concept of attraction without committing himself to admit it as a real, physical force. Thus:

As every moving body tends (*conatur*) to recede by the tangent from the curved line that it describes, we can well call this conatus "*excussorius*" [extruding], as in the motion of the sling, in which there is required an equal force which compels the moving body not to run away. *We can represent this conatus by the perpendicular to the next point of the tangent, insensibly distant from the preceding point.* And as the line is circular, the famous Huygens, who was the first to deal with it geometrically, called it *centrifugal* [force].[1]

Indeed, the infinitesimal curve from a point on the tangent to the "next point" can be considered as circular, and therefore Huygens's law of centrifugal force can be used for determining the *conatus* in question. Leibniz deduces therefrom that: "The *centrifugal* or extruding *conatus* of the circulation can be expressed by the *sinus versus* of the angle of the circulation,"[2] that is, of the angle formed by the radii drawn from the center to the moving body.

Thence, using the methods of the infinitesimal calculus and making some rather heavy blunders – such as "The centrifugal *conatus* of a body in harmonic circulation is in the inverse cube proportion of the radii" – he can finally assert:

If a mobile that has gravity, or is drawn toward a certain center, as is the case of the planets in respect to the sun, *moves in an ellipse* (or in another section of the cone) *in a harmonic circulation, and if the focus of the ellipse is the center of the circulation as well as of the attraction, the attractions or solicitations of gravity will be directly as the squares of the circulations, or as the squares of the radii or distances from the center reciprocally.*[3]

In other words:

The same planet is differently attracted by the sun, and namely in the duplicate ratio of its nearness, so that [being] twice nearer [to the sun]

[1] *Mathematische Schriften*, VI, 152, 169.   [2] *Ibid.*, 153, 170.
[3] *Ibid.*, 156, 176.

it is perpetually solicited to descend towards the sun by a certain new impression four times more strongly, and [being] three times nearer, nine times more strongly. This is obvious because of what precedes, namely, because the planet has been posited as describing an ellipse, as circulating harmonically, and furthermore as being continuously impelled towards the sun.[1]

As we see, the inverse-square law of attraction (about the *modus producendi* of which, however, we learn nothing) is deduced by Leibniz from Kepler's *first* law, and not from the *third* law, as was done by Newton (and also by Hooke, Wren, and Halley). Moreover, it is deduced despite the erroneous assumption that the motion of the planets is a "harmonic" one – a truly marvelous achievement – which can only be compared with Kepler's own: two errors cancel out.

There can, therefore, be no doubt about Leibniz's originality, though we have to admit – as he does himself – that he knew that the inverse-square proportion[2] had already been recognized also by the very famous Isaac Newton, since this was mentioned in the review in the *Acta eruditorum*, and we must suspect that, though "therefrom [he] could not find out how he [Newton] arrived at it," it was this review that not only prompted his writing of the *Tentamen* but also incited him to borrow from Newton the concept of attraction which Newton himself so successfully used. Alas, in doing so he committed a number of rather appalling errors, as we have seen. Yet as they can only be explained by the haste with which he composed his *Tentamen*, I shall not deal with them here, all the more so as some of them were corrected by him in 1706 and all of them were enumerated by Newton in his (unpublished) review of Leibniz's *Tentamen*, written sometime in 1712.[3]

Let us now turn our attention to the "second" version of the *Tentamen*. As I have mentioned, its text is practically identical with that of the first one; it contains, however, an important addition about the concepts of gravity and attraction that Leibniz inserted between the passage in which he expressed his hope of having advanced toward the true explanation of the celestial motions and the passage which contains the exposition of his theory.[4]

---

[1] *Mathematische Schriften*, VI, 157, 181.

[2] *Ibid.*, 157, 181; letter to Huygens, 13 October 1690, *ibid.*, 189; Huygens, *Oeuvres complètes*, IX, 522 sq.

[3] See J. Edleston, *Correspondence of Sir Isaac Newton and Professor Cotes* (London, 1850), App. XXXII, pp. 308 sq.

[4] *Mathematische Schriften*, VI, 163–166.

From the considerations of the famous Gilbert it is clear that every larger body of the world insofar as it is known to us, has the nature of a magnet, and that, besides the directing power (*vis directiva*) [in virtue of which] it looks at certain poles, it has a force of attracting the parent [similar] bodies [placed] inside its sphere [of force], which [force] in things terrestrial we call gravity, and which, by a certain analogy, we attribute to the stars. But it is not sufficiently clear, what is the true cause of this very obvious phenomenon, and whether this cause is the same as in the magnet.

Leibniz admits that this problem cannot "yet" receive a demonstrative solution; he thinks, however, that he can formulate a probable one.

In any case it can be asserted that attraction is produced by a certain corporeal radiation; indeed, immaterial [causes] must not be used for the explanation of corporeal phenomena. Furthermore, it conforms to reason that there is in the globe a *conatus* to drive out [from itself] the inconvenient or perturbing matter, or [matter] not sufficiently apt to perform freely its motions in the [interior] place assigned to it [in the globe]; wherefrom [it results] that other [matter] is attracted by circumpulsion, matter agreeing with the inner motion of the attracting body or having a motion of a kind that disturbs it less. An example of this is the flame, which to the sense perception itself shows the expulsion of the one and the attraction of the other.

Yet we can pursue this "example" further and conceive a fluid globe swimming in the aether as a drop of oil does in water. (A rather amusing example: where did Leibniz see a drop of oil swimming *in* water?) Now

it is in the nature of a fluid to have various internal motions, which, where they are restrained by the ambient [medium] so that the matter does not fly away, turn back, are transformed into circular motions, and strive to describe great circles, for in this way they retain most of their *conatus* to recede. By this [*conatus*] those bodies in which less of this fluid is included, or in which there is a lesser *conatus* to recede, are pushed down.

Thus far, Leibniz's explanation of gravity follows the lines of the Cartesian vortex conception, in which centripetal forces are deduced from centrifugal ones, the "outward" pressure of the driven-out matter pushing back in its place other matter which thereby is driven or drawn in toward the "attracting" body or its center. Leibniz, however, improves the explanation, and in exactly the same way Huygens did, substituting for the circular motion around the axis a multitude of such motions around the center of the globe:

But if the centrifugal [an obvious error: it should be centripetal] force is to be explained by the device of Kepler, it must not be deduced from the motion of the aether along the equator and the parallels which would drive [bodies] toward the axis of the earth, but, as I remember having observed already long ago, [from motions] along great circles having the same center as that of the globe, analogous to the motions that appear in the atmosphere of the magnet... In this way the diverse causes... coincide one with the other ... in our explanation [of gravity] and we have at the same time the spherical radiation, the attraction of the magnet, the driving away of the perturbing [matter], the internal motion of the fluid, the circulation of the atmosphere, [all of them] conspiring [in the production] of the centrifugal [centripetal] force. Yet whatever the cause of gravity it is sufficient for us [to admit] that the attracting globe pushes out material rays analogous to the rays of light or emits lines of impulses receding in all directions from the center; not, however, [in such a way] that it should be necessary for parts of the earth to reach the heavy body, but that, matter impelling matter, the *impetus* be propagated, as in light and sound and moved liquids.

These "rays of impulse" originate in the centrifugal forces developed in the innumerable vortices of aetherial matter that turns with great speed around the center of the "attracting body," both inside and outside of it, which forces exert a pressure on the surrounding medium. Leibniz warns us, however, that this pressure, or impulse, is propagated in time, and not in an instant, as had been erroneously assumed (by Descartes): no sensible effect can be propagated in an instant – in any case, not in the world of Leibniz, who denies the existence of absolutely hard bodies and who knows, moreover, that the propagation of light is not instantaneous.

But let us go back to the, so to say, magnetic rays, by which attraction is produced. They consist in the recessive *conatus* of a certain insensible fluid, the parts of which are most closely pressed together, although the fluid itself is divisible in a most subtle way; when porous bodies, such as terrestrial bodies, which contain less matter tending to recede from the center than does an equal volume of the insensible fluid and thus are endowed with less levity, are introduced into the sensible fluid, it follows with necessity that, the emitted fluid prevailing, the terrestrial [bodies] are pushed down towards the center.

It is interesting to note that Leibniz defines heavy bodies as those that have "less levity," in opposition to the prevailing conception that sees in light bodies those that have less gravity. But he is perfectly right: it is centrifugal motion and centrifugal pressure, that is, motion and pressure "upward," that are to be considered as primary factors; motion "downward," or "toward the center," is only a secondary effect of motions and pressure "upward."

The *causa gravitatis* seems thus to be determined with sufficient probability (though, to tell the truth, with by no means sufficient clarity). Leibniz, however, is not satisfied and, in order to explain different *specific* gravities of terrestrial bodies, he deems it necessary to postulate a second, and much more subtle, fluid, a fluid that can penetrate pores of solid bodies too small to admit the particles of the gravitational fluid. But he does not insist upon this and continues:

But, *caeteris paribus*, the specific gravity being the same, the solicitation to tend towards the center will nonetheless be greater or less, according to the quantity of radiation [received by the body] which is to be estimated as in the case of light. Indeed, as was demonstrated some time ago by learned men [as a matter of fact, by Kepler], just as bodies are illuminated in the inverse square ratio of their distances from the source of light, so also must attracted bodies gravitate so much less as the square of the distance from the attracting one is greater. The reason of both is the same and is obvious. [Indeed, both spread uniformly in space, and therefore] illuminations and solicitations of gravity are reciprocally as the squares of distances from the radiating or the attracting center.[1]

Thus far we have proceeded a priori, and it is by pure reasoning that the inverse-square law of gravitation has been determined. But that is not enough, and Leibniz announces that the same law will be established by him a posteriori, that is, "deduced by the analytical calculus from the common phenomena of the planets" (that is, from their elliptical orbits), thus producing "a marvelous consensus of reason and observations and an extraordinary confirmation of truth." No doubt. Yet – and this is rather astonishing and utterly unexpected – Leibniz concludes this (second) preface to the *Tentamen* by a hyper-positivistic pronouncement that leaves those of Newton far behind:

What follows [that is, the *Tentamen*] is not based on hypotheses, but is deduced from phenomena by the laws of motion; whether there is an attraction of the planets by the sun, or not, it is sufficient for us to be able to determine [their] access and recess, that is, the increase or decrease of their distance [from the sun] which they would have if they were attracted according to the prescribed law. And whether in truth they do circulate around the sun, or do not circulate, it is enough that they change their positions in respect to the sun as if they moved in a harmonic circulation; we obtain therefrom the *Principles of Understanding*, wonderfully simple and fertile, such as I do not know whether of yore men ever dared even to hope for.

But what herefrom must be concluded about the very causes of the motions we leave to be estimated by the wisdom of each one; indeed it is

[1] *Mathematische Schriften*, VI, 165.

possible that the thing is already brought so far that an understanding poet will not dare any longer to tell astronomers that they are searching in vain.[1]

I have mentioned already that Huygens did not like the Leibnizian orb-vortices . . . which is rather natural: he felt that his own were sufficient, and that Leibniz, as a matter of fact, had been inspired by them. Thus, making himself *advocatus diaboli* and willfully misunderstanding Leibniz as accepting fully the Newtonian attraction, and disregarding Leibniz's contention that attraction could be explained mechanically – indeed, Huygens could think that compared to him Leibniz did not even attempt to give a mechanical explanation (but did not Newton himself tell his readers that attraction could be pressure or impulse?) – he tells Leibniz that his endeavor to reconcile Newton and Descartes by using both attraction and harmonic circulation is perfectly redundant, the latter being completely superfluous:

I see that you [and M. Newton] have met in what concerns the natural cause of the elliptic trajectories of the planets; but as in dealing with this matter you have seen only an extract of his book and not the book itself, I would very much like to know whether you did not change your theory since, because you introduce into it the vortices of M. Descartes [not a very nice remark] which to my mind are superfluous if one admits the system of M. Newton in which the movement of the planets is explained by the gravity towards the sun and the *vis centrifuga* that counterbalance each other.[2]

Huygens's objection (he will repeat it in another letter to Leibniz of 11 August 1693)[3] seems rather pertinent (the editors of Huygens's *Oeuvres complètes* even believe that it convinced, or at least impressed, Leibniz himself).[4]

As a matter of fact, neither for Leibniz nor even for Huygens himself is the objection as impressive as it seems at first glance, because it implies the acceptance not only of the Newtonian attraction, but also of the Newtonian vacuum, which neither of them has ever admitted. Indeed, it is only in empty spaces, that is, in spaces where bodies move without encountering any resistance, that planets subjected to Newton's laws would be able to move in elliptical orbits; in spaces full of matter (Leibniz), or even only half full (Huygens), they would not be able to move even in circles; they would all be

---

[1] *Mathematicshe Schriften*, VI, 166.
[2] See Huygens to Leibniz, 8 February 1690, *ibid.*, II, 41; Huygens, *Oeuvres complètes*, IX, 367 sq.
[3] *Mathematische Schriften*, II, 187; Huygens, *Oeuvres complètes*, X, 267 sq.
[4] *Oeuvres complètes*, IX, 368, n. 10.

drawn into the sun. Huygens neglects this problem. Leibniz, however, is fully aware of it. Thus in a desperate endeavor to save the plenum he makes an attempt to eliminate the resistance of the surrounding medium. Now, the only way to do this is to endow the medium with the same movement as that of the body in question. In this case, as Descartes has already explained, the body will be at rest in the moving medium, it will be "carried along" by or "freely swim" in it. Thus Leibniz is perfectly right in maintaining that his "harmonic circulation" is not superfluous but absolutely necessary,[1] because he believes (wrongly, alas) that a body which moves in such a way moves "as if it were moved in the void by its simple impetuosity [inertial motion] joined to gravity. And the same body is also moved in the aether as if it swam quietly in it without having its own impetuosity . . . and did only obey in an absolute manner the aether that surrounds it." As for the "paracentric" motion, that is, the motion toward the center, it is true that Leibniz does not explain it; but Huygens himself gives such an explanation only for terrestrial gravity, not for cosmic attraction or gravitation.

The result of Leibniz's attempt is to reconcile vortices with attraction, that is, Descartes with Newton; making the Cartesian vortex move in a "harmonic circulation" is, of course, not successful and Huygens is right in pointing out that, in this case, planets would not observe Kepler's third law. To attempt to save the situation by the postulation – as in the case of gravity – of a second subtle matter is, as Leibniz suggests, to indulge in "hypotheses" of a kind that Huygens does not even condescend to discuss. And yet, we cannot blame Leibniz for not succeeding in doing something that could not be done. And, in any case, it was not Huygens who could reproach him for not doing it.[2]

[1] Letter to Huygens, 13 October 1690, *Mathematische Schriften*, VI, 189; Huygens, *Oeuvres complètes*, IX, 525.

[2] On the discussion between Huygens and Leibniz, see F. Rosenberger, *Isaac Newton und seine physikalischen Principien* (Leipzig, 1895), pp. 235 sq.; and R. Dugas, *Histoire de la mécanique au XVIIe siècle* (Paris: Dunod, 1954), esp. pp. 491 sq.

Attraction an Occult Quality?

As a matter of fact, it was Leibniz who, in spite – or because – of his own use of – or play with – the concept of attraction in his *Tentamen de motuum coelestium causis* of 1689,[1] stressed the analogy between Newtonian attraction and an occult quality and reinforced his analogy by asserting attraction to be a miracle. He did this, however, rather late. At first, in 1690,[2] he only expressed his astonishment that Newton seemed to consider gravity a certain incorporeal and inexplicable virtue and did not believe in the possibility of explaining it mechanically – had not Huygens done it very well? But in 1690 Leibniz did not speak about occult qualities, or about miracles. As a matter of fact, it was Huygens whom he reproached for introducing miracles into natural philosophy: is not the indivisibility of atoms, which Huygens believed in, a perpetual miracle? It is only in 1703, in his *Nouveaux essais* (which, however, he did not publish because of Locke's death: he did not want to attack a dead adversary) that he mentions "occult qualities" and "miracles." Thus, referring to Locke's letter to Stillingfleet,[3] Leibniz writes:

He cites the example of the attraction of matter [p. 99, but especially p. 408], where he speaks of the gravitation of matter towards matter attributed to M. Newton . . . confessing that one would never be able to conceive its "how." This is, in effect, to return to occult qualities, and even, which is worse, to inexplicable ones.[4]

Having explained that God does not attribute to things properties that are not compatible with their essence, but only those that are natural to them and that can be understood (except in the case of a miracle), Leibniz goes on:

[1] C. J. Gerhardt, ed., *Leibnizens mathematische Schriften* (Halle, 1860), VI, 144 sq., 161 sq.
[2] Letter to Huygens, October 1690, in Huygens, *Oeuvres complètes* (The Hague: M. Nijhoff, 1901), IX, 521.
[3] See *Mr. Locke's Reply to the Right Reverend Lord Bishop of Worcester, Answer to his Second Letter* . . . (London, 1699), *infra*, p. 155, n. 1.
[4] Erdmann, ed., *Nouveaux essais sur l'intendement humain*, Avant propos (Berlin, 1840), 202 sq. Also, C. J. Gerhardt, ed., *Die philosophischen Schriften von G. W. Leibniz* (Berlin, 1875–1890), V, 58 sq.

Thus we can assert that matter will not naturally have [the faculty of] attraction, mentioned above, and will not move by itself in a curved line because it is not possible to conceive how this could take place there, that is, to explain it mechanically; whereas that which is natural must be able to become distinctly conceivable . . . This distinction between what is natural, and what is unexplainable and miraculous, solves all the difficulties. By rejecting it one would maintain something worse than occult qualities; one would renounce Philosophy and Reason, opening an asylum for ignorance and laziness by a dead system which admits not only that there are qualities which we do not understand – of which there are only too many – but also that there are such [qualities] which the greatest mind, even if God gave him every possible opening, could not understand, that is, they would be either miraculous or without rhyme or reason; and it would also be without rhyme or reason that God should work miracles; thus this lazy hypothesis would destroy equally our philosophy which seeks reasons and divine wisdom which furnishes them.[1]

It is only in 1711, in a letter to N. Hartsoeker,[2] that he does this. As a matter of fact, the three letters published in the *Mémoires de Trévoux* and the *Memoirs of Literature* are only part of the correspondence between Leibniz and Hartsoeker. This correspondence started in 1706 and became active in 1710 after the publication by Hartsoeker of his *Éclaircissements sur les conjectures physiques* (Amsterdam, 1710). In one of the letters that precede the published one (of 1711) Leibniz tells Hartsoeker that he does not admit the existence of atoms,[3] which Hartsoeker asserts; Hartsoeker[4] nastily replies by associating the "conspiring motions" of Leibniz with the "small vortices of the very Reverend Father Malebranche"; Leibniz then states[5] that to assume the existence of atoms, that is, the original and primordial indivisibility of certain parts of matter, is to have recourse to a miracle or an occult quality; Hartsoeker[6] answers that the "conspiring motions" of his opponent are a much greater, and even a perpetual, miracle, and that there is no reason why God could not have created atoms. Once more Leibniz[7] explains that "God cannot create natural atoms, or indivisible bodies" as it would be absurd, that "atoms are effects of the weakness of our imagination,"

---

[1] *Nouveaux essais*, pp. 203 sq.

[2] 6 February 1711, published first in the *Mémoires de Trévoux* (1711), and then in an English translation, in the *Memoirs of Literature* of 1712; see *Die philosophischen Schriften*, III, 516 sq., letter XI.

[3] *Ibid.*, p. 497, letter V.

[4] *Ibid.*, p. 498, letter VI, 8 July 1710.

[5] *Ibid.*, p. 306, letter VII.

[6] *Ibid.*, pp. 501 sq., letter VIII.

[7] *Ibid.*, pp. 506 sq., letter IX, 30 October 1710.

and that "it is easy to make fictions, but difficult to make them reasonable"; Hartsoeker, however,[1] does not agree that atoms are unreasonable, and adds that if one were to call them miraculous one could, not without reason, maintain that everything is a perpetual miracle.

Answering this letter,[2] Leibniz re-expressed his astonishment at Hartsoeker's inability to understand his conception of "conspiring motions," renewed his attack on atoms, the existence of which he reasserted to be unreasonable, and demanded an explanation; he then goes on:

If you allege only the will of God for it, you have recourse to a miracle, and even to a perpetual miracle; for the will of God works through a miracle whenever we are not able to account for that will and its effects from the nature of the objects. For example, if any one should say, it is God's will that a planet should move round in its orb without any other Cause of its Motion, I maintain that it would be a perpetual miracle: for by the nature of things, the planet going round tends to move from its orb along the tangent, if nothing hinders it; and God must continually prevent it, if no natural cause does . . .

It may be said in a very good sense, that everything is a continued miracle that is, worthy of admiration: but it seems to me that the example of a planet, which goes round, and preserves its motion in its orb without any other help but that of God, being compared with a planet kept in its orb by the matter which constantly drives it towards the sun, plainly shows what difference there is between natural and rational miracles, and those that are properly so called, or supernatural; or rather between a reasonable explication, and a fiction invented to support an ill-grounded opinion. Such is the method of those who say, after M. de Roberval's *Aristarchus*, that all bodies attract one another by a law of nature, which God made in the beginning of things. For alleging nothing else to obtain such an effect, and admitting nothing that was made by God, whereby it may appear how he attains to that end, they have recourse to a miracle, that is, to a supernatural thing, which continues for ever, when the question is to find out a natural cause . . .

Thus the ancients and the moderns, who own that gravity is an *occult quality*, are in the right, if they mean by it that there is a certain mechanism unknown to them, whereby all bodies tend towards the center of the earth. But if they mean, that the thing is performed without any mechanism, by a simple *primitive quality*, or by a law of God, who produces that effect without using any intelligible means, it is an unreasonable occult quality, and so very occult, that 'tis impossible it should ever be clear, tho' an Angel, or God himself, should undertake to explain it.[3]

[1] *Die philosophischen Schriften*, III, p. 514, letter X, 10 December 1710.
[2] *Ibid.*, pp. 516 sq., letter XI, 6 February 1711, the first of the letters published in the *Mémoires de Trévoux*.
[3] *Ibid.*, pp. 517 sq.

I have mentioned already that it was this letter, to which Cotes drew Newton's attention, that motivated Newton's statements in the *Scholium Generale* which he instructed Cotes to insert in the second edition of the *Principia* (see Appendix C). Cotes did, of course, but, in addition, he lumped together Cartesians and Leibniz, and answered them in his preface by an impassioned counterblast:

Some I know . . . mutter something about occult qualities. They continually are cavilling with us, that gravity is an occult property, and occult causes are to be quite banished from philosophy. But to this the answer is easy: that those are indeed occult causes whose existence is occult, and imagined, but not proved; but not those whose real existence is clearly demonstrated by observations. Therefore gravity can by no means be called an occult cause of the celestial motions, because it is plain from the phenomena that such a power does really exist. Those rather have recourse to occult causes who set imaginary vortices of matter entirely fictitious and imperceptible by our senses to direct those motions . . . Some there are who say that gravity is praeternatural and call it a perpetual miracle. Therefore they would have it rejected, because praeternatural causes have no place in physics. It is hardly worthwhile to spend time in answering this ridiculous objection which overturns all philosophy. For either they will deny gravity to be in bodies, which cannot be said, or else they will therefore call it praeternatural because it is not produced by the other properties of bodies and therefore not by mechanical causes. But certainly there are primary properties of bodies; and because they are primary, they have no dependence on the others. Let them consider that all these are in like manner praeternatural, and in like manner to be rejected. And then what kind of philosophy are we like to have?[1]

Moreover, having already in his letter to Bentley of 10 March 1712/13 offered to attack Leibniz for "his want of candour" exemplified in his *Tentamen de motuum coelestium causis*, Cotes added, not naming Leibniz, of course, a parody of Leibniz's "harmonic circulation":

Galileo has shown that when a stone projected moves in a parabola, its deflection into that curve from its rectilinear path is occasioned by the gravity of the stone towards the earth, that is, by an occult quality. But now somebody, more cunning than he, may come to explain the cause after this manner. He will suppose a certain subtile matter, not discernible by our sight, our touch, or any other of our senses, which fills the spaces which are near and contiguous to the surface of the earth, and that this matter is carried with different directions, and various, and often contrary, motions, describing parabolic curves. Then see how easily he may account for the deflection of the stone spoken of above. The stone, says he, floats in this

[1] *Principia*, Motte–Cajori, p. xxvi.

subtile fluid, and following its motion, can't choose but describe the same figure. But the fluid moves in parabolic curves, and therefore the stone must move in a parabola, of course. Would not the acuteness of this philosopher be thought very extraordinary, who could deduce the appearances of Nature from mechanical causes, matter and motion, so clearly that the meanest man may understand it? Or indeed should not we smile to see this new *Galileo* taking so many mathematical pains to introduce occult qualities into philosophy, from whence they have been so happily excluded? But I am ashamed to dwell so long upon trifles.[1]

And since Hartsoeker also had rejected void and attraction, though in a manner different from that of Leibniz – he filled space with an immaterial, living, and even intelligent fluid – and had been guilty of criticizing Newton in his *Éclaircissements sur les conjectures physiques* (Amsterdam, 1710), Cotes wrote a paragraph about Hartsoeker:

Allowing men to indulge in their own fancies, suppose any man should affirm that the planets and comets are surrounded with atmospheres like our earth, which hypothesis seems more reasonable than that of vortices; let him then affirm that these atmospheres by their own nature move about the sun and describe conic sections, which motion is much more easily conceived than that of the vortices penetrating one another; lastly, that the planets and comets are carried about the sun by these atmospheres of theirs: and then applaud his own sagacity in discovering the causes of the celestial motions. He that rejects this fable must also reject the other; for two drops of water are not more alike than this hypothesis of atmospheres, and that of vortices.[2]

It is rather tempting to compare the angry diatribe of Cotes with the rather mild and serene answer of Newton in the General Scholium. Yet, as a matter of fact, Newton's first reaction to Leibniz's attack was neither mild nor serene. He was deeply angered by it, especially by Leibniz's association of his attraction with that of Roberval,[3] "which was the same as to call it romantic," and he started to write a reply to be published in the *Memoirs of Literature*, though, on second thought, he did not send it to them; he also wrote a bitter criticism of the *Tentamen de motuum coelestium causis*, and of some other works of Leibniz concerning physics; but did not publish them either.[4]

[1] J. Edleston, *Correspondence of Sir Isaac Newton and Professor Cotes* (London, 1850), p. 149.

[2] *Principia*, Motte–Cajori, p. xix.

[3] See *supra*, p. 59, n. 2.

[4] See I. B. Cohen and A. Koyré, "Newton and the Leibniz-Clarke Correspondence," *Archives Internationales d'Histoire des Sciences 15* (1962), 63-126; and for the criticism of the *Tentamen*, Edleston, *Correspondence*, pp. 308 sq.

In 1715 (November or December), in a letter to the Abbé Conti, Leibniz renewed his attack:

His philosophy appears to me rather strange and I cannot believe it can be justified. If every body is heavy, it follows (whatever his supporters may say, and however passionately they deny it) that Gravity will be a scholastic occult quality or else the effect of a miracle . . . It is not sufficient to say: God has made such a law of Nature, therefore the thing is natural. It is necessary that the law should be capable of being fulfilled by the nature of created things. If, for example, God were to give to a free body the law of revolving around a certain center, he would have either to join to it other bodies which by their impulsion would make it always stay in a circular orbit, or to put an Angel at its heels; or else he would have to concur extraordinarily in its motion. For naturally it would go off along a tangent . . . I am strongly in favour of experimental philosophy, but M. Newton is departing very far from it when he claims that all matter is heavy (or that every part of matter attracts every other part) which is certainly not proved by experiment . . . And because we do not yet know in detail how gravity is produced, or elastic force, or magnetic force, this does not give us any right to make of them scholastic occult qualities or miracles; but it gives us still less right to put bounds to the wisdom or power of God.[1]

The Abbé Conti having communicated this letter to him, Newton answered:

As for philosophy, he colludes in the signification of words, calling those things miracles which create no wonder, and those things occult qualities whose causes are occult, though the qualities themselves be manifest.[2]

Nearly at the same time, the problem of attraction, that is, the question whether it is an occult quality and a miracle, or a respectable force and law of nature, formed one of the main topics of the famous polemics between Leibniz and Clarke,[3] together with the problem of the reality or impossibility of void space, absolute motion, and other problems of metaphysics and natural philosophy.[4]

---

[1] Raphson, *Historia fluxionum* (London, 1715 [actually 1717]); and Des Maiseaux, *Recueil de diverses pièces sur la philosophie, la religion naturelle, l'histoire, les mathématiques, etc., par Mss Leibniz, Clarke, Newton et autres auteurs célèbres* (Amsterdam, 1720), vol. II.

[2] 26 February 1716; see Des Maiseaux, *Recueil*, II, 22.

[3] *A Collection of Papers which passed between the late learned M. Leibniz and Dr. Clarke in the years 1715 and 1716 relating to the Principles of Natural Philosophy and Religion* (London, 1717), republished in 1720 as vol. I of Des Maiseaux, *Recueil*; today available in English in the excellent edition of H. G. Alexander, *The Leibniz–Clarke Correspondence* (Manchester: Manchester University Press, 1956), and in the original in the critical edition of A. Robinet, *Correspondance Leibniz–Clarke*, présentée d'après les MS originaux des bibliothèques de Hannovre et de Londres (Paris: Presses Universitaires de France, 1957).

[4] On this correspondence see A. Koyré, *From the Closed World to the Infinite Universe* (Baltimore: Johns Hopkins Press, 1956), and A. Koyré and I. B. Cohen, "The Case of the Missing *Tanquam*," *Isis* 52 (1961), 555–566.

Leibniz's death (14 November 1716) did not put an end to the polemics; Newton, indeed, continued them. Thus, in the second English edition of his *Opticks*, he added to the text of Query XXIII (which became Query XXXI), which I have quoted,[1] after "by rest, that is, . . . by nothing," the words ". . . and others that they stick together by conspiring motions, that is by relative rest among themselves";[2] and to that which states that the active principles of nature are not occult qualities but general laws of nature,[3] he added the following explanation:

> For these are manifest qualities and their causes only are occult. And the *Aristotelians* gave the name of occult qualities, not to manifest qualities, but to such qualities only as they supposed to lie hid in bodies, and to be the unknown causes of manifest effects: such as would be the causes of gravity, and of magnetick and electrick attractions, and of fermentations, if we should suppose that these forces or actions arose from Qualities unknown to us, and uncapable of being discovered and made manifest. Such occult qualities put a stop to the improvement of natural philosophy, and therefore of late years have been rejected.[4]

Finally, at the end of the review of the *Commercium epistolicum* that he published anonymously in the *Philosophical Transactions* (which review – *recensio* – translated into Latin was published as a preface to the second edition of the *Commercium*, in 1722), Newton settled his account with Leibniz:

> The Philosophy which Mr. *Newton* in his *Principles* and *Optiques* has pursued is Experimental; and it is not the Business of Experimental Philosophy to teach the Causes of things any further than they can be proved by Experiments. We are not to fill this Philosophy with Opinions which cannot be proved by Phaenomena. In this Philosophy Hypotheses have no place, unless as Conjectures or Questions proposed to be examined by Experiments. For this Reason Mr. *Newton* in his *Optiques* distinguished those things which were made certain by Experiments from those things which remained uncertain, and which he therefore proposed in the End of his *Optiques* in the Form of Queries. For this Reason, in the Preface to his *Principles*, when he had mention'd the Motions of the Planets, Comets, Moon and Sea as deduced in this Book from Gravity, he added: *Utinam caetera Naturae Phaenomena ex Principiis Mechanicis eodem argumentandi genere derivare liceret. Nam multa me movent ut nonnihil suspicer ea omnia ex viribus quibusdam pendere posse, quibus corporum particulae per causas nondum cognitas vel in se mutuo impelluntur et secundum regulares figuras cohaerent, vel ab invicem fugantur et recedunt: quibus viribus ignotis Philosophi hactenus Naturam frustra tentarunt.* And in the End of

---

[1] See *supra*, p. 56, n2.   [2] See *supra*, p. 56, n2.
[3] *Optice*, p. 335; *Opticks* (1952), p. 364. [4] *Optice*, p. 344; *Opticks* (1952), p. 401.

this Book in the second Edition, he said that for want of a sufficient Number of Experiments, he forbore to describe the Laws of the Actions of the Spirit or Agent by which this Attraction is performed. And for the same Reason he is silent about the Cause of Gravity, there occurring no Experiments or Phaenomena by which he might prove what was the Cause thereof. And this he hath abundantly declared in his *Principles*, near the Beginning thereof, in these Words: *Virium causas et sedes Physicas iam non expendo.* And a little after: *Voces Attractionis, Impulsus, vel Propensionis cuiuscunque in centrum indifferenter et pro se mutuo promiscue usurpo, has Vires non Physice sed Mathematice tantum considerando. Unde caveat Lector ne per huiusmodi voces cogitet me speciem vel modum actionis, causamve aut rationem physicam alicubi definire, vel Centris (quae sunt puncta Mathematica) vires vere et physice tribuere, si forte aut Centra trahere aut vires Centrorum esse dixero.* And in the End of his *Opticks: Qua causa efficiente hae attractiones* [sc. *gravitas, visque magnetica & electrica*] *peragantur, hic non inquiro. Quam ego Attractionem appello, fieri sane potest ut ea efficiatur impulsu vel alio aliquo modo nobis incognito. Hanc vocem Attractionis ita hic accipi velim ut in universum solummodo vim aliquam significare intelligatur qua corpora ad se mutuo tendant, cuicunque demum causae attribuenda sit illa vis. Nam ex Phaenomenis Naturae illud nos prius edoctos esse oportet quaenam corpora se invicem attrahant, et quaenam sint leges et proprietates istius attractionis, quam in id inquirere par sit quanam efficiente causa peragatur attractio.* And a little after he mentions the same Attractions as Forces which by Phaenomena appear to have a Being in Nature, tho' their Causes be not yet known; and distinguishes them from occult Qualities which are supposed to flow from the Specifick Forms of things. And in the Scholium at the End of his Principles, after he had mentioned the Properties of Gravity, he added: *Rationem vero harum Gravitatis proprietatum ex Phaenomenis nondum potui deducere, et Hypotheses non fingo. Quicquid enim ex Phaenomenis non deducitur Hypothesis vocanda est; et Hypotheses seu Metaphysicae seu Physicae, seu Qualitatum occultarum, seu Mechanicae, in Philosophia experimentali locum non habent. ——Satis est quod Gravitas revera existet et agat secundum leges à nobis expositas, et ad Corporum coelestium et Maris nostri motus omnes sufficiat.* And after all this, one would wonder that Mr. *Newton* should be reflected upon for not explaining the Causes of Gravity and other Attractions by Hypotheses; as if it were a Crime to content himself with Certainties and let Uncertainties alone. And yet the Editors of the *Acta Eruditorum*[1] (a) have told the World that Mr. *Newton* denies that the cause of Gravity is Mechanical, and that if the Spirit or Agent by which Electrical Attraction is performed, be not the *Ether* or *subtile Matter* of *Cartes*, it is less valuable than an Hypothesis, and perhaps may be the Hylarchic Principle of Dr. *Henry Moor:* and Mr. *Leibnitz* (b) hath accused him of making Gravity a natural or essential Property of Bodies, and an occult Quality and Miracle. And by this sort of Railery they are perswading the *Germans* that Mr. *Newton* wants Judgment, and was not able to invent the Infinitesimal Method.

[1] March 1714, pp. 141–142.

It must be allowed that these two Gentlemen differ very much in Philosophy. The one proceeds upon the Evidence arising from Experiments and Phaenomena, and stops where such Evidence is wanting; the other is taken up with Hypotheses, and propounds them, not to be examined by Experiments, but to be believed without Examination. The one for want of Experiments to decide the Question, doth not affirm whether the Cause of Gravity be Mechanical or not Mechanical; the other that it is a perpetual Miracle if it be not Mechanical. The one (by way of Enquiry) attributes it to the Power of the Creator that the least Particles of Matter are hard: the other attributes the Hardness of Matter to conspiring Motions, and calls it a perpetual Miracle if the Cause of this Hardness be other than Mechanical. The one doth not affirm that animal Motion in Man is purely mechanical: the other teaches that it is purely mechanical, the Soul or Mind (according to the Hypothesis of an *Harmonia Praestabilita*) never acting upon the Body so as to alter or influence its Motions. The one teaches that God (the God in whom we live and move and have our Being) is Omnipresent; but not as a Soul of the World: the other that he is not the Soul of the World, but INTELLIGENTIA SUPRAMUNDANA, an Intelligence above the Bounds of the World; whence it seems to follow that he cannot do any thing within the Bounds of the World, unless by an incredible Miracle. The one teaches that Philosophers are to argue from Phaenomena and Experiments in the Causes thereof, and thence to the Causes of those Causes, and so on till we come to the first Cause: the other that all the Actions of the first Cause are Miracles, and all the laws imprest on Nature by the Will of God are perpetual Miracles and occult Qualities, and therefore not to be considered in Philosophy. But must the constant and universal Laws of Nature, if derived from the Power of God or the Action of a Cause not yet known to us, be called Miracles and occult Qualities, that is to say, Wonders and Absurdities? Must all the Arguments for a God taken from the Phaenomena of Nature be exploded by *new hard Names*? And must Experimental Philosophy be exploded as *miraculous* and *absurd*, because it asserts nothing more than can be proved by Experiments, and we cannot yet prove by Experiments that all the Phaenomena in Nature can be solved by meer Mechanical Causes? Certainly these things deserve to be better considered.[1]

One would think that after this protracted discussion nothing would remain of Leibniz's sly and mischievous accusations and that everyone would be persuaded that Newtonian attraction was *toto coelo* different from any "occult" quality of the scholastics. And yet, ten years after the conclusion of the debate, Fontenelle was still not convinced, and in the *Elogium* of Newton he says:

He declares very freely that he lays down this attraction, only as a cause which he knows not, and whose effects he only considers, compares and calculates; and in order to avoid the reproach of reviving the *Occult*

[1] Pp. 55 sq.; *Opera omnia*, ed. Horsley, IV, 492 sq.

qualities of the Schoolmen, he 'says, that he establishes none but such Qualities as are *manifest* and very visible by their phenomena, but that the causes of these Qualities are indeed occult, and that he leaves it to other Philosophers to search into them; but are they not properly causes which the Schoolmen called *occult Qualities*; since their effects are plainly seen? besides, could Sir Isaac think that others would find out these *Occult causes* which he could not discover? with what hopes of success can any other man search after them?[1]

[1] *The Elogium of Sir Isaac Newton* (London, 1728), p. 21; reprinted in *Isaac Newton's Papers and Letters on Natural Philosophy*, ed. I. Bernard Cohen (Cambridge, Massachusetts: Harvard University Press, 1958), p. 463.

Gravity an Essential Property of Matter?

It is well known that Newton did not believe gravity to be an "innate, essential and inherent property of matter"; indeed, in 1675, in his *Hypothesis Explaining the Properties of Light*,[1] and in 1679, in a letter to Boyle (28 February 1678/9),[2] he attempted to explain gravity by mechanical means – that is, by the motions of subtle matter or an ethereal medium – but he did not pursue these hopeless attempts, at least for some time; in 1692, in a letter to Bentley,[3] he asked Bentley not to ascribe to him that Epicurean notion; attraction as action at a distance through vacuum without mediation, he told Bentley,[4] was an utter absurdity that nobody could believe in, stating moreover rather clearly that this mediation had to be performed by something which is not material, that is, by God.

Yet the *Letters to Bentley* were written about five years after the publication of the *Principia*, and published only in 1756; thus they could not enlighten readers of the *Principia*, who, especially those of the first edition (London, 1687), could hardly fail to misunderstand Newton's position and to ascribe to him just those opinions which he so vehemently rejected in these letters. All the more so as Bentley, in spite of Newton's admonition, said in his *Confutation of Atheism* that "a constant Energy [is] infused into Matter by the Author of all things" and that "Gravity may be essential to Matter."[5] As for Newton himself, he did not, in the *Principia*, express his own views about the "nature" of gravitation, nor did he tell his readers that action at a distance, without mediation, was an impossibility and that bodies could not, in this sense, attract each other. He took, how-

---

[1] Thomas Birch, *The History of the Royal Society of London* (London, 1757), III, 250 sq.; I. B. Cohen, ed., *Isaac Newton's Papers and Letters on Natural Philosophy* (Cambridge, Massachusetts: Harvard University Press, 1958), pp. 180 sq.

[2] Thomas Birch, *The Works of the Honourable Robert Boyle* (London, 1744), I, 70 sq.; Cohen, *Newton's Papers and Letters*, pp. 250 sq.; Newton, *Correspondence*, II, 288.

[3] *Four Letters from Sir Isaac Newton to Doctor Bentley* (London, 1756), p. 20; Cohen, *Newton's Papers and Letters*, p. 298.

[4] *Ibid.*, p. 25; p. 302.

[5] Richard Bentley, *A Confutation of Atheism from the Origin and Frame of the World* (London, 1693), part III, p. 11; Cohen, *Newton's Papers and Letters*, p. 363.

ever, great pains to explain that the forces of attraction and repulsion dealt with in natural philosophy, forces by which bodies either approach each other or, on the contrary, flee and recede from each other, are not to be taken as "causes" of these phenomena of motion, but as "mathematical forces," the causes of which are yet unknown.

Thus in the *Praefatio ad lectorem*, having explained that common mechanics takes its origin from the practical arts, he continues:

> But I consider philosophy rather than arts . . . and consider chiefly those things which relate to gravity, levity, elastic force, the resistance of fluids, and the like forces, whether attractive or impulsive; and therefore I offer this work as the mathematical principles of philosophy, for the whole burden of philosophy seems to consist in this—from the phenomena of motions to investigate the forces of nature, and then from these forces to demonstrate other phenomena . . . for I am induced by many reasons to suspect that they may all depend upon certain forces by which the particles of bodies, by some causes hitherto unknown, are either mutually impelled towards one another, and cohere in regular figures, or are repelled and recede from one another. These forces being unknown, philosophers have hitherto attempted the search of Nature in vain; but I hope the principles here laid down will afford some light either to this or some truer method of philosophy.

Later on he explains that all the expressions which he uses in order to designate centripetal forces, or forces by which bodies approach one another, are devoid of physical meaning and are to be taken only as mathematical terms that can be substituted one for the other:

> I . . . use the words attraction, impulse, or propensity of any sort towards a center, promiscuously, and indifferently, one for another; considering those forces not physically, but mathematically: wherefore the reader is not to imagine that by those words I anywhere take upon me to define the kind, or the manner of any action, the causes or the physical reason thereof, or that I attribute forces, in a true and physical sense, to certain centers (which are only mathematical points); when at any time I happen to speak of centers as attracting, or as endued with attractive powers.[1]

And in the introduction to Section XI of Book I, dealing with the motion of spherical bodies which tend to each other by centripetal forces, and which, therefore, revolve about a common center of gravity, Newton says that he will consider "the centripetal forces as if they were attractions [*tanquam attractiones*] though perhaps, if we used the language of physics [*physice loquendo*], they would more

---

[1] *Principia* (1687), Definitio VIII, pp. 3–4; Motte–Cajori, pp. 5–6.

truly be called impulses [*verius dicantur impulsus*]."[1] He will do this because he is dealing with mathematical problems and has therefore to use a way of speaking more easily understood by mathematical readers.

Rather interesting and strange this: *verius dicantur impulsus*. Strange because, as a matter of fact, attraction and impulse are not equivalent, at least not completely equivalent, as Huygens and Fontenelle did not fail to observe[2] and as Newton himself hints in the General Scholium added to the second edition of the *Principia*, where he states that attraction or gravitation has properties that mechanical forces do not possess;[3] thus it is strange that he nonetheless consistently asserts their equivalence. Interesting because it reveals that for Newton – just as for his mechanistic opponents – *impulse* is the only acceptable mode of action for a physical force, and that he himself is conscious of the danger implied in the use of the term "attraction." Yet the term "impulse" is no less dangerous if taken in its literal sense: it suggests a real, *physical*, mechanism; it yields too much to Cartesians. Newton, accordingly, explains that, like "attraction," "impulse" is not to be taken as implying a definite *physical* meaning: both terms are to be understood in a purely mathematical way, that is, as being devoid of any reference to the *modus producendi* of the effects ascribed to them, or else as being neutral with respect to any such *modus*.

Thus, in the Scholium which concludes this same section, Newton explains:

I here use the word *attraction* in general for any endeavor [*conatu*] whatever, made by bodies to approach to each other, whether that endeavor arise from the action of the bodies themselves, as tending [*petentium*] to each other or agitating each other by spirits emitted; or whether it arises from the action of the ether or of the air, or of any medium whatever, whether corporeal or incorporeal, in any manner impelling bodies placed therein towards each other. In the same general sense I use the word *impulse*, not defining in this treatise the species or physical qualities of forces, but investigating the quantities and mathematical proportions of them; as I observed [*explicui*] before in the Definitions.[4]

Newton's position seems thus to be perfectly clear: the forces he is dealing with are "mathematical" forces; or else he is dealing with them insofar and only insofar as they are subjected, or subjectable, to

[1] *De motu corporum sphericorum viribus centripetis se mutuo petentium*, p. 162, p. 164.
[2] See *supra*, pp. 121–122 and 57–58.   [3] See *infra*, p. 158.
    Principia (1687), p. 191; Motte–Cajori, p. 192.

mathematical treatment. We do not care, or at least do not inquire, what they are in themselves; our aim is not to speculate about their true nature (or about the causes that produce them) but to investigate the manner in which they are acting; or, to express it in a slightly modernized way, to find out the "how" and not the "why," to establish the "laws" and not look for the "causes."

It may seem rather surprising, in spite of these very decided and definite declarations by Newton, which are not very different, moreover, from those that were made by him in connection with his optical work and which the very contents of the *Principia* (*Philosophiae naturalis principia mathematica*) – a book on rational mechanics and mathematical astronomy – seemed fully to confirm, that his teaching could be, and was, interpreted as positing action at a distance by an attractive force residing in the bodies. This all the more so as the positivistic indifference toward explanatory hypotheses, together with the skeptical admission of the multiplicity of such possible explanations of the phenomena, was by no means a surprising and unheard-of attitude; quite the contrary, it was rather widespread and was adopted by such well-known figures as Boyle and Hooke.

As for gravity proper, it was long before, in 1636, that Galileo proclaimed that we do not know what it is – we know only the name – that all explanations of it given by philosophers are merely words, and that it is not profitable to inquire into the nature of gravity: it is sufficient to know that its action follows precise mathematical laws.[1] And John Wallis, in 1669, declared in his *Mechanics* that he would not inquire about the cause of gravity; he would instead take it simply as a force (whatever it might be) due to which bodies go down:

Gravitas est vis motrix, deorsum, sive ad Centrum Terrae. Quodnam sit, in consideratione Physica Gravitatis Principium, non hic inquirimus. Neque etiam, an qualitas dici debeat, aut Corporis Affectio, aut quo alio nomine censeri par sit. Sive enim ab innata qualitate in ipso gravi corpore; sive a communi circumstantium vergentia ad centrum; sive ab electrica vel magnetica Terrae facultate quae gravia ad se alliciat (de quo non est ut hic moveamus litem:) sufficit ut Gravitatis nomine eam intelligamus, quam sensu deprehendimus, Vim deorsum movendi tam ipsum corpus grave, tam quae obstant minus efficatia impedimenta.[2]

Yet the very fact that Newton used the term "attraction" along

[1] Galileo, "Dialogo II," in *Opere*, Edizione nazionale, ed. A. Favaro (Florence, 1897), VII, 260.
[2] J. Wallis, *Mechanica sive de motu tractatus geometricus* (London, 1669), Def. XII, p. 3; *Opera mathematica* (Oxford, 1695), I, p. 576.

with and even in preference to "impulse" could not but rehabilitate this expression – and with it the conception – which had been so radically rejected by the Cartesians; and the consistent parallelism of attraction and impulse (in the texts I have quoted and in many others that I have not, such as the Optical Section [XIV], of the First Book) maintained by Newton, could not fail to produce the impression that he was dealing in both cases with analogous *physical* forces, even though he might disregard, or make an abstraction of, their *physical* reality and consider only their mathematical aspect.

Moreover, Newton's example of "mathematical" force as distinguished from "physical" force was by no means convincing. It is certain that we cannot attribute forces to mathematical points, that it is not the central point of a spherical body that attracts bodies placed outside of it, and that two bodies which describe similar orbits around their common center of gravity are not attracted by their common center of gravity – though they behave *as if* they were and *as if* all the mass of each spherical body was concentrated in its center.[1] Yet is it not obvious that, if bodies do so behave, they do so because the force that acts upon them, and which we well may call "mathematical," results from the by no means "mathematical" forces that we ascribe to the innumerable particles of the central spherical body, or the revolving bodies themselves?

Finally, as Huygens had noticed, "impulse" or "pressure" is not interchangeable with "attraction": the former are not "toward a body," and can be directed as well or even better toward a void. And even if they are directed toward a body they do not give rise to *mutual* forces and – as Newton himself will recognize[2] – they do not depend on the mass of this body. Besides, the Newtonian justification of his use of the term "attraction" is rather misleading; as a matter of fact, it is not a mathematical concept, and for the "mathematical reader" the expression *vis centripeta* (formed on the pattern of Huygens's *vis centrifuga* and as homage to him) would be just as good, and even much better. Indeed, in the first ten sections of Book I, where Newton discusses the motion of bodies describing all sorts of curves, and especially conic sections, he consistently uses the term *vis centripeta*.[3]

[1] *Principia* (1687), Book I, Sec. XII, pp. 192 sq. and 200 sq.; Motte–Cajori, pp. 193 sq. and 200 sq.

[2] See *infra*, p. 157.

[3] For example, *Principia* (1687), Sec. III, Prop. XI, Prob. VI, p. 50, and Prop. XII, Prob. VII, p. 51, where he determines the law for centripetal forces directed to one focus for bodies moving on ellipses or hyperbolas; or Sec. VIII, p. 128, which deals with the orbits of bodies acted upon by centripetal forces of any kind.

Moreover, in order to designate these centripetal forces by which bodies tend (*petunt*) toward each other, Newton as often as not does not use the term *attractio* alone, but uses it in connection with the much more concrete Keplerian term *tractio*, giving *tractio* an active meaning, and *attractio* a passive one; thus bodies *trahunt* each other and are *attracta* by each other (the English translation that renders both words by "attraction," though countenanced by Newton himself,[1] blurs this rather important nuance).

Thus even the mathematical reader, learning that *attractiones . . . fieri solent ad corpora* (and not *ad puncta mathematica*) and are proportional to their masses; that *corporum trahentium & attractorum actiones semper mutuae sunt & aequales*;[2] that *corpora duo se invicem trahentia describunt . . . figuras similes*;[3] that *vires quibus corpora se mutuo trahunt* diminish with distance; that, in particular, "if each of the bodies of the System A, B, C, D, etc., do each singly pull (*trahunt*) all the others with accelerative forces that are either inversely or directly in the ratio of any power whatever of the distances from the pulling body (*a trahente*) . . . [then] it is plain that the absolute forces of these bodies are as the bodies themselves," because "it is conformable to reason that forces which are directed to bodies depend on their nature and quantity as they do in magnets,"[4] and so forth; learning this, then, the mathematical reader will doubtless understand – or misunderstand – Newton as asserting the existence in bodies of forces by which they act upon each other (pull each other, *trahunt*), in spite of the distance that separates them. And, as he never encounters a mention of any medium that transmits this action, the reader will conclude, like Huygens and Liebniz, and also Cotes, that Newton postulates action at a distance, not wanting, however, to commit himself, just as in 1672 in his *New Theory about Light and Colors* he asserted the corpuscular structure of light, at the same time denying that he did so.

As for the nonmathematical reader, he accepted the nonunderstandable attraction as one of the ways in which God acts upon the world. Indeed, God did not have to conform this action to our understanding of it. Thus Locke:

---

[1] See his letter to Cotes of 28 March 1713 in J. Edleston, *Correspondence of Sir Isaac Newton and Professor Cotes* (London, 1850), p. 154.

[2] *Principia* (1687), p. 162; Motte–Cajori, p. 164.

[3] *Ibid.*

[4] *Principia* (1687), Prop. LXIX, Th. XXIX, and *scholium*, pp. 190 sq.; Motte–Cajori, pp. 191 sq.

If God can give no Power to any parts of Matter, but what Men can account for from the Essence of Matter in general: If all such Qualities and Properties must destroy the Essence or *change the essential Properties* of Matter, which are to our Conceptions above it, and we cannot conceive to be the natural Consequence of that Essence; it is plain, that the Essence of Matter is destroyed and its *essential Properties changed* in most of the sensible parts of this our System: For 'tis visible, that all the Planets have Revolutions about certain remote Centers, which I would have any one explain, or make conceiveable by the bare Essence or natural Powers depending on the Essence of Matter in general, without something added to that Essence, which we cannot conceive; for the moving of Matter in a crooked Line, or the attraction of Matter by Matter, is all that can be said in the Case; either of which, it is above our Reach to derive from the Essence of Matter or Body in general; though one of these two must unavoidably be allowed to be superadded in this instance to the Essence of Matter in general. The Omnipotent Creator advised not with us in the making of the World, and his ways are not the less Excellent, because they are past our finding out.[1]

Locke recognizes that Newton had made him change his mind:

I admit that I said (*Essay on Human Understanding*, Book II, ch. VIII, par. 11) that body acts by impulse and not otherwise. This also was my view when I wrote it and even now I cannot conceive its action in any other way. But since then I have been convinced by the judicious Mr. Newton's incomparable book that there is too much presumption in wishing to limit the power of God by our limited conceptions. The gravitation of matter toward matter in ways inconceivable to me is not only a demonstration that God, when it seems to Him good, can put into bodies powers and modes of acting which are beyond what can be derived from our idea of body or explained by what we know of matter; but it is furthermore an incontestable instance that He has really done so. I shall therefore take care to correct this passage in the new edition of my book.[2]

Which, by the way, he did. Indeed, as noticed already by A. C. Fraser in his edition of the *Essay:*

In the first three editions this section stands thus: "The next thing to be considered, is how bodies operate on one another; and that is manifestly by impulse, and nothing else. It being impossible to conceive that body should operate on *what it does not touch* (which is all one as to imagine it can operate where it is not), or when it does touch operate any other way than by motion." In the subsequent edition, Locke suppressed this passage and replaced it by: "The next thing to be considered is how bodies produce ideas in us; and that is manifestly by impulse, the only way we can conceive bodies to operate in."[3]

---

[1] See *Mr. Locke's Reply to the Right Reverend Lord Bishop of Worcester, Answer to his Second Letter* . . . (London, 1699), pp. 398 sq.

[2] *Ibid.*, p. 408.

[3] J. Locke, *Essay Concerning Human Understanding*, ed. A. C. Fraser (Oxford, 1894), I, 171, note 1.

The appearance of the *Opticks* (London, 1704) did not improve the situation; quite the contrary. Indeed, though in order to explain the "fits" of easy reflection and easy refraction, and even reflection and refraction in general, Newton made an appeal to the "hypothesis" of a vibrating medium (which finally, in the second English edition, turns out to be a luminiferous elastic aether), he at the same time "asked" in Query I (and IV) whether bodies do not act upon light at a distance. Moreover, Dr. George Cheyne (who was considered as a follower of Newton and expressed, concerning the relation of God, space, and the world, views pretty similar to those that Newton held himself but did not want to profess) asserted that, though not *essential* in the full meaning of the term, gravity or attraction was nevertheless a primary quality of matter. Thus he wrote:

> Attraction or Gravitation is not essential to matter but seems rather an original Impress which continues in it by virtue of the Omnipresent Activity in the Divine Nature of which it is a Copy or an Image in the low degree suitable for the gross creatures and so may be now recon'd among the primary Qualities of Matter without which as it is now constituted matter cannot be.[1]

Cheyne added[2] that attraction could not be explained mechanically.

Confronted with this glaring "misinterpretation" of his teaching, Newton reacted. He did not, however, state outright that for him gravity was in no sense a "property" of body but was produced by the action of an immaterial cause – as Clarke had done meanwhile;[3] Newton preferred to explain that he did not mean what he seemed to say. Thus in the Latin edition of his *Opticks* (London, 1706), in which he reprinted without change Query I asserting an action at a distance of bodies upon light, and in Query XXII, in which he explained that mutual attraction of light particles and gross bodies was 1,000,000,000,000,000 times as strong as that between the gross bodies themselves, he published a Query (XXIII; XXXI in the second English edition) in which, having discussed the various forces – gravitational, chemical, electrical – by which bodies act upon one another at a distance and having said that there may be in nature other attractive powers, he added (p. 322 of the 1706 Latin edition, p. 351

---

[1] G. Cheyne, *Philosophical Principles of Natural Religion* (London, 1705; 2nd ed., 1715), p. 41. On Cheyne, see Mme. Hélène Metzger, *Attraction universelle et religion naturelle chez quelques commentateurs anglais de Newton* (Paris: Hermann, 1937).
[2] *Ibid.*, p. 42.
[3] In a note to pars I, cap. XI, par. 15, of Rohault's *Physica*; see *infra*, p. 171.

of the 1717 second English; these texts being somewhat different, I quote them both):

Qua causa efficiente hae Attractiones peragantur, in id vero hic non inquiro. Quam ego Attractionem appello, fieri sane potest ut ea efficiatur *Impulsu* vel alio aliquo modo nobis ignoto. Hanc vocem Attractionis ita hic accipi velim ut in universum solummodo vim aliquam significare intelligatur qua Corpora ad se mutuo tendant cuicunque demum causae attribuenda sit illa vis. Nam ex phaenomenis Naturae illud nos prius edoctos oportet quaenam corpora se invicem Attrahant et quaenam sint Leges et Proprietates istius Attractionis quam in id inquirere par sit, quanam efficiente causa peragatur Attractio. Attractiones gravitatis, virtutisque magneticae et electricae, ad satis magna se extendunt illae quidem intervalla; adeoque etiam sub vulgi sensum notitiamque ceciderunt. At vero fieri potest ut sint praeterae aliae quoque aliquae quae tam augustis finibus contineantur, ut usque adhuc omnem observationem fugerint.

How these Attractions may be performed I do not here consider. What I call attraction may be performed by impulse, or by some other means unknown to me. I use that word here to signify only in general any force by which Bodies tend towards one another, whatsoever be the cause. For we must learn from the Phaenomena of Nature what bodies attract one another, and what are the Laws and Properties of the Attraction, before we inquire the Cause by which the Attraction is performed. The Attractions of Gravity, Magnetism, and Electricity, reach to very sensible distances, and so have been observed by vulgar Eyes, and there may be others that reach to so small distances as hitherto escape observation; *and perhaps electrical Attraction may reach to such small distances, even without being excited by Friction* [italicized words added in the third English edition].

In the second edition of the *Principia*, in the third of his *Regulae philosophandi*,[1] in which he deals with the essential properties of bodies, that is, with those which *intendi et remitti nequeunt* (it is curious to see Newton use the medieval terminology of the Oxford and Parisian schoolmen), he lists as such *extensio, durities, impenetrabilitas, mobilitas*, and *vis inertiae* – but not gravity – though stating at the same time that it is a universal force. Indeed, he said that *corpora omnia in se mutuo gravitant* was just as certain or even more so than that they are extended.

In the *Scholium Generale* by which he enriched this second edition[2] he stated that, though he had explained the phenomena of the heavens and of our sea *per Vim gravitatis*, he did not assign the cause of gravity because he could not deduce from the phenomena its rather peculiar properties and was not prepared to feign hypotheses to do so. Indeed,

[1] *Principia* (1713), pp. 357 sq.; Motte–Cajori, pp. 398 sq.
[2] *Ibid.*, p. 483; p. 546.

this is certain, that it must proceed from a cause that penetrates to the very centres of the sun and planets, without suffering the least diminution of its force; that operates not according to the quantity of the surfaces of the particles upon which it acts (as mechanical causes use to do), but according to the quantity of the solid matter which they contain, and propagates its virtue on all sides to immense distances, decreasing always as the inverse square of the distances . . . But hitherto I have not been able to discover the cause of those properties of gravity from phenomena, and I feign no hypotheses.

To which weighty statement he added (on Cotes's suggestion and in order to defend himself against the attack of Leibniz, who, in a letter to Hartsoeker, accused him of reintroducing into natural philosophy not only occult qualities but even a perpetual miracle):

For whatever is not deduced from the phenomena is to be called a hypothesis, and hypotheses, whether metaphysical or physical, whether of occult qualities or mechanical have no place in experimental philosophy. In this philosophy particular propositions are inferred from the phenomena and afterwards rendered general by induction. Thus it was that the impenetrability, the mobility, and the impulsive force of bodies, and the laws of motion and gravitation, were discovered. And to us it is enough that gravity does really exist, and act according to the laws which we have explained, and abundantly serves to account for all the motions of the celestial bodies, and of our sea.[1]

This celebrated pronouncement, which on one hand seemed to reassert, more strongly than ever, the pure empiricism professed in the first edition and in the third "Rule of Reasoning in Philosophy," which seemed to reject all causal explanation of the phenomena and, in a positivistic-agnostic manner, to accept gravity – or gravitation – as a mere fact, and, on the other hand, associated it with such truly essential properties of bodies as impenetrability, mobility, and inertia, asserting at the same time that it was not to be explained "mechanically," did not, and obviously could not, achieve the effect desired by Newton, any more than the hints of the Latin *Opticks*. His readers remained convinced not only that gravity, or universal attraction, was a real cosmic force – which according to Newton it was – but also that it was a *physical* one – which according to him it was not – and even that it was a real, though perhaps not "essential," property of matter. And Cotes (who, by the way, expressed his doubts about Newton's assertion of a mutual attraction of bodies, objecting that it implied that Newton "tacitly [made] this supposition that

[1] *Principia* (1713), p. 484; p. 547. See Edleston, *Correspondence*, pp. 153, 155.

ye Attractive force resides in the Central Body"[1]) in his famous Preface to the second edition of the *Principia* – which everyone, with good reason, considered to have been, if not written under Newton's direction, at least read and approved by him and thus to constitute an authoritative expression of his views – seemed to confirm this conviction. He did not, of course, assert that gravity was an *essential* property of body – he was taught not to do so – yet, like Cheyne, he called it a *primary* one and asserted that

either gravity will have a place among the primary qualities of all bodies, or Extension, Mobility and Impenetrability will not. And the nature of things will either be rightly explained by gravity of bodies or it will not be rightly explained by their extension, mobility and impenetrability.[2]

As a matter of fact, Cotes first wrote "essential" – this, by the way, shows how easy it was for a serious and well-informed student of Newton to misunderstand him – and only when corrected by Clarke, to whom he submitted the draft of his preface, did he recognize his error and improve his text. At the same time, in his letter to Clarke, he expressed a rather far-reaching anti- and pre-Cartesian skepticism, shared, as a matter of fact, by Newton himself, concerning our knowledge, or understanding, of the relation between substance and property, a skepticism that, owing to the influence of Locke, was to become general in the seventeenth century. Newton, indeed, in the *Scholium Generale* added to the second edition of the *Principia*, stated that

what the real substance of anything is we know not. In bodies we see only their figures and colours, we hear only the sounds, we touch only their outward surfaces, we smell only the smells, and taste the savours; but their inward substances are not to be known either by our senses, or by any reflext act of our minds.[3]

In the unpublished drafts of this passage he went even further in his rejection of the "moderns" and in going back to the traditional Aristotelian-scholastic views:

Substantias rerum non cognoscimus. Nullas habemus earum ideas. Ex phaenomenis colligimus earum proprietates solas & ex proprietatibus quod sint substantiae. Corpora se mutuo non penetrare colligimus ex solis phaenomenis: substantias diversi generis se mutuo non penetrare ex

---

[1] See Edleston, *Correspondence*, p. 153, and *infra*, Chapter VII, "Attraction, Newton, and Cotes."
[2] *Principia*, Motte–Cajori, p. xxvi.
[3] *Principia* (1713), p. 483; Motte–Cajori, p. 546.

phaenomenis minime constat. Et quod ex phaenomenis minime colligitur temere affirmare non debet.

Ex phaenomenis cognoscimus proprietates rerum & ex proprietatibus colligimus res ipsas extare easque vocamus substantias sed ideas substantiarum non magis habemus quam caecus ideas colorum . . .

Ideas habemus attributorum ejus sed quid sit rei alicujus substantia minime cognoscimus.[1]

As for Cotes, he wrote to his censor Clarke:

Sir: I return you my thanks for Your correction of the Preface and particularly for Your advice in relation to that place where I seemed to assert Gravity to be Essential to Bodies. I am fully of Your mind that it would have furnish'd matter for Cavilling and therefore I struck it out immediately upon Dr. Cannon's mentioning Your Objection to me, and so it never was printed . . . My design in that passage was not to assert Gravity to be essential to Matter, but rather to assert that we are ignorant of the Essential properties of Matter and that in respect to our Knowledge Gravity may possibly lay as fair a claim to that Title as the other Properties which I mention'd. For I understand by Essential Propertys such propertys without which no other belonging to the same substance can exist: and I would not undertake to prove that it were impossible for any of the other Propertys of Bodies to exist without even extension. (Cambridge, June 25, 1713.)[2]

Cotes, as we have seen, replaced "essential" by "primary." Strictly speaking, "primary" and "essential" do not mean the same thing. An *essential* property is a property without which a thing can neither be, nor even be thought of; such, for instance, is the case of extension, but not that of gravity, as we cannot think of a body as being deprived of extension but can very well think of it as possessing no gravity. Yet, *in praxi*, it was hardly better; all the more, or all the less, so as Cotes, suppressing the term "essential" altogether, characterized as *primary* not only gravity but also extension, mobility, and impenetrability, thus putting all these "qualities" on the same level and making "gravity" a quality of the body, just as Dr. Cheyne had done. Thus it was rather natural that he was understood, or misunderstood, as placing gravity among the essential properties of matter and as endowing matter with the force of attraction.

Once more, or even twice more, Newton protested. Thus in the Queries added to the second English edition of his *Opticks* (1717), he revived the aethereal conceptions developed in his *Hypothesis of*

---

[1] See A. R. Hall and M. Boas Hall, *A Selection from the Unpublished Scientific Papers of Sir Isaac Newton in the Portsmouth Collection, Cambridge University Library* (Cambridge, England: Cambridge University Press, 1962), pp. 356 sq.

[2] See Edleston, *Correspondence*, pp. 151 sq.

1675; indeed, he enhanced the role of the aether, explaining by aethereal pressure phenomena such as reflection and refraction that formerly (especially in the *Principia*, Book I, Sec. XIV) were explained by the action at a distance of attractive and repulsive forces; he also presents – hypothetically, of course – an explanation of gravity by aethereal pressure which he announced in the Preface to this edition: "And to shew that I do not take Gravity for an Essential Property of Bodies, I have added a question (Qu. XXI) concerning its Cause, chusing to propose it by way of a Question because I am not yet satisfied about it for want of Experiments." Furthermore, in order to make his new aethereal theories more acceptable and to reduce the glaring contradictions between them and the assertions of the Queries that postulate action at a distance, Newton suppressed part[1] of Query XXII in the Latin *Optice* (Qu. XXX of the English), where he asserted that attraction between light particles and gross matter is 10^{15} times stronger than terrestrial gravity, and added at the end of Query XXIX: "What I mean in this question by *vacuum* and by Attraction of the Rays of Light towards glass or crystal may be understood" as meaning aether and action of the aether.[2] And in the third edition of the *Principia* (1727) he added to the text of the third *regula philosophandi* the following statement: "Attamen Gravitatem corporibus essentialem esse minime affirmo. Per vim insitam intelligo solam vim inertiae. Haec immutabilis est. Gravitas recedendo a Terra diminuitur."

Yet it was too late. It seems that nobody paid much attention to the "hypothesis" of the *Opticks*, which, on one hand, explained gravitation by postulating an aethereal medium of a most improbable structure, a medium which was

much rarer within the dense bodies of the Sun, Stars, Planets and Comets than in the empty celestial Spaces between them [and which] passing from them to great distances grows denser and denser perpetually . . . and thereby causes the gravity of those great Bodies towards one another and of their parts towards the Bodies,

and on the other hand suggested in Query XXII (a hypothesis not more probable than that of Query XXI) that such a medium should be 700,000 times rarer, being, nevertheless, as many times more elastic than the air, in order not to disturb the motions of the planets and

---

[1] *Optice*, pp. 320 sq.
[2] See my "Études newtoniennes II: Les Quéries de *L'Optique*," *Archives Internationales d'Histoire des Sciences 13* (1960), 15–29.

to oppose to them so small a resistance "as would scarce make any sensible alteration . . . in ten Thousand years." Indeed, it explained. or explained away, the action at a distance of the attractive forces, but only by replacing them by repulsive ones, which was not much better; besides, the Newtonian hypothesis (not very different from that which Hooke examined and rejected fifty years earlier, and even, *horribile dictu*, from that which Roberval proposed in his *Aristarchus*[1]) was obviously unable to explain the *mutual* attraction of bodies. And as to the statement of the third edition of the *Principia*, it certainly was beside the point: it was not *gravitas* as weight (*pondus*) that was in question but *gravitas* as an attracting power, the *pondus* of which was only an effect. Thus it could – and according to Newton himself did – remain constant, all changes of *weight* notwithstanding.

Furthermore – and this seems to me to be more important still – the subtle differences maintained by Newton between "physical" and "nonphysical" (transphysical) forces, "essential" and "nonessential" properties of matter, were lost for the eighteenth-century reader; they distinguished, of course, fundamental or "primordial" properties of bodies, as extension, hardness, and so on, from the "more particular ones, as figure, colour, odour, etc." but they felt that, as Maupertuis in his *Discours sur la différente figure des astres* has very aptly formulated it,

the manner in which the properties reside in a subject is always inconceivable for us. People are not astonished when they see a body in motion communicate this motion to others; the habit that they have of seeing this phenomenon prevents them from seeing how marvellous it is [Maupertuis hints at Malebranche, who thought such communication impossible: Malebranche, indeed, denied all causality and all action to bodies, and, generally speaking, to creatures, and referred all effectivity to God], but philosophers will not make the error of believing that the impulsive force is more conceivable than the attractive one. [Indeed], is it more difficult for God to make bodies tend or move towards each other, these bodies being at a distance, than to wait, in order to move them, that one body be met by the other [as, according to Malebranche, he had to do]? If we had complete ideas of bodies, if we knew well what they are in themselves and what are their properties, how and in what number they reside in them, we would not be embarrassed to decide whether attraction is a property of matter. But we are very far from having such ideas: we know bodies only by sense, without any knowledge of the subject in which these properties find themselves united . . . It would be ridiculous to want to assign to bodies other properties besides those that experience has taught us are found in them; but it would, perhaps, be still more ridiculous to pronounce

[1] See *supra*, p. 59, n. 2.

dogmatically the exclusion of all others: as if we had the measure of the capacity of the subjects while we know them only by this small number of properties. [Accordingly], attraction is, so to say, no more than a question of fact: it is into the system of the Universe that we have to look in order to find out whether it is a principle that effectively has a place in nature, how far it is necessary [to admit it] in order to explain the phenomena, or, finally, whether it is gratuitously introduced for explaining facts that are as well explained without it.[1]

As we see, for Maupertuis – and it is the same for Voltaire – gravity, or attraction, has become a purely factual question. But it ceased to be a problem as it was for Newton himself.

Eighteenth-century thought became reconciled to the ununderstandable – with very few exceptions.[2] As Ernst Mach expressed it: "It became accustomed to use forces acting at a distance as a given starting point of explanation, and the incentive to inquire about their origin disappeared nearly completely."[3] Later, the problem was very successfully hidden in the concept of field.[4]

[1] Maupertuis, *Discours sur la différente figure des astres* (Paris, 1732); *Oeuvres* (Lyons, 1756), I, 98, 94, 96, 103.

[2] See C. Isenkrahe, *Das Rätsel von Schwerkraft* (Brunswick: Vieweg, 1879).

[3] Ernst Mach, *Die Mechanik in ihrer Entwicklung* (9th ed.; Leipzig: Brockhaus, 1933), p. 185.

[4] See M.-A. Tonnelat, "De l'idée de milieu à la notion de champ," *Archives Internationales d'Histoire des Sciences 12* (1959), 337–356.

The Void and Extension

The conception of void space was repudiated by Descartes as strongly as, or even more strongly than, by Aristotle. For the latter, indeed, void space merely did not exist *in rerum natura*, or at most was actually impossible; for the former it was much more than that: it was a *contradictio in adjecto*. Indeed, having established that "the nature of body consists not in weight, hardness, colour or similar things, but only in extension,"[1] Descartes was bound to identify extension (space) and matter and to assert that

space or internal locus and corporeal substance do not differ, in reality, but only in the way in which they are apt to be conceived by us. But in truth, extension in length, breadth and depth that constitutes space is clearly the same that constitutes body.[2]

Wherefrom it followed immediately that "it is repugnant that there be a vacuum or [a place] where there would be absolutely no thing," and that

it is clear that vacuum in the philosophical sense, that is [a place] in which there would be absolutely no substance, cannot exist, because the extension of space, or internal place, does not differ from the extension of body. For just as from the fact alone that body is extended in length, breadth and depth we conclude that it is a substance, because it is totally repugnant that there be any extension of nothing, we have in the same way to conclude also about space which is supposed to be void: namely, as there is extension in it, there is also necessarily substance.[3]

The concept of absolute void arises from an erroneous extension of the vulgar use and acceptance of the word, which, as a matter of fact, "does not mean a space where there is nothing, but only a space where we do not find something that, as we think, should be there, as when we call a bottle 'empty,' though it is full of air, or when we

---

[1] Descartes, *Principia philosophiae*, pars II, art. 4, in *Oeuvres*, ed. C. Adam and P. Tannery (Paris, 1897–1913), VIII, 42; French translation, *Principes de philosophie, ibid.*, IX 65; and already in *Le Monde, ibid.*, XI, 35 sq., and *Discours de la méthode, ibid.*, VI, 42 sq.

[2] *Principia philosophiae*, pars II, art. 10, *ibid.*, VIII, 45; IX, 68.

[3] *Ibid.*, art. 16, VIII, 49; IX, 71.

say that there is nothing in a fish pond, if there are no fish, though it is full of water,"[1] and so on. Accustomed to this way of thinking, or not thinking, we go on and assume that a container could be made empty of all contents, so that there would really be *nothing* in it. Which is completely absurd:

in truth we can no more conceive a vessel with nothing in it than we can conceive a mountain without a valley: it would mean conceiving the inside of that vessel without its extension, or that extension without the extended substance: of nothing, indeed, there can be no extension . . .

Thus, if one asked, what would happen if God destroyed all body that is contained in a certain vessel, and would not allow any other [body] to come into the *locus* of the destroyed, we have to answer: the walls of that vessel would, *eo ipso*, be contiguous. This is so because if there is nothing between two bodies, it is necessary that these bodies mutually touch each other; and it is manifestly repugnant that they be distant, or that there be distance between them, and that, nonetheless, this distance be nothing; for all distance is a mode of extension and therefore cannot be without the extended substance.[2]

Indeed, Rohault, having in cap. VII of his *System of Natural Philosophy* posited Descartes's determination of the essence of matter – identification of extension and body – cannot but conclude the non-existence of void. Thus, for example, "Ex his, quae de Natura materiae posuimus, colligere licet . . . inane, quod vocant Philosophi nullum esse posse,"[3] and "Nihilum sive inane nullas habet proprietates,"[4] not even that of existence. To which Clarke replies, "Consentaneum hoc quidem ei dicere qui essentiam materiae extensionem dicit. Verum ex gravitatis natura . . . constat jam omnino aliquod inane et multo id quidem maxime in rebus esse";[5] moreover, according to Clarke, the Cartesians – Rohault – are making a logical error in identifying the *vacuum* with *nihil*: space void of matter is undoubtedly space in which there is nothing, but this does not make it itself nothing; furthermore, the identification of extension and matter leads to very awkward and even absurd consequences, namely, its necessity and eternity; indeed, infinity implies necessity (it is rather interesting to see Clarke, as Newton did before him,[6] accept this Cartesian axiom as a premise of his reasoning, a premise so certain and evident that

---

[1] *Ibid.*, art. 17, VIII, 49; IX, 72.
[2] *Ibid.*, art. 18, VIII, 50; IX, 73.
[3] Rohault, *Physica*, pars I, cap. 8, p. 26; *Rohault's System of Natural Philosophy*, trans. John Clarke (London, 1723), Book I, cap, VIII, p. 27.
[4] *Ibid.*, cap. XII, par. 26, p. 64.
[5] *Ibid.*, cap. VIII, p. 27.
[6] See *infra*, p. 94.

they do not even feel the need to formulate it, or, of course, to mention its Cartesian origin). Accordingly,

Si Extensio esset materiae Essentia, ideoque Materia idem quod Spatium ipsum; sequeretur ubique et infinitam esse materiam et necessario aeternam, quae neque creari poterit, nec possit in Nihilum redigi, quod est absurdum.[1]

Thus it is clear that space is different from matter, and that it is not *extensio, sed extensio solida* that should be considered as the essence of matter. Furthermore, the unhindered motion of planets and comets in the celestial spaces clearly leads to the conclusion that these spaces are empty.

Some years later the problem of the void became one of the topics of the polemics between Clarke and Leibniz.[2] Clarke defended the distinction of space from matter and the existence of a vacuum; Leibniz accepted the former and rejected the latter. Matter being finite and space infinite, argued Clarke, there must necessarily be a void. Moreover, from the very infinity of space followed its necessary existence; and this, in turn, implied a direct and immediate relation to God. Clarke, therefore, asserted that space was an attribute, a quality, or a property of God. Somewhat later, in the Avertissement published in the preface to Des Maiseaux's edition of the *Correspondence*,[3] and, as a matter of fact, written by Newton himself, he somewhat toned down his assertions – probably because of their Spinozistic flavor – explaining that they should not be taken literally and that space and duration are not *qualities* or *properties*, but modes of existence of the substance which is really necessary and substantially omnipresent and eternal. This, according to him – and to Henry More, whom he follows closely in his conception of space – does not imply a divisibility of God's substance, as space itself is indivisible or "indiscerptible."[4]

As for Leibniz, who denied the metaphysical reality of both space and time and reduced them to a set of relations in order of coexistence for space and of succession for time – he based his reasoning on the

[1] *Rohault's System*, note to cap. VII, par. 8, p. 24.
[2] *A Collection of Papers which passed between the late learned M. Leibniz and Dr. Clarke in the Years 1715 and 1716 relating to the Principles of Natural Philosophy and Religion* (London, 1717).
[3] *Recueil de diverses pièces sur la philosophie, la religion naturelle, l'histoire, les mathématiques, etc., par Mss Leibniz, Clarke, Newton et autres auteurs célèbres* (Amsterdam, 1720), vol. I.
[4] On Newton, Clarke, and More, see A. Koyré, *From the Closed World to the Infinite Universe* (Baltimore: Johns Hopkins Press, 1957).

principle that Professor Lovejoy has so aptly called the "principle of plenitude" and contended that the existence of the vacuum was in contradiction to God's infinite perfection and implied a limitation of his power of creation. Indeed, it is obvious that there is more reality in the *plenum* than in the *vacuum*. Accordingly it would be unworthy of God not to create matter wherever it was possible to do so, that is, everywhere, and thus to create a poorer and less perfect world though being able to create a more perfect one. Besides, according to Leibniz, the existence of a void space, with some chunks of matter dispersed in it here and there, contradicted the principle of sufficient reason: why, indeed, space being homogeneous and isoform, should God create matter here and not there?

Needless to say, Leibniz's arguments did not convince the Newtonians. They did not think that by their conception they impoverished the world or put a limitation on God's creative power. Quite the contrary, they felt elated by the discovery that there was in the world so much more void than matter: it seemed to them to reduce this latter's importance to nothing, or almost nothing, and to administer a hard blow to materialism. Thus already Bentley in his *Confutation of Atheism* explains enthusiastically that "the empty Space of our Solar Region . . . is 8575 hundred thousand million million times more ample than all the corporeal substance in it" and that "the Summ of Empty Spaces within the Concave of the Firmament is 6860 million million million times bigger than All the Matter contain'd in it,"[1] and it is obviously with great satisfaction that Voltaire informs us that "it is not certain that there is a cubic inch of solid matter in the whole universe."[2] Moreover, Newtonians thought that God should not, and could not, be bound by the principles of plenitude and sufficient reason, and that Leibniz, by imposing them upon God, limited or even destroyed his freedom and subjected him to necessity. Or, to express it somewhat differently, though agreeing that everything must have a reason, Clarke maintained that God's will was a more than sufficient one.[3]

Thus for Clarke. As for Voltaire, he naturally defends the void, combining a positivistic-agnostic attitude toward matter, obviously

[1] Richard Bentley, *A Confutation of Atheism from the Origin and Frame of the World* (London, 1693), part II, pp. 14 sq.; I. B. Cohen, *Isaac Newton's Papers and Letters on Natural Philosophy* (Cambridge, Massachusetts: Harvard University Press, 1958), pp. 326 sq.

[2] Voltaire, *Lettres philosophiques*, édition critique par Gustave Lanson (Paris: Edouard Cornély, 1909, and later editions), letter 16, vol. II, p. 20.

[3] *Rohault's System of Natural Philosophy*, I, 20 sq., Clarke's second reply.

inspired by Maupertuis, with a theory of space that follows closely the teaching of Clarke. In his *Éléments de la philosophie de Newton* he writes:

> Those who cannot conceive the *Void*, object that this *Void* would be nothing, that nothing can have no properties, and that, thus, nothing can take place in the *Void*.
>
> One answers that it is not true that the *Void* is nothing; it is the *locus* of bodies, it is space, it has properties, it is extended in length, breadth and depth, it is penetrable, it is inseparable, etc.[1]

It is true, concedes Voltaire, that we cannot form an image of the *Void*; "but I cannot form an image of myself as a thinking being either, and this does not preclude me from being convinced that I think." Indeed, "We can form images only of what is corporeal; and *Space* is not corporeal." Nevertheless, "I conceive Space very well." "There is no other possible answer to this argument," continues Voltaire, "than to say that matter is infinite; that is what several philosophers asserted, and that is what Descartes did after them."[2] Yet this infinitization of matter is based only on the supposition that matter and extension are identical, and proves only how dangerous it is to rely, in your reasoning, upon suppositions. Indeed,

> it is false that matter and extension are the same thing: all matter is extended, but all extension is not matter . . . we do not know at all what matter is; we know only some properties of it and nobody can deny that it is possible that there are millions of other extended substances different from what we call Matter.[3]

In identifying extension and matter Descartes not only made an error, he also contradicted himself, "for he admitted a God; but where is God? He is not in a mathematical point, he is immense; what is his immensity if not the immense Space?" Indeed, "the existence of an infinite matter is a contradiction in terms." Not, however, that of an infinite space:

> Space exists necessarily, because God exists necessarily; it is immense, it is, as duration, a mode, an infinite property of a necessary and infinite Being. Matter is nothing of that kind: it does not exist necessarily; and if this substance were infinite, it would be an essential property of God, or God himself: but it is neither the one nor the other; therefore it is not and cannot be infinite.[4]

[1] Voltaire, *Éléments de la philosophie de Newton, mis à la portée de tout le monde par Mr. de Voltaire* (Amsterdam, 1783), ch. XVII, p. 210.
[2] *Ibid.*, p. 211.
[3] *Ibid.*, pp. 212 sq.
[4] *Ibid.*

It is interesting to note that, whereas in the first and second editions of the *Éléments* Voltaire, as we have seen, completely espoused the views of Newton and Clarke and presented them as his own, in the third edition (1748), which he modified and enlarged by a whole book (the first) devoted to "The Metaphysics of Newton," he presents them as those of Newton, and of Clarke, "a philosopher as great or even greater than Newton himself."[1]

[1] *Ibid.*

Rohault and Clarke on Attraction

The Cartesians rejected attraction, whether magnetic or gravitational, together with a number of other analogous concepts, because of their inherent obscurity: they were not "clear and distinct," as, according to Descartes, all our concepts should be, and therefore had no place in philosophy. Thus Rohault, having explained that in the world, which is full of matter without any void, all motion of a body implies a circular motion of a certain part of the surrounding matter – it pushes away, or aside, that of which it takes the place and its own place is taken by that which is behind it – which leads to very important consequences, namely, the mechanical explanation of a series of different phenomena, continues:

14. *That this Motion in a Circle, is the Cause of many surprizing Motions:*
This Truth, though it was known long ago, yet Philosophers, for want of duly attending to it, and well weighing and considering its Consequences, have thought it impossible to account for all the Motions we see in Nature by Impulse alone, which is the only way that we can conceive clearly, by which one Body moves another by pushing it; and which so naturally follows from the Impenetrability of Matter, which all the World agree in. And this is the Reason why they introduced into their Philosophy Things, indeed very specious, such as *Attraction, Sympathy, Antipathy, the Fear of a* Vacuum, etc. but which, at the Bottom, are mere Chimera's, invented to make them appear to give a Reason of that which they did not at all understand, and therefore ought not to be used in the better sort of Natural Philosophy.
15. *The obscurity of the Words Attraction, Sympathy and Antipathy:*
For as to (1) Attraction, Sympathy, and Antipathy, they ought not to be allowed at all, by reason of their Obscurity. That they are obscure, is very evident; for if we take a Loadstone, for Example, It is manifest to all the World, that to say it has an *attractive Vertue* or a *Sympathy* with the Iron, does not at all explain the Nature or the Properties of it. And as to the *Fear of a* Vacuum, I reserve the Notion of That to the following Chapter, where we shall compare the Reasoning of the Antients and our own together.[1]

To this statement of Rohault's Samuel Clarke replies:

[1] *Physica*, pars I, cap. XI, §14, p. 49; *System*, I, 54.

Note 1: *Attraction*: Since nothing acts at a Distance, that is, nothing can exert any Force in acting where it is not; it is evident, that Bodies (if we would speak properly) cannot at all move one another, but by Contact and Impulse. Wherefore *Attraction* and *Sympathy* and all *occult Qualities*, which are supposed to arise from the *Specifick Forms* of Things are justly to be rejected. Yet because, besides innumerable other Phaenomena of Nature, that universal Gravitation of Matter, which shall be more fully handled afterwards, can by no means arise from the mutual impulse of Bodies (because all Impulse must be in proportion to the Superficies, but Gravity is always in proportion to the Quantity of solid Matter, and therefore must of Necessity be ascribed to some Cause that penetrates the very inward Substance it self of solid Matter) therefore all such *Attraction*, is by all means to be allowed, as is not the Action of Matter at a Distance, but the Action of some immaterial Cause which perpetually moves and governs Matter by certain Laws.[1]

As for gravity proper, Rohault explains[2] that it is produced by the circular (vortex) motion of matter which recedes from the center and pushes back toward it its more sluggish parts, as Descartes has explained and as Huygens has very well demonstrated in his famous experiment.[3] He then proceeds to expose that experiment and concludes: "The Matter will recede from the Center, and force the Body to approach towards the Center, in the same Manner as they who affirm all Bodies to be heavy, say that the water forces Cork to rise up."[4]

Once more, Clarke replies:

(1) *Force the Body to approach towards the Center*, etc. This was a very ingenious Hypothesis, and so long as the World was thought to be full, a very probable one. But since it has been made appear by a great many very exact Observations of modern Philosophers, that the World is not full; and that Gravity is the most ancient and most universal Property of Matter, and the principal of all in maintaining and keeping together the whole Universe; we must proceed in another Method, and find out another Theory of Gravity. To be short, the celebrated Sir *Isaac Newton* has pursued this Enquiry with that Success, that the most simple Nature of Gravity, being supposed, he has established the true System of the World beyond all Controversy, and most clearly explained the most considerable Phaenomena of all Nature. And his Opinion of the Nature and Properties of Gravity is this.

Every *single* Particle of all Bodies whatever, *gravitates* to every *single* Particle of all Bodies whatsoever; that is, they are impelled towards each other by Gravity, *See the Notes on Part I, Chap. II, Art. 15*.

[1] *Ibid.*
[2] *Physica*, pars II, cap. XXVIII, §13, pp. 328 sq.; *System*, II, 96.
[3] See *supra*, pp. 119 sq.
[4] *Physica*, pars II, cap. XXVIII, §13, pp. 328 sq.; *System*, II, 96.

This gravitating Force is *Universal as to the Extent of it*; that is, all Bodies whatsoever, so far as we know, where-ever they are placed, not only on the Earth, but also in the Heavens, whether in the Moon or Planets, in the Sun or any other Place, are endued with this Power.

This Force is also *universal as to the Kinds of Bodies;* that is, all Bodies, whatever their Figure, Form or Texture be whether they be simple or compound, fluid or solid; whether they be great or small; whether they be in Motion or at Rest, are endued with this Power.

This Force is also *universal as to Time;* that is, all other Conditions being the same, it never increases or diminishes.

The Quantity of this Gravity at equal Distances, is always exactly in Proportion to the Quantity of Matter·in the gravitating Bodies. For instance, *if a cubick Foot of Gold has a Thousand Pound Weight* upon the Superficies of the Earth, *two cubick Feet* will have *two Thousand Pound Weight* upon the same Superficies; and if the Earth contained but half the quantity of Matter that it does now, the same cubick Foot of Gold which has now *a thousand Pound Weight* upon the Superficies of the Earth, would have *but Five Hundred only*.

This Gravity in given Bodies is greater or less according to the Distance of those Bodies from each other; for Example a Stone which near the Superficies of the Earth, is very heavy, if it were carried up as high as the Moon would be very light.

Lastly, The Proportion of the Increase or Decrease of this Gravity in Bodies approaching to or receding from each other is such that its Force is reciprocally in a duplicate Proportion or as the Squares of their Distances. For Example, a Body which at the Distance of ten Diameters of the Earth, weighs a hundred Pounds; would, if its Distance were but half so far, weigh four Times as much; and if but a third Part so far, nine Times as much. So likewise, the Force which upon the Superficies of the Earth, could support a Hundred Pound Weight; if it were twice as far off the Center, could support four times the Weight, if three Times as far off, it could support nine Times the Weight.[1]

---

[1] *Physica*, pars II, cap. XXVIII, §13, pp. 328 sq.; *System*, II, 96.

Copernicus and Kepler on Gravity

For pre-Copernican physics and cosmology, gravity was a natural tendency of heavy bodies to move toward the center of the world, which coincided with the center of the earth. Having removed this latter from its central position, Copernicus had, accordingly, to modify the theory of gravity. He did it by substituting for the unique cosmic gravity several planetary ones. Thus he writes:

> I myself think that Gravity or heaviness is nothing else but a natural Appetency implanted in the parts by the divine providence of the Universal Artisan in order that they should unite with one another in their oneness and wholeness and come together in the form of a Globe. It is believable that this affect is present in the Sun, Moon and the other bright planets and through its efficacy they remain in the Spherical figure in which they are visible, though they nevertheless accomplish their circular movements in many different ways.[1]

It is quite an analogous conception that we encounter in William Gilbert: he does not explain gravity by magnetic attraction – the magnetic virtue of the earth explains its rotation – but by the presence in each of the cosmic globes – the earth, the moon, the sun, and the planets – of particular and proper "forms" that make their parts come together (*coacervatio* and *coitio*), and parts separated from the whole tend toward their whole, terrestrial to the earth, lunar to the moon, solar to the sun.[2]

As for Kepler, he shares Copernicus' and Gilbert's conviction that gravitational forces, properly so called, are particular to each of the celestial bodies; the planets do not attract each other, nor does the sun, in this sense, attract them; there is no universal gravitation. On the other hand (*a*) he stresses the active character of the gravitational attraction which he interprets as being analogous to the magnetic one (sometimes he calls it "magnetic") and (*b*) he asserts that this mutual gravitational attraction takes place between the

---

[1] *De revolutionibus orbium coelestium* (Thorn, 1873), lib. I, cap. 9, p. 24.

[2] W. Gilbert, *De magnete, magneticisque corporibus et de magno magnete tellure physiologia nova* (London, 1600), pp. 65, 225, 227; *De mundo nostro sublunari philosophia nova* (Amsterdam, 1651), pp. 115 sq.

earth and the moon because of their fundamental similarity, so that the attractive virtue of the moon reaches as far as the earth (and thus causes the tides) and that of the earth even much farther than the moon. Thus he writes:

A mathematical point, be it the center of the world or not, cannot move heavy bodies, either effectively or objectively, so that they approach it . . . It is impossible that the [natural] form of a body, moving its body, should seek a mathematical point, or the center of the world . . . Thus the common theory of gravity appears to be false . . . As for the true theory of gravity, it is based upon these axioms: all corporeal substance insofar as it is corporeal is apt to remain at rest at any place in which it is placed alone, outside of the virtue of a cognate body . . . Gravity is a mutual corporeal affection of cognate bodies toward their reunion or conjunction (of a similar kind is also the magnetic faculty) such that the Earth drags [*trahat*] the stone much more than the stone tends toward the Earth.

Heavy bodies (even if we place the Earth in the center of the world) do not move toward the center of the world as to the center of the world, but toward the center of a cognate round body, that is, the Earth. Thus, wherever the Earth be placed, or wherever it should transport itself by its animal [vital] faculty, always the heavy bodies will move toward it. If the Earth were not spherical, heavy bodies would not move from everywhere toward the central point of the Earth, but would move from divers directions toward divers points.

If two stones were placed in a certain place of the world, near each other and outside the orb of the virtue of a third cognate body, these stones, in a manner similar to two magnetic bodies, would meet in an intermediate place, each nearing the other by an interval proportional to the bulk [*moles*] of the other.

If the Moon and the Earth were not retained each in its circuit by an animal [vital] force, or by some other, equivalent, the Earth would ascend toward the Moon by a fifty-fourth part of the interval [separating them], and the Moon would descend by fifty-three parts, or about, of this interval; and there they would meet; provided, however, that their substance is of the same density.[1]

In this case, indeed, the mass (*moles*) of the earth would be about fifty-three times that of the moon, and it will attract the moon fifty-three times as strongly as it will be attracted by it. This because, as Kepler informed his friend Fabricius, "gravity is a magnetic force that reunites similar [bodies], which is the same in a large and a small body, is divided according to the *moles* of the bodies, and receives the same dimensions as these."[2]

[1] *Astronomia nova*, Introductio, *Opera omnia*, ed. Frisch, III, 151; *Gesammelte Schriften*, ed. M. Caspar, III, 24 sq.
[2] Letter of 10 November 1608, *Opera omnia*, III, 459; *Gesammelte Schriften*, XVI, 193 sq.

How does this "attraction" act? Kepler, of course, does not know; but in the letter to Fabricius just quoted, discussing the traditional arguments against the motion of the earth revived by Tycho Brahe (a body thrown upward would not fall on the same place, and so forth), he suggests an image,[1] which, perhaps, is more than an image, as he also makes use of it in the *Epitome*: bodies do not "lag behind" the rotating Earth because it drags them with it by the force of gravity, as if they were attached to it by innumerable chains or sinews. Indeed, "if there were no such chains or sinews stretched the stone would remain in its place and not follow the motion of the Earth."[2] But there are; or at least gravity acts as if there were. Thus he tells us in the *Epitome astronomiae Copernicanae*:

Heavy bodies seek the body of Earth as such and are sought by it; therefore they will move more strongly toward the parts of the Earth that are nearer, than toward those that are farther away . . . just as if they were attached to the parts above, which they are by the very perpendicular and also by infinite oblique lines or sinews, less strong than this [perpendicular] that all of them contract in themselves.[3]

[1] *Opera omnia*, III, 458; *Gesammelte Schriften*, XVI, 196.
[2] *Opera omnia*, III, 461; *Gesammelte Schriften*, XVI, 197.
[3] *Epitome astronomiae Copernicanae*, lib. I, pars V; *Opera omnia*, VII, 181; *Gesammelte Schriften*, VII, 96.

Gassendi on Attraction and Gravity

Gassendi was a not very good physicist, a bad mathematician – he did not understand Galileo's deduction of the law of falling bodies and wanted to supplement the action of gravity by that of a pressure of the air – and a rather second-rate philosopher. Yet, in his own time, and even through the whole seventeenth century, he was both very famous and very influential; even Newton speaks about him with great favor and it may be[1] that he was influenced by him. Moreover, from the point of view of the history of science he has the merit of having, in a most effective and spectacular way, in a series of experiments performed in the harbor of Marseille on a galley that the governor of the province, the Count d'Allais, put at his disposal (in 1641), demonstrated the truth of the assertion of Galileo (and Bruno) that a stone, or a bullet, let fall from the mast of a moving ship will fall at the foot of the mast, and not lag behind. He was not the first to make this experiment;[2] yet he was the first to make it publicly and to describe it, in his *De motu impresso a motore translato* (Paris, 1641); he has also the great merit of having been able to go beyond Galileo in freeing himself from the spell of circularity and to give, in the same *De motu*, a correct formulation of the principle of inertia.[3] As I have shown elsewhere,[4] and as we shall see,[5] it was because of his conception of gravity as an effect of attraction that he was able to do it. As for this conception he obviously formed it under the joint influence of Copernicus and Kepler, though he modified both of them by an admixture of the notion of *effluvia*.

Thus, having explained that attraction is not very different from *impulsus*, since "to attract is nothing else than to push (*impellere*) something toward oneself by an incurved instrument,"[6] while this

---

[1] See *supra*, p. 85, n. 4.
[2] A. Koyré, "Gassendi savant," *Actes du Congrès du Tricentenaire de Gassendi* (Paris, 1957).
[3] See *supra*, p. 68.
[4] *Études galiléennes* (Paris: Hermann, 1939), part III.
[5] See *infra*, Appendix I.
[6] *De motu*, ep. I, cap. XVII, p. 68.

pushing implies the pulling of that instrument, he tells us that he considers

gravity, which is in the very parts of the Earth, and in the terrestrial bodies, to be not so much an innate force [*vis insita*], as a force impressed by the attraction of the Earth; indeed, we can understand it from the here-adjoined example of the magnet: let us take and hold in the hand a small plate of iron of some ounces; if then a most powerful magnet should be put under the hand, we would experience a weight no longer of ounces, but of several pounds. And because we will have to admit that this weight is not so much innate [*insitum*] to the iron, as impressed [in it] by the attraction of the magnet placed under the hand; thus also where we deal with the weight or the gravity of a stone or of another terrestrial body, we can understand that this gravity is in this kind of body not so much from itself [its own nature] as from the attraction of Earth that is below it.[1]

How does this "attraction" act? Gassendi, taking Kepler's image of chains, strings, or sinews as expressing the literal truth of the matter, assumes that each particle of the heavy body is linked with the earth by thin strings that pull it toward it. Which, by the way, makes clear the cause of the difference in weight of small and large bodies – more particles, more strings – and explains, at the same time, why small and large bodies fall to the ground in the same time: the heavier one is pulled down with a force proportional to the *moles*, that is, the number of particles, it includes, and it resists this pull in the same proportion:

Thus it happens, that if two stones or two globes [made] of the same material, for instance, of lead, the one small and the other very large, were simultaneously let fall from the same altitude, they will reach the Earth at the same moment—and with a not lesser speed, the small one, though it should be not heavier than one ounce, and the large one, though it [should weigh] a hundred or more pounds; it is evident that the large one is attracted by a greater number of small strings, and that there are more particles that attract it; so that there results therefrom a proportion between the force and the mass [*moles*] and from both of them [the force and the mass] results in both cases [a force] sufficient for the accomplishment of the motion in the same time. Most astonishing: if the globes were of different material, for instance the one of lead and the other of wood, the one will reach the Earth hardly later than the other, that is the wooden than the leaden; for the proportion will take place in the same manner, as long as to the same number of particles will be attached the same number of strings.[2]

How far does this attractive power reach? Very far, possibly to the

[1] *Ibid.*, ep. II, cap. VIII, p. 116. [2] *Ibid.*, ep. I, cap. XV, p. 61.

planets;[1] but, assuming that the attraction is produced by the magnetic rays emanating from the earth, the bodies in the region of the planets will be drawn much less strongly, because in these regions the density and the number of these rays will decrease with the distance. For the same reason it will not extend to the fixed stars, as no rays, or hardly any, will reach so far: "For, if the cause [of the fall] be the attraction produced by the magnetic rays, as these rays are so much rarer and become so much lesser in number as the distance from the Earth increases, it may be that they pull the globe from the region of the Planets, but not so strongly; but not from the region of the fixes."[2]

Strangely enough, or perhaps characteristically for Gassendi, from these considerations he does not draw the conclusion that bodies falling to the earth from the region of the planets will move, at least at the beginning, much more slowly than they do on earth, and that, from the region of the fixed stars, they will not come down at all. Quite the contrary; he proceeds to the determination of the incredible speed with which bodies would move if we admitted that they will fall to the earth from everywhere. In this case, he says, they will start with the velocity that they have here, and increase it gradually, as here, and will come from the moon in two and a half hours, from the sun in less than eleven and a quarter hours, and from the fixed stars in one day, eleven and a quarter hours.

Gassendi's conception of gravity as strings pulling bodies toward the earth – a rather naïve one, but after all not very much more so than that of Faraday's lines of force – entails a rather interesting and unexpected consequence: for him no more than for Descartes is there an action through the void. In order that a body be attracted by, or tend toward, another – for instance, a heavy body by the earth – something, some kind of *effluvium* from the attracting one, must reach the attracted. Indeed, let us

conceive a stone in those imaginary spaces that are extended beyond this world, and in which God could create other worlds; do you think that, at the very moment that it [the stone] would be formed there, it would fly towards the Earth and not, rather, remain unmoved where it was first placed, as if, so to say, it had no *up*, nor *down* where it should tend and wherefrom it should withdraw?

But if you think that it will come here, imagine that not only the Earth

---

[1] *Syntagma philosophicum physicae*, sec. I, lib. V, cap. III, p. 352; *Opera omnia* (Lyons, 1657), vol. I.
[2] *Syntagma*, sec. I, lib. V, cap. III, p. 352.

but the whole world is reduced to nothing, and that these spaces are completely empty as [they were] before God created the world; then, indeed, as there will be no center, all the spaces will be similar; it is obvious that the stone will not come here, but will remain motionless in its place. Now let the world, and in it the Earth be put back again: will the stone immediately drive here? If you say that it will, it is necessary [to admit] that the Earth will be felt by the stone, and therefore the Earth must transmit to it a certain force, and send out the corpuscles, by which it gives to it an impression of itself, in order, so to say, to announce to it that it [the Earth] is restored in being and put back in the same place. How, otherwise, could you understand that the stone should tend towards the Earth?[1]

It is difficult to tell whether these "particles" that reach the body "excite" it and make it "tend" or "drive" toward the earth, or whether they build the "string" that pulls it. Probably both. Why not? After all, even Kepler speaks about bodies "seeking" the earth; and do not magnets that pull small bodies toward them move themselves toward the large ones? In any case,

if some space of the air that surrounds it should, by God, be made completely void, so that neither from the Earth, nor from elsewhere could anything penetrate it: would a stone placed in it move toward the Earth, or its center? Assuredly not more than [the stone] placed in the ultramundial spaces; because for this stone, which would have no communication whatever either with the Earth or with any other thing in the world, it would be the same as if the world, and the Earth, or the center were not and as if nothing whatever existed.[2]

[1] *De motu*, ep. I, cap. XV, p. 59.
[2] *Ibid.*, ep. I, cap. XV, p. 60. On Gassendi, see B. Rochot, *Les Travaux de Gassendi sur Épicure et l'atomisme* (Paris: Vrin, 1944), and of course K. Lasswitz, *Geschichte der Atomistik* (Hamburg and Leipzig, 1890), vol. II.

Hooke on Gravitational Attraction

In May 1666, Hooke presented to the Royal Society "a paper . . . concerning the inflexion of a direct motion into a curve by a supervening attractive principle," in which, curiously enough, he devises, and rejects, a possible explanation of gravitational attraction by aetheric pressure, quite analogous to that which Newton formulated fifty years later in Query XXI of his English *Opticks* of 1717:[1]

I have often wondered, why the planets should move about the sun according to *Copernicus'* supposition, being not included in any solid orbs (which the ancients possibly for this reason might embrace) nor tied to it, as their centre, by any visible strings; and neither depart from it beyond such a degree, nor yet move in a straight line, as all bodies, that have but one single impulse, ought to do: For a solid body, moved in a fluid, towards any part (unless it be protruded aside by some near impulse, or be impeded in that motion by some other obviating body; or that the medium, through which it is moved, be supposed not equally penetrable every way) must preserve in its motion in a right line, and neither deflect this way nor that way from it. But all the celestial bodies, being regular solid bodies, and moved in a fluid, and yet moved in circular or elliptical lines, and not straight, must have some other cause, besides the first impressed impulse, that must bend their motion into that curve. And for the performance of this effect I cannot imagine any other likely cause besides these two: The first may be from an unequal density of the medium, through which the planetary body is to be moved; that is, if we suppose that part of the medium, which is farthest from the centre, or sun, to be more dense outward, than that which is more near, it will follow, that the direct motion will be always deflected inwards, by the easier yielding of the inward, and the greater resistance of the outward part of that medium. This hath some probabilities attending it; as, that if the ether be somewhat of the nature of the air, 'tis rational that that part, which is nearer the sun, the fountain of heat, should be most rarefied; and consequently that those, which are most remote, should be most dense: But there are other improbabilities, that attend this supposition, which being nothing to my present purpose I shall omit.

But the *second* cause of inflecting a direct motion into a curve may be from an attractive property of the body placed in the centre, whereby it continually endeavours to attract or draw it to itself. For if such a principle

[1] See pp. 160–161.

be supposed, all the phenomena of the planets seem possible to be explained by the common principle of mechanic motions; and possibly the prosecuting this speculation, may give us a true hypothesis of their motion, and from some few observations their motions may be so far brought to a certainty that we may be able to calculate them to the greatest exactness and certainty that can be desired.[1]

Hooke endeavored to "explicate" this inflection by the example of the conical pendulum, stating, however, that in this case "the *conatus* of returning to the centre . . . is greater and greater according as it is farther and farther removed from the centre, which seems to be otherwise in the attraction of the sun." In spite of this very important difference between the law of gravitational attraction and that of the conical pendulum, this latter presented indeed a very good analogy of the planetary motions: its bob described circles, or variously directed ellipses, according to the force of the *impetus* conferred to it:

May 23d. 1666. There was read a Paper of Mr. *Hooke's* explicating the Inflexion of a direct motion into a Curve, by a supervening, attractive Principle, which was order'd to be Register'd. The Discourse contain'd therein is an Introduction to an Experiment to shew that Circular Motion, is compounded of an indeavour by a direct motion by the Tangent, and of another indeavour tending to the Center: To which purpose there was a *Pendulum* fastened to the Roof of the Room with a large wooden Ball of *Lignum Vitae* on the end of it; and it was found, that if the *Impetus* of the indeavour by the Tangent, at the first setting out, was stronger than the indeavour to the Center, there was generated such an Elliptical Motion, whose longest Diameter was parallel to the direct indeavour of the Body at the first Impulse: But if that *Impetus* were weaker than that indeavour to the Center, there was generated such an Elliptical Motion, whose shorter Diameter was parallel to the direct indeavour of the Body in the first point of the Impulse; if both were equal there was made a perfect Circular Motion. There was also made another Experiment, by fastening another Pendulous Body by a short String on the lower part of the Wire, by which the greater weight was suspended, that it might freely make a Circular or Elliptical Motion round the bigger, whilst the bigger mov'd Circularly or Elliptically about the first Center. The intention whereof was to explicate the manner of the Moons motion about the Earth, it appearing evidently thereby, that neither the bigger Ball, which represented the Earth, nor the less which represented the Moon, were mov'd in so perfect a Circle or Ellipsis, as otherwise they would have been, if either of them had been suspended and mov'd singly: But that a certain Point which seem'd to be

---

[1] See Richard Waller, "The Life of Dr. Robert Hooke," in *The Posthumous Works of Robert Hooke* (London, 1705), p. xii; Thomas Birch, *History of the Royal Society* (London, 1757), I, 90 sq.; E. Gunther, *Early Science in Oxford* (Oxford, 1930), VI, 265 sq.

the Center of Gravity of the two Bodies (howsoever posited and consider'd as one) seem'd to be regularly mov'd, in such a Circle or Ellipsis, the two Balls having other peculiar motions in small Epicicles about the said Point.[1]

Hooke rightly concluded therefrom that

by this hypothesis the phenomena of the comets, as well as of the planets, may be solved; and the motions of the secondary as well as of the primary planets. The motions also of the progression of the apsides are very evident, but as for the motion of libration or latitude that cannot be so well made out by this way of pendulum; but by the motion of a wheel upon a point is most easy.[2]

Somewhat later, in his lectures given to the Royal Society at Gresham House in 1670, Hooke wrote:

I shall . . . hereafter explain a system of the world differing in many particulars from any yet known, but answering in all things to the common rules of mechanical motions. This depends upon three suppositions: *First*, That all celestial bodies whatsoever have an attraction or gravitating power towards their own centres, whereby they attract not only their own parts, and keep them from flying from them, as we may observe the Earth to do, but that they also do attract all the other celestial bodies that are within the sphere of their activity, and consequently that not only the Sun and Moon have an influence upon the body and motion of the Earth, and the Earth upon them, but that Mercury, Venus, Mars, Jupiter, and Saturn also, by their attractive powers, have a considerable influence upon its motion, as in the same manner the corresponding attractive power of the Earth hath a considerable influence upon every one of their motions also. The *second* supposition is this, that all bodies whatsoever that are put into a direct and simple motion, will so continue to move forward in a straight line till they are, by some other effectual powers, deflected, and sent into a motion describing a circle, ellipsis, or some other more compounded curve line. The *third* supposition is, that these attractive powers are so much the more powerful in operating by how much the nearer the body wrought upon is to their own centres. Now, what these several degrees are, I have not yet experimentally verified, but it is a notion which, if fully prosecuted, as it ought to be, will mightily assist the astronomers to reduce all the celestial motions to a certain rule, which I doubt will never be done without it. He that understands the nature of the circular pendulum, and of circular motion, will easily understand the whole of this principle, and will know where to find directions in nature for the true stating thereof. This I only hint at present to such as have ability and opportunity of prosecuting this inquiry, and are not wanting of industry for observing and calculating, wishing heartily such may be found, having myself many other things in hand which I would first complete, and therefore cannot so well attend it.

[1] Birch, *History of the Royal Society*, I, 90 sq.
[2] *Ibid.*

But this I durst promise the undertaker, that he will find all the great motions of the world to be influenced by this principle, and that the true understanding thereof will be the true perfection of astronomy.[1]

Hooke was right, of course, in stating that the "true understanding" of the principle of universal attraction would lead to "the true perfection of astronomy"; it is precisely what Newton did in his *Principia*. His explanation, however, of why he does not himself "prosecute" this inquiry, and thus did not himself make "the greatest discovery in nature that ever was made since the world's creation,"[2] sounds rather lame: the truth of the matter is that Hooke did not "understand the nature of the circular pendulum and of circular motion" (something for which we cannot blame him: at that time – 1670 – nobody but Huygens and Newton did) and failed in his unworkable attempts to verify the law of attraction experimentally. Still it is rather surprising that he not only published in 1674 (that is, after the publication in 1673 of Huygens's *Horologium oscillatorium*, where the nature of the circular pendulum and of circular motion was stated for the first time) his lectures of 1670 but even let them be included, without alteration, in the *Lectiones Cutlerianae* in 1679. All the more so as it is well known that some time in the late seventies (certainly long after the perusal of Huygens's *Horologium oscillatorium* of 1673, which contained the formulation of the law of centrifugal force that he was unable to deduce himself), Hooke – as also Halley and Wren – discovered the inverse-square law of gravitational attraction and even mentioned it in a letter to Newton of 6 January 1680. Yet he could not deduce from it the elliptical trajectory of the planets (*a*) because he lacked sufficient mathematical ability and (*b*) because he accepted as correct Kepler's erroneous assumption that the speed of a planet was, in each point of the trajectory, inversely proportional to its distance from the sun. This latter point seems to me to invalidate his claims to the discovery of the law of universal gravitation before Newton.[3] Curiously enough, it has been missed by the latest defenders of Hooke's priority rights.[4] It is, how-

---

[1] *An Attempt to prove the motion of the Earth by Observation* (London, 1674), pp. 27 sq., republished in the *Lectiones Cutlerianae* (London, 1679), and in Gunther, *Early Science in Oxford*, vol. VIII.

[2] Letter of T. Aubrey to Antony Wood, 15 September 1689; see Hooke's *Diary* in Gunther, *Early Science in Oxford*, VII, 714.

[3] A. Koyré, "An Unpublished Letter of Robert Hooke to Isaac Newton," *infra*, Chapter V.

[4] Miss D. Patterson, "Hooke's Gravitation Theory," *Isis 40* (1949), 327–341; *41* (1950), 32–45; Johs. Lohne, "Hooke versus Newton," *Centaurus 7* (1960), 6–52.

ever, interesting to note that in 1680 Hooke devised an extremely ingenious mechanical theory of gravitational attraction, which he
explained by the action of quick vibrations of the aether on the bodies
immersed in it.

Suppose then that there is in the Ball of the Earth such a Motion, as I,
for distinction sake, will call a *Globular Motion*, whereby all the Parts
thereof have a Vibration towards and fromwards the Center, or of Expansion and Contraction; and that this vibrative Motion is very short and very
quick, as it is in all very hard and very compact Bodies: That this vibrative
Motion does communicate or produce a Motion in a certain Part of the
Aether, which is interspersed between these solid vibrating Parts; which
communicated Motion does cause this interspersed Fluid to vibrate every
way in *Orbem*, from and towards the Center, in Lines radiating from the
same. By which radiating Vibration of this exceeding Fluid, and yet exceeding dense, Matter, not only all the Parts of the Earth are carried or forced
down towards the Center; but the Motion being continued into the Aether,
interspersed between the Air and other kinds of Fluids, it causeth those
also to have a tendency towards the Center; and much more any sensible
Body whatsoever, that is anywhere placed in the Air, or above it, though at
a vast Distance; which Distance I shall afterwards determine, and shew
with what proportioned Power it acts upon Bodies at all Distances both
without and within the Earth: For this Power propagated, as I shall then
shew, does continually diminish according as the Orb of Propagation does
continually increase, as we find the Propagations of the *Media* of Light
and Sound also to do; as also the Propagation of Undulation upon the
Superficies of Water. And from hence I conceive the Power thereof to be
always reciprocal to the *Area* or Superficies of the Orb of Propagation, that
is duplicate of the Distance; as will plainly follow and appear from the consideration of the Nature thereof, and will hereafter be more plainly evinced
by the Effects it causes at such several Distances.[1]

Though Hooke's role in the history of science is better understood
today than it was in the eighteenth and nineteenth centuries,[2] and
though his works and diaries have been published and republished,[3]
he still has not received the full monographical treatment to which
he is doubtless entitled.[4]

[1] "Of Comets and Gravity," *Posthumous Works*, pp. 184 sq.
[2] E. N. da C. Andrade, "Robert Hooke," *Proceedings of the Royal Society (London
[A] 201* (1950), 439–473.
[3] Gunther, *Early Science in Oxford*, vols. V-VIII, X, XIII; and *The Diary of
Robert Hooke, 1672–1680*, ed. H. Robinson and W. Adams (London: Taylor and
Francis, 1935).
[4] For the literature on Hooke, see Lohne, cited on p. 183, n. 4; for his "vibrational"
theory of gravitation, see J. Zennek, "Gravitation", *Encyclopädie der mathematischen
Wissenschaften* (Leipzig, 1903–1921), Bd. V, *Physik*.

Gassendi and Horizontal Motion

As I have mentioned,[1] it is his belief in attraction, that is, his explanation of gravity by attraction, that enables Gassendi to go beyond Galileo and not only to free himself from the spell of circularity, but also to deny the privileged character of "horizontal" and "vertical" ("up and down") directions and to assert the equivalence of all of these.

Gassendi starts by suggesting that though, of course, nothing violent can be perpetual, this famous dictum does not apply to horizontal motion;[2] quite the contrary: horizontal motion could and even should be considered a natural motion, and this not only in the case in which the earth turns on its axis and stones and other terrestrial objects participate in this motion, but also if it stood still. Horizontal motion is, as a matter of fact, a circular one, a motion that follows the surface of the earth, and thus does not change its distance from the center: it moves neither "up" nor "down." Let us imagine, continues Gassendi, a perfectly round ball placed on a horizontal surface – that is, the surface of the earth – that we assume to be perfectly smooth and polished (an example used already by Nicolaus of Cusa and Galileo):[3] is it not clear that it will never cease to move, and will never slow down or accelerate its motion, as we have supposed all external obstacles removed from its path and as at every instant of its motion it will be in the same position in respect to the surface upon, and to the center around, which it moves?

A body thrown horizontally in the air will not, of course, behave in this manner, because with its horizontal motion will be admixed a perpendicular one; in other words, because of its gravity, it will go down and describe a curve.

Galileo, who still thought of gravity as pertaining to the body itself, could not go further: he could not make an abstraction from it; he needed therefore a surface – be it spherical as in the *Dialogo*

---

[1] *Supra*, p. 176.
[2] *De motu impresso a motore translato*, cap. X, pp. 38 sq.
[3] A. Koyré, *Études galiléennes* (Paris: Hermann, 1939), part III, pp. 148, 149.

or truly horizontal, that is, plane, as in the *Discorsi* – that had to support the bodies in order to prevent them from going "down."

Gassendi, however, for whom gravity was only an effect of an "attraction," that is, of a force external to the body, could very well make an abstraction from it: in order to deprive a body of its gravity he had only to suppress (in thought or in imagination) all other bodies that could act upon it, and place it in the void, for instance, in the imaginary spaces that extend *ad infinitum* beyond the world.[1] Vice versa, in order to explain the real behavior of heavy bodies, that is, their not continuing their motion in a horizontal line, in other words, the admixture of the perpendicular motion that incurves it toward the earth, "it is necessary, besides the impellent cause, to recur to an attracting one which accomplishes this task. Indeed, what else is this power than that which pertains to the whole Earth and can be called magnetic?"[2] But in the imaginary spaces the body will not be subjected to this attraction; moreover, there will be no center around which to turn; the "horizontal" motion will therefore become rectilinear and the body, once put in motion, will move forever, in the same direction and with the same speed.

You ask me, what will happen to that body which I assumed can be conceived [to exist] in these void spaces, if, removed from rest, it should be impelled by a certain force? I answer that it is probable that it will move uniformly and incessantly; and that slowly or quickly according to whether a small or a great impetus will be impressed upon it. As for the argument, I take it from the uniformity of the horizontal motion already explained. Indeed this latter seems not to cease but for the admixion of the perpendicular motion; so that, as in the void spaces there is no admixion of the perpendicular motion, in whatever direction the motion should begin, it would be akin to the horizontal, and will neither accelerate, nor slow down, and therefore, will never cease.[3]

Thus, in the imaginary void spaces, motion is conserved. But not only there: as a matter of fact, it is conserved on this very earth. In order to demonstrate it, Gassendi gives a careful description and analysis of the pendular motion, of which, following Galileo, he asserts the perfect isochronism, and concludes:

All that has no other aim than to make us understand that motion impressed [on a body] through void space where nothing either attracts, or resists, will be uniform, and perpetual; and that, therefrom, we conclude

---

[1] See *supra*, p. 178.
[2] *De motu*, ep. I, cap. XIII, p. 46.
[3] *Ibid.*, ep. I, cap. XVI, pp. 62 sq.

that all motion that is impressed on a body is in itself of that kind; so that in whatever direction you throw a stone, if you suppose that, at the moment in which it leaves the hand, by divine power, everything besides this stone is reduced to nothing, it would result that the stone will continue its motion perpetually and in the same direction in which the hand has directed it. And if it does not do so [in fact], it seems that the cause is the admixion of the perpendicular motion which intervenes because of the attraction of the Earth, which makes it deviate from its path (and does not cease until it arrives at the Earth), just as iron scrapings thrown near a magnet do not move in a straight line but are deviated toward the magnet.[1]

[1] *Ibid.*, ep. I, cap. XVI, pp. 69 sq.

The State of Motion and the State of Rest

I would like to point out that the expressions "state of motion" and "state of rest" are used neither by Huygens, nor by Wallis, nor even by Hooke. Thus Huygens, in his *De motu corporum ex percussione*[1] (published only posthumously in 1703, but written in 1656), states as Hypothesis I: "A body in motion, when it does not encounter any obstacle, tends to move perpetually with the same speed and in a straight line"; and in the *Horologium oscillatorium* of 1673, Hypothesis I asserts: "If there were no gravity, and the air did not oppose the motion of bodies, any body, having once started its motion, would continue it with a uniform speed in a straight line."[2]

Wallis, as a matter of fact, does not even give a special formulation of the principle of inertia. He states, at the very beginning of his *De motu*, that

under motion we understand local motion; though logicians deal with several kinds of motion, such as generation, augmentation, alteration, etc. (I do not want to discuss here whether all these can be reduced to the local motion); we shall take here *Motus* in its more common acceptance as meaning *local motion* that is usually called φορά, or *latio*.[3]

Having then explained that he will call *momentum* that which produces motion and *impedimentum* that which opposes it, that if the *momentum* is stronger than the *impedimentum* motion will be produced, or accelerated, and contrariwise, retarded or arrested if the *impedimentum* is stronger than the *momentum*, and that, if the *momentum* and the *impedimentum* are of equal strength (*si aequipollent*) motion will neither be produced nor arrested, but that whatever was there before, whether motion or rest, will persevere,[4] he says in a *scholium*:

It seems that the last part of this proposition, that is, that motion once begun (provided no obstacle be posited) will persevere by its own force

[1] Huygens, *Oeuvres complètes*, XVI, 30.
[2] Pars II, *De descensu gravium et motu eorum in cycloide, ibid.*, XVII, 125.
[3] *Mechanica, sive tractatus de motu geometricus* (London, 1670), pars I, cap. I, def. II, p. 2.
[4] *Ibid.*, pars I, cap. II, prop. XI, p. 18.

(spontaneously) without a motor adjoined, no less than the already existing rest (if no motor be joined), was postulated by Galileo, Descartes, Gassendi, and others; and herefrom they drew conclusions of no small importance. But I do not remember any one that has seen it demonstrated.[1]

However, he later says, "Motion, if there be no *impedimentum*, will persevere with the same speed, even if there were no cause of motion joined to it."[2] Hooke[3] makes only the "supposition" "that all bodies whatsoever that are put into a direct and simple motion will so continue to move forward in a straight line," and so forth.[4]

As for Newton, in his *Waste Book* of 1664 he writes: "*Ax. 2.* A quantity will always move in the same straight line (nor changing the determination or celerity of its motion) unless some external cause divert it." He states, however, following Descartes, that "everything perseveres in its actual state unless disturbed by some external cause."[5]

In the *De gravitate et aequipondio fluidorum*, Newton uses the Cartesian formula in his definition of force (*vis*) and *inertia*:

Def. V. Force is the causal principle of motion and rest. And it is either an external principle, which generates or destroys or in some way changes the motion impressed on any body, or it is an internal principle by which the existing motion or rest is conserved in a body, and by which any being endeavours to persevere in its state and opposed resistance . . .

Def. VIII. Inertia is the internal force of a body, so that its state cannot be easily changed by an externally applied force.[6]

In the *Propositiones de motu* sent to the Royal Society in 1684, he states that he will call inherent or innate force the force owing to which a body tends to persevere in its rectilinear motion (*vim corporis, seu corpori insitam, qua id conatur perseverare in motu suo*

---

[1] *Ibid.*, pars I, cap. I, prop. XI, *scholium*, p. 19.

[2] *Ibid.*, pars III, cap. X, p. 645, where he refers to pars I, cap. I, prop. XI.

[3] See *supra*, p. 182.

[4] *Mechanica*, pars III, cap. X, p. 645.

[5] Cambridge University Library MS. Add. 4004. See J. W. Herivel, "Sur les premières recherches de Newton en dynamique," *Revue d'Histoire des Sciences 15* (1962), 110.

[6] A. R. Hall and M. B. Hall, editors, *A Selection from the Unpublished Scientific Papers of Sir Isaac Newton in the Portsmouth Collection, Cambridge University Library* (Cambridge, England: Cambridge University Press, 1962), p. 114:

"Def 5. Vis est motus et quietis causale principium. Estque vel externum quod in aliquod corpus impressum motum ejus vel generat vel destruit, vel aliquo saltem modo mutat, vel est internum principium quo motus vel quies corpori indita conservatur, et quodlibet ens in suo statu perseverare conatur & impeditum reluctatur . . .

"Def 8. Inertia est vis interna corporis ne status ejus externa vi illata facile mutetur."

secundum lineam rectam)[1] and that every body by the innate force alone advances *in infinitum* along a straight line provided nothing external hinders it (*corpus omne sola vi insita uniformiter secundum lineam rectam in infinitum progredi, nisi aliquid extrinsecus impediat*).[2]

In the *De motu sphaericorum corporum in fluidis*,[3] which must be somewhat later than the *Propositiones de motu* (its beginning – the definitions – is identical with that of the *Propositiones de motu*), MSS *B* and *C* have Hypothesis I: "By the innate force alone the body moves uniformly in a straight line perpetually if nothing hinders it (*sola vi insita corpus uniformiter in linea recta semper pergere si nil impediat*). But Hypothesis II introduces the term "state of motion or rest": "The changing of the state of motion or rest is proportional to the impressed force and occurs in the straight line that the [said] force impresses." MS *D* has the same text as *B* and *C*, but changes *hypothesis* into *lex*:

Law I: A body always continues uniformly in a straight line by its innate force alone if nothing impedes it.
Law II: Change in the state of motion or rest is proportional to the impressed force and occurs along the right line in which that force is impressed.[4]

Finally, the *De motu corporum*, which I believe to be still later, has the full formula of the *Principia*:

Def. 3: The innate force of matter is the power to resist, by which the body, so far as in it is, perseveres in its state either of being at rest or moving uniformly in a straight line. And it is proportional to its body and does not differ at all from the *inertia* of the mass, but in the manner of our conception. And the body exercises this force only in the changes of its state produced by an external force impressed upon it. And in its action the Resistance and *Impetus* are only respectively distinct from each other in this respect: it is *Resistance* in so far as the body opposed the impressed force, *Impetus* in so far as a body yielding with difficulty endeavours to change the state of the other body. The vulgar, moreover, attribute resistance to [bodies] at rest, and *impetus* to the moving [ones]; but motion and rest, as they are commonly conceived, are only respectively distinct from

---

[1] Def. II. See W. W. Rouse Ball, *An Essay on Newton's Principia* (Cambridge, 1892), pp. 35 sq.
[2] Hypothesis II, *ibid.*, pp. 36.
[3] *Unpublished Scientific Papers*, pp. 243 sq.
[4] *Ibid.*, p. 243:
"*Lex I: Sola vi insita corpus uniformiter in linea recta semper pergere si nil impediat,*
"*Lex II: Mutationem status movendi vel quiescendi proportionalem esse vi impressae et fieri secundum lineam rectam qua vis illa imprimitur.*"

each other; nor do those [bodies] truly rest that are commonly regarded as at rest.[1]

[1] MS *A*, "De motu corporum," *ibid.*, pp. 239 sq.:

"3. *Materiae vis insita* est potentia resistendi qua corpus unumquodque quantum in se est perseverat in statu suo vel quiescendi vel movendi uniformiter in directum. Estque corpori suo proportionalis, neque differt quicquam ab *inertia* massae nisi in modo conceptus nostri. Exercet vero corpus hanc vim solummodo in mutatione status sui facta per vim aliam in se impressam estque Exercitium ejus *Resistentia* et *Impetus* respectu solo ab invicem distincti: Resistentia quatenus corpus reluctatur vi impressae, *Impetus* quatenus corpus difficulter cedendo conatur mutare statum corporis alterius. Vulgus insuper resistentiam quiescentibus & impetum moventibus tribuit: sed motus et quies ut vulgo concipiuntur respectu solo distinguuntur ab invicem: neque vere quiescunt quae vulgo tanquam quiescentia spectantur."

Descartes on the Infinite and the Indefinite

Though Giordano Bruno[1] had stated that the concept of the actual infinite (*in actu*) is perfectly accessible to human *intellect* (not, however, to human senses or imagination), it was left to Descartes to assert not only that this concept is a positive one, whereas that of finitude is negative (and not vice versa), but also that the concept of the infinite not only is accessible but is even the *first* one that is given to the human mind, which can conceive finitude only by the negation of it. Accordingly, in contradistinction to the traditional teaching which places the idea of God beyond the reach of human intelligence (whence the rejection of Saint Anselm's proof by Saint Thomas and the Thomistic scholastics), Descartes asserts that the idea of God as the absolutely, that is, infinitely, perfect being (*ens infinitum et infinite perfectum*) is the very first, innate, idea of the human mind, prior even to that of self. Indeed, I cannot conceive myself, that is, a finite thought, if not in opposition to the idea of infinite thought, that is, of God!

I must not think that I do not perceive the infinite by a true idea, but only by the negation of the finite, as I perceive rest and darkness by the negation of motion and light; but on the contrary I obviously understand that there is more reality in the infinite substance than in a finite one, and therefore in a certain manner the perception of the infinite is prior in me to [that of] the finite, that is of God to that of myself. By what reason, indeed, could I understand that I doubt, that I desire, that is, that I am lacking something, and that I am not wholly perfect, if I had no idea of a perfect being by comparison to which I recognize my defects?[2]

In a letter to Clerselier, 23 April 1649, Descartes says:

I never use the word infinite [*infini*] in order to signify only not having an end, which is negative, and to which I have applied the word indefinite, but to signify a real thing which is incomparably greater than all those

---

[1] *De l'infinito universo et mondi* (Venice [actually London], 1584); see Mrs. D. W. Singer's English translation, *On the Infinite Universe and the Worlds*, adjoined to her *Giordano Bruno, His Life and Thought* (New York: Abelard-Schuman, 1950), First Dialogue, pp. 250 sq.

[2] See *Meditationes*, III, in *Oeuvres*, VII, 45.

that have an end. The notion that I have of the infinite is in me before that of the finite because, from that alone that I conceive *being* or *that which is* without thinking whether it is finite or infinite, it is the infinite being that I conceive; but, in order that I could conceive a finite being, it is necessary that I remove something from this general notion of being, which, consequently, must precede.[1]

Descartes's position concerning the infinite has often been misunderstood by historians, who have even deemed it to be inconsistent. Descartes, on the one hand, firmly maintains the priority of the concept of the infinite, and, accordingly, its perfect validity, asserting that there is no contradiction in the idea of an infinite number and that matter not only is indefinitely divisible (which implies the impossibility of atoms) but is even actually divided into an infinite number of parts; and, on the other hand, he just as firmly refuses to deal with problems concerning the composition of the continuum or to answer questions such as whether the infinite number is odd or even, whether there are infinities larger or smaller than others, and so on.[2] This because, though it is a *clear* and therefore *true* idea, it is however not a *distinct* one, and even cannot be distinct for finite minds. This being so:

We have to observe two things carefully: the first being that we always keep before our eyes that God's power and goodness are infinite, in order that this should make us understand that we must not fear to fail in imagining His works too great, too beautiful, or too perfect; but that, on the contrary, we can fail if we suppose in them any boundaries or limits of which we have no certain knowledge ... We must always keep before our eyes that the capacity of our mind is very mediocre, and that we must not be so presumptuous as it seems we would be if we supposed that the universe had any limits, without being assured of it by divine revelation or, at least, by very evident natural reasons; because it would [mean] that we want our thoughts to be able to imagine something beyond that to which God's power has extended itself in creating the world.[3]

It may be, of course, that, besides the systematic reasons for not applying the term "infinite" to the world, Descartes had also "tactical" ones. Thus, answering a letter of Chanut (11 May 1647), who informs him about a "doubt" of Queen Christina of Sweden concerning the compatibility of the "hypothesis" of an infinite world with the Christian religion, Descartes writes:

[1] *Oeuvres*, V, p. 356.
[2] *Principia philosophiae*, pars I, Sec. 26, in *Oeuvres*, IX, 36.
[3] *Ibid.*, pars III, Secs. 1 and 2; pp. 80 sq. and 103 sq.

I remember that the Cardinal of Cusa and several other Doctors have supposed the world infinite, without having ever been reproved by the Church on this subject; on the contrary, it is believed that to conceive His works very great is to honor God. And my opinion is less difficult to receive than theirs; for I do not say that the world is *infinite*, but *indefinite*. In which there is a rather remarkable difference; for [in order] to say that a thing is infinite, one has to have some reason which makes it known [to be] such, and this can be the case concerning God alone; but for saying that it is indefinite, it is sufficient not to have any reason by which one could prove that it has limits. Thus it seems to me that one cannot prove, nor even conceive, that there should be limits to the matter of which the world is composed. Not having thus any reason for proving, and even being unable to conceive, that the world has limits, I call it indefinite. But I cannot deny . . . that it may have some that are known by God, though they are incomprehensible to me, and that is why I do not say absolutely that it is *infinite*.[1]

[1] *Oeuvres*, V, 19 sq.

God and the Infinite

It is well known that in contradistinction to the Greek philosophical tradition in which – at least usually and mostly – the concept of the infinite – ἄπειρων – means imperfection, indetermination, lack (privation) of form, in the Christian one this concept acquires a positive meaning denoting the highest perfection of God, who in his essence and being surpasses all limitation and finitude. Or, as St. Thomas explains it, this concept is to be understood *negative et non privative*. Accordingly, the traditional division of being (*divisio entis*) into *necessarium* and *contingens*, *creans* and *creatum*, is closely paralleled by that of the *ens* into *finitum* and *infinitum*, the infinity being the privilege of God's perfection, and the finiteness the unavoidable *defectum* of the necessarily imperfect creature. The idea of an infinite creature is therefore felt to be a *contradictio in adjecto* and the question whether God could have made an infinite creature usually receives a negative answer, which, moreover, is not considered as imposing a limitation upon God's (infinite) creative power: the impossible is not a limit. It is not God who, so to say, is unable to make an infinite creature, it is the creature (*ens creatum*) that is unable to sustain its infinitization. Even those who, like St. Thomas, admitted the possibility of an actually infinite multitude of (finite) things and also considered that the ontological structure of the created being (*ens creatum*) was not incompatible with a certain kind of successive infinity – thus the world, once created, could be considered as able to exist *in aeternum* and even, creation in time being impossible to demonstrate, as having existed forever[1] – did not assert the possibility of its actual infinity,[2] but maintained its actual finitude. We have to mention, however, that in the wake of the protracted, intensive, and very interesting discussions on the concept of the infinite – in both of its aspects, that is, the infinitely small and the infinitely great – by the philosophers and logicians of the fourteenth century, quite a number of them went far beyond St. Thomas and even Duns Scotus

[1] Thomas Aquinas, *Summa theologiae*, pars I, qu. X, art. 5, *ad* 4.
[2] *Ibid.*, pars I, qu., VII, art. 3.

and, rejecting outright the condemnation of the infinite by Aristotle, accepted unreservedly not only the infinite *in potentia* (which, making a sharper logical analysis of the concept, they called "syncategorematic") but also of the infinite *in actu* (that they called "categorematic"). Thus, for example, François de Meyronne, Jean de Bassols, Robert Holkot, and especially Nicolas Bonnet and Gregorius of Rimini, the last of whom was one of the greatest logicians of the age, asserted the divisibility of the continuum into an actually infinite number of parts, which, moreover, Aristotle's contention notwithstanding, could be and even were, all of them, traversed in any finite movement; they also asserted the possibility – for God – of drawing an actually infinite line, and so forth. They concluded, accordingly, that it was possible for God to produce an actually infinite number of things, for instance of stones, and even to reunite them all in an infinitely large one. The best formulation of this "infinitistic" standpoint is to be found in Gregorius of Rimini, who, discussing the question – "Utrum Deus per infinitam suam potentiam posset producere effectum aliquem infinitum" – affirms that God can produce not only an infinite multiplicity of things, existing at the same time (actual infinity), but also an infinite magnitude as, for instance, a *corpus infinitum* (something that St. Thomas had denied and Kepler will deny), and even raise to infinity, that is, to an infinite intensity, a certain form or quality, such as heat, or charity, whatever that may mean, if it means anything.[1]

It is rather clear that a large part of these discussions about the possibility, for God, of producing an infinite stone or an infinite degree of charity – in contradistinction to those that deal with the composition of the continuum and the eternity of the world – are logico-metaphysical exercises and deal with purely logico-metaphysical possibilities. Indeed, even Gregorius of Rimini did not assert that God had, in fact, done all that he could do; he only maintained that he *could* have done it, though he did not.

It is only with Nicolaus of Cusa that we encounter the idea that God did everything that he could do in order to "explicate" in the world his *infinitas complicata*. Yet though the idea of "Creation"

---

[1] On these medieval discussions see Jean Mair (Johannes Majoris), a late follower of Gregorius of Rimini, *Le Traité de l'infini*, nouvelle édition, avec traduction et notes par Hubert Elie (Paris, 1938); and Pierre Duhem, *Le Système du monde* (Paris, 1956), vol. VII; on the history of the idea of infinity, see Jonas Cohn, *Geschichte des Unendlichkeitsproblems im abendländischen Denken* (Leipzig, 1896; Hildesheim, 1960), and Louis Couturat, *De l'infini mathématique* (Paris, 1896).

may be considered as strongly attenuated with him, he never asserts the infinity of the creature (nothing determinate as such can be infinite: an infinite line is not a line, but infinity; an infinite quantity is not quantity, but infinity, and so on;[1] and he never affirms the infinity of the world (as Descartes mistakenly assumed him to do) but always calls it "interminate" and opposes its limitlessness to the positive infinity of God. And if Giordano Bruno does it, though distinguishing the utterly simple "incorporeal infinitude" of God from the corporeal infinitude of the Universe in which the former becomes explicit, this latter, "the infinite and boundless image" of the Prime Origin,[2] becomes its necessary adjunct and can hardly be called *creatum*.[3]

As for Descartes, his fundamental proof of God's existence from the idea of God – a modification of St. Anselm's argument foreshadowed already by Duns Scotus – is based explicitly upon the necessary connection of infinity and existence: God exists, and exists as *causa sui* in virtue of his infinity, that is, his infinite perfection.[4] But, since at the same time Descartes maintains as strongly as possible the contingent character of the world fully dependent in its being and structure on God's creative will, he has to distinguish, as he does in fact, God's positive and absolute infinity, which implies unity, simplicity, and indivisibility from the mere boundlessness (indefinity) of the world, consistent with multiplicity, divisibility, and change. Thus, for instance, he says:

By an infinite substance I understand a substance having true and rea and actually infinite and immense perfections. This [infinity] is not an accident superadded to the concept of substance, but the very essence of the substance taken absolutely, and not limited (terminated) by any defects; these defects, with respect to the substances, are accidents; but not the infinity or infiniteness.[5]

[1] *De visione Dei*, cap. XIII; on Nicolaus of Cusa see M. de Gandillac, *La Philosophie de Nicolas de Cues* (Paris: Montaigne, 1942).
[2] *De infinito universo e mondi* (Venice [actually London], 1584); see Mrs. D. W. Singer's English translation, *On the Infinite Universe and the Worlds*, adjoined to her *Giordano Bruno, His Life and Thought* (New York: Abelard-Schuman, 1950), First Dialogue, p. 257.
[3] A. O. Lovejoy, *The Great Chain of Being* (Cambridge, Massachusetts: Harvard University Press, 1936; New York, 1960), and A. Koyré, *From the Closed World to the Infinite Universe* (Baltimore: Johns Hopkins Press, 1957).
[4] A. Koyré, *Essai sur l'idée de Dieu et les preuves de son existence chez Descartes* (Paris: Leroux, 1922).
[5] *Meditationes*, III, in *Oeuvres*, VII, 40.

Motion, Space, and Place

Newton's friend Samuel Clarke discussed motion, space, and place in his notes to *Rohault's System of Natural Philosophy*:

The Dispute about the Nature and Definition of *Motion*, amongst the Writers of Philosophy, has always been very perplexed. I suppose, because, not sufficiently attending to the different Senses of an ambiguous Word, they endeavoured to comprehend that in one Definition, which ought to have been very exactly distinguished into its different Parts. That *Motion* (or rather the Effect of Motion) in general, *is a Translation of a Body from one Place to another*, is pretty well agreed amongst them all. But what is meant by *being translated from one place to another* here the Controversy lies and Philosophers differ widely. They who define Motion by comparing the Thing which is moved, not with the Bodies that encompass it, but only with Space which is immoveable and infinite, can never know or understand, whether any Body at all rests, nor what the absolute Celerity of those Bodies that are moved is; for besides, that this whole Globe of the Earth revolves about the Sun, it can never be known whether or no the Center of this whole System, in which all the Bodies relating to us is contained, rests, or is moved uniformly in a streight Line. Again, they who define Motion, by comparing the Thing which is moved, not with infinite Space, but with other Bodies, and those at a very great Distance, these necessarily make some Body the Mark by which all Motion is to be measured, which, whether it self is at rest, or, with respect to Bodies at a still greater distance, is moved, is impossible to be known likewise. Lastly, They who define Motion by comparing the Thing which they say is moved, not with distant Bodies, but only with that Superficies which immediately touches it; it is very weak in them to say, that those Things are truly at rest, which being connected with the Particles of other Bodies, are moved with the greatest Swiftness; as the Globe of the Earth which is incompassed with Air, and revolves about the Sun. And on the contrary, that *they* only can be said to be moved, that with the utmost Force, and Resistance which they can make, can do no more than barely hinder themselves from being carried along with other Bodies, as Fishes which strive against the Stream.

But if we rightly distinguish the different Sense of the ambiguous Word, this whole Mist will immediately vanish. For a Thing in Motion, may be considered in three Respects, by comparing it with *the Parts of infinite and immoveable Space*, or with *Bodies that surround it at a distance*, or with *that Superficies which immediately touches it*. If these three Considerations be exactly distinguished into their several Parts, all future Disputes about Motion will be very easy. First then, a Thing in Motion may be compared with the Parts of *Space*: And, because the parts of Space are infinite and immoveable, and cannot undergo any Change like Matter, therefore that Change of Situation, which is made with respect to the Parts of Space, without any regard had to the Bodies which encompass it, may rightly be called, *absolutely and truly proper Motion*. Secondly, a Thing in Motion may be compared with distant Bodies, and because a Body may in this manner be transferred along with other Bodies which immediately surround it; therefore that Change of Situation which is made with respect to those Bodies which are at a distance, and not to those which are near, may properly be called, *relatively common Motion*. Lastly, a Thing in Motion, may be compared with the Superficies of those Bodies which immediately touch it: And because, whatsoever is thus moved, may possibly have no *absolute* or *common* Motion at all (as if an Arrow were shot towards the West, with the same Swiftness, that the Earth turns towards the East;) and on the contrary, that which in this respect is at rest, may really be transferred with both *absolute* and *common* Motion (as Bodies hid in the Bowels of the Earth) therefore that Change of Situation which is made with respect to those Superficies, which immediately touch the Thing moved, may rightly be called *Motion relatively proper*.

First, *Absolutely and truly proper Motion*, is *the Application of a Body, to the different parts of infinite and immoveable Space*. And this is indeed alone absolute and proper Motion, which is always generated and changed by the Forces impressed upon the Body that is moved, and by them only; and to which alone are owing the real Forces of all Bodies to move other Bodies by their impulse, and to which they are in proportion (*See Newt. Princip. Book I. Def. 2, — 8*). But this *only true Motion* cannot be found out or determined by us, nor can we distinguish, when two Bodies any way strike against each other, which the *true Motion*, and consequently the true Force from whence that Impulse arises, belongs to; whether to that which seems to us to move swiftest, or to that which moves slowest, or perhaps seems to be quite at rest; because it cannot be demonstrated whether the Center of Gravity, as was said before, or of the whole System (which we may properly enough define to be, *One Point in Infinite Space*,) be at rest or no.

Secondly, *Motion relatively common is the Change of Situation which is made with respect, not to those Bodies which are nearest, but to some that are at a distance*. And this sort of Motion we mean, when we say, that Men, and Trees, and the Globe of the Earth it self revolve about the Sun: And we mean this Motion also when we consider the Quantity of Motion, or the Force of a Body in Motion to strike against any Thing. For Example, when a Ball of Wood, with a piece of Lead in it to make it heavy, is thrown out of our Hand, we commonly reckon the Quantity of Motion, or the Force with which the Ball strikes, from the Celerity of the Ball, and the Weight of the included Lead together. I say we *commonly* reckon it so, and indeed truly, with respect to the Force it self, or any sensible Effect of it; but whether that *Force or true Motion* be *really* in the Ball that strikes, or in the Earth which seems to be struck, this, as was said before, we cannot certainly determine.

Lastly, *Motion relatively proper, is the successive Application of a Body to the different Parts of Bodies which immediately touch it.* And this is the Motion we generally mean in Philosophical Disputes, where we enquire into the Nature of particular Things, as when we say, that Heat, or Sound, or Liquidness, consist in Motion. But particular notice ought to be taken, that the *successive Application of a Body* is so to be understood, that it is to be applied successively to the different Parts of the Bodies immediately touching it, *with its whole Superficies taken together* (*par tout ce qu'il a d'extérieur*, as the *French* expresses it;) as when a Ball that is thrown, glides against the different Parts of the Air with its whole Superficies; and when our Hand is moved up and down, it is successively applied with its whole Superficies, to the different Parts of the Air on the one Side, and of the Joint by which it is fastned to the Body on the other Side. It was to no purpose therefore for Mr. *Le Clerc* to find fault with this Definition, in his *Phys. lib. 5. Chap. 5. It will follow,* says he, *that the Banks and the Channel of the River are as much moved as the Water, because they are as far removed from the Water that runs by, as the Water is from the other Parts of the Channel and Banks.* But the Case of the Water is very different from that of the Banks. The whole Superficies of the Water is successively applied to different Parts of the Bodies which surround it, and immediately touch it, and therefore is transferred from some of those surrounding Bodies to others. But the Banks are partly fixed to the Earth, and therefore are not transferred from those Bodies which immediately surround them. For when we say, that a Body is transferred, we mean that the Whole of it is transferred. Wherefore an Island sticking up in the middle of a River, is not moved (not so much as with this *mere relative Motion*) tho' the Water slides by it, because it is firmly fixed in the Earth, and is not transferred from that which immediately touches it. So a Body equally poised in a Liquor whose Parts run upon it with equal Force, is not moved; because though every particular Part of the Superficies of it be every Moment applied to different Parts of the Liquid that surrounds it, yet the whole Superficies of it is not transferred at once from the concave Superficies of the Parts which surround it, considered as one whole Superficies.

Further, according to these different Definitions of *Motion*, are we to understand the Word *Place* in different Senses. For when we speak of *truly or absolutely proper Motion* (or *Rest*;) then by *Place* we mean, *that Part of infinite and immoveable Space which the Body possesses;* when we speak of *Motion relatively common*, then by Place is meant, a *Part of some particular Space or moveable Dimension*, which Place it self is truly and properly moved, along with that which is placed in it: And when we speak of *Motion relatively proper* (which indeed is very improper) then by *Place*, is meant *the Superficies of the Bodies* (or *sensible Spaces*) *which immediately surround the thing moved.*[1]

---

[1] Rohault, *Physica*, pars I, cap. X, sec. 2, p. 36; *Rohault's System of Natural Philosophy*, trans. John Clarke (London, 1723), I, 39, n. 1.

IV

Newton, Galileo, and Plato

The year of grace 1692 marks an important date in the history of Newtonianism: this is the year in which the Reverend Mr. Richard Bentley,[1] chaplain to the bishop of Worcester, addressed to the famous author of the *Philosophiae naturalis principia mathematica* a series of questions concerning the most profound problems of natural philosophy which the latter had neglected to treat – or had avoided – in his work. The reason for Bentley's step was serious indeed. It was especially serious for him owing to the great honor that had befallen him of having to inaugurate the Boyle Lectures, which had been established under a bequest of the great and pious "Christian philosopher," Robert Boyle.[2] The Boyle Lecture, actually a series of eight lecture-sermons given during one year, each in a different London church, had to be, according to the wish of their founder, devoted to the defense of the Christian religion and the

[1] To be exact, since he did not become *Doctor Divinitatis* until 1696, Mr. Richard Bentley, M.A. One of the greatest philologists of the age, Bentley (1662–1742) became Master of Trinity College (Newton's college) in Cambridge University in 1700. It was Bentley who, first on his own and then as enterpreneur (directing Roger Cotes), undertook the publication of the second edition of the *Principia*. The standard biography is James Henry Monk, *The Life of Richard Bentley, D.D.* (London, 1830). The most recent study on Bentley is G. P. Goold, "Richard Bentley: A Tercentenary Commemoration," *Harvard Studies in Classical Philology*, No. 67 (1963), pp. 285–302.

[2] Robert Boyle died on 30 December 1691 and left, according to his will, an income of £50 per annum to reimburse the author of a series of lectures or sermons on the proofs of the truths of the Christian religion. Bentley's lectures, *Eight Sermons Preached at the Honourable Robert Boyle Lecture in the First Year MDCXCII* (London, 1693), had a tremendous influence upon eighteenth-century apologetics. The first of these lectures was intended to prove "The folly of atheism and deism even with respect to the present life," the second demonstrates that "Matter and motion cannot think," the third, fourth, and fifth present "A confutation of atheism from the structure of the human body," while the sixth, seventh, and eighth present "A confutation of atheism from the origin and frame of the world." These sermons were reprinted in Alexander Dyce, ed., *The Works of Richard Bentley, D.D.* (London, 1836–1838), vol. III. This collection went through at least nine editions in English and one in Latin (Berlin, 1696). Sermons seven and eight (preached at St. Mary-le-Bow on 7 November and 5 December 1692), which treat of cosmology, have been reproduced in facsimile in I. B. Cohen, ed., *Isaac Newton's Papers and Letters on Natural Philosophy* (Cambridge, Mass.: Harvard University Press, 1958), pp. 313–394, where they are preceded by a very interesting essay, "Bentley and Newton," by Perry Miller (pp. 271–278); a note on the printing of Bentley's sermons appears on p. 23.

refutation of atheism, the ravages of which, especially the pernicious influence of Thomas Hobbes, had placed true faith in danger. They therefore had to demonstrate, among other things, that the new science – that is to say, the "mechanical philosophy" of which Boyle had been so firm an adherent and the heliocentric astronomy – which had been assured a definitive victory over ancient views by Newton's work, could not possibly lead to materialism, but on the contrary offered a solid base for rejecting and confuting it.

What a glorious assignment! But also, what a difficult one! All the more so since Bentley, a good theologian and an admirable philologist, was not prepared to deal with scientific questions. So, after having tried to acquaint himself with the difficulties and to surmount them by his own means, he decided to appeal to the master himself, and to ask him whether or not the mathematical philosophy, and particularly Newtonian cosmology, could do without the intervention of a creative God or whether on the contrary they implied such intervention.

This proved to be a very happy inspiration, for Newton gave himself with good grace to the request of the young theologian. The four letters which Newton addressed to Bentley in response to his questions – in which he explained how Bentley could, and also how he could not, use the principles of modern science as foundations of a natural theology – constitute one of the most precious and most important documents for the study and interpretation of Newtonian thought.[1] As such, these letters merit and demand a long and detailed commentary, which however I will not undertake here.[2] I will limit myself to the study of a curious position – in itself of minimal importance – of this correspondence, namely, to the reference made by Newton to "Platonic" cosmological theory.

[1] Carefully preserved by Bentley, these letters were found among his papers by his executor and published under the title *Four Letters from Sir Isaac Newton to Dr. Bentley* (London, 1756). They were reprinted by S. Horsley in the edition of the *Opera omnia* of Newton (London, 1782), vol. IV, and also reprinted (in facsimile, from the first printing) with an excellent introduction by Perry Miller in Cohen, *Newton's Papers and Letters*. It is in these letters that Newton enjoins Bentley not to ascribe to him the notion that gravity is essential to matter (letter II, Horsley, *Opera omnia*, IV, 437; Cohen, *Newton's Papers and Letters*, p. 298), and tells him that action at a distance of one body upon another "without mediation of something which is not material" as if "gravity should be innate, inherent and essential to matter" is an absurdity (letter III, *ibid.*, p. 438; p. 302).

It is to be noted that in the original printing, as well as in the edition of them by Horsley, letters III and IV were interchanged. They were published in the correct order in *Bentley's Correspondence* (London, 1892).

[2] I have done this, in part, in my *From the Closed World to the Infinite Universe* (Baltimore: Johns Hopkins Press, 1957).

The problem which, more than any other, seems to have preoccupied Bentley was to know whether, supposing an initial uniform distribution of matter in space,[1] the system of the world could be produced from it as a result of the action of purely natural causes and also whether the motions of the planets, once created by God, could not result from the action of gravitation alone. Newton replied as follows:

I answer, that the Motions which the Planets now have could not spring from any natural Cause alone, but were impressed by an intelligent Agent. For since Comets descend into the Region of our Planets, and here move all manner of ways, going sometimes the same way with the Planets, sometimes the contrary way, and sometimes in cross ways, in Planes inclined to the Plane of the Ecliptick, and at all kinds of Angles, 'tis plain that there is no natural Cause which could determine all the Planets, both primary and secondary, to move the same way and in the same Plane, without any considerable Variation: This must have been the Effect of Counsel. Nor is there any natural Cause which could give the Planets those just Degrees of Velocity, in Proportion to their Distances from the Sun, and other central Bodies, which were requisite to make them move in such concentrick Orbs about those Bodies.[2]

It is certainly curious to note, we must observe in passing, that Newtonian cosmology, which, with respect to those that preceded it, represents a unification and an admirable simplification of the laws that regulate the universe, does not diminish, but on the contrary increases, at least apparently, the accidental and irrational character of the planetary system. In fact, for Kepler, for example, the dimensions and the distances of the bodies which make up the solar system are found to be determined by the action of structural "archetypical" laws: as a consequence of which their motions, that is to say, the form of their orbits and their speeds of revolution, are determined by purely natural laws. Nothing of this sort is found in Newton. Without doubt the distances, the speeds, and the shapes of the planetary orbits are for Newton linked together even more tightly than for Kepler, whose three laws Newton reduced to a single one, the law of attraction, from which they may be derived. On the other hand, the given dimensions and distances of the bodies of the system of the world are arbitrary: the planets could have been bigger or smaller, and could have been placed nearer to or farther from the sun. They could also have been moved more quickly or more slowly. They

---

[1] The official target of Bentley's attack is the materialism of Lucretius; in fact, it is Hobbes and also Descartes.

[2] Horsley, *Opera omnia*, IV, 431; Cohen, *Newton's Papers and Letters*, p. 284.

would then have described orbits very different from those which they actually describe: circles, or very eccentric ellipses; they would then not even have obeyed the same laws. As Newton explained the matter to Bentley,

Had the Planets been as swift as Comets, in Proportion to their Distances from the Sun (as they would have been, had their Motion been caused by their Gravity, whereby the Matter, at the first Formation of the Planets, might fall from the remotest Regions towards the Sun) they would not move in concentrick Orbs, but in such eccentrick ones as the Comets move in.[1]

It follows then that the distribution and the speeds of the planets do not arise from a purely natural cause, such as the action of gravity, and that

to make this System therefore, with all its Motions, required a Cause which understood, and compared together, the Quantities of Matter in the several Bodies of the Sun and Planets, and the gravitating Powers resulting from thence; the several Distances of the primary Planets from the Sun, and of the secondary ones from *Saturn, Jupiter*, and the Earth; and the Velocities with which these Planets could revolve about those Quantities of Matter in the central Bodies; and to compare and adjust all these Things together, in so great a Variety of Bodies, argues that Cause to be not blind and fortuitous, but very well skilled in Mechanicks and Geometry.[2]

Newton's reply does not seem to have satisfied Bentley.[3] It may be that he had not fully grasped the import of Newton's reasoning, according to which matter subjected only to the law of gravity could not engender the planetary system. Perhaps Bentley had judged New-

[1] Letter I, Horsley, *Opera omnia*, IV, 431; Cohen, *Newton's Papers and Letters*, p. 285.

[2] *Ibid.*, pp. 431–432; pp. 286–287. Newton also explains to Bentley that if, originally, matter were evenly scattered through space, it would be inconceivable that it "should divide itself into two sorts, and that Part of it, which is fit to compose a shining Body, should fall down into one Mass and make a Sun, and the rest, which is fit to compose an opaque Body, should coalesce, not in one great Body, like the shining Matter, but into many little ones; or if the Sun at first were an opaque Body like the Planets, or the Planets lucid Bodies like the Sun, how he alone should be changed into a shining Body, whilst all they continue opaque, or all they be changed into opaque ones, whilst he remain unchanged." All that, says Newton, "I do not think explicable by meer natural Causes, but am forced to ascribe it to the Counsel and Contrivance of a voluntary Agent" (p. 430; p. 282). To admit anything of that kind is to fall into the Cartesian hypothesis, and "is plainly erroneous."

On the other hand, Newton does not appreciate Bentley's attempt to show the teleology of the creation by the inclination of the axis of the earth, in which he sees nothing extraordinary "unless you will urge it as a Contrivance for Winter and Summer (p. 433; p. 289). It is only a minor feature in the Harmony of the System which "was the Effect of Choice rather than Chance."

[3] In his first letter he had evidently asked Newton whether the planets could not be moved by the rays of the sun – the hypothesis of Borelli of which Bentley may have had some knowledge – which Newton bluntly denied.

ton's reasoning to be too feeble to upset the Cartesian teaching which asserted that random movements of matter are spontaneously transformed into ordered vortical motions and finally give birth to the planetary systems as well as to comets. It is also possible that Newton's conception of a "Cause" that was "very well skilled in Mechanicks and Geometry" and that indulged in com plicated computations to determine the masses, the distances, and the speeds which he would have to give to the sun and to the planets in order to produce our world, seemed to Bentley a little too anthropomorphic. However that may be, he turned to Newton once again, and, among other things, probably asked Newton if it would not have been possible for God to create the planets, for example the earth, at a given distance from the sun, letting them somehow acquire their orbital motions by purely natural means; namely by infusing into them "both a gravitating Energy towards the Sun, and a transverse Impulse of a just Quantity."[1] Newton replied that there was no value in this argument:

To the last Part of your Letter, I answer, First, that if the Earth (without the Moon) were placed any where with its Center in the *Orbis Magnus*, and stood still there without any Gravitation or Projection, and there at once were infused into it, both a gravitating Energy towards the Sun, and a transverse Impulse of a just Quantity moving it directly in a Tangent to the *Orbis Magnus*; the Compounds of this Attraction and Projection would, according to my Notion, cause a circular Revolution of the Earth about the Sun. But the transverse Impulse must be a just Quantity; for if it be too big or too little, it will cause the Earth to move in some other Line. Secondly, I do not know any Power in Nature which would cause this transverse Motion without the divine Arm.[2]

Newton obviously is right: there exists no natural force which could in an instant confer on the earth (or on one of the planets) a determined degree of tangential speed. The reason is at once simple and general: no possible natural force can in an instant give a determined degree of speed to any body whatsoever. Because this is something that is naturally impossible, it is something that only a supernatural agent may accomplish. But could not one avoid the necessity of having to call in divine action, by letting the bodies in question – the planets – acquire their speeds progressively rather than instantaneously, by the action of their weights? To this, Newton replies:

[1] In his second letter, apparently lost.
[2] Letter II, Horsley, *Opera omnia*, IV, 436 sq.; Cohen, *Newton's Papers and Letters*, pp. 296 sq.

Blondel tells us somewhere in his Book of Bombs, that *Plato* affirms, that the Motion of the Planets is such, as if they had all of them been created by God in some Region very remote from our System, and let fall from thence towards the Sun, and so soon as they arrived at their several Orbs, their Motion of falling turned aside into a transverse one.[1]

Newton's reference to Blondel is exact – and most curious. In the latter's work on *L'Art de jetter les bombes*, after having explained that according to Galileo the acquisition of movement (or of speed) can be made only progressively, Blondel tells us:

For the rest, it is difficult to conceive that a moving body can at once acquire a determined degree of speed, without having passed through all the preceding degrees of less speed; one can thus judge for what reason the ancients were persuaded that the sentiments of Plato partook of something divine. This philosopher said on this subject that God, having perhaps created the heavenly bodies in an identical place of rest, had then given them the freedom to move in a straight line toward a single point (in the manner in which heavy objects are carried toward the center of the earth) to the point at which having in their descent passed through all the stages of speed they will have acquired that of their destined state; after which he would have converted this rectilinear and accelerated motion into circular motion to make it equal and uniform, so that these bodies would be able to preserve it infinitely.

That which is most admirable in this thought is that the proportions which are found among the distances of the heavenly bodies, and the differences in speed of their movements, are found to conform to the results of this reasoning; and that it would not be absolutely impossible to determine the location of this first place of rest, from which they all would have begun their movement.[2]

The "Platonic" mechanism reported by Blondel was not exactly the same as that which Newton had already discussed, and rejected, in his first letter to Bentley. In the latter, the planets had been supposed to be subject to the action of gravity alone, but according to Blondel their falling motion is found to be interrupted and deviated *before* they have acquired the maximum speed that the attraction of the sun could give them. Thus one is to suppose that at the moment when this deviation occurs – or is made to occur – that is to say, at the moment when, in their descent toward the sun, they arrive at their orbits, they possess the "proper" speed, precisely that speed which allows them to turn around the sun on their concentric trajec-

[1] Letter II, Horsley, *Opera omnia*, IV, 436; Cohen, *Newton's Papers and Letters*, p. 297.

[2] *L'Art de jetter les bombes*, par Monsieur Blondel, Maréchal de Camp aux Armées du Roy (Amsterdam, 1683), troisième partie, livre premier, *Doctrine de Galilée sur le mouvement*, chap. VIII, p. 166: "Suites admirables des propriétés du mouvement."

tories. So much is affirmed by Blondel. Newton comments as follows:

And this is true, supposing the gravitating Power of the Sun was double at that Moment of Time in which they all arrive at their several Orbs; but then the divine Power is here required in a double respect, namely, to turn the descending Motions of the falling Planets into a side Motion, and at the same time to double the attractive Power of the Sun. So then Gravity may put the Planets into Motion, but without the divine Power it could never put them into such a circulating Motion as they have about the Sun; and therefore, for this, as well as other Reasons, I am compelled to ascribe the Frame of this System to an intelligent Agent.[1]

The "Platonic" mechanism is then unworkable, and the assertion of Blondel is false. How amusing it is to see Newton, by a refinement of politeness, proclaim the assertion of Blondel to be true at the moment when he demonstrates that it is not! The fact of the matter is that the solar attraction confers on the planets, and this throughout the whole distance of their fall, a motion too rapid for them to remain on the circular orbits with the speeds acquired during their fall. To counterbalance the centrifugal force which they would develop in turning around the sun, and to prevent them from running off along a tangent, there must be a force of attraction twice as great. We may note in passing that this is rather curious.

Not less curious – from a totally different point of view, to be sure – is the fact that Newton attributes his knowledge of the "Platonic" theory only to Blondel. For this leads us to suppose that he ignored the source on which Blondel himself had drawn, namely, Galileo. Or, since Galileo expounds the "Platonic" conception in his *Dialogo* as well as in his *Discorsi*, one is tempted to conclude therefrom that Newton had never studied either of these works. That would explain furthermore why Newton could, in good faith without doubt, have attributed to the great Florentine the discovery of the law of inertia – which he had not made – while passing entirely in silence over Descartes, to whom we owe that law. It is also possible – such things happen – that, having read Galileo in his youth, Newton meanwhile had completely forgotten his presentation of the "Platonic" conception, and thus did not recognize the source of Blondel. Which of these two possibilities have we to admit? We must, for the moment at least, reserve our judgment. After all, the name of

[1] Letter II, Horsley, *Opera omnia*, IV, 436 sq.; Cohen, *Newton's Papers and Letters*, pp. 297 sq.

Galileo does appear in the fourth and last letter from Newton to Bentley.

It is truly a pity that the letters from Bentley to Newton – save for the third, which is preserved among Newton's papers – have been lost without ever having been published and that, as a result, one can do no more than reconstruct their contents from Newton's replies. Having received Newton's letter,[1] Bentley a month later (18 February 1692/3) sends Newton a hastily drawn résumé of his seventh lecture, containing a *Confutation of Atheism from the Origin and Frame of the World*. In this third letter, the one that is now in the Trinity College Library, Bentley assures Newton that he does not hold gravity to be an "innate" property of matter, that he did not ascribe that doctrine to Newton, and that if he used this expression it was for brevity's sake.[2] Indeed, he holds

[1] Newton's second letter, referring to Blondel, is dated from Trinity College, 17 January 1692/3. Newton followed this with a short letter to Bentley dated 11 February 1693, but in it he does not discuss the question of Blondel and Plato. Then on 18 February 1692/3 Bentley wrote again to Newton, being encouraged, as he said, by Newton's "unexpected and voluntary favour by the last post." Newton answered on 25 February 1692/3.

[2] This letter is printed as part of Appendix X to David Brewster, *Memoirs of the Life, Writings, and Discoveries of Sir Isaac Newton* (Edinburgh, 1855), II, 463–470. Bentley asks Newton to examine an "abstract and thread of my first unpublished sermon; and to acquaint me with what you find in it y^t is not conformable to truth and your hypothesis. My mind would be very much at ease, if I had that satisfaction, before ye discourses are out of my power." Following the outline, Bentley raises a question about how the planets might acquire their "transverse motions" about the sun: "Now, therefore, suppose the planets to be formed in some higher regions, and first descend toward the sun, wherby they would acquire their velocities; but then they would have continued their descent to ye sun unless a Divine power gave them a transverse motion against y^t vast impetus y^t such great bodies must fall with; so y^t on all accounts there's a necessity of introducing a God." Then Bentley turns to the argument that Newton raised from Blondel, remarking that he had already encountered it in Fabri's *Astronomia physica* and in Galileo: "As to what you cite from Blondel, I have read ye same in Hon. Fabri's *Astronomia Physica*, and Galilæo's *System*, p. 10 and 17, who adds, y^t by the velocity of Saturn, one may compute at what distance from ye sun it was formed, according to ye degrees of acceleration found out by himself in the progression of odd numbers. (But he must surely have erred, not knowing w^t you have since shewn, y^t ye velocity of descent as well as weight of bodies decreases as ye square of ye distance increases,) and y^t there is y^t proportion of ye distances and velocities of all ye planets *quam proxime*, as if they all dropt from ye same hight. (But you seem to reject this, saying, y^t the gravitation of ye sun must be doubled at ye very moment they reach their orbs.) I confess I could make no use of ye passage of Galilæo and Fabri, because I could not calculate, so y^t I said no more, but in general as above, and ye rather because I knew that there must be some given hights, from whence each of them descending, might acquire their present velocities. But I own, y^t if I could understand ye thing, it would not be only ornamental to ye discourse, but a great improvement of ye argument for a Divine power; for I think it more impossible y^t they should be all formed naturally at ye same y^n at various distances; and 'tis ye miracle of all miracles if they were naturally formed at such intervals of time, as all of them to arrive at their respective orbs at ye very same moment, which is necessary, if I rightly conceive your meaning about doubling ye sun's attraction; for if Mercury fell first, and when he

that it is impossible that "gravity should either be coeternal and essential to matter or ever acquired by it" in any natural way, which is "self evident if gravitation be true attraction." Nay, Bentley holds that, according to Newton, whom he follows, universal gravitation cannot be explained mechanically.

In the same letter Bentley informs Newton that "as what you cite from Blondel, I have read ye same in Hon. Fabris *Astronomia Physica* and Galileo's *System*" but could not use it (*a*) because Galileo obviously made a mistake in not recognizing that the force of gravity and therefore the acceleration of falling bodies was not constant but varied with the distance and (*b*) because he himself (Bentley) was unable to make the necesssary calculations. Bentley recognizes, however, that it would be a good argument for a divine power, as "it is more impossible" that the planets would all be "formed naturally" at the same time at various distances and that it would be "a miracle of miracles" if they would naturally be formed at this distance in different intervals of time that would enable them to arrive at their present position at the same moment.

Having received Bentley's letter outline and having been reminded by him that the "passage of Plato" is to be found in Galileo, Newton, in his reply, comes back to this passage, which he subjects, once more, to a severe criticism:

> As for the Passage of *Plato*, there is no common Place from whence all the Planets being let fall, and descending with uniform and equal Gravities (as *Galileo* supposes) would at their Arrival to their several Orbs acquire their several Velocities, with which they now revolve in them. If we suppose the Gravity of all the Planets towards the Sun to be of such a Quantity as it really is, and that the Motions of the Planets are turned upwards, every Planet will ascend to twice its Height from the Sun. *Saturn* will ascend till he be twice as high from the Sun as he is at present, and no higher; *Jupiter* will ascend as high again as at present, that is, a little above the Orb of *Saturn*; *Mercury* will ascend to twice his present Height, that is,

---

reached his own orb, ye sun's attraction was doubled. That continuing doubled, ye descents of ye succeeding planets would be proportionably accelerated, which would disturb ye supposed proportion betwixt Mercuries velocity and theirs." (This letter is reprinted in H. W. Turnbull and J. F. Scott, eds., *The Correspondence of Isaac Newton* (Cambridge, England: Cambridge University Press, 1959, III, 251 sq.) As Bentley quotes pp. 10 and 17 of Galileo's *System*, it seems to indicate that he used the second Latin edition of the *Dialogo Systema cosmicum*, published by Johanne Antonius Huguetan in Leiden in 1641. As for the *Astronomia physica* of Honoré Fabri, I do not know what work of Fabri he has in mind, as among the works of the latter there is none bearing this title. Fabri deals indeed with astronomy in the fourth volume of his *Physica, id est scientia rerum corporearum* (Leiden, 1669–1671), but the *tractatus* in which he does it (*tractatus* VIII) is called *De corpore coelesti*. Moreover, in this *tractatus*, Fabri does not develop the "Platonic" theory.

to the Orb of *Venus*; and so of the rest; and then by falling down again from the Places to which they ascended, they will arrive again at their several Orbs with the same Velocities they had at first, and with which they now revolve.

But if so soon as their Motions by which they revolve are turned upwards, the gravitating Power of the Sun, by which their Ascent is perpetually retarded, be diminished by one half, they will now ascend perpetually, and all of them at all equal Distances from the Sun will be equally swift. *Mercury* when he arrives at the Orb of *Venus*, will be as swift as *Venus;* and he and *Venus*, when they arrive at the Orb of the *Earth*, will be as swift as the *Earth;* and so of the rest. If they begin all of them to ascend at once, and ascend in the same Line, they will constantly in ascending become nearer and nearer together, and their Motions will constantly approach to an Equality, and become at length slower than any Motion assignable. Suppose, therefore, that they ascended till they were almost contiguous, and their Motions inconsiderably little, and that all their Motions were at the same Moment of Time turned back again; or, which comes almost to the same Thing, that they were only deprived of their Motions, and let fall at that Time, they would all at once arrive at their several Orbs, each with the Velocity it had at first; and if their Motions were then turned Sideways, and at the same Time the gravitating Power of the Sun doubled, that it might be strong enough to retain them in their Orbs, they would revolve in them as before their Ascent. But if the gravitating Power of the Sun was not doubled, they would go away from their Orbs into the highest Heavens in parabolical Lines. These Things follow from my *Princ. Math. Lib.* i. *Prop.* 33, 34, 36, 37.[1]

I do not know whether this second exposition by Newton was clearer for Bentley than the first had been, nor whether he took the pains to study Propositions 33, 34, 36, and 37 of the *Principia* to understand the course of Newton's reasoning. Personally, I strongly doubt it. As a matter of fact, in the seventh sermon or lecture of his *Confutation of Atheism*, devoted precisely to the demonstration of the existence of God from the evidence of the structure of the solar system, Bentley limited himself to affirming on the whole the im-

---

[1] Letter III, Horsley, *Opera omnia*, IV, 440 sq.; Cohen, *Newton's Papers and Letters*, pp. 306 sq. (Printed as letter III in the original edition and also by Horsley, this should be letter IV according to dates.) Newton simplifies things a little. As a matter of fact, as Newton himself remarked, the ascending movement of the planets will never cease and they will never attain the common limit of their ascent; vice versa, leaving this common limit they would never be able, in a finite time, to descend to the actual orbits along which they now move. But as it is in general impossible that the planets could be created in the *same* place, and therefore it could only be a question of places very near to one another, Newton held that he had the right to substitute a proximity of place for identical place, and to stop the rising motion "before" the planets had attained their limit. The rest would follow automatically.

possibility of the planets' acquiring, by falling toward the sun, the speeds necessary to move around the sun as they actually do; he did not go into details nor did he refer to "the passage of Plato."[1] Without doubt he considered it useless to enter into any reasoning of such difficulty; it is possible also that, an excellent philologist though a bad mathematician, he knew that the theory which Newton, placing his faith in Blondel, had presented as one of Plato's could not be found (at least as such) in Plato's writings. Indeed, he knew that it could be found, on the other hand, in the writings of Galileo, and thus had indicated this to Newton.

If all the planets are "let fall," and descend "with uniform and equal Gravities (as *Galileo* supposes)," they cannot, Newton tells us, all start out from the same position. We agree. We must, however, make precise the sense of the expression "descending with uniform and equal Gravities." In effect, Newton's statement could be made to say two very different things. The first is that, according to Galileo,

---

[1] In his seventh sermon, Bentley discussed the question of where the planets might have been made. Bentley had approved the impossibility of a "Supposition [that] the Matter of the Chaos could never compose such divided and different Masses as the Starrs and Planets of the present World." Then he changed his subject: "But allowing our Adversaries, that The Planets might be composed: yet however they could not possibly acquire such Revolutions in Circular Orbs, or (which is all one to our present purpose) in Ellipses very little Eccentric. For let them assign any place where the Planets were formed. Was it nearer to the Sun, than the present distances are? But that is notoriously absurd: for then they must have ascended from the place of their Formation, against the essential property of mutual Attraction. Or were each formed in the same Orbs, in which they now move? But then they must have moved from the Point of Rest, in an horizontal Line without any inclination or descent. Now there is no natural Cause, neither Innate Gravity nor Impulse of external Matter, that could beget such a Motion. For Gravity alone must have carried them downwards to the Vicinity of the Sun. And that the ambient Æther is too liquid and empty, to impell them horizontally with that prodigious celerity, we have sufficiently proved before. Or were they made in some higher regions of the Heavens; and from thence descended by their essential Gravity, till they all arrived at their respective Orbs; each with its present degree of Velocity, acquired by the fall? But then why did they not continue their descent, till they were contiguous to the Sun; whither both Mutual Attraction and Impetus carried them? What natural Agent could turn them aside, could impell them so strongly with a transverse Sideblow against that tremendous Weight and Rapidity, when whole Worlds are a falling? But though we should suppose, that by some cross attraction or other they might acquire an obliquity of descent, so as to miss the body of the Sun, and to fall on one side of it: then indeed the force of their Fall would carry them quite beyond it; and so they might fetch a compass about it, and then return and ascend by the same steps and degrees of Motion and Velocity, with which they descended before. Such an eccentric Motion as this, much after the manner that Comets revolve about the Sun, they might possibly acquire by their innate principle of Gravity: but circular Revolutions in concentric Orbs about the Sun or other central Body could in no-wise be attain'd without the power of the Divine Arm" (Cohen, *Newton's Papers and Letters*, pp. 345–347). It is worth noting that in this passage Bentley uses the term "innate gravity," and in his eighth sermon (p. 363) defines "Gravitation toward the Sun" as "a constant Energy infused into Matter by the Author of all things."

the action of gravity is everywhere uniform and constant and that, as a consequence, bodies – all bodies, large and small, heavy and light – fall everywhere with the same acceleration, no matter where they are placed, whether far from or near to the earth (or, as it may happen, from the sun), in other words, that the acceleration of free fall *due to gravity* is a universal constant, having the same value everywhere in the solar system. The second possibility is that, according to Galileo, all bodies, and therefore also all planets, "fall" with the same acceleration – whether that acceleration is constant or not – so that, as a consequence, if they start from the same place, and fall together through identical spaces, they will have at the same "height" from the sun equal speeds; this assertion, far from implying any constancy of the acceleration, allows it to vary with the distance, as the force of attraction does, and even allows the same variation with the distance.

Which interpretation shall we give to the Newtonian formulation? That is to say: what sense do these words have in the mind of Newton? This is not an irrelevant question. Actually, the first interpretation represents the Galilean theory of falling bodies truly and historically. The second, on the contrary, is a later adaptation and actually a misinterpretation. Thus the first implies a correct and precise knowledge of the work of Galileo; the second does not imply that at all. Now it seems clear that it is the second sense which Newton adopts, in spite of Bentley's rather penetrating remarks on this subject, because he uses it and deduces the consequences of it – for example, that, if the orbital movement of the planets is turned "upwards," they will ascend to a "height" double their actual "height" – which it is impossible to deduce from the authentic Galilean concept. Thus there seems to be confirmation of the hypothesis which I formulated earlier in this work, namely, that Newton had never *studied* Galileo. And that if he had read Galileo's works in his youth, he had in the meanwhile forgotten what is to be found therein.[1]

Let us now turn to Galileo.

The first mention of the "Platonic" theory of the "fall" of the planets, or more exactly of their rectilinear motion prior to their cir-

---

[1] It is this last "hypothesis" that proves to be the true one. Indeed, in the third volume of *The Correspondence of Isaac Newton* we find a MS by Newton from the year 1665 or 1666 (pp. 46 sq.) proving without possibility of doubt that Newton had read the *Dialogo*; in this MS Newton discusses – though without naming him – Galileo's assertion that a falling body will traverse 100 braces (cubits) in 5 seconds (p. 219 of

cular motion, is to be found in the *Dialogue Concerning the Two Chief World Systems*, first published in Florence in 1632. In the course of the first "day," Salviati, after having explained the structure and respective roles of circular and rectilinear motion, addresses himself to the subject as follows:

We may therefore say that straight motion serves to transport materials for the construction of a work; but this, once constructed, is to rest immovable – or, if movable, is to move only circularly. Unless we wish to say with Plato that these world bodies, after their creation and the establishment of the whole, were for a certain time set in straight motion by their Maker. Then later, reaching certain definite places, they were set in rotation one by one, passing from straight to circular motion, and have ever since been preserved and maintained in this. A sublime concept, and worthy indeed of Plato, which I remember having heard discussed by our friend, the Lincean Academician.[1]

The discussion of the "Academician" – which we have seen Blondel expound faithfully – concerns the impossibility of a body at rest acquiring any degree of motion whatever without having passed previously through all the degrees of speed – or of slowness – intermediate between the said degree and rest. From which it follows that, in order to confer on a body at rest a certain degree of speed, nature makes it move during a certain time in a rectilinear and accelerated motion:

This assumed, let us suppose God to have created the planet Jupiter, for example, upon which He had determined to confer such-and-such a velocity, to be kept perpetually uniform forever after. We may say with Plato that at the beginning He gave it a straight and accelerated motion; and

---

the original edition; p. 219 of the Salusbury translation; see *Correspondence*, III, 52, note 2). In the same note the editor of the *Correspondence* mentions that Dr. Herivel "has pointed out to us" that Newton himself in an early notebook (1661–1665) said that "according to Galilaeus an iron ball of 100 florentine [pounds] descends 100 braces Florentine or cubits . . . in 5″ of an hower."

The *Dialogo* was translated into English by Thomas Salusbury under the title *Mathematical Collections and Translations* (London: Printed by William Leybourn, 1661). The first part containing: *The System of the World by Galileus Galileus Linceus*. Nearly all the edition perished in the great London fire; however, a copy has been preserved in the library of Trinity College. Moreover, Newton could have read it in Latin, all the more so as a Latin edition of the *Dialogo Systema cosmicum* was published in London (by Thomas Dicas) in 1663.

[1] Galileo Galilei, *Dialogo sopra i due massimi sistemi del mondo* (edizione nazionale), vol. VII, Giornata prima, p. 44; in English translation, *Dialogue on the Great World Systems*, ed. Giorgio de Santillana (Chicago: University of Chicago Press, 1953), pp. 24–25, or *Dialogue Concerning the Two Chief World Systems – Ptolemaic and Copernican*, trans. Stillman Drake (Berkeley and Los Angeles: University of California Press, 1953), p. 20.

later, when it had arrived at that degree of velocity, converted its straight motion into circular motion whose speed thereafter was naturally uniform.[1]

Sagredo objects, however, that, since the gradations of speed and slowness are infinite, it would not have been possible for nature to have conferred all of these on the body of Jupiter, and that it would therefore be more probable that the circular motion of the latter would have been created instantaneously with the determined speed. To this Salviati replies prudently:

I did not say, nor dare I, that it was impossible for Nature or for God to confer [on the body of Jupiter] immediately that velocity which you speak of. I do indeed say that *de facto* Nature does not do so – that the doing of this would be something outside the course of nature, and therefore miraculous.[2]

A few pages later on, Salviati explains that the downward motion – either free fall or along an inclined plane – is a motion that is produced and accelerates naturally and must therefore always precede circular motion which, once acquired, continues perpetually with a constant speed.[3] To quote from Galileo, "circular motion is never acquired naturally without straight motion to precede it; but, being once acquired, it will continue perpetually with uniform velocity." Then Salviati returns to the concept of Plato and in order to embellish it says that to the illustration of this "Platonic" concept he will add "one particular observation of our academic friend which is quite remarkable."

Let us suppose that among the decrees of the divine Architect was the thought of creating in the universe those globes which we behold continually revolving, and of establishing a center of their rotations in which the sun was located immovably. Next, suppose all the said globes

---

[1] *Dialogo*, p. 45; Santillana, pp. 25–26; Drake, p. 21.

[2] *Ibid.*, p. 45; Santillana, p. 26; Drake, p. 21.

[3] *Ibid.*, p. 53; Santillana, p. 34; Drake, p. 28. A marginal note reads: "Circular motion can never be acquired naturally without straight motion preceding it." It is interesting to observe here that, for Galileo, the eternal continuation of circular movement, at least when it is a question of celestial phenomena, poses no problem. Movement along a straight line is presented essentially as a movement with variable speed – accelerated or decelerated – while circular movement enjoys, on the contrary, all the peculiarities of inertial movement; it is "perpetually uniform." Also, when in and by their "descending" motions the planets attain the speeds which God had assigned to them, and their rectilinear motions are replaced by their circular motions, they can then follow their circular paths eternally by themselves without – in contrast to the Newtonian conception – the need of any force of attraction whatever to keep them in the neighborhood of the sun, and this because their motions do not give rise to any centrifugal force. See my *Études galiléenes* (Paris: Hermann, 1939), pp. 236 sq.

to have been created in the same place, and there assigned tendencies of motion, descending toward the center until they had acquired those degrees of velocity which originally seemed good to the Divine mind. These velocities being acquired, we lastly suppose that the globes were set in rotation, each retaining in its orbit [cerchio] its predetermined velocity. Now, at what altitude and distance from the sun would have been the place where the said globes were first created, and could they all have been created in the same place?

To make this investigation, we must take from the most skillful astronomers the sizes of the orbits in which the planets revolve, and likewise the times of their revolutions. From these data we deduce how much faster Jupiter (for example) moves than Saturn; and it being found (as in fact it is) that Jupiter does move more swiftly, it is necessary that Jupiter, departing from the same height, descended more than Saturn – as we know is actually the case, its orbit being inferior to that of Saturn. And going still further one may determine, from the proportions of the two velocities of Jupiter and Saturn and from the distance between their orbits, and from the natural ratio of acceleration of natural motion, at what altitude and distance from the center of their revolutions must have been the place from which they originally departed. This place determined and agreed upon, it is asked whether Mars, descending from there to its orbit, is found to agree in size of orbit and velocity of motion with what is found by calculation; and the same is done for the earth, Venus, and Mercury, the size of whose orbits and the velocities of whose motions agree so closely with those given by the computations that the matter is truly wonderful.[1]

Sagredo does not fail to agree, saying, "I have heard this idea with extreme delight and if I did not believe that making these calculations accurately would be a long and painful task, and perhaps one too difficult for me to understand, I should ask to see them." Galileo (Salviati) replies that the "procedure is indeed long and difficult." Furthermore, he says, "I am not sure I could reconstruct it offhand. Therefore we shall keep it for another time" – a time which, alas, will never come. Moreover, in place of "alas" should we not perhaps say "by good luck"? For these computations would have caused Galileo great disappointment.

The comparison of the presentations – and above all the appreciations – of the "Platonic" cosmology by Galileo and by Newton allows us to see certain rather significant and curious differences between these two men. Thus, for Newton, adopting this "Platonic" cosmology produces no gain, that is to say, it does not result in any economy of supernatural actions for God. It is rather the opposite that is true. It is, in effect, as difficult to confer instantaneously a

[1] *Ibid.*, pp. 53 sq.; Santillana, pp. 35–36; Drake, p. 29.

determined velocity upon a body as to change instantaneously the direction of its movement. Neither of these operations is possible in the natural order of things; in either case one must suppose a miracle. Furthermore, the "Platonic" cosmology implies another miracle of its own in addition to the preceding one, since in order that the planets may retain their orbits, or even initially describe those orbits, it is necessary that the force of attraction of the sun be doubled at the very moment when a motion "toward the side" is substituted for the "downward" motion.

It would seem that these considerations do not hold for Galileo, and that according to him these two operations are not of the same level: to confer motion on a body at rest is one thing, whereas to change the direction – *while preserving the speed* – of a body *already in motion* is another.[1] The law of continuity must be invoked in one case but not in the other. In one it is a question of producing something new, but in the other there is merely a change which affects only an accidental and superficial characteristic of motion without modifying its profound reality, and without producing something that has not already been there. Furthermore, he reckons that the "Platonic" cosmology does not demand any miracles beyond, properly understood, that of creation. As to the doubling of the force of attraction, Galileo has no need of it whatsoever, since, first of all, for him the sun does not attract the planets; instead they tend toward the sun in virtue of an inclination which is characteristic of them and which has its origin in their bodies;[2] and further – or even in the first place – their circular movement around the sun *does not engender centrifugal forces*, so that no force of attraction from the sun is necessary to keep them in their orbits or to make them describe those orbits. And this follows because for Galileo the circular motion of the planets, which turn around a center without approaching or receding from it, is a motion arising from the force of inertia.

---

[1] Galileo would probably have protested against the assertion that according to him gravity is a "tendency" or "inclination," and would have recalled the celebrated passage in which he said that "gravity" is only a word, and no one knows – nor even has need to know – what it is. It suffices to know how it acts, that is, how bodies fall. Now it is just this refusal to attempt to make an explanation of gravity, or even to make a theory, and its acceptance as a simple fact, which led Galileo – and the Galileans – to conceive of it as something which belongs to bodies, and to attribute to it a constant magnitude (and thus, to bodies, a constant acceleration) and even to continue to use – as Galileo does in the passage which I have cited – expressions such as "inclination" or "desire."

[2] The change in direction, as in the case of the planets, is made instantly and without the intervention of any force whatever.

Galileo seems to have attributed a certain importance, and even an important certainty, to the resurrection of the "Platonic" cosmology. Actually, he did not limit himself to an exposition of it by Salviati in the *Dialogo*. He returns to it in the *Discorsi* (*Discourses and Demonstrations Concerning Two New Sciences*, published in 1638), this time having Sagredo recall for the reader the marvelous agreement between the ideas of the "Academician" and those of Plato. The occasion this time is a discussion of the motion – along a parabola – of projectiles. Galileo explains that if the accelerated motion of a body falling from a certain height, which he designates by the term *sublimity*, is turned from a vertical line and made to move in a direction perpendicular to it, along a horizontal line, the result will be a parabola. This provokes the following discussion by Sagredo:

SAGR. Allow me, please, to interrupt in order that I may point out the beautiful agreement between this thought of the Author and the views of Plato concerning the origin of the various uniform speeds with which the heavenly bodies revolve. The latter chanced upon the idea that a body could not pass from rest to any given speed and maintain it uniformly except by passing through all the degrees of speed intermediate between the given speed and rest. Plato thought that God, after having created the heavenly bodies, assigned them the proper and uniform speeds with which they were forever to revolve; and that He made them start from rest and move over definite distances under a natural and rectilinear acceleration such as governs the motion of terrestrial bodies. He added that once these bodies had gained their proper and permanent speed, their rectilinear motion was converted into a circular one, the only motion capable of maintaining uniformity, a motion in which the body revolves without either receding from or approaching its desired goal. This conception is truly worthy of Plato; and it is to be all the more highly prized since its underlying principles remained hidden until discovered by our Author who removed from them the mask and poetical dress and set forth the idea in correct historical perspective. In view of the fact that astronomical science furnishes us such complete information concerning the size of the planetary orbits, the distances of these bodies from their centers of revolution, and their velocities, I cannot help thinking that our Author (to whom this idea of Plato was not unknown) had some curiosity to discover whether or not a definite "sublimity" might be assigned to each planet, such that, if it were to start from rest at this particular height and to fall with naturally accelerated motion along a straight line, and were later to change the speed thus acquired into uniform motion, the size of its orbit and its period of revolution would be those actually observed.

SALV. I think I remember his having told me that he once made the computation and found a satisfactory correspondence with observation. But he did not wish to speak of it, lest, in view of the odium which his many new discoveries had already brought upon him, this might be adding fuel to the fire. But if any one desires such information he can obtain it for himself from the theory set forth in the present treatment.[1]

The resurrection, or the rediscovery, by Galileo of the sublime conception of Plato provoked a rather lively curiosity among the learned. It has also stirred up a certain skepticism, because no one has actually been able to find a passage in which Plato described the cosmological ideas attributed to him by Galileo.[2]

Even among modern scholars there has been no success in finding either in Plato or in the writings of his successors the cosmological doctrine in question.[3] A passage in the *Timaeus*[4] – the only one that can be invoked – discusses only the transformation by the demiurge of chaos into cosmos; but it does not mention either the naturally accelerated motion of planets or their "fall" in the direction of the sun and their circular motion around the sun. Thus it has been necessary to submit to the evidence: however sublime it may be, the theory in question is not in Plato.

On very close examination, furthermore, it appears that Galileo himself does not affirm that he has simply discovered the Platonic cosmology. Salviati in the *Dialogo* specifically says that he wishes to "adorn" a Platonic concept ("per adornare un concetto Platonico"), and in the *Discorsi* Sagredo actually says:

[1] Galileo Galilei, *Discorsi e dimostrazioni matematiche intorno due nuove scienze* (edizione nazionale), vol. VIII, Giornata quarta, pp. 283 sq.; in English translation, *Dialogues Concerning Two New Sciences*, trans. Henry Crew and Alfonso de Salvio (New York: Macmillan, 1914; Dover, n.d.), pp. 261–262.

[2] Thus on 4 December 1644, Mersenne, who had not been able to find it either, wrote to Peiresc to ask him to inquire of Gassendi or others "si Platon dit ce que Galilée lui fait dire dans ses *Dialogues du mouvement de la Terre*"; *Correspondance du P. Marin Mersenne*, ed. Cornelius de Waard (Paris: Presses Universitaires de France, 1955), IV, 403. Gassendi replied (p. 415) that "il n'a pas de souvenance d'en avoir rien leu dans le text même de Platon" and "faut que ce soit dans quelque autre autheur ancien qui l'aye veu en d'autres oeuvres de Platon de celles qui ne se trouvent plus." Furthermore, Platonic or not, the conception expounded by Galileo was impossible (as was quickly shown by Frénicle and Mersenne, who performed the calculations which Galileo no doubt had neglected to make); see *Harmonicarum libri* (Paris, 1636), tome I, "Praefatio," prop. 2. The planets could not all start from the same place. That the assertion of Galileo is false was confirmed 250 years later by M. P. Mansion: "Sur une opinion de Galilée relative à l'origine commune des planètes," *Annales de la Société Scientifique de Bruxelles 18* (1894), 46, 90; see also the note of de Waard, *Correspondance de Mersenne*, IV, 409.

[3] A. E. Taylor believed he had discovered the source in Eusebius, *Praeparatio evangelica*, XV, but he was wrong. See Stephen Hobhouse, "Isaac Newton and Jacob Boehme," *Philosophia 2* (1937), 36: "Professor A. E. Taylor writes to me that this may be a development by Blondel of a theory ascribed to Plato by Atticus, and preserved in Eusebius, *Praeparatio evangelica*, XV."

[4] *Timaeus* 30A.

Stop, if you please, because it seems to me that it is suitable to adorn this thought by our Author by its conformity with the conception of Plato concerning the determination of the different speeds of uniform revolution of the celestial motions. [Fermate, in grazia, perchè qui mi par che convenga adornar questo pensiero dell' Autore . . .]

In both books, we are told specifically that the "Academician" had "adorned," that is to say, embellished, developed, leaped to his own conceptions from, the sublime idea of Plato. If Sagredo seems so positive in his attribution to Plato of certain characteristic traits of the doctrine, is he not saying that it was presented by Plato only under a mask, as a poetic allegory, and that it is the Academician who, in revealing the foundations about which Plato was "silent" or ignorant, has transformed it into a scientific theory? Thus, speaking twice through the voice of a *porte-parole*, Galileo actually says to us: "I attribute this doctrine to Plato; but, as a matter of fact, it is I who have invented it." Why then does he present it as Platonic? Is it only to announce, at the very beginning of the *Dialogo*, that in the great debate between Aristotle and his master Galileo has taken the part of Plato? Did he really believe he had found in Plato the germ of the system which he had elaborated? Or was he only amused to cloak an ingenious idea with a prestigious name and thus to present it as coming from a great philosopher – an ingenious idea which he obviously believed but which was all the same a little too extravagant and by the same token a little too risky?

To these questions it is not easy to give a reply. Still more difficult is it to know exactly what this conception represented for Galileo. Was it a "jest," a pleasantry,[1] as according to him the "circular" theory of the fall of heavy bodies on a rotating earth had been? Or was it on the contrary a serious speculation (as, moreover, the circular theory seems to have been[2]) for explaining the structure of the planetary system – a theory that, without claiming to represent the

---

[1] This was the opinion of Emil Strauss in his translation of the *Dialogo: Dialog über die beiden hauptsächlichsten Weltsystem, das ptolemäische und das kopernikanische* (Leipzig, 1891), p. 499, n. 23; and see Galileo's letter of 5 June 1637 to Pietro Carcavy, ed. naz., VII, 89, where Galileo refers to his circular theory as "un capriccio et una bizzaria, cioe *iocularis quaedam audacia*"; also see de Waard, *Correspondance de Mersenne*, III, 572.

[2] On this theory, see de Waard, *Correspondance de Mersenne*, IV, 438 sq., App. II, "La Spirale de Galilée"; and also my "De motu gravium naturaliter cadentium," *Transactions of the American Philosophical Society 45* (1956), 333 sq. Santillana (pp. 181–182, note 57) and Drake (pp. 476–477) each discuss briefly Galileo's circular theory of free fall on a rotating earth. In a recent note on "Galileo's Attempt at a Cosmogony," *Isis 53* (1962), 460–464, S. Sambursky argues that Galileo may have intended to imply that he had "given a liberal interpretation to some passage in Plato."

manner in which things had actually happened, did not represent any the less the manner in which they could have happened? I admit freely that I lean toward this latter interpretation. How actually can one otherwise explain the insistence with which Galileo presents it and the extraordinary expression "true history" (*verace istoria*) which he puts in the mouth of Sagredo?

The objection will perhaps be raised that one really cannot understand how Galileo could have believed in the possibility of so unreal a method as that which he had invented. And still less, certainly, in its reality. Surely that would appear very improbable. Let us not forget, however, that for the minds of the seventeenth century the frontier between the believable and the unbelievable did not lie exactly where it does for us. Did they not believe, the majority at least, in a finite world bounded by the celestial vault outside of which there was rigorously and absolutely nothing? Furthermore, did they not hold that the world had been created at a given moment, and not very long ago, in the past? Did not Newton himself believe that God had placed the heavenly bodies at their "proper" distances from the sun and that he had conferred upon them, later or at the same time, the "proper" speeds which would be necessary for them to accomplish their revolutions? Why could Galileo not have believed that God had – or, at least, that he could have – used the mechanism of falling? Is this not a most elegant way, and the only natural one, to give to a body a particular speed? Did not Galileo himself use it in his own theory of projectiles when, as we have seen, in order to give his projectiles a *horizontal* speed, he has them fall from a given height instead of giving them this speed directly? The term "sublimity" itself which he uses – is it not revealing and significant?

It seems to me therefore that only one conclusion is possible. For Galileo the "Platonic" cosmology is not a simple μῦθος, like that of the *Timaeus*, but a possible if not a "true" story.

V

An Unpublished Letter of
Robert Hooke to Isaac Newton

Robert Hooke's letter to Isaac Newton of 9 December 1679 forms a part of a very interesting correspondence exchanged between the two great scientists during the winter months of 1679-1680. This correspondence, which played an important, perhaps a decisive, role in the development of Newton's thought,[1] was discovered, some sixty years ago, by W. W. Rouse Ball in the Library of Trinity College, Cambridge, and was published by him in his precious *Essay on Newton's Principia*.[2] Unfortunately, the collection in Trinity College was not complete, and contained only five of the seven letters written by Newton and Hooke; the remaining two – namely, Hooke's letter to Newton of 9 December 1679 and Newton's reply of 13 December 1679 – were missing.

The latter turned up at a public sale at Messrs. Sotheby and Co., on 29 June 1904, and was acquired by the British Museum. It was published, with an extremely careful and scholarly commentary, by Professor Jean Pelseneer, in 1929.[3]

The former also appeared at a sale at Sotheby's, in April 1918, came into the possession of Dr. Erik Waller of Stockholm, and finally was acquired by the Yale University Library, New Haven.[4] With the kind permission of the librarian, Mr. James T. Babb, I have been enabled to print it here for the first time.[5] Thus the gap that remained

[1] In his letter to Halley of 14 July 1686, Newton writes: "This is true, that his letters occasioned my finding the method of determining figures, which when I had tried in the ellipsis, I threw the calculations by, being upon other studies." See W. W. Rouse Ball, *An Essay on Newton's "Principia"* (London, 1893), p. 165.

[2] Rouse Ball, *Essay*, "Appendix A: Correspondence between Hooke and Newton, 1679-1680, and memoranda relating thereto," pp. 139–153.

[3] Jean Pelseneer, "Une Lettre inédite de Newton," *Isis 12* (1929), 237–254; reprinted in H. W. Turnbull and J. F. Scott, ed., *The Correspondence of Isaac Newton* (Cambridge, England: Cambridge University Press, 1959), II, 307 sq.

[4] See Ernest Weil, "Robert Hooke's Letter of 9 December 1679 to Isaac Newton," *Nature 158* (1946), 135.

[5] One passage only – "I could add many other considerations consonant to my

221

open even after Professor Pelseneer's publication seems now to be definitely closed.[1]

The relationship between Newton and Hooke was never friendly, though it is only after the last – the third – clash, which followed the publication of Newton's *Principia*, that it degenerated into a bitter and burning hatred.[2] The second clash occurred in 1679, and is the subject matter of this paper. As for the first – and in many respects the most important one – it took place at the very beginning of Newton's public career, in 1672, when Hooke produced a somewhat hasty and rather sharp criticism of Newton's optical discoveries, announced by him in his *New Theory about Light and Colors*,[3] claiming, more-

theory of circular motions compounded by a direct motion and an attractive one to the center . . ." – has been preserved by Hooke himself (see his *True state of the Case and Controversy between Sᵣ Isaac Newton and Dr. Robert Hooke as to the Priority of that Noble Hypothesis of Motion of the Planets about the Sun as Their Center* in Rouse Ball, *Essay*, pp. 151 sq.). The contents of this letter, however, were not completely unknown, since Hooke had read it to the Royal Society at their meeting on 4 December 1679, and inserted a short report of it in the *Minutes* of the Society, which was published by Thomas Birch, *History of the Royal Society* (London, 1757), III, 512 sq.

[1] An entry in Hooke's *Journal*, quoted by Pelseneer, "Lettre inédite de Newton," p. 238, seems to imply that there may have been two more letters; "peut-être de simples billets," says Professor Pelseneer. No trace has ever been found of them, nor have they ever been mentioned by anybody, not even by Newton. Since the original writing of this article, a memorandum by Hooke and some letters have been published in the Royal Society's edition of *The Correspondence of Isaac Newton*, as follows: vol. I: memorandum by Hooke, 19 June 1672, pp. 195–197; *Hooke to Lord Brouncker, c. June 1672, pp. 198–203; Hooke to Newton, 20 January 1675/6, pp. 412–413; Newton to Hooke, 5 February 1675/6, pp. 416–417; Hooke to Oldenburg, 15 February 1671/2, pp. 110–114; vol. II: Newton to Hooke, 18 December 1677, p. 239; Hooke to Newton, 24 December 1677, p. 240; *Newton to Hooke, 5 March 1677/8, p. 253; Newton to Hooke, 18 May 1678, p. 264; Hooke to Newton, 25 May 1678, p. 265; *Newton to Hooke, 8 June 1678, p. 266; Hooke to Newton, 24 November 1679, p. 297; Newton to Hooke, 28 November 1679, p. 300; Hooke to Newton, 9 December 1679, p. 304; Newton to Hooke, 13 December 1679, pp. 307–308; Hooke to Newton, 6 January 1679/80, pp. 309–310; Hooke to Newton, 17 January 1679/80, pp. 312–313; Newton to Hooke, 3 December 1680, p. 314; *Hooke to Newton, 18 December 1680, p. 317; vol. III: Aubrey and Hooke to Anthony à Wood, 15 September 1689, pp. 40–42. The asterisk in each case indicates that the letter in question has "not been previously published, so far as can be ascertained." The new letter from Newton to Hooke, 5 March 1677/8, is very short and deals only with Newton's controversy with Lucas concerning the theory of light and colors. The one of 8 June 1678 is brief and merely acknowledges a letter of Hooke, and replies to a question concerning the topography of the Fens; it concludes by saying, "If I can serve you at any time pray be free with Sᵣ Your obliged & humble Servant Is. Newton." The new letter from Hooke to Newton, 18 December 1680, is again brief and is unrelated to any Hooke–Newton controversy. Hooke's letter to Brouncker, c. June 1672, is related to the earlier controversy at the time of the publication of Newton's theory of light and colors.

[2] It is well known that Newton obstinately refused to publish his *Opticks* during the lifetime of Hooke. He therefore held back his manuscript, awaiting patiently and confidently the disappearance of his foe, and printed it in 1704, the year of Hooke's death.

[3] *Philosophical Transactions*, No. 80, pp. 3075 sq., reproduced in I. B. Cohen, ed., *Isaac Newton's Papers and Letters on Natural Philosophy* (Cambridge, Massachusetts: Harvard University Press, 1958), pp. 47 sq.

over, priority for the best part of them.[1] It is natural that this unexpected attack, as well as the tone adopted by Hooke – already a
well-known man, the celebrated author of the very famous *Micrographia*[2] – toward the obscure Cambridge professor could not fail to

[1] See Sir David Brewster, *Memoirs of the Life, Writings and Discoveries of Sir Isaac
Newton* (Edinburgh, 1855), I, 78–79; Louis Trenchard More, *Isaac Newton, a Biography* (New York: Scribner, 1934), pp. 82–89. As a matter of fact, Hooke's criticism
was rather profitable to Newton; it made him improve his theory by incorporating
undulatory components into it. See T. J. Kuhn, "Newton's Optical Papers," in Cohen,
Newton's Papers and Letters, pp. 27 sq.

[2] *Micrographia: or some physiological descriptions of minute bodies made by magnifying glasses, with observations and inquiries thereupon* by R. Hooke, Fellow of the
Royal Society (London, 1665). The *Micrographia*, a first-rate work of quite outstanding
importance, is characterized by the *Dictionary of National Biography* as "a book full
of ingenious ideas and singular anticipations. It contained the earliest investigation
of the 'fantastical colours' of thin plates with a quasi-explanation by interference (p.
66), the first notice of the 'black spot' in soap-bubbles, and a theory of light, as a 'very
short vibrative motion' transverse to straight lines of propagation through a 'homogeneous medium.' Heat was defined as 'a property of a body arising from the motion
or agitation of its parts' (p. 37), and the real nature of combustion was pointed out
(p. 103) in detail, eleven years before the publication of Mayow's similar discovery."
Professor E. N. da C. Andrade, in his Wilkins Lecture, "Robert Hooke," *Proceedings
of the Royal Society* [A] *201* (1950), 445, says: "The plates of the *Micrographia* are
beautiful in themselves but also record a number of fundamental discoveries . . .
Sachs, the historian of botany, puts Hooke with Malpighi, Grew and Leeuwenhoek as
'endeavouring by earnest reflection to apply the powers of mind to the objects seen
with the assisted eye, to clear up the true nature of the microscopic objects, and to
explain the secrets of their constitution.' The figures of the gnat, the flea and the louse
were long famous. But microscopic pictures and their discussion form but a small part
of the book. In it we find important theoretical discussions of the nature of light and
heat . . . further discussion of capillarity on the lines of his earlier tract [*An attempt for
the explication of the phenomena observable in an experiment published by the Honor-
able Robert Boyle* (London, 1661)]; experiments on the thermal expansion of solids and
liquids; shrewd speculations on tempering of metals; observations on crystal structure;
astronomical discussions, including attempts to form artificially craters like those of
the moon; and accounts of the magnitudes of stars, in which occurs the statement that
more powerful telescopes would discover fresh stars . . . Further, we must note that
the book contains a very full discussion of the colours of thin plates, such as flakes of
mica, air films between glasses, and bubbles not only of soapy water but of rosin and
several other substances. These observations were a cause of subsequent dispute
with Newton. The *Micrographia* gained Hooke considerable fame at home and abroad."
There have been three modern reprints of Hooke's *Micrographia*: (1) in R. T. Gunther,
ed., *Early Science in Oxford* (Oxford: Printed for the Subscribers, 1938), vol. XIII;
(2) a paperbound reprint of the above-cited reference, with preface by R. T. Gunther
(New York: Dover, 1961); (3) reproduction of the London edition of 1665, *Historiae
naturalis classica*, ed. J. Cramer and H. K. Swann (Weinheim: J. Cramer, 1961), vol.
XX. To these merits of Hooke could be added the kinetic theory of matter developed
by him in his *Lectures de potentia restitutiva, or, Of the spring: Experiments on the
power of springing bodies* (London, 1678), reissued in the *Lectiones Cutlerianae* (Lon-
don, 1679), and also the very ingenious theory of gravity based on this theory; see
Chapter III, "Newton and Descartes," Appendix H, *supra*. Some publications relat-
ing to Hooke which have appeared since this article was originally written are:
Louise D. Patterson, "Pendulums of Wren and Hooke," *Osiris 10* ((1952), 277–321;
"The Royal Society's Standard Thermometer 1663–1709," *Isis 44* (1953), 51–64;
Margaret Espinasse, *Robert Hooke* (London: Heinemann, 1956); Sir Geoffrey Keynes,
A Bibliography of Dr. Robert Hooke (Oxford: Clarendon Press, 1960); Johs Lohne,
"Newton's 'Proof' of the Sine Law and His Mathematical Principles of Colors,"

engender a deep resentment in Newton's proud and sensitive mind.[1] The wounds inflicted in this long-drawn and heated polemic are doubtless responsible for the nearly pathological aversion to all publications, the nearly invincible resistance to being drawn out of his shell, that Newton developed in his later years.

In the year 1675/6, when Newton presented to the Royal Society his *Hypothesis Explaining the Properties of Light*,[2] the bitterness of the polemic reached its climax; Hooke once more asserted that the main part of Newton's work "was contained in his *Micrographia*, which Mr. Newton had only carried farther in some particulars."[3] Newton replied by pointing out Hooke's indebtedness to Descartes and others and his inability to apply exact measurement to the problems of optics, especially to that of the colors in thin plates:

He left me to find out and make such experiments about it, as might inform me of the manner of the production of those colours, to ground an hypothesis on; he having no further insight to it than this, that the colour depended on some certain thickness of the plate; though what that thickness was at every colour, he confesses in his Micrography, he had attempted in vain to learn; and therefore, seeing I was left to measure it myself,[4] I suppose he will allow me to make use of what I took the pains to find out.

Archive for History of Exact Sciences 1 (1961), 389–405; Richard S. Westfall, "The Development of Newton's Theory of Color," *Isis 53* (1962), 339–358; "Newton's Reply to Hooke and the Theory of Colors," *Isis 54* (1963), 82–96; "Newton and His Critics on the Nature of Colors," *Archives Internationales d'Histoire des Sciences 15* (1962), 47–58.

[1] It made him abandon the project of his *Lectiones opticae*; see *Correspondence*, I, 146, Collins to Newton, and p. 161, Newton to Collins. On Newton's character, see the paper of Professor Kuhn quoted in note 1, p. 223.

[2] Newton sent it to the Royal Society on 9 December 1675, expressly stating that he did not want it to be published in the *Transactions*. See Birch, *History of the Royal Society*, III, 247–305, reproduced in Cohen, *Newton's Papers and Letters*, pp. 177–235. In this paper (pp. 263 sq.; pp. 193 sq.) Newton studies, *inter alia*, the phenomena of colors in thin plates and air laminae ("rings") that, indeed, had been extensively treated by Hooke in his *Micrographia* (Observ. IX, "Of the Colours observable in Muscovy Glass [mica] and other thin bodies," pp. 47–67) Hooke is therefore right in claiming priority. On the other hand, Newton is right in pointing out that Hooke did not, and could not, measure the thickness of these plates and laminae and left it to him to do so.

[3] Birch, *History of the Royal Society*, III, 269; Cohen, *Newton's Papers and Letters*, p. 199.

[4] Newton did it by substituting – a stroke of genius – convex and planoconvex lenses (object glasses) of known curvature pressed together for the thin plates of mica and the like used by Hooke; the measure of the radii of the rings enabled him to calculate the corresponding distance separating the lenses. As for the "hypothesis" he "grounded" on his experiments, it consisted – *horribile dictu* – in a combination of Hooke's undulatory theory of light and his own corpuscular conception. See F. Rosenberger, *Newton und seine physikalischen Prinzipien* (Leipzig, 1895).

And this I hope may vindicate me from what Mr. Hooke has been pleased to charge me with.[1]

Yet, instead of meeting Newton's attack with a countercharge, Hooke, though maintaining the superiority of his own theory over that of his rival, quite unexpectedly made a step toward reconciliation. Professor L. T. More assumes "that pressure was put on Hooke to appease the wounded feelings of the younger man,"[2] an assumption that goes far toward explaining the otherwise unintelligible fact that Hooke sent Newton a letter which Professor Pelseneer, who likewise attributes it to pressure – on the part of Oldenburg[3] – characterizes as "so courteous and so humble that it looks like a child's letter of excuses."[4]

Sir [writes Hooke][5], The hearing a letter of yours read last week in the meeting of the Royal Society, made me suspect that you might have been some way or other misinformed concerning me; and this suspicion was the more prevalent with me, when I called to mind the experience I have formerly had of the like sinister practices.[6] I have therefore taken the freedom, which I hope I may be allowed in philosophical matters to acquaint you of myself. First, that I doe noe ways approve of contention, or feuding or proving in print, and shall be very unwillingly drawn to such kind of warre. Next, that I have a mind very desirous of, and very ready to embrace any truth that shall be discovered, though it may much thwart or contradict any opinions or notions I have formerly embraced as such. Thirdly, that I do justly value your excellent disquisitions, and am extremely well pleased to see those notions promoted and improved which I long since began, but had not time to compleat. That I judge you have gone farther in that affair much than I did, and that as I judge you cannot meet with any subject more worthy your contemplation, so I believe the subject cannot meet with a fitter and more able person to enquire into it than yourself, who are every way accomplished to compleat, rectify, and reform what were the sentiments of my younger studies, which I designed to have done somewhat at myself, if my other more troublesome employments would have permitted,[7] though I am sufficiently sensible it would have been with

---

[1] Birch, *History of the Royal Society*, III, 279; Cohen, *Newton's Papers and Letters*, p. 209.

[2] See More, *Isaac Newton*, p. 175.

[3] It seems to me more probable that this pressure was exerted not by Oldenburg, but by Lord Brouncker; see Hooke's letter to Brouncker of *c.* June 1672, *Correspondence*, I, 198 sq.

[4] See Jean Pelseneer, "Lettres inédites de Newton," *Osiris* 7 (1939), 541. On this subject, see A. Rupert Hall and Marie Boas Hall, "Why Blame Oldenburg?" *Isis 53* (1962), 482–491.

[5] See Brewster, *Memoirs*, I, 140-141; More, *Isaac Newton*, pp. 175–176; *Correspondence*, I, 412.

[6] An obvious hint at Oldenburg, and not an unjust one.

[7] It is perfectly true that Hooke, who, as Curator of Experiments of the Royal

abilities much inferior to yours. Your design and mine are, I suppose, both at the same thing, which is the discovery of truth, and I suppose we can both endure to hear objections, so as they come not in the manner of open hostility, and have minds equally inclined to yield to the plainest deductions of reason from experiment. If, therefore, you will please to correspond about such matters by private letters, I shall very gladly embrace it; and when I shall have the happiness to peruse your excellent discourse, (which I can as yet understand nothing more of by hearing it cursorily read), I shall, if it be not ungrateful to you, send you freely my objections, if I have any, or my concurrences, if I am convinced, which is the more likely. This way of contending, I believe, to be the more philosophical of the two, for though I confess the collision of two hard-to-yield contenders may produce light, [yet] if they be put together by the ears by other's hands and incentives, it will [produce rath]er ill concomitant heat,

---

Society, was supposed "to furnish the Society every day [they met once a week] with three or four considerable experiments," never enjoyed the blessing of leisure of which Newton, at least in his Cambridge years, had so large a share. Yet it was certainly not only outward pressure that prevented Hooke from thinking out his extremely numerous and original ideas; it was just as much, or even more, the inner pressure of a feverish and ebullient mind. Let us quote once more the *DNB:*

"The registers of the Royal Society testify to the eagerness with which Hooke hurried from one inquiry to another with brilliant but inconclusive results. Among those which early engaged his attention were the nature of the air, its function in respiration and combustion, specific weights, the laws of falling bodies, the improvement of land-carriage and diving bells, methods of telegraphy, and the relation of barometrical readings to changes in the weather. He measured the vibrations of a pendulum two hundred feet long attached to the steeple of St. Paul's; invented a useful machine for cutting the teeth of watch-wheels; fixed the thermometrical zero at the freezing-point of water; and ascertained (in July 1664) the number of vibrations corresponding to musical notes." This characterization of Robert Hooke is not so very different from that of Professor Andrade, who says ("Robert Hooke," p. 439): "Probably the most inventive man who ever lived, and one of the ablest experimenters, he had a most acute mind, and made astonishingly correct conjectures, based on reason, in all branches of physics. Physics, however, was far from being his only field: he is the founder of scientific meteorology; as an astronomer he has observations of great significance to his credit; he did fundamental work on combustion and respiration; he was one of the founders of modern geology." And (p. 441) "From now on [1660] we are to be confronted with the difficulty of coping with the stream of inventions, notions, brilliant suggestions, accurate observations, daring speculations and prophetic conjectures that poured from Hooke's fertile brain and contriving hands. It will be impossible even to mention them all; to classify them will be difficult; in many cases, in view of the scanty record, it will be hard to decide what exactly was done. Practically everything, however, will bear witness to a truly extraordinary inventiveness and a truly modern outlook. Sometimes Hooke is wrong, but he is wrong in a strictly scientific and not a medieval way. Very often the ideas which he tumbled out in such profusion were taken by others; sometimes his findings were reached quite independently by others, which Hooke found hard to believe. At every stage we are witnessing the workings of a mind so active, so fertile in expedients, so interrupted at every hour, at every endeavour, by the inrush of new concepts, new projects, that it is hard to disentangle his doings. Newton said that he made his discoveries by keeping the subject constantly before him and waiting until the first dawnings opened little by little into the full light. This Hooke was quite unable to do; he totally lacked Newton's powers of concentration. His mind was restless, continually disturbed by fresh ideas, but they were nearly all good and many were of first importance."

which served for no other use but . . . kindle-cole. S^r, I hope you will pardon this plainness of, your very affectionate humble serv^t,

ROBERT HOOKE[1]

1675/6

Newton's reply, likewise written, most probably, under pressure, though very courteous and even conciliatory, is by no means as meek and humble as Hooke's letter. Quite the contrary: while recognizing the merits of his predecessors, Descartes and Hooke, even calling them "giants," he quite unmistakably insists on his own:

Dear Sir,—

At the reading of your letter I was exceedingly pleased and satisfied with your generous freedom, and think you have done what becomes a true philosophical spirit. There is nothing which I desire to avoyde in matters of philosophy more than contention, nor any kind of contention more than one in print; and, therefore, I most gladly embrace your proposal of a private correspondence. What's done before many witnesses is seldom without some further concerns than that for truth; but what passes between friends in private, usually deserves the name of consultation rather than contention; and so I hope it will prove between you and me. Your animadversions will therefore be welcome to me; for though I was formerly tyred of this subject by the frequent interruptions it caused to me, and have not yet, nor I believe ever shall recover so much love for it as to delight in spending time about it; yet to have at once in short the strongest objections that may be made, I would really desire, and know no man better able to furnish me with them than yourself. In this you will oblige me, and if there be any thing else in my papers in which you apprehend I have assumed too . . .

. . . If you please to reserve your sentiments of it for a private letter, I hope you [will find that I] am not so much in love with philosophical productions, but that I can make them yield. . . .

But, in the mean time, you defer too much to my ability in searching into this subject. What Descartes did was a good step.[2] You have added much several ways, and especially in considering the colours of thin plates. If I have seen farther, it is by standing on the shoulders of giants.[3] But I make no question you have divers very considerable experiments beside those

---

[1] This letter is addressed "to my much esteemed friend, Mr. Isaak Newton, at his chambers in Trinity College in Cambridge." *Correspondence*, I, 412 sq.

[2] If one considers that Descartes established the law of refraction and gave a complete theory of the rainbow, one must confess that the praise bestowed on him by Newton is not very lavish.

[3] As is pointed out by L. T. More, *Isaac Newton*, p. 177, n. 28, this celebrated saying, which is usually quoted as being original with Newton and as expressing his magnanimous modesty, is, as a matter of fact, a commonplace. It is used by Burton in his *Anatomy of Melancholy* as a quotation from Didacus Stella, *In Luc*. 10 tom. 2: *Pigmaei Gigantum humeris impositi plusquam ipsi gigantes vident.*

you have published, and some, it's very probable, the same with some of those in my late papers.[1]

This celebrated correspondence has been, since its publication, greatly admired and praised by the historians and biographers of Newton. Thus Brewster exclaims: "These beautiful letters, emulous of good feeling and lofty principle, throw some light on the character and position of two of the greatest of our English philosophers."[2] I must confess that I do not share this common admiration. Both letters seem to me to be too full of rhetoric. The mutual praise (though very carefully guarded by Newton) and the subtle distinction between contention in public and friendly discussion in private (a commonplace since Prodicos, or at least since Plato) give much more the impression of conforming to a conventional pattern than of following a free inspiration. Or, to quote Professor More: "These two letters have all the earmarks of an attempt towards a formal reconciliation which had been urged by others, and recognised as proper by themselves. Each of the writers expresses great admiration for the other's ability; each deprecates the public and partisan discussion of their opinions; and each requests the other to criticise rigourously his work, but to do it privately."[3] – Neither, of course, availed himself of the magnanimous and high-sounding invitation.

The official reconciliation did not heal the wounds inflicted by the conflict. Bitterness and resentment on both sides, and especially on Newton's, remained; to quote Professor More once more:

Two such men may indulge in general sentiments of a high and abstract order, and use elaborate expressions of personal esteem; but there could not be found two men, who were so temperamentally incapable to form a lasting friendship. Both were suspicious and sensitively vain. In Hooke these qualities showed themselves by wrathful explosions and by reiterated accusations that he had been robbed of the fruits of his work; in Newton, when opposed, they were equally apparent in a cold assumption of a disdain for fame and a silent retirement into his ivory tower. It is needless to say that their correspondence was limited to official communications; the embers of hostility still existed and needed only a new occasion to make them blaze in public. They never forgave each other: Hooke continued to claim that he had anticipated Newton's work, and Newton maintained his

[1] See Brewster, *Memoirs*, I, 141; More, *Isaac Newton*, 176; *Correspondence*, I, 416 sq. Newton's letter is dated "Cambridge, 5 February 1675/6." The rest of this letter deals with special optical questions of no interest in the present context.
[2] See Brewster, *Memoirs*, I, 143.
[3] See More, *Isaac Newton*, p. 177.

aloof attitude towards the Society till Hooke's death relieved him from the fear of his insinuations.[1]

Yet, outwardly and formally, cordial, or at least courteous, relations were re-established and, though no real scientific correspondence had followed the exchange of the letters of reconciliation, still, as has been shown by Professor Pelseneer, in the years 1677–1688 Newton and Hooke actually exchanged a couple of (rather insignificant) letters.[2] Newton even went so far as to congratulate Hooke on his election, after Oldenburg's death, to the secretaryship of the Royal Society.[3]

Thus it was perfectly natural that, having been, two years later, entrusted with holding and promoting the correspondence of the Royal Society with its members as well as with foreign scientists, Hooke, on 24 November 1679, addressed to Newton an invitation to resume his former relations with the Royal Society, and to participate in the exchange of scientific information with its members:

Sir – Finding by our registers that you were pledged to correspond with Mr. Oldenburg, and having also the happiness of receiving some letters from you my self make me presume to trouble you with this present scribble – Dr. Grew's more urgent occasions having made him decline the holding correspondence. And the Society hath devolved it on me. I hope therefore that you will please to continue your former favours to the Society by communicating what shall occur to you that is philosophicall, and for returne, I shall be sure to acquaint you with what we shall receive considerable from other parts or find out new here. And you may be assured that whatever shall be soe communicated shall be noe otherwise further imparted or disposed of than you yourself shall praescribe. I am not ignorant that both heretofore, and not long since also, they have been some who have indeavoured to misrepresent me to you, and possibly they or others have not been wanting to doe the like to me,[4] but difference in opinion if such there be (especially in philosophicall matters where interest hath little concerne) me thinks should not be the occasion of enmity – 'tis not with me I am sure. For my part I shall take it as a great favour if you shall please to communicate by letter your objections against any hypothesis or opinion of mine; and particularly if you will let me know your thoughts of that of compounding the celestiall motions of the planetts of a direct motion by the

[1] *Isaac Newton*, p. 177.
[2] See Pelseneer, "Lettres inédites de Newton."
[3] See *Correspondence*, II, 239; Pelseneer "Lettres inédites de Newton," p. 542, Newton to Hooke, 18 December 1677: "I wish you much happiness in yor new employmt & that the R. Society may flourish yet more by the labours of so able a member." Hooke was elected secretary of the Royal Society on 25 October 1677.
[4] Once more a hint at Oldenburg.

tangent and an attractive motion towards the centrall body,[1] or what objections you have against my hypothesis of the lawes or causes of springynesse.[2]

I have lately received from Paris a new hypothesis invented by Mo Mallement de Messanges,[3] D[r] of the Sorbon, who desires much to have what can be objected against it. He supposes then a center of this our vortex about which all the primary planets move in perfect circles, each of them in his aequall spaces in aequall times. The next to it he places the Sun; and about the Sun, Mercury as a satellit; the next Venus; the next the earth, about which the Moon as a satellit; then Mars; then Jupiter and his satellits; and Saturn with his. He supposes the Sun to make its revolution in about half the time the earth makes its, and the plaine of it to be inclined to the plaine of the ecliptick as much as the trepidation requires. He is not precise in defining any thing, as reserving a liberty to himself to help him out where objections might stick.

I am informed likewise from Paris that they are there about another work, viz. of setling the longitude and latitude of the most considerable places: the former of those by the eclipses of the satellites of Jupiter. M[r] Picart and De la Hire travell, and Mo[r] Cassini and Romer observe at Paris. They have already found that Brest in Britaigne is 18 leagues nearer Paris than all the mappes make it. I have written to a correspondent in Deavonshire to see if we can doe somewhat of that kind here, and I should be glad if by perpendicular observations, we could determine the difference of latitude between London and Cambridge. If you know of any one that will observe at Cambridge, I will procure it to be done here very exactly.

M[r] Collins shewed me a book he received from Paris of De la Hire containing first a new method of the conick sections[4] and secondly a treatise De locis solidis. I have not perused the book but M[r] Collins commends it. M[r] Flamstead by some late perpendicular observations hath confirmed the paralax of the orb of the earth.

But I fear I have too much trespassed, and therefore to put an end to your further trouble I shall subscribe my self, Sir,

Your very humble Servant

R. H.

---

[1] Hooke's ideas on celestial mechanics were expounded at the end of his *Attempt to Prove the Motion of the Earth by Observation* (London, 1674). I quote the relevant passage *infra*, p. 233.

[2] Hooke deals with the laws of elasticity (springiness) in his *Lectures de potentia restitutiva*.

[3] Claude Mallemont (or Mallemans) de Messanges, professor of philosophy in the Collège de Plessis. He published a *Nouveau système du monde inventé par M. Mallemont de Messanges* (Paris, 1678), followed by a *Nouveau système du monde, par lequel, sans excentricité, trépidation et autres inventions d'astrologues on explique mécaniquement tous les phénomènes* (Paris, 1679); a *Dissertation sur les comètes*, in 1681; and a solution of the quadrature of the circle in 1686. All his writings are a tissue of absurdities.

[4] Probably Philippe de la Hire's *Nouveaux éléments des sections coniques, les lieux géometriques, la construction ou effection des équations* (Paris, 1679).

[5] See Rouse Ball, *Essay*, pp. 139 sq.; More, *Isaac Newton*, pp. 220 sq.; *Correspondence*, II, 297.

Hooke's letter barely needs a comment. Having been, as I have already mentioned, newly entrusted with the correspondence of the Royal Society, he is performing his duty – or playing his part – in (a) informing Newton of his new appointment, (b) asking him, in a very courteous and dignified way, to resume his scientific co-operation with the Society, and (c) giving to Newton news about the recent developments in the field of science. Of course, one could ask oneself why Hooke finds it necessary to inform Newton about the obviously worthless "hypothesis" of Mallemont de Messanges. Yet it is possible that its worthlessness was somewhat less striking in 1679 than it is now, or even only a hundred years later: the *Philosophical Transactions* are full of things as manifestly worthless and absurd or even worse. Absurdity, as well as truth, is a daughter of time.

On the other hand, we should ask ourselves why Hooke asks Newton for a criticism of his work, quite particularly of his theory of elasticity and his celestial mechanics. Does he really want to learn the objections which Newton could formulate against them? This does not seem very probable: Hooke bears criticism as badly as Newton himself; to me it appears much more like a piece of rhetoric aimed at convincing Newton of the sincerity of his friendly feelings and at dissipating the apprehension and mistrust that Newton may still feel against him. We may assume, too, that Hooke is trying to induce Newton to acknowledge the value of his brilliant pioneer work in these two fields of study that seemed to lie outside of Newton's own preoccupations; Hooke did not – and could not – know that Newton had been interested in celestial mechanics for some fifteen years and that in this field, as in optics, Newton was already far ahead of him. Finally, it is even not impossible that Hooke expected, or at least hoped, that Newton would be able to bring his celestial mechanics to a completion, that is, to work out mathematically the ratio of the variation (as a function of the distance) of that attractive power of which he was the first to assert the cosmic universality and fundamental role.[1]

Hooke's merits in the development of the theory of elasticity have been recognized by history and rewarded by the naming of its cardinal law: Hooke's law; his contributions to celestial mechanics, on the other hand, are so completely overshadowed by the work of

---

[1] See my paper, "La Gravitation universelle, de Kepler à Newton," *Archives Internationales d'Histoire des Sciences 4* (1951), 638–653.

Newton that it is nearly impossible for us to appreciate them justly and to determine their value and importance in, and for, their own time.[1] In order to do so, we should compare Hooke's attempts not with Newton's achievements – there is between them no common measure – but with those of *his* contemporaries, or immediate predecessors, for example, with those of Borelli.[2]

Such a comparison would show that in the very first paper – read by Hooke before the Royal Society on 23 May 1666 – in which he deals with the problems of planetary motions, a paper in which Borelli's influence is unmistakable, Hooke's superiority is quite obvious.[3] The replacement of Borelli's "tendency" or "natural instinct" of the planets to move toward the sun (or, in the case of the satellites, toward their primary planet) by an attractive power of the central body that draws the planets (or the satellites) to itself enables Hooke to make a decisive step, and to consider this attractive power not as a constant force – like Borelli's "tendency" or "instinct" – but as a force which is some function of the distance. Hooke, it is true, does not know the exact law of variation of this force. Yet we must not overlook the fact that his conception is only incomplete and no longer simply false, as was Borelli's. In 1670, in his *Cutlerian Lectures*, Hooke seems to have taken a step further: a step of tremendous importance. The attractive power is now conceived not as a special force (or set of forces) that binds the planets to the sun or the satellites to their planet, but as a universal factor that binds all the

[1] A very able and scholarly attempt to vindicate for Hooke a much more important role in the development of celestial mechanics than is usually attributed to him has been made recently by Miss L. D. Patterson, "Hooke's Gravitation Theory and Its Influence on Newton," *Isis 40* (1949), 327–341; *41* (1950), 32–45. Unfortunately, Miss Patterson – who, in order to magnify Hooke (as a matter of fact, Hooke has been rather badly treated by Newton-inspired historians) charges Newton with all the capital sins, including plagiarism and falsification of documents – does not seem to me to appreciate at its just value the difference between an *idea* and a *theory*. A much more balanced and just account of Hooke's scientific work – the best that we have today – has been given by Andrade, "Robert Hooke."

[2] See A. Amitage, " 'Borell's Hypothesis' and the Rise of Celestial Mechanics," *Annals of Science 6* (1952), 268–282, and my paper, "La Mécanique céleste de Borelli," *Revue d'Histoire des Sciences 5* (1952), 101–138.

[3] See Birch, *History of the Royal Society*, II, 90; R. T. Gunther, "The Life and Work of Robert Hooke," *Early Science in Oxford*, VI, 245–266. In this paper Hooke (*a*) sketched – and rejected – an explanation of the incurvation of the planetary motions by aethereal pressure, and (*b*) suggested that "the inflecting of direct motion of a body into a curve" may be the result of "an attractive property of the body placed in the centre; whereby it continually endeavours to attract or draw it to itself." Hooke illustrated his conception by an experiment with a conical pendulum which, depending on the strength of the impetus (tangential) given to it, described circles or differently oriented ellipses; see Chapter III, "Newton and Descartes," Appendix H, *supra*.

celestial bodies (at least those of our solar system) together, and that, moreover, is identical with our terrestrial gravity.[1]

In 1674, in his *Attempt to Prove the Motion of the Earth by Observation* (London, 1674), pp. 27 sq., which, according to Hooke, reproduces the text, or the contents, of his 1670 lectures,[2] and which he says was read to the Royal Society in 1671, he announces

a system of the world differing in many particulars from any yet known answering in all things to the common rules of mechanical motions. This depends upon three suppositions.

First, that all celestial bodies whatsoever have an attraction or a gravitating power towards their own centers, whereby they attract not only their own parts, and keep them from flying from them, as they may observe the earth to do, but that they do also attract all the other celestial bodies that are within the sphere of this activity;[3] and consequently that not only the sun and moon have an influence upon the body and motion of the earth; and the earth upon them, but that Mercury, Mars, Saturn and Jupiter by their attractive power have a considerable influence upon its motions, and in the same manner the corresponding attractive power of the earth hath a considerable influence upon every one of their motions also.

The second supposition is this, that all bodies whatsoever that are put into a direct and simple motion will so continue to move forward in a straight line, till they are by some other effectual powers deflected and bent into a motion describing a circle, ellipsis or some other more compound curve line.

The third supposition is that these attractive powers are so much the more powerful in operating by how much the nearer the body wrought upon is to their own centers. Now what these several degrees are, I have not yet experimentally verified;[4] but it is a notion which, if fully prosecuted

---

[1] Miss L. D. Patterson, *Isis 40* (1949), 330, gives Hooke the credit for having discovered the inverse-square law as far back as 1664, though not having stated it explicitly in his *Micrographia*, and the law of centrifugal force nearly at the same time, in any case, prior to the experiments of 23 May 1666. In my opinion such is by no means the case. See p. 183 and Chapter III. Let us not forget, however, that universal attraction was asserted by Roberval already in 1644 in his *Aristarchi Samii de mundi systemate partibus et motibus ejusdem libellus* (Paris, 1644), reissued by Mersenne in his *Cogitata physicomathematica* (Paris, 1647), vol. III.

[2] Robert Hooke, *Lectiones Cutlerianae*, preface: "I have begun with a Discourse composed and read in Gresham College in the year 1670, when I designed to have printed it, but was diverted by the advice of some Friends to stay the repeating the Observation, rather than publish it upon the Experience of one Year only. But finding that Sickness hath hitherto hindered me from repeating the tryals, and that some Years Observations have already been lost by the first delay: I do rather hast it out now, though imperfect, then detain it for a better compleating, hoping it may be at least a Hint to others to prosecute and compleat the Observations, which I much long for."

[3] The sphere of activity of the attracting or gravitating power is thus considered by Hooke as finite.

[4] In his letter to Newton of 6 January 1680, Hooke writes that Halley, "when he returned from St Helena, told me that his pendulum at the top of the hill went slower than at the bottom" and thus "had solved me a query I had long desired to be answered

as it ought to be will mightily assist the astronomer to reduce all the celestial motions to a certain rule which I doubt will never be done without it. He that understands the nature of the circular pendulum and circular motion[1] will easily understand the whole ground of this principle and will know where to find direction in nature for the true understanding thereof, etc. This, I dare promise the undertaker, that he will find all the great motions in the world to be influenced by this principle, and that the true understanding thereof will be the true perfection of astronomy.

The boldness and the clarity of Hooke's thought and the depth of his intuition are nothing less than admirable; the near similarity of his world view with that of Newton is striking – Hooke certainly is perfectly right in insisting on his priority. Yet it cannot be denied that the lacuna which we discovered in his earlier work has not been filled up: Hooke still does not know "what the several degrees are" by which the attractive power varies with the distance. In 1678, when he publishes his *Cometa*, he is as far from the solution of that problem as in 1674,[2] and that is probably why, feeling that he is unable to keep his promise and to "explain" his "system of the world," he simply reissues, in 1679, his old *Attempt* under the new cover of *Lectiones Cutlerianae*.

Did he still believe in the possibility of determining the law of attraction "experimentally"? In any case, when in the same year 1679 he finally found out the inverse-square law, he certainly did not do it by experiment.[3] It is even possible that his appeal to astronomers and to those who "understand the nature of the circular pendulum and

but wanted opportunity, and that was to know whether the gravity did actually decrease at a greater height from the center. To examine this decrease of attraction I have formerly made many experiments on Paule's steeple and Westminster Abby, but none that were fully satisfactory." See Rouse Ball, *Essay*, p. 148. Besides the experiments at St. Paul's and Westminster Abbey, Hooke also made experiments in a deep mine at Banstead Downes; see Gunther, *Early Science in Oxford*, VI, 257.

[1] In spite of Miss L. D. Patterson's able defense of Hooke, "A Reply to Professor Koyré's Note on Robert Hooke," *Isis 41* (1950), 304–305, I still believe, as I pointed out in "Note on Robert Hooke," *Isis 41* (1950), 195, that it is not the "conatus to descend" but the "conatus of returning to the centre" in the plane of the motion – as, besides, Miss Patterson states herself in her paper on Hooke's gravitational theory, *Isis 40* (1949), 333, that Hooke assumes to be proportional to the sine of the vertex angle, and that, therefore, he is not among those who "understand the nature of the circular pendulum and circular motion." See also Johs Lohne, "Hooke versus Newton," *Centaurus 7* (1960), 6–52.

[2] The assertions (in the *DNB* and elsewhere) that the inverse-square law is stated in the *Cometa* are based on a misinterpretation of a passage in a letter of Newton to Halley of 20 June 1686 (Rouse Ball, *Essay*, p. 157): "I am almost confident by circumstances, that Sir Chr. Wren knew the duplicate proportion when I gave him a visit; and then Mr. Hooke (by his book Cometa written afterwards) will prove the last of us three that knew it." Newton does not mean that the "duplicate proportion" is to be found in the *Cometa*, but, on the contrary, that it does not appear even there.

[3] By the means at his disposal it was utterly impossible.

circular motion" reveals some doubt about the value, in this case, of purely experimental research.

I have said already and I want to repeat: it is only justice to recognize the outstanding value of Hooke's vision and to defend him against Newton's accusation of having only plagiarized from Borelli.[1] And yet one can well understand Newton's outburst when, having completely worked out the *Principia*, he was confronted with Hooke's claims:

Borell did something in it, and wrote modestly. He has done nothing, and yet written in such a way, as if he knew and had sufficiently hinted all but what remained to be determined by the drudgery of calculations and observations, excusing himself from that labour by reason of his other business, whereas he should rather have excused himself by reason of his inability. For 'tis plain, by his words, he knew not how to go about it. Now is not this very fine? Mathematicians, that find out, settle, and do all the business, must content themselves with being nothing but dry calculators and drudges; and another, that does nothing but pretend and grasp at all things,[2] must carry away all the invention, as well of those that were to follow him, as of those that went before.[3]

If, as I am inclined to believe, Robert Hooke, in writing to Newton, expected, or at least hoped, to start a friendly discussion, and to obtain some help, the answer must have been deeply disappointing

---

[1] Newton to Halley, 20 June 1686 (Rouse Ball, *Essay*, p. 159; *Correspondence*, II, 437): "I cannot forbear, in stating the point of justice, to tell you further, that he has published Borell's hypothesis in his own name."

[2] Newton is certainly more than unjust in not recognizing the amazing fecundity of Hooke's restless mind. Hooke is not a mere "pretender" and "grasper"; if he was nicknamed "the universal claimant" because "there is scarcely a discovery made in his time which he did not conceive himself entitled to claim" (*DNB*) it was because his mind was "so prolific" that he had really some reason to claim a great number of these discoveries, or at least the ideas on which they were based. Yet, it was this very restlessness, the inability of concentration, and therefore, of obtaining conclusive results, that made him unacceptable to Newton. Newton, to speak with Professor Pelseneer, was a "classical" mind and must have shuddered when reading Hooke's "profession de foi" (*Lectiones Cutlerianae*, preface), where he explained that "there is scarce one Subject of millions that may be pitched upon, but to write an exact and compleat History thereof, would require the whole time and attention of a man's life, and some thousands of Inventions and Observations to accomplish it: So on the other side no man is able to say that he will compleat this or that Inquiry, whatever it be, (The greatest part of Invention being but a luckey bitt of chance, for the most part not in our own power, and like the wind, the Spirit of Invention bloweth where and when it listeth, and we scarce know whence it came, or whether 'tis gone.) 'Twill be much better therefore to imbrace the influences of Providence, and to be diligent in the inquiry of everything we meet with. For we shall quickly find that the number of considerable Observations and Inventions this way collected, will a hundred fold out-strip those that are found by Design. No man butt hath some luckey hints and useful thoughts on this or that Subject he is conversant about, the regarding and communicating of which, might be a means to other Persons highly to improve them." See *supra*, p. 225, n. 7.

[3] See Rouse Ball, *Essay*, p. 159; *Correspondence*, II, 438.

to him. It is even possible that it was this disappointment – and irritation – that determined his subsequent behavior, namely, the fact that, though he promised Newton to keep his correspondence to himself, he immediately made it public by a reading at a meeting of the Royal Society: both Newton's letter and his own answer. Most probably, though he knew only too well – by experience – that Newton, to quote the expression of Locke, was a man "nicely to deal with," he could not resist the temptation of publicly correcting and thus humiliating his rival.

Indeed, Newton's answer to Hooke's invitation to correspond with him and the Royal Society, though by no means as harsh and as forbidding as, some years later, in a letter to Halley, he pretended it to be[1] – quite on the contrary, it is, in form, extremely courteous and urbane – aimed obviously at discouraging Hooke's attempts. It is quite clear that Newton does not want to resume his former relation with the Royal Society: perhaps less than ever, since it means dealing with Hooke, whom he still dislikes and does not trust.[2] Thus, in order to cut short all further approaches, he tells Hooke that he has completely renounced philosophy and has never even heard about Hooke's theories of celestial motions; that he has no time to lose in correspondence, though he is perfectly willing to "communicate in oral discourses" with him – should they ever have "familiar converse." Still, being a well-bred man and, besides, a Fellow of the Royal Society, Newton feels that he cannot give Hooke's request, made in the name of the Society, a purely negative answer and, to sweeten the pill, he proposes to him a carefully thought-out project of a very interesting experiment which should enable one "to prove the motion of the earth by observation."[3] It is

[1] Newton to Halley, 20 June 1686, Rouse Ball, *Essay*, p. 157: "In my answer to his first letter I refused his correspondence, told him I had laid philosophy aside, sent him only the experiment of projectiles (rather shortly hinted than carefully described), in compliment to sweeten my answer, expected to hear no further from him."

[2] According to Professor More, *Isaac Newton*, p. 297, "Newton . . . with great ingenuity, relieved his feelings of resentment for past injustice, and insinuated every reason for making Hooke so angry that he would drop any further correspondence."

[3] Though Newton calls it "a fancy" and, in his letter to Halley (quoted *supra*, n. 1), pretends it to be "rather shortly hinted than carefully described," it is, as Professor Pelseneer rightly remarks ("Lettre inédite de Newton," pp. 240 sq.), "en dépit de la négligence de l'exposé, un magnifique exemple de la conception d'un problème scientifique chez Newton"; besides, adds he (p. 241, n. 11), "cette négligence concerne surtout la forme; au contraire, certains détails de l'expérience proposée par Newton révèlent un sens admirable de l'importance relative des causes d'erreurs dont Hooke allait avoir à tenir compte au cours de l'expérimentation, par exemple la dissymétrie causée dans les couches d'air du puits par la chute de la bille." I would go even further: in my opinion, Newton, in instructing Hooke about the manner in which the proposed

in describing this experiment that Newton made the fateful blunder[1] which occasioned the flare-up of his second polemic with Hooke and finally led him to the elucidation of the inverse-square law of universal gravitation.

Newton's letter to Hooke has been considered by all Newton's historians – even by such careful and critical ones as Professor Pelseneer and Professor More – as an invaluable document about its author's spiritual development. In my opinion it is by no means worthy of such confidence. Newton – a suspicious and secret mind – had no reason whatever to be sincere and "candid" with Hooke. Most probably, he was not. Thus, all he says – even, or perhaps just, the famous phrases in which he describes his aversion for science, though seemingly supported by comparable assertions in 1676 and confirmed by his letters to Halley in 1686 – is not to be taken as gospel truth. It is, of course, quite possible that, at the time when he received Hooke's letter, he was "busy" "upon other things," and "thought no farther of philosophical matters than his letters put me up."[2] He may have been occupied with pure mathematics or chemical experiments, or with theology, or even with something else,[3] but it is impossible to admit that this aloofness lasted long years and was as strong as he tells Hooke. Indeed, some months before (in February 1679), he sends to Locke a very elaborate paper, in which he develops – as a hypothesis – a physical explanation of gravitation. Moreover he contradicts and betrays himself: at the same moment when he tells Hooke (in the letter of 28 November 1679) that he has "shook hands with philosophy" and that he has never so much as heard of Hooke's "hypothesis of compounding the celestial motions of the planets, of a direct motion by the tangent to the curve" (which means that he not only has never heard of the famous pendulum experiments of 1666 but also has never read his *Attempt to Prove the Motion of the Earth by Observation* of 1674 and of 1679), he informs him of having ordered two pieces of metal for a reflecting tube and congratulates him on the

---

experiment is to be performed, and in analyzing the possible sources of error, wants to give a lesson to Hooke, and to show him his own ability as an experimenter. Moreover, he is, in a certain sense, reversing the roles: it is he, Newton, who gives the idea, and Hooke who has the drudgery of finding out.

[1] In describing the trajectory of a falling body, he told Hooke that it would be a spiral.

[2] Newton to Halley, 20 June 1686; Rouse Ball, *Essay*, p. 157; *Correspondence*, II, 436.

[3] Professor Pelseneer, "Lettre inédite de Newton," suggests that he was studying law.

confirmation by Flamsteed of the discovery of the earth's parallax which Hooke announced in his book.[1]

Small wonder that Hooke did not believe him.[2] It was not so much a lack of affection for philosophy as a lack of affection for Hooke – and fear of being "embroiled" in discussions – that inspired Newton. But let the reader judge for himself.

Sir,

I cannot but acknowledge my self every way by the kindness of your letter tempted to concur with your desires in a philosophical correspondence. And heartily sorry I am that I am at present unfurnished with matter answerable to your expectations – for I have been this last half year in Lincolnshire cumbered with concerns amongst my relations till yesterday when I returned hither; so that I have had no time to entertain philosophical meditations, or so much as to study or mind any thing else but country affairs. And before that, I had for some years last been endeavouring to bend myself from philosophy to other studies[3] in so much that I have long grutched the time spent in that study unless it be perhaps at idle hours sometimes for a diversion; which makes me almost wholy unacquainted with what philosophers at London or abroad have of late been imployed about. And perhaps you will incline the more to believe me when I tell you that I did not, before the receipt of your last letter, so much as heare (that I remember) of your hypothesis of compounding the celestial motions of the planets, of a direct motion by the tangent to the curve, and of the laws and causes of springyness, though these no doubt are well known to

[1] See *An Attempt to Prove the Motion of the Earth by Observation*, p. 25: "'Tis manifest then by the observations of July the Sixth and Ninth: and that of the One and twentieth of October that there is a sensible parallax of the Earths Orb to the first Star in the head of *Draco*, and consequently a confirmation of the Copernican System against the *Ptolomaick* and *Tychonic*." It is difficult to admit that these assertions of ignorance of Hooke's work are anything else but irony.

[2] Hooke was perfectly right in disbelieving Newton, and in inserting before the last paragraph of Newton's letter the words: "he here pretends he knew not H's hypothesis." There seems to be very little doubt, if any, about the fact that Newton *knew* "Hooke's hypothesis," as, besides the slip I have already pointed out, he quite definitely says so in his letter to Halley of 20 June 1686, where, protesting against Hooke's claim of having taught him "the duplicate proportion," he adds, "That by the same reason he concludes me then ignorant of the rest of the duplicate proportion, he may as well conclude me ignorant of the rest of that theory I had read before in his book" (Rouse Ball, *Essay*, p. 157); and "That when Hugenius [in 1673] put out his Horol-[ogium] Oscil[latorium] . . . I had then my eye upon comparing the forces of the planets arising from their circular motion, and understood it; so that a while after, when Mr. Hooke propounded the problem solemnly, in the end of his Attempt to prove the Motion of the Earth, if I had not known the duplicate proportion before, I could not but have found it now." In the postscript to this letter (p. 160) Newton writes: "For his extending the duplicate proportion down to the centre (which I do not) made him correct me, and tell me the rest of his theory as a new thing to me, and now stand upon it, that I had all from that his letter, notwithstanding that he had told it to all the world before, and I had seen it in his printed books, all but the proportion."

[3] "Philosophy" in the language of the seventeenth century includes natural science (*philosophia naturalis*), but not mathematics.

the philosophical world. And having thus shook hands with philosophy, and being also at present taken of with other business, I hope it will not be interpreted out of any unkindness to you or the R. Society that I am backward in engaging my self in these matters, though formerly I must acknowledge I was moved by other reasons[1] to decline, as much as Mr Oldenburg's importunity and ways to engage me in disputes would permit, all correspondence with him about them. However I cannot but return my hearty thanks for your thinking me worthy of so noble a commerce and in order thereto francly imparting to me several things in your letter.

As to the hypothesis of Monsr Mallemont, though it should not be true yet if it would answer to phaenomena it would be very valuable by reason of its simplicity. But how the orbits of all the primary planets but Mercury can be reduced to so many concentric circles through each of which the planet moves equal spaces in equal times (for that's the hypothesis if I mistake not your description) I do not yet understand. The readiest way to convince the world of this truth would be I conceive to set forth first in some two of the planets, suppose Mars and earth, a specimen thereof stated and determined in numbers.[2]

I know no body in the University addicted to making astronomical observations: and my own short sightedness and tenderness of health makes me something unfit. Yet it's likely I may sometime this winter when I have more leisure than at present attempt what you propound for determining the difference of latitude between Cambridge and London.

I am glad to hear that so considerable a discovery as you made of the earth's annual parallax is seconded by M Flamstead's observations.

In requital of this advertisement I shall communicate to you a fancy of my own about discovering the earth's diurnal motion. In order thereto I will consider the earth's diurnal motion alone, without the annual, that having little influence on the experiment I shall here propound. Suppose then, *BDG* represents the globe of the earth [see Fig. 3] carried round once a day about its centre *C* from west to east according to the order of the letters *BDG*; and let *A* be a heavy body suspended in the air, and moving round with the earth so as perpetually to hang over the same point thereof *B*. Then imagine this body *A* let fall, and its gravity will give it a new motion towards the centre of the earth without diminishing the old one from west to east. Whence the motion of this body from west to east, by reason that before it fell it was more distant from the centre of the earth than the parts of the earth at which it arrives in its fall, will be greater than the motion from west to east of the parts of the earth at which the body arrives in its fall; and therefore it will not descend the perpendicular *AC*, but outrunning the parts of the earth will shoot forward to the east side of the perpendicular describing in its fall a spiral line *ADEC*, quite con-

---

[1] Newton believed himself to have been unfairly treated by the Royal Society in general and by Hooke in particular.

[2] Professor Pelseneer comments on this passage as follows ("Lettre inédite de Newton," p. 240): "Ces derniers mots expriment de fort heureuse façon l'idée qui est à la base de l'oeuvre newtonienne: la traduction dans le langage mathématique des faits d'expériences et le contrôle des hypothèses ainsi réalisé en toute sûreté."

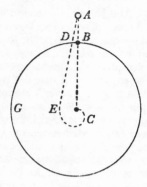

Fig. 3

trary to the opinion of the vulgar who think that, if the earth moved, heavy bodies in falling would be outrun by its parts and fall on the west side of the perpendicular. The advance of the body from the perpendicular eastward will in a descent of but twenty or thirty yards be very small, and yet I am apt to think it may be enough to determine the matter of fact. Suppose then in a very calm day a pistol bullet were let down by a silk line from the top of a high building or well, the line going through a small hole made in a plate of brass or tinn fastened to the top of the building or well, and the bullet when let down almost to the bottom were setled in water so as to cease from swinging, and then let down further on an edge of steel lying north and south to try if the bullet in setling thereon will almost stand in aequilibrio but yet with some small propensity (the smaller the better) decline to the west side of the steel as often as it is so let down thereon. The steel being so placed underneath, suppose the bullet be then drawn up to the top and let fall by cutting, clipping or burning the line of silk, and if it fall constantly on the east side of the steel it will argue the diurnall motion of the earth.[1] But what the event will be I know not, having never attempted to try it.[2] If any body would think this worth their trial, the best way in my opinion would be to try it in a high church or wide steeple, the windows being first well stopped; for in a narrow well the bullet possibly may be apt to receive a ply from the straitened air neare the sides of the well, if in its fall it come nearer to one side than to another. It would be convenient also that the water into which the bullet falls be a yard or two deep or more, partly that the bullet may fall more gently on the steel, partly that the motion which it has from west to east at its entering into the water may by meanes of the longer time of descent through the

---

[1] The reader may judge if these elaborate prescriptions are really "rather hinted than carefully described."

[2] Newton, of course, cannot doubt his analysis of the movement of the falling body and its "outrunning" the parts of the earth that are below it, and he does not need an experiment in order to be certain of it; the only thing he can doubt is the possibility of ascertaining this outrunning by experiment.

water, carry it on further eastward and so make the experiment more manifest.

If I were not so unhappy as to be unacquainted with your hypothesis abovementioned[1] (as I am with almost all things which have of late been done or attempted in philosophy) I should so far comply with your desire as to send you what objections I could think of against them, if I could think of any. And on the other hand I could with pleasure heare and answer any objections made against any notions of mine in a transient discourse for a divertisment.[2] But yet my affection to philosophy being worn out, so that I am almost as little concerned about it as one tradesman is to be about another man's trade or a country man about learning, I must acknowledge my self averse from spending that time in writing about it which I think I can spend otherwise more to my own content and the good of others: and I hope neither you nor any body els will blame me for this aversness. To let you see that it is not out of any shyness, reservedness, or distrust that I have of late and still do decline phi[losophi]call commerce but only out of my applying my self to other things, I have communicated to you the notion above set down (such as it is) concerning the descent of heavy bodies for proving the motion of the earth; and shall be as ready to communicate in oral discourse anything I know, if it shall ever be my happiness to have familiar convers frequently with you.[3] And possibly if any thing usefull to mankind occurs to me I may sometimes impart it to you by letter. So wishing you all happiness and success in your endeavours, I rest,

Sir,
Your humble Servant
to command

Is. NEWTON

P.S. Mr. Cock has cast two pieces of metal for me in order to a further attempt about the reflecting tube which I was the last year inclined to by the instigation of some of our Fellows. If I do any thing you may expect to hear from me. But I doubt the tool on which they were to be ground, being in the keeping of one lately deceased who was to have wrought the metals, is lost.

Cambridge.

Novemb. 28, 1679

Endorsed: For his ever Hon^d ffriend Mr Robert Hooke at his Lodgings in Gresham College in London[4]

The problem Newton is dealing with in the experiment he suggests to Hooke, namely, the problem of the trajectory of a heavy body falling to the earth, or to the center of the earth, has a very long and

---

[1] Newton rubs it in!

[2] ". . . in a transient discourse for a divertisment," that is, not taking any serious account of them. It was by no means what Hooke aimed at.

[3] As Newton lived in Cambridge and practically never went to London, the probability of such a "familiar converse" was, obviously, not very great.

[4] See Rouse Ball, *Essay*, pp. 141 sq.; *Correspondence*, II, 300 sq.; see also L. T. More, *Isaac Newton*, pp. 223 sq.

intricate story – unfortunately too long and too intricate to be dealt with here. Edmund Hoppe, in his *History of Physics*,[1] seeks the source of "the opinion of the vulgar who think that, if the earth moved, heavy bodies in falling would be outrun by its parts and fall on the west side of the perpendicular" in Tycho Brahe, who "in his *De mundi aetherei recentioribus phenomenis* (1588–1610) presented as the principal objection against the rotation of the earth the fact that a stone falling on the west side of a tower would deviate to the west, for during its fall the earth flees beneath it to the west." It is perfectly true that Tycho Brahe used this argument as well as several others, based on the same fundamental conception – that of the Aristotelian dynamics. Yet he did not invent them, but only clothed them, sometimes, in modern garb.[2] As to the argument of the body falling from a tower, it belongs to the stock in trade of the objections against the movement of the earth and can be traced back to its discussion, and rejection, by Ptolemy and, farther back, by Aristotle himself, who asserts that, if the earth were moving, a stone thrown perpendicularly upward would never fall back on the place wherefrom it departed because that place would, meanwhile, move away from beneath it.[3]

The Aristotelian (Ptolemaic, Tychonian) argument is by no means stupid. Quite the contrary: on the basis of the Aristotelian dynamics, or even, more exactly, on the basis of the Aristotelian conception of motion, according to which the motion of a body, especially its natural motion, is perfectly independent of, and not influenced by, the motion of its point of origin *we* believe it to be the case in the propagation of the rays of light – it *is* perfectly sound and even irrefutable. In order to disprove it, a new conception of motion (and of space, physical reality, and so on) was needed, and before it had been developed – by Galileo and Descartes – the attempts made by the Copernicans to answer the argument in question were bound to be weak and rather unconvincing.[4] Copernicus, for instance, asserted that, the circular motion of the earth being a "natural" and not a "violent" one, it would be "participated in" by all the earthly objects; Kepler explained that all the "earthly" bodies were drawn from west to east by the same "magnetical" attractive power

[1] See Edmund Hoppe, *Histoire de la physique* (Paris: Payot, 1928), p. 54.

[2] See my *Études galiléennes* (Paris: Hermann, 1939), part III, "Galilée et la loi d'inertie," pp. 22 sq.

[3] See Aristotle, *De coelo*, I, 2: *Physica*, II, 1, and V, 2; Ptolemy, *Almagest*, I, 7.

[4] By far the best defense of the Copernican position, from the point of view of the theory of *impetus*, was devised by Giordano Bruno; see my *Études galiléennes*, part III, pp. 11 sq.

or strains that drew them toward the earth.[1] It is, therefore, hardly surprising that the anti-Copernicans – and anti-Copernicanism was by no means supported only by the condemnation of the heliocentric system by the Roman church and restricted to Catholic countries[2] – continued to make use of the old objection throughout the seventeenth century. Thus, among countless others, this objection is raised by the celebrated author of the widely read, and very influential, *Almagestum novum*, the Jesuit J. B. Riccioli.[3]

The Galilean "New Science" destroyed, of course, the very basis of the Aristotelian reasoning. Yet, as a matter of fact, Galileo himself did not give a correct solution of the problem. He asserted, indeed, in his *Dialogue on the Two Greatest World Systems*, that, whether the earth moved or stood still, all the phenomena that may happen on it, with the sole exception of the tides (which he explained by a combination of the effects of the earth's diurnal and annual motions), would take place in a perfectly identical manner. A rather sad conclusion – it precluded the finding out of a physical proof of the Copernican doctrine – which seemed unbelievable, and, besides, was false. Moreover, in his deduction of the true ("absolute") motion of the falling body, as distinguished from its motion relative to the moving earth (a question that every Copernican had to consider) he made an error – which, it is true, he recognized later that he had made – stating it to be *circular*.[4]

The error of the Galilean solution was discovered by Mersenne,[5] who subjected it to a very searching criticism, and tried to devise a better one. This, in turn, led to a very interesting discussion about the trajectory of a falling body, a discussion in which Fermat took a prominent part.[6]

[1] *Ibid.*, pp. 26 sq.

[2] Even Isaac Barrow, Newton's master, was by no means sure of the verity of the Copernican doctrine, and, on his deathbed, expressed the hope that he would learn the truth in the other world. About the spread of Copernicanism in England, see F. R. Johnson, *Astronomical Thought in Renaissance England* (Baltimore: Johns Hopkins Press, 1937).

[3] Johannes Baptista Riccioli, S.J., *Almagestum novum* (Bologna, 1651); *Astronomia reformata* (Bologna, 1665).

[4] See *Dialogo . . . sopra i due massimi sistemi del mondo*, in *Le Opere di Galileo Galilei* (edizione nazionale, VII, pp. 190 sq.)

[5] See Marin Mersenne, *Harmonices mundi* (Paris, 1636); *Harmonie universelle* (Paris, 1636); *Cogitata physicomathematica* (Paris, 1644).

[6] The very interesting discussions about the trajectory of a body falling onto a rotating earth are unfortunately too intricate to be dealt with here. I have studied this history in "A Documentary History of the Problem of Fall from Kepler to Newton," *Transactions of the American Philosophical Society*, new series, *45* (1955), 329–355. Here I shall only mention that according to Fermat this trajectory will have

On the other hand, the partial acceptance of Galileo's erroneous theory by Riccioli induced the latter to present a new objection against the motion of the earth, an objection that gave birth to a heated polemic in Italy, of which polemic Newton's friend James Gregory published a very carefully written report in the *Philosophical Transactions* in 1668.[1]

---

the form of a spiral, and that this view was held also by Stephano degli Angeli (see next note). Fermat developed his theory in a letter to Galileo which has remained unpublished. Yet, since he communicated it to Mersenne, Mersenne gave an account of it in his *Cogitata physicomathematica*, pp. 57 sq., and even added to the text a drawing (Fig. 4) which is not without some resemblance to that of Newton; in both of them, for

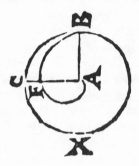

Fig. 4

instance, in spite of the fact that the deviation of the falling body from the perpendicular is to the east, the spiral is drawn from the right to the left. Newton may have been acquainted with Fermat's thesis and with Mersenne's drawing.

[1] "An Account of a controversy betwixt Stephano de Angelis, professor of the mathematics in Padua, and Joh. Baptista Riccioli, Jesuite; as it was communicated out of their lately Printed Books by that learned mathematician, Mr. Jacob Gregory, a Fellow of the R. Society," *Philosophical Transactions of the Royal Society I* (1668), 693 sq. Gregory does not quote the titles of the books he is reporting about. It seems worthwhile to reproduce them in full:

[i] Stefano degli Angeli: *Considerationi sopra la forza/di alcune raggioni/ fisicomatte-matiche/ addotte dal M. R. P./Gio. Battista Riccioli della Compagnia di Giesù nel suo Almagesto Nuova/et Astronomia Riformata contro il/Sistema Copernicano/espresse in due dialogi da F./ Stefano degli Angeli/Venetiano, Mattematico nello Studio di Padova,* Apreso Bartolo Bruni, Venetia 1667;

[ii] Michele Manfredi, replying to Angeli in the name of Riccioli, who did not want to enter himself into the polemics, or, at least, to do it under his own name (according to Carlos Sommervogel, S.J., *Bibliothèque de la Compagnie de Jésus* [Brussels, Paris, 1895], VI, 1803, s.v. "Riccioli," "Manfredi" is only a pseudonym of Riccioli): *Argomento fisicomattematico/del padre Gio. Battista Riccioli Della Compagnia di Giesù/contro il moto diurno della terra,/Confirmato di nuovo con l'occasione della Ris-posta alle Conside-/razioni sopro la Forza del dello Argomento, etc./Fatte dal M. R. Fr. Stefano De gil Angeli,/Mattematico nello Studio di Padova,/All'Illustriss. Signore il Sig. Co: Francesco Carlo Caprara,/Conte di Pantano,/Confaloniere di Giustizia/del Popolo e Commune di Bologna,\ n Bologna, Per Emilio Maria, e Fratelli de' Manolesi, 1668;*

[iii] Angeli, defending himself against Manfredi, and counterattacking: *Seconde/ considerationi/sopra la forza/dell' argomento fisico-mattematico/del M. Rev. P./Gio.*

Thus it is not particularly surprising that Newton too, perhaps as early as when reading Gregory's paper, turned his attention to the problem; nor is it astonishing that, having done so, he found the true answer: a body falling from a high tower will not "lag behind," but "outrun" it, that is, fall not to the *west* but to the *east* of its initial position.

Now let us go back to Newton and to Hooke.

Upon receiving Newton's letter above discussed, Hooke immediately presented it to the Royal Society. At its meeting on 4 December 1679,

Mr. Hooke produced and read a letter of Mr. Newton to himself, dated 28th November, 1679, containing his sentiments of Mons. Mallemont's new hypothesis of the heavens; and also suggesting an experiment, whereby to try, whether the earth moves with a diurnal motion or not, viz. by the falling of a body from a considerable hight, which, he alledged, must fall to the eastward of the perpendicular, if the earth moved.

This proposal of Mr. Newton was highly approved of by the Society;

Battista Riccioli/della Compagnia di Gésù,/contra il moto diurno della terra,/spiegato dal Sig. Michel Manfredi nelle sue "*Risposte, e/Riflessioni sopra le prime Considera-tione/di/F. Stefano degl' Angeli/ Venetiano/Mattematico nello Studio di Padova*"/ *Espresse da guesti in due altri Dialoghi III, e. IV./Per Mattio Bolzetta de Cadorini, in Padova*, 1668.

Besides the books reported about by Gregory there are four others on the same subject:

[iv] *Risposta/di Gio: Alfonso/Borelli/Messinese Matematico della Studio di Pisa/Alle considerazioni fatte sopra alcuni luoghi del suo/Libro della Forza della Percossa/Dell R. P. F. Stefano De Gl. Angeli/Matematico nello Studio di Padova. All' Illustrissimo, e Dottissimo Sig./Michel Angelo Ricci.* Messina, 29 Febraio, 1688;

[v] *Terze/Considerationi/Sopra una lettera/Del Molto illustre, et eccelentissimo Signor/Gio: Alfonso Borelli Messinese Mattematico nello Studio di Pisa/Scritta da Questi in replica/Di a'cune dottrine incidamente tocche/Da Fra/Stefano degli Angeli/Venetiano/ Mattematico Nello Studio di Padova/Nelle sue prime considerationi sopra la forza di certo Argomento/contro il moto diurno Terra/Espresse da questo in un Dialogo/Quinto in ordine,* In Venetia M.DC.LXVIII, Apresso li Heredi Leni con licenza de' Superiori;

[vi] *Confermazione/d'una sentenza/del Signor/Gio Alfonso/Borelli M./Matematico dello Studio di Pisa/di nuovo contradetta/Dal/M. R. P. Fra Stefano/de Gl' Angeli/ Matematico dello Studio di Padova/nelle sue terze considerationi/Prodotta da/ Diego Zerilli./*In Napoli. per Ludovico Cauallo, 1668;

[vii] *Quarte/Considerationi/Sopra la Confermatone/D'una Sentenza dal Sig. Gio. Alfonso Borelli M./Matematico nello Studio di Pisa/Prodotta da Diego Zerilli/contro le terze Considerationi/ Di Stefano degli Angeli/E sopra l'Apologia del M. R. P. Gio. Battista Riccioli/Della Compagnia di Giesù/A favore d'un suo Argomento detto Fisico-Matematico/Contro il sistema Copernicano/Espresse dal medesimo de gl' Angeli Venetiano Matematico/nello Studio di Padova in due Dialoghi VI. e. VII.* In Padova, Per Mattio Cadorin detto Bolzetta, 1669, con Licenza de' Superiori.

According to Sommervogel, "Riccioli," the *Apologia* of R. P. G. B. Riccioli is the same book as that of Manfredi quoted under [ii]. See my paper, "Le De motu gravium de Galilée," *Revue d'Histoire des Sciences 13* (1960), 197–245.

and it was desired, that it might be tried as soon as could be with convenience.[1]

Newton's proposal was not only approved, but also discussed. And nothing is more illuminating than this discussion; it shows us the scientific climate, or, if one prefers, the level of the scientific understanding – or lack of understanding – of even the best minds of the time. Thus we read that

Sir Christopher Wren supposed, that there might be something of this kind tried by shooting a bullet upwards at a certain angle from the perpendicular round every way, thereby to see whether the bullets so shot would all fall in a perfect circle round the place, where the barrell was placed. This barrell he desired might be fixed in a frame upon a plain foot, and that foot placed upon a true plain every way, and the mouth of the gun be almost in the same point over the plain which way soever shot.

Mr. Flamstead hereupon alledged, that it was an observation of the gunners, that to make a ball fall into the mouth of the piece, it must be shot at eighty-seven degrees; and that he knew the reason thereof; and that it agreed with his theory: and that a ball shot perpendicularly would never fall perpendicularly: and he mentioned the recoiling of a perpendicular jet of waters. But this was conceived to arise from some mistake of the gunners, in not well taking notice of all circumstances; since a body shot perpendicularly would also descend perpendicularly; and a body shot at eighty-seven degrees would fall considerably distant from the place where it was shot.[2]

A week later, on 11 December 1679, Hooke once more deals with Newton's letter. This time it is not the experiment, but Newton's solution of the problem of the trajectory of the falling body that is in question:

Upon the mentioning of Mr. Newton's letter, and the experiment proposed in it, Mr. Hooke read his answer to him upon that subject, wherein he explained what the line described by a falling body must be supposed to be, moved circularly by the diurnal motion of the earth,[3] and perpendicularly by the power of gravity: and he shewed, that it would not be a spiral line, as Mr. Newton seemed to suppose, but an excentrical elliptoid, supposing no resistance in the medium: but supposing a resistance, it would be an excentric ellipti-spiral, which, after many revolutions, would rest at last in the centre: that the fall of the heavy body would not be directly east, as Mr. Newton supposed: but to the south-east, and more

---

[1] Minutes of the Royal Society, 4 December 1679; Birch, *History of the Royal Society*, III, pp. 512 sq.; Rouse Ball, *Essay*, p. 145.

[2] *Ibid.* The criticism of Wren's and Flamsteed's opinions is probably due to Hooke.

[3] Even Hooke, in spite of the fact that he had given to the principle of inertia a pretty good formulation, falls into the error of considering the falling bullet as moved circularly by the rotation of the earth.

to the south than the east. It was desired, that what was tryable in this experiment might be done with the first opportunity.[1]

The problem whether by "elliptoid" Hooke meant an ellipse or simply some kind of oval curve has always been a crux for the historians.[2] The finding of Hooke's letter to Newton at last enables us to give a definitive answer to this vexed question: Hooke did *not* mean the curve to be an ellipse.[3]

To the second *questio vexata,* by what kind of reasoning Hooke arrived at the conviction that the falling body – supposing, as always had been done, no resistance in the medium – would describe a curve closed upon itself, and thus assert, *for the first time and in violent opposition to the whole preceding tradition,*[4] that a body falling onto a moving earth will *not* arrive at its center, in contradistinction to what would happen if the earth remained immobile, this letter, unfortunately, gives us no information, and we are still reduced to hypotheses.

It is nevertheless extremely interesting to see that Hooke, though deploring Newton's "desertion of philosophy," is more than skeptical about the reality of this desertion. But, of course, the chief value of this letter lies in its scientific part, as it gives us the first, though not quite correct – but we cannot blame him for that[5] – application to the problem of the trajectory of falling bodies of Hooke's theory of "compounding a curve by a direct [tangential] Motion and an attractive one to the centre."

Hooke's letter is dated 9 December 1679:[6]

For his much honoured freind Mr Isaac Newton Lucasion Professor at Cambridge

S^r

Your Deserting Philosophy in a time when soe many other Eminent freinds have also left her (Steno, De Graft and now newly Signor Brorus

---

[1] See Birch, *History of the Royal Society,* III, p. 516; Rouse Ball, *Essay,* p. 146.

[2] See L. D. Patterson, *Isis 41* (1950), 32 sq. and 42.

[3] Hooke to Newton, 9 December 1679, *Correspondence,* II, 304 sq. This letter was published for the first time in the original version of this article, *Isis 43* (1952), 329 sq.

[4] Even Borelli, who asserted that a planet gravitating toward the sun and animated by a motion along the tangent will not fall into the sun but will move around it and describe an ellipse, never asserted that a heavy body on the earth will behave in the same manner.

[5] The problem that Hooke and Newton are dealing with is extremely difficult and was solved only in 1835 by Coriolis.

[6] In this letter only the superscription and the signature are in Hooke's own handwriting. The rest is written by an amanuensis, and a very bad and ignorant one. I am reproducing it as faithfully as possible, without correcting either the spelling or the punctuation, even where the words are obviously misspelled or make no sense.

Borellij Vivians[1] and some others) Seems a little Unkind yet tis to be hoped her allurements may sometimes make you (as well as them) alter your resolutions, though never soe Deleberately & positively made: for my one part I confesse that I may tell you my opinion frankly. I doe not despare of you at all for I find by your letter you doe sumetimes for your divertisements spend an Hower or soe, in conversing And I know that you that have soe fully known those Dilights cannot chuse but sumetime have a hankering after them and now and then Desire a tast of them, And I would never wish any thing more from a Person of your ability: I hate Drudges or Devotons[2] at any thing. Covetousness Slavery or Supersticon act them and they produce nought but Molas or chymeras sume what with out life or Sole. I wish I were as sure of your Correspondence and Communicating as I am of your Yet remaining affection to Philosophy. However S[r] I must thanke you for what I am sure of for that (they say) is one way to gett more. Let this therefore assure you that I very much Value the great favor & kindness of your Letter and more Especially for communicateing your Notion about the Descent of heavy Bodys: tis certainly right & true soe far as concerns the falling of the body Let fall from a great hight to the Eastwards of the perpendicular and not to the westward of it as most have hitherto Imagined. And in this opinion concurred S[r] Christopher Wren S[r] John Hoskins M[r] Henshaw and most of those that were present at our meeting on Thursday Last to whom I read soe much of your letter (and not more) as conserned Monsieur Mallement and this Experiment. But as to the curve Line which you seem to suppose it to Desend by (though that was not then at all Discoursed of) Vizt a kind of spirall which after sume few revolutions Leave it in the Center of the Earth my theory of circular motion makes me suppose it would be very differing and nothing att all akin to a spirall but rather a kind Elleptueid. At least if the falling Body were supposed in the plaine of the equinoxciale supposing then y[e] earth were cast into two half globes in the plaine of the equinox and those sides separated at a yard Distance or the lilke to make Vacuity for the Desending Body and that the gravitation to the former Center remained as before and that the globe of the earth were supposed to move with a Diurnall motion on its axis and that the falling body had the motion of the superficiall parts of the earth from whence it was Let fall Impressed on it, I conceive the line in which this body would move would resemble An Elleipse: for Instance Let ABDE [Fig. 5] represent the plaine of the equinox litmited by the superficies of the earth: C the Center therof to which the lines of Gravitation doe all tend. Let A represent the heavy Body let fall at A and attracted towards C but Moved also by the Diurnall

---

[1] I do not understand the meaning of Hooke's assertion that Steno (Nicolaus Stenonius), De Graft (doubtless Regnerus de Graaf), Signor Brorus, Borelli (J. A. Borelli), and Vivians (Vincenzo Viviani) left philosophy. De Graaf, of course, did when he died on 17 August 1673; Borelli died on 31 December 1679, but at the time of Hooke's letter he was still alive. Steno lived until 25 November 1686, and Viviani until 22 September 1703; both were active until their deaths. As for Signor Brorus, Hooke means the Italian alchemist Giuseppe Francesco Barri (Borro, Burrhus), who was alive at the time (d. 1695). See *Correspondence*, II, p. 306, n. 5.

[2] Devosons or Devotons. I do not know what is meant. Perhaps devotees.

Revolution of the earth from A towards BDE &c I conceive the curve that will be described by this desending body A will be AFGH and that the body A would never approach neerer the Center C then G were it not for the Impediment of the medium as Air or the like but would continually proceed to move round in the Line AFGHAFG &c But w[h]ere the

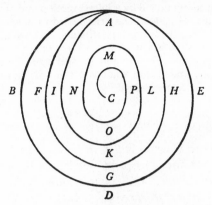

FIG. 5

Medium through which it moves has a power of impeding and destroying its motion the curve in wch it would move would be some what like the Line AIKLMNOP&c and after many resolutions would terminate in the Center C. But if the Body litt [?] fall be not in the aquinochill plain as

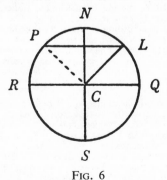

FIG. 6

here at London Ja 51°.32′ the elleipsed will be made in a plain inclined to the plaine of the Equinox: 51.32 soe that the fall of the Ball will not be exactly east of the perpendicular but south East and indeed more to the south then the east; as lett NLQS represent ye Meridian of London and Q the equinox L London and PL the parrallel in w^h it moves about the

R   249

Axis NS: the body let fall at L would desend in the plaine LC supposed at Right angles with the plaine of that Meridion NLQSR and not in the superficies of the cone pLC [Fig. 6] whose apex is C the Center of the earth and whose base is the plaine of the parrallel circle PL.[1] I could adde many other conciderations which are consonant to my Theory of Circular motions compounded by a Direct motion and an attractive one to a Center. But I feare I have already trespassed to much upon your more Usefull thoughts with these my impertinants yet I would desire you not to look upon them as any provacations to alter your mind [to] more mature and serious Resolutions. Goe on and Prosper and if you succed and by any Freind Let me understand what you think fit to impart, any thing from you will be Extremly Valued by

Sr Your very Humble Sarvant
RO: HOOKE

Gresham Colledg Dec. 9th 1679[2]

Hooke's letter to Newton is – or at least pretends to be – written in an amiable and friendly spirit. But it was by no means in this spirit that it was received by the latter: quite the contrary, it made him exceedingly angry.[3] After all, it is easy to understand Newton's reaction; nobody, and Newton less than anybody, likes his blunders to be pointed out to him, and "corrected," even if the corrections are based – at least partially – upon a misunderstanding. And Hooke not only "corrected" Newton, but also exposed his blunder to the Royal Society, that is, to the world.[4]

---

[1] It is interesting to note that Newton did not assert that the falling body will describe a spiral on a cone. Hooke misunderstands him or, rather, reconstructs Newton's views. He obviously believes Newton to hold a certain theory about the fall of heavy bodies onto a rotating earth according to which these bodies will describe spirals, a plane spiral when falling on the equator, and conical spirals when falling from a point placed on some parallel. This theory, reported by Mersenne and Galileo, goes back to John George Locher's *Disquisitiones mathematicae* (Ingolstadt, 1614). The *Disquisitiones* of Locher, having been held *sub praesidio Christophori Scheineri*, are usually misquoted as a work of the latter.

[2] See *Correspondence*, II, 304.

[3] "Could scarce persuade myself to answer his second letter; did not answer his third," reports Newton to Halley, 20 June 1686; Rouse Ball, *Essay*, p. 157; *Correspondence*, II, 436; this "third" by the way, was perhaps the most important of the lot: it was the letter in which Hooke told Newton that "the attraction always is in duplicate proportion to the distance from the center reciprocall."

[4] From a formal point of view, Hooke's actions were perfectly correct: he did not read to the Royal Society the "personal part" of Newton's letter (about his estrangement from philosophy, etc.); as for the scientific part, it was addressed to Hooke as the secretary of the Royal Society, and had to be presented to its members, as well as the answer (scientific) that Hooke sent to Newton. Still, having repeatedly asked Newton for a *private* correspondence and having assured him of secrecy, Hooke, in making this correspondence public, certainly demonstrated a lack of tact. As for Newton's reaction, it is expressed in the following passage of the postscript of his letter to Halley quoted in note 3: "Should a man who thinks himself knowing, and loves to show it in correcting and instructing others, come to you, when you are busy, and notwithstanding your excuse press discourses upon you, and through his own mistakes

Small wonder, therefore, that Newton's answer should be as dry and terse as a solicitor's writ. He wants to make his blunder good somehow and, at the same time, to teach Hooke a lesson, show him his own error, tell him what, in the case imagined by him (a fall through a void space which yields without resistance), the real path of the falling body would be.

Newton admits that, if there is no resistance, the body in question will not arrive at the center of the earth. But in that case, and contrary to Hooke's supposition, it will not describe a closed curve "resembling an ellipse" but an open[1] and very complicated one – a curve which he, Newton, is able to determine, but Hooke is not. Thus he writes:

S^r

I agree wth you y^t ye body in o^r latitude will fall more to ye south then east if ye height it falls from be any thing great. And also that if its gravity be supposed uniform it will not descend in a spiral to ye very center but circulate wth an alternate ascent & descent made by its *vis centrifuga* & gravity alternately overballancing one another. Yet I imagin ye body will not describe an Ellipsoeid but rather such a figure as is represented by A F O G H J K L [Fig. 7] etc.[2]

At the end of the letter, Newton, imitating Hooke's manner, concludes:

Your acute Letter having put me upon considering thus far ye species of this curve,[3] I might add something about its description by points *quam proxime.* But the thing being of no great moment I rather be[g] yor pardon for having troubled you thus far wth this second scribble wherin

---

correct you, and multiply discourses: and then make this use of it, to boast that he taught you all he spake, and oblige you to acknowledge it, and cry out injury and injustice if you do not; I believe you would think him a man of strange unsociable temper. Mr Hooke's letters in several respects abounded too much with that humour, which Hevelius and other complain of."

[1] As a matter of fact, Newton does not say that the curve will be an open one; nor does he say that it will be closed; he does not say anything about it. His very careful drawing is made in such a way as to leave the question open.

[2] See Pelseneer, "Lettre inédite de Newton"; *Correspondence*, II, 307. This letter is dated 13 December 1679.

[3] A moment of very great importance, because, as Newton himself later told Halley (letter of 27 July 1686, Rouse Ball, *Essay*, p. 167; *Correspondence*, II, 447): "His correcting my spiral occasioned my finding the theorem, by which I afterwards examined the ellipsis," and (letter of 14 July 1686, *ibid.*, p. 165; p. 444): "His letters occasioned my finding the method of determining figures, which when I had tried in the ellipsis, I threw the calculations by, being upon other studies; and so it rested for about five years, till upon your request I sought for that paper; and not finding it, did it again."

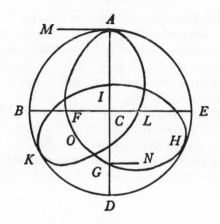

FIG. 7

if you meet wth any thing inept or erroneous I hope you will pardon y former & y^e latter I submit & leave to yor correction remaining S^r

Yo^r very humble Servant

Is. NEWTON

Newton's solution is not quite correct – which, as a matter of fact, is not surprising. The problem he deals with is very difficult,[1] and its solution implies the use of mathematical methods that Newton probably did not possess at the time, perhaps not even later. Much more surprising is the very problem Newton is treating – the problem of a body submitted to a *constant* centripetal force. In other words, Newton assumes, or at least seems to assume, that gravity is something *constant* – an assumption that enabled Hooke to "correct" him once more by pointing out that Newton misunderstood the question.

"Your calculation of the curve described by a body attracted by an aequall power at all distances from the center, such as that of a ball rolling in an inverted concave cone," writes Hooke to Newton on 6 January 1680, "is right,[2] and the two auges will not unite by about a third of a revolution: but my supposition is that the attraction

---

[1] See Pelseneer, "Lettre inédite de Newton," pp. 250 sq., for a discussion of the problem and its solution.

[2] *Ibid.*, p. 251: "Hooke a donc observé qu'on peut ramener au problème traité par Newton l'étude du mouvement d'un point pesant assujetti à se mouvoir sur un cône de révolution, d'axe vertical et de rayon CA, reposant sur la point en C. On sait que cette équivalence des deux problèmes est une conséquence des équations intrinsèques du mouvement du point sur la surface conique. Si l'on songe que Hooke ne s'est probablement livré à aucun calcul, sa remarque donne une mesure exacte de la profondeur et de la sûreté de son intuition."

always is in duplicate proportion to the distance from the center reciprocall."[1]

Years later, on 27 May 1686, at the height of a new quarrel with Hooke – the last one, the quarrel about the priority in the discovery of the inverse-square law – Newton tried to explain (or to explain away) his blunder in the following way or ways:

The summe of what past between Mr Hooke and me (to the best of my remembrance) was this. He solliciting me for some philosophicall communications or other I sent him this notion, that a falling body ought by reason of the earth's diurnall motion to advance eastward and not fall to the west as the vulgar opinion is. And in the scheme wherein I explained this I carelessly described the descent of the falling body in a spirall to the center of the earth:[2] which is true in a resisting medium, such as our air is. Mr Hooke replyed it would not descend to the center but at a certaine limit returne upwards againe. I then took the simplest case for computation, which was that of gravity uniform in a medium not resisting – imagining he had learned the limit from some computation, and for that end had considered the simplest case first.[3] And in this case I granted what he contended for, and stated the limit as nearly as I could. He replyed that gravity was not uniform but increased in descent to the center in a reciprocall duplicate proportion of the distance from it, and thus the limit would be otherwise than I had stated it, namely, at the end of every intire revolution, and added that according to this duplicate proportion the motions of the planets might be explained and their orbs defined.[4]

And in a letter of 20 June 1686 (which I have already and repeatedly quoted) Newton adds that at the time of this correspondence he "thought no further of philosophical matters than his letters put me upon it, and therefore may be allowed not to have had my thoughts of that kind about me so well at that time."[5]

Newton's explanations, to tell the truth, do not seem very convincing. It is hard to believe that, if he ever had had "thoughts" about the problem, that is, if he had really thought out a theory about the complete trajectory of the falling body, he could have forgotten it so much as to form, on the spur of the moment, another and quite a different one.

It is difficult to admit too that it was mere "carelessness" that made

---

[1] Hooke's letter to Newton of 6 January 1680; Rouse Ball, *Essay*, p. 147; *Correspondence*, II, 309.

[2] This is not quite true: the drawing is by no means careless and is backed by the text.

[3] Newton probably thought that Hooke was following Borelli, who, though admitting a constant power of gravity, believed that the resulting curve will be an ellipse.

[4] See Rouse Ball, *Essay*, p. 155; *Correspondence*, II, 433.

[5] *Ibid.*, p. 157; p. 436.

Newton describe (that is, draw) the descent of the falling body in a spiral; the drawing only illustrates the text of the letter. A more careful one would, perhaps, add some spires to the line; it would not have changed its essential nature. Besides, that the falling body would describe a spiral in the interior of the earth was, as I have said, a rather widely held belief. Moreover, as Newton himself points out, for a resisting medium it is quite a correct one.

It seems to me, therefore, most probable that Newton never had given many "thoughts" to the problem.[1] It may have appeared to him not only devoid of reality – bodies do not fall through the earth – but also of no importance whatever (he tells us so himself). He may even have felt that it lacks any (or, at least, any definite) meaning. How was the earth to be considered in this case – as a material body that would differ from our earth only by being penetrable like our air? In this case, the medium would oppose resistance. Or, should all matter be thought away, leaving behind it pure space and its former center? But in this case, why should the body go down toward it? The answer was quite clear for those who, like Fermat, still believed that bodies "seek" the center of the earth, but for those who did not and who believed that bodies were "attracted by" or "pushed toward" the earth, the situation was quite different. They had to find out how this attraction, whether a pull or a push, would vary in the interior of the earth. And that was a problem that nobody could master, not even Newton, who, as he confesses to Halley, held pretty uncertain views about it until 1685;[2] thus he "never extended the duplicate proportion lower than to the superficies of the earth, and before a certain demonstration I found the last year, have suspected it did not reach accurately enough down so low."[3]

---

[1] For the solution of the problem of the trajectory of a body falling *to the earth* from a point placed above its surface – the problem he deals with in his first letter to Hooke – he did not need such a theory. It is perfectly true that, as he says to Halley (letter of 20 June 1686, postscript, *ibid.*, p. 162; p. 440), "In the small ascent and descent of projectiles above the earth, the variation of gravity is so inconsiderable, that Mathematicians neglect it. Hence the vulgar hypothesis with them is uniform gravity." Yet, of course, this did not entitle Newton to admit, as in his second letter to Hooke, that gravitation was constant below the earth's surface, down to the center of the earth. And to say as Newton does, "And why might not I, as a Mathematician, use it frequently without thinking on the philosophy of the heavens, or believing it to be philosophically true?" does not explain or justify his procedure. Nor does it explain away his blunder and thoughtlessness.

[2] *Ibid.*, pp. 156 sq.; pp. 435 sq.

[3] *De motu* (Rouse Ball, *Essay*, p. 56): "Ex horologii oscillatorii motu tardiore in cacumine montis praealti quam in valle liquet etiam gravitatem ex aucta nostra a terrae centro distantia diminui, sed qua proportione nondum observatum est." Newton does not tell us why he suspected that the "duplicate proportion" did not

Newton was interested in gravity as a cosmic factor. He endeavored to find a physical explanation of this "force," because he never, as well we know, believed in an "attractive power." He did not achieve his purpose. Indeed, he found out something else, namely, the impossibility of doing it:[1] a discovery of tremendous importance (though usually not recognized as such) which liberated his mind to transform "attraction" from a physical into a "mathematical" force.

As for terrestrial gravity, though he suspected, and even believed in, its identity with the cosmic one, he never, before Hooke put it to him, made it a subject of special study. As to terrestrial gravity, he was even less sure than in the case of that "gravity" or "attraction" which regulated the movements of the planets, that the inverse-square proportion which he deduced from Kepler's third law was anything more than a mere approximation. Nay, he was rather certain that it was just that: a mere approximation – because, as he tells Halley, "There is so strong an objection against the accurateness of this proportion, that without my demonstrations, to which Mr Hooke is yet a stranger, it cannot be believed by a judicious philosopher."[2]

---

reach accurately below the surface of the earth, but it seems to me possible to guess the reasons: (*a*) the near parts of the earth could (and at first glance should) exert a greater influence than those that are far away, and (*b*) a body which is in the atmosphere of the earth is already, in a certain sense, below its surface.

[1] He found that in order to explain attraction mechanically, as an action of the surrounding medium (aethereal push), he had to postulate an elastic aether; and this implied the postulation of a force of repulsion between the particles of the aether. Thus attraction could be explained only by repulsion, that is, by something philosophically just as bad.

[2] Letter to Halley, 20 June 1686, Rouse Ball, *Essay*, p. 158; *Correspondence*, II, 437. The importance of this passage has been pointed out by F. Cajori, "Newton's Twenty Years' Delay in Announcing the Law of Gravitation," in *Sir Isaac Newton, a Bicentenary Evaluation of His Work* (Baltimore: Williams and Wilkins, 1928), p. 182. Cajori drew from it the conclusion that "before 1685 Newton suspected that the law of inverse squares was a mere approximation to the truth." Newton thought, rather reasonably, that the parts nearest to the falling body exerted a stronger attraction, and that the mass of the earth could not be considered as concentrated in its center. He once more does not tell us what the objection is, nor what demonstration he has in mind; once more we are obliged to guess. I think that the reason why Newton felt that his deduction of the inverse-square proportion from Kepler's third law was valid only *quam proxime* and not absolutely was that it had been made under the assumption that the orbits of the planets are circular, and not elliptic. Now, how could a proportion valid for circles be at the same time valid for eccentric ellipses? Should not the trajectory, even if not circular, be at least one with the sun in the center, and not in a focus of the orbits? It is obvious that these objections could be met only by a factual demonstration that from attraction following the inverse-square law, "compounded with a direct motion by the tangent," there would result a motion in an ellipse, and vice versa that such a motion implied an attraction inversely proportional to the square of the distance and directed to one of the foci of the elliptic trajectory. It is this demonstration which constitutes, according to Newton himself, his great discovery, and not

As for the inside of the earth, he only knew that the inverse-square proportion could not be applied there. But he was not able – being probably not sufficiently interested in the problem – to determine what was the one that has to be applied. And it was only when Hooke – erroneously – asserted that the inverse-square law was valid even there (though at the same time acknowledging that he did not believe it seriously), that Newton applied himself to solving the problem. This he did, as we know, in 1685 when he found out (solving two problems at the same time) that the inverse-square law had to be applied primarily not to the wholes, but to the particles which compose them, and that the resulting (mathematical) attraction of a spherical body, such as the earth, had to be computed as if its whole mass was concentrated in its center.[1] There was the surprising, but nevertheless necessary and evident, result that a particle placed outside of a sphere will be attracted by a force inversely proportional to the square of its distance from the center,[2] and a particle placed inside a sphere will be attracted by a force proportional to its distance from the center.[3] Of these deliberations Newton tells us:

After I had found that the force of gravity towards a whole planet did arise from and was compounded of the forces of gravity towards all its parts, and towards every one part was in the inverse proportion of the squares of the distances from the part, I was yet in doubt whether that proportion inversely as the square of the distance did accurately hold, or but nearly so, in the total force compounded of so many partial ones; for it might be that the proportion which accurately enough took place in greater distances should be wide of the truth near the surface of the planet, where the distances of the particles are unequal, and their situation dissimilar. But by the help of the Prop. LXXV and LXXVI, Book I, and their Corollaries, I was at last satisfied of the truth of the Proposition, as it now lies before us.

[From Book III, proposition VIII, Theorem VIII: *In two spheres gravitating each towards the other, if the matter in places or all sides round about and equidistant from the centres is similar, the weight of either sphere towards the other will be inversely as the square of the distance between their centres.*][4]

---

the invention of the inverse-square law as such – an easy thing since the work of Huygens and even earlier.

[1] The decisive role played by this discovery was recognized by J. A. Adams and J. W. L. Glaisher in 1887 (see Cajori, "Newton's Twenty Years' Delay," pp. 127 sq.), and in 1927 by H. H. Turner (see *Sir Isaac Newton, a Bicentenary Evaluation of His Work*, p. 187), who points out that this result "came as a complete surprise" to Newton.

[2] *Sir Isaac Newton's Mathematical Principles of Natural Philosophy.* Andrew Motte's translation revised by Florian Cajori (Berkeley: University of California Press, 1947), p. 199: Proposition LXXVI, Theorem XXXIV.

[3] *Ibid.*, p. 196, Proposition LXXIII, Theorem XXXIII.

[4] *Ibid.*, pp. 415 sq.

But in 1679, when proposing to Hooke an experimental proof of the motion of the earth, he seems to have simply followed the lead of the tradition in considering gravity as constant,[1] and in assuming that a heavy body, if it were not arrested by the earth, would finally arrive at its center. Each of these two conceptions is strictly incompatible with the other.

Let us now go back to Hooke. It cannot be denied that his attempt to deal with the problem of the trajectory of the falling body is extremely ingenious; the device of cutting the earth in two in order to give to this body the space it needs for moving down toward the center (and around it) is plainly brilliant; the endeavor to combine the idea of attraction, inherited from Gilbert, Kepler, and Bacon, with the principles of the Galilean mechanics, already announced in the *Attempt to Prove the Motion of the Earth by Observation*,[2] and to apply the resulting pattern not only to celestial but also to terrestrial physics, points in the right direction. Once more we have to admire Hooke's depth of vision and energy of thought. Once more we are obliged to recognize that he is unable to arrive at a precise, quantitative, mathematical solution. Once more, though at this time he is in possession of the inverse-square law, he misses the point.

He does not recognize that, in the case imagined by him, the falling body will describe not an "elliptoid," that is, some kind of oval curve, but an exact ellipse. This is all the more surprising since the situation in which he places his heavy body (falling through a split made through the equator of the earth) is very nearly similar to that which he realized in his famous experiments performed before the Royal Society on 23 May 1666. The imagined case leads to a result exactly similar to that which, at that time, he believed the Royal Society experiments to indicate: the power by which the body is attracted toward the center is directly proportional to its distance from that center.[3]

It is rather strange that Hooke seems not to have recognized this analogy. It is all the more strange since he knew (or, more precisely, assumed) – as anyone who accepted the explanation of gravity by

---

[1] It is a strange paradox of history that the strongest supporters of this conception were Galileo and the Galileans.

[2] See *supra*, p. 233.

[3] Newton, therefore, is perfectly right in reproaching Hooke (letter to Halley, 20 June 1686, Rouse Ball, *Essay*, pp. 159 sq.; *Correspondence*, II, 435 sq.) for extending the inverse-square proportion down to the center of the earth.

attraction was bound to assume – that the attractive power was at its maximum on the earth's surface, and that it diminished above as well as below it.[1] He even tried, as we know, to determine the rate of this diminishing by experiment.

One could argue, of course, that this analogy did not escape Hooke, and that it was just because he had no means of ascertaining the ratio of the variation of the force of attraction according to the distance of the attracted body from the center of the earth – he could not determine it theoretically and the experiments failed to give a result[2] – that he confined himself to stating in a vague manner that the curve in question will be a kind of "elliptoid," resembling an ellipse, but not an ellipse. But in this case he would have had no reason to speak of an "excentrical elliptoid";[3] moreover, he would not be able to assert to Newton, as he did in his letter of 6 January 1680, that his "supposition is that the attraction always is in duplicate proportion to the distance from the center reciprocall." Indeed, in his device of cutting the earth in two "in the plaine of the equinox" he supposed "that the gravitation to the former center remained as before."

One could assume, on the other hand, that, having discovered the inverse-square law (as did everybody else) from Kepler's third law, and the law of centrifugal force – which, as Newton did not fail to point out,[4] was rather easy, this latter having been published by Huygens in 1673[5] – Hooke transferred to his falling body the scheme of motion prevailing in the skies. The mention of Kepler[6] in the very

---

[1] See Cornelis de Waard's introduction to the supplementary volume of the *Oeuvres* of Fermat (Paris: Gauthier-Villars, 1922).

[2] This was not Hooke's fault. With the instruments at his disposal, a successful direct measurement was impossible.

[3] In the experiments of 23 May 1666, the ellipses described by the ball of the conical pendulum were, of course, not eccentric.

[4] In the postscript of his letter to Halley of 20 June 1686 (Rouse Ball, *Essay*, p. 160; *Correspondence*, II, 438), Newton says that to find the inverse-square law from Kepler's third law was pretty easy and something that any mathematician could have done (and told Hooke) five years before: "For when Hugenius had told how to find the force in all cases of circular motion, he has told 'em how to do it in this as well as in all others."

[5] In his *Horologium oscillatorium* of 1673 Huygens announced the laws of centrifugal force (which he had possessed since 1659), but without giving their demonstrations – a nasty trick played on his contemporaries, since it obliged them to find the proofs by themselves. It is well known that Newton recognized Huygens's priority and that his demonstrations – one of which he found, independently, in 1665–66 – are quite different from those of Huygens. See J. W. Herivel, "Sur les premières recherches de Newton en dynamique," *Revue d'Histoire des Sciences 15* (1962), 106–140, especially pp. 117–129.

[6] Hooke to Newton, 6 January 1680 (Rouse Ball, *Essay*, p. 147; *Correspondence*, II, 309): "My supposition is that the attraction always is in duplicate proportion to the distance from the center reciprocall, and consequently that the velocity will be in a sub-

letter in which the inverse-square law is formulated by Hooke makes this assumption by no means improbable.[1] It is all the more probable in that it would give an explanation also of Hooke's avoidance of the simple transfer of the astronomical scheme to terrestrial phenomena. Indeed, in this same letter (an answer to Newton's letter of 13 December 1679, published by Professor Pelseneer), he writes:

What I mentioned in my last concerning the descent within the body of the earth was but upon the supposall of such an attraction, not that I really believe there is such an attraction to the very center of the earth, but on the contrary I rather conceive that the more the body approaches the center the lesse will it be urged by the attraction, possibly somewhat like the gravitation on a pendulum or a body moved in a concave sphere where the power continually decreases the nearer the body inclines to a horizontal motion which it hath when perpendicular under the point of suspension or in the lowest point ... But in the celestiall motions the sun, earth, or centrall body are the cause of the attraction, and though they cannot be supposed mathematicall points yet they may be conceived as physicall, and the attraction at a considerable distance may be computed according to the former proportion as from the very center.[2]

In the celestial motions, because of the great distance that separates the attracted bodies, they can be conceived as points; but this is

duplicate [proportion] to the attraction, and consequently as Kepler supposes reciprocall to the distance." Hooke does not recognize the error committed by Kepler, which shows sufficiently well the very imperfect character of his "theory of circular motion compounded by a direct motion and an attractive one to the center" and explains his inability to solve the problem of deducing the elliptic trajectory from the inverse-square law of attraction. See Halley's letter to Newton of 29 June 1686 about Sir Christopher Wren's challenge to Hooke (Rouse Ball, *Essay*, pp. 162 sq.; *Correspondence*, II, 441 sq.)

[1] It is to be mentioned, however, that Newton suggests another explanation of Hooke's discovery of the inverse-square law, not improbable either (letter to Halley, 20 June 1686, postscript: Rouse Ball, *Essay*, p. 160; *Correspondence*, II, 438): "Nor do I understand by what right he claims it [the inverse-square proportion] as his own; for as Borell wrote, long before him, that by a tendency of the planets towards the sun, like that of gravity or magnetism, the planets would move in ellipses, so Bullialdus wrote that all force, respecting the sun as its centre, and depending on matter, must be reciprocally in a duplicate ratio of the distance from the centre, and used that very argument for it, by which you, sir, in the last Transactions, have proved this ratio in gravity. Now if Mr. Hooke from this general proposition in Bullialdus, might learn the proportion in gravity, why must this proportion here go for his invention?"

The passage of Bullialdus (Ismael Bouillaud) which Newton evidently has in mind is contained in his *Astronomia philolaica* (Paris, 1645), pp. 21 sq., and his explanation of the origin of Hooke's views on gravitation seems to be confirmed by a passage of the *Posthumous Works* (London, 1705), p. 185 (dated 1682) where the inverse-square law of gravitation is deduced from an analogy with the inverse-square law of the intensity of illumination. I have to point out, however, that Bullialdus does not assert the inverse-square law of attraction, but uses the argument reported by Newton, adding to it, moreover, the analogy between magnetic forces and light, as a refutation of Kepler's celestial mechanics.

[2] Hooke to Newton, 6 January 1680, Rouse Ball, *Essay*, p. 147; *Correspondence*, II, 309.

obviously impossible in the case of a terrestrial motion,[1] even of such an impossible motion as that of a body falling to the center of the earth. In this case, the real variation of the attractive "urge," which becomes weaker and not stronger when the body approaches the center, should be taken into account. How? Hooke does not know, any more than he knows what the resulting line will actually be. It is not an ellipse, of course, but something resembling it.

Yet it would be very interesting and even very useful (for astronomy as well as for navigation) to know it. And once more, in his letter of 17 January 1680, Hooke urges Newton to solve the problem:

"It now remains to know the proprietys of a curve line (not circular nor concentricall) made by a centrall attractive power which makes the velocitys of descent from the tangent line or equall straight motion at all distances in a duplicate proportion to the distances reciprocally taken.[2] I doubt not that by your excellent method you will easily find out what that curve must be, and its proprietys, and suggest a physicall reason of this proportion."[3]

I must confess that this appeal for help, backed by an honest and straightforward admission of Newton's mathematical superiority, should have met a better reception on Newton's part than it did. Newton, indeed, solved the problem, but he never said a word about it to Hooke.

[1] As I have already pointed out, to discover that this was not impossible, but on the contrary, necessarily true was one of the main achievements of Newton.

[2] Hooke to Newton, 17 January 1680, Rouse Ball, *Essay*, p. 149; *Correspondence*, II, 312 sq. Hooke, once more, repeats his error: an attractive power which conforms to the inverse-square law will not make "the velocitys of descent from the tangent line or equall straight motion at all distances in a duplicate proportion to the distances reciprocally taken." Moreover, this proposition, if taken *verbatim*, implies the proportionality of the velocity – and not of the acceleration – to the force acting on the body.

[3] As we see, even in this pure case, Hooke does not suggest that the resulting curve will be a conic section.

VI

Newton's "Regulae Philosophandi"

In an earlier article,[1] I drew the attention of historians of Newton to the differences, sometimes very important, between the texts of the three editions of the *Philosophiae naturalis principia mathematica*, and to the interest which a comparative analysis of these editions might have.[2] The study of Newton's manuscripts[3] – neglected until only very recently – shows that the actual labor of Newton in preparing the successive editions of the *Principia*[4] was actually much greater than one might suppose from a mere comparison of the printed texts. This would be true even if such a comparison were complemented by the information given in the correspondence between

[1] A. Koyré, "Pour une édition critique des oeuvres de Newton," *Revue d'Histoire des Sciences 8* (1955), 19–37.

[2] Such a systematic analysis – surprisingly – has never yet been made. However, a critical and variorum edition of Newton's *Principia*, prepared by I. Bernard Cohen and myself, will soon be published.

[3] The history of Newton's manuscripts is very complex. He left them to his niece, Catherine Conduitt, who in turn left them to her only daughter, Catherine, Viscountess Lymington, who left them to her son, the second Earl of Portsmouth. The Portsmouth family preserved the papers in their castle at Hurtsbourne Park. About 1872, after a fire in their castle, the Portsmouth family decided to give the scientific papers to Cambridge University but stipulated that the papers on theology, chronology, history, and alchemy must be returned to Hurtsbourne. A commission, composed of H. R. Luard, G. G. Stokes, J. C. Adams, and G. D. Liveing, was appointed to choose, classify, and describe the manuscripts for Cambridge University. They discharged their task to the general satisfaction, and published in 1888 a small book: *A Catalogue of the Portsmouth Collection of Books and Papers Written by or Belonging to Sir Isaac Newton, the Scientific Portion of which has been Presented by the Earl of Portsmouth to the University of Cambridge* (Cambridge, 1888). Alas, despite the presence of distinguished scientists on the commission, the publication of the *Catalogue* did not encourage the study of Newton's manuscripts; even the opposite. Only in the last few years has this research been undertaken, by I. B. Cohen, F. Manuel, A. R. and M. B. Hall, J. W. Herivel, R. S. Westfall, D. T. Whiteside, H. W. Turnbull, J. F. Scott, and myself. Those manuscripts which the Portsmouth family retained were sold at public auction in 1936. Lord Keynes bought nearly half of them, and left them after his death (in 1946) to King's College, Cambridge.

[4] The *Philosophiae naturalis principia mathematica* was published in 1687 under the care of Edmond Halley; a second edition appeared in 1713, edited by Roger Cotes, Newton's successor in his chair at Cambridge; and a third edition was published in 1726, edited by Henry Pemberton. Roger Cotes, who took his assignment as editor very seriously, exchanged an extremely interesting correspondence with Newton (part of which is, alas, lost). The surviving letters were published by J. Edleston, *Correspondence of Sir Isaac Newton and Professor Cotes* (London, 1850).

261

Newton and Roger Cotes, Plumian Professor of Astronomy at Cambridge, who prepared under Newton's direction the second edition of the *Principia*.

Newton's manuscripts – thousands upon thousands of pages – show a curious aspect of his mentality. He seems to have been incapable of thinking without pen in hand, and even to have found pleasure in the mere mechanical exercise of writing. Thus he copied at length and in his own hand authors whom he had read,[1] and even copied his own writings.[2] His manuscripts inform us equally of the extreme care which he took in the redaction of his works: he writes, crosses out, corrects, copies it all again, crosses out, recorrects . . . and recopies. Having finished, he starts all over again: thus, he made at least eight drafts of the *Scholium generale* for the second edition.

One of the most interesting examples of the evolution of the text and of the thought of Newton is offered by the *Regulae philosophandi*,[3] which are a succinct résumé of the logical and epistemological views of Newton, placed at the beginning of Book III of the *Principia*, which bears the title *De systemate mundi*.

Let us note first of all that the expression *Regulae philosophandi* appears only in the second and third editions of the *Principia*. In the first, in a corresponding place, one finds a series of propositions, nine in all, which are entitled *Hypotheses*. This is all the more curious, given the hostility to "hypotheses" so often proclaimed by Newton from the beginning of his scientific career, and given also that famous slogan, *Hypotheses non fingo*, to which frequently the whole Newtonian epistemology is reduced.[4]

The list of these "hypotheses," to tell the truth, is not very logical and can only be explained by the haste with which the *Principia* was composed. They comprehend, in effect, two methodological "hypotheses" (I and II), a "hypothesis" (III) that affirms the unity of matter and the possibility of transforming any given body into any

---

[1] A large portion of Newton's MSS contain citations from alchemical books.

[2] Thus, for example, he recopied five and six times his own theological MSS.

[3] It is interesting to note that Andrew Motte, in his English translation of the *Principia – Sir Isaac Newton's Mathematical Principles of Natural Philosophy and His System of the World* (London, 1729) – translates this expression by: "Rules of Reasoning in Philosophy." And Mme. du Châtelet, in her *Principes mathématiques de la philosophie naturelle* (Paris, 1757–1758), renders it: "Règles qu'il faut suivre dans l'étude de la physique."

[4] On the sense of this slogan, as well as on the sense of the term "hypothesis," see Chapter II, and also I. B. Cohen, *Franklin and Newton* (Philadelphia: The American Philosophical Society, 1956), pp. 129 sq. and Appendix I, "Newton's use of the word: HYPOTHESIS," pp. 575–589.

other,[1] and six "hypotheses" concerning the structure of the solar system. One may easily understand why Newton did not maintain this incongruous assemblage and why, in the second edition of his work, he quite properly distributed these "hypotheses" into three classes. At least this is what he did for those he kept: actually, the third, the one that affirms the unity of matter, disappeared[2] and was replaced by something else. Furthermore, of the eight propositions remaining, there is but one, "Hypothesis IV" (which affirms the immobility of the center of the system of the world), that continues to be presented as a hypothesis: it appears as "Hypothesis I" of the second and third editions.[3] The last six "hypotheses" concerning the structure of the solar system are found in the later editions to have been promoted to the rank of "Phaenomena." And the original first two hypotheses, which propose formal and general principles of the science of nature, are from the second edition denominated "Rules," rules of reasoning, *Regulae philosophandi*. As such, they keep their numbers: I and II. In the second edition, Newton adds a third rule; in the third and last edition he adds a fourth rule. And he had, at a certain moment, the intention of adding yet a fifth.

---

[1] Hyp. III: *Corpus omne in alterius cujuscunque generis corpus transformari pone, et qualitatem gradus omnes intermedios successive induere:* "Any body can be transformed into another, of whatever kind, and all the intermediate degrees of qualities can be induced in it."

[2] The reason for this disappearance is not very clear. It may be that having affirmed in the Queries of the Latin edition of his *Opticks* (in 1706) that God had in all probability created in the beginning atoms of different shapes and masses – which implies the nontransformability of one kind into another – Newton was obliged to suppress his Hypothesis III, which affirms the contrary.

A "hypothesis" likewise appeared in Book II, Sec. IX, "*De motu circulari fluidorum,*" of the *Principia*: HYPOTHESIS: *Resistentiam, quae oritur ex defectu lubricitatis partiuem Fluidi, caeteris paribus, proportionalem esse velocitati, qua partes Fluidi separantur ab invicem:* "The resistance arising from the want of lubricity in the parts of a fluid, is, other things being equal, proportional to the velocity with which the parts of the fluid are separated from one another."

[3] In the second and third editions, it appears after Proposition X, Theorem X, of Book III: *Hyp. I: Centrum Systemates Mundo quiescere. Hoc ab omnibus concessum est, dum alii Terram, alii Solem in centro quiescere contendant:* "Hypothesis I: That the centre of the system of the world is immovable. This is acknowledged by all, while some contend that the earth, others that the sun, is fixed in that centre." This "hypothesis" is all the more curious, since for Newton neither the earth nor the sun is immobile; but the immobility of the center of gravity of the solar system – in which Newton seems to have believed – cannot effectively be demonstrated from phenomena, and is therefore in this sense a hypothesis.

Hypothesis II of Book III of the *Principia*, which follows Lemma III of Proposition XXXVII, says that if the earth were replaced by a ring turning on its own axis with a diurnal motion and around the sun with an annual motion, the axis itself being inclined to the plane of the ecliptic by an angle of $23\frac{1}{2}°$, the precession of the equinoxes would be the same whether the ring were liquid or rigid. This too was a proposition which Newton believed to be true – he was right – but which he could not demonstrate.

We shall not, here, occupy ourselves with the "Phaenomena,"[1] but merely with the "Rules." The change of terminology is to be explained, without doubt, by the increasing aversion of Newton to "hypotheses," as well as by a certain alteration in the sense in which he used this expression.[2] In the first edition of the *Principia*, he gave it the traditional sense: a fundamental assumption or supposition in a theory. Thus, in his unpublished treatise *De motu*[3] he followed the *Definitiones* of centripetal force, the force of a body, and the force of resistance by a series of four "hypotheses," which comprehend among others the law of inertia and the law of the composition of motions – hypotheses which, in the *Principia*, were to become *Axiomata seu leges motu* ("Axioms or laws of motion"); similarly, at the beginning of *De systemate mundi* (Book III of the *Principia*) he listed the "hypotheses," that is to say, the fundamental assumptions of his cosmological system. Yet we must keep in mind, as I have remarked above, that this list of hypotheses in which the general principles of reasoning are found mixed up with empirical data could not be a model of logical coherence.

Twenty or twenty-five years later,[4] Newton no longer used the term "hypothesis" in the sense of *principle* – nor in the sense of a possible, or probable but not certain, explanation of phenomena (the sense in which he had used this term since his youth).[5] Now he would use it in a much narrower sense, one that was clearly pejorative, of a gratuitous assertion that was undemonstrable and extrascientific. In short, henceforward a hypothesis is to be neither an axiom nor even a conjecture, but a fiction.[6] Thus he writes to Roger Cotes:

As in Geometry the word Hypothesis is not taken in so large a sense as to include the Axiomes & Postulates, so in Experimental Philosophy it is not

[1] See my study cited on p. 261, n. 1.

[2] See Professor Cohen's study cited on p. 262, n. 4.

[3] The short treatise *De motu*, the first version of Book I of the *Principia*, written in late 1684 and early 1685, was published by S. P. Rigaud, *Historical Essay on the First Publication of Newton's "Principia"* (London: Oxford University Press, 1938), and by W. W. Rouse Ball, *An Essay on Newton's "Principia"* (London, 1893).

[4] In the Queries appended to the Latin edition of the *Opticks* (1706), the sense of the term "hypothesis" is already the same as in the second and third editions of the *Principia*.

[5] In 1676, Newton sent the Royal Society a long treatise entitled, *An Hypothesis explaining the Properties of Light, discoursed of in my several Papers.* This treatise was published by Thomas Birch, *History of the Royal Society of London* (London, 1757), III, 248–305, and reprinted in facsimile in *Isaac Newton's Papers and Letters on Natural Philosophy*, edited by I. Bernard Cohen (Cambridge, Massachusetts: Harvard University Press, 1958), pp. 178–235.

[6] The famous *Hypotheses non fingo* does not mean "I do not make hypotheses," but "I do not feign hypotheses." See Chapter II.

to be taken in so large a sense as to include the first Principles or Axiomes wch I call the laws of motion. These Principles are deduced from Phaenomena & made general by Induction: wch is the highest evidence that a Proposition can have in this philosophy. And the word Hypothesis is here used by me to signify only such a Proposition as is not a Phaenomenon nor deduced from any Phaenomena but assumed or supposed w^thout any experimental proof.[1]

And in order to render absolutely clear the sense which he attributes to this expression, Newton enjoins Cotes to add at the end of the next paragraph the following discussion:

For whatever is not deduced from the phenomena is to be called an hypothesis; and hypotheses, whether metaphysical or physical, whether of occult qualities or mechanical, have no place in experimental philosophy. In this philosophy particular propositions are inferred from the phenomena, and afterwards rendered general by induction. Thus it was that the impenetrability, the mobility, and the impulsive force of bodies, and the laws of motion and of gravitation, were discovered. And to us it is enough that gravity does really exist, and act according to the laws which we have explained, and abundantly serves to account for all the motions of the celestial bodies, and of our sea.[2]

Let us now consider the first two "hypotheses" or "rules." In the first edition of the *Principia* (E₁) they are presented as follows:

Hyp. I: Causas rerum naturalium non plures admitti debere, quam quae et vera sunt et earum Phenomenis explicandis sufficiunt. Natura enim simplex est et rerum causis superfluis non luxuriat.

Hyp. II: Ideoque effectuum naturalium ejusdem generis ejusdem sunt causae.

Uti respirationis in Homine et in Bestia; descensus lapidis in Europa et in America; Lucis in Igne culinari et in Sole; reflexionis lucis in Terra et in Planetis.

Hyp. I: We ought to admit no more causes of natural things than such as are both true and sufficient to explain their appearances. For nature is simple and does not luxuriate in superfluous causes of things.

Hyp. II. Therefore the causes of natural effects of the same kind are the same.

Thus the respiration of man and of beasts; of the descent of stones in

---

[1] See Edleston, *Correspondence*, pp. 154–155.

[2] *Ibid.*, p. 155. This paragraph also appears in the General Scholium added to the second edition of the *Principia*. As early as 1706, in Query 24 of the Latin edition of his *Opticks* (Query 31 of the second [1717] and later English editions), Newton had written: "For hypotheses are not to be regarded in experimental Philosophy. And although the arguing from Experiments and Observations by Induction be no Demonstration of general Conclusions; yet it is the best way of arguing which the Nature of Things admits of, and may be looked upon as so much the stronger, by how much the Induction is more general."

Europe and in America; of the light in culinary fire and in the sun; of the reflection of light on the earth and in the planets.

In the second edition of the *Principia* (E_2) Newton does not modify the wording of Hypothesis I. In making it Regula I, however, he amplifies his statement a little by placing in front of the formula which expresses the fundamental principle of the simplicity of nature a much more explicit statement:

> Dicunt utique Philosophi: Natura nihil agit frustra, et frustra fit per plura quod fieri potest per pauciora.

> To this purpose the philosophers say: Nature does nothing in vain, and it is in vain to do by more [means] that which can be done by fewer.

E_2 has no further modification to the rule thus formulated.

As to Rule II, the second edition of the *Principia* reproduces without change the text of the first. But the third edition (E_3) introduces a rather curious emendation. It reads from now on:

> Ideoque effectum naturalium ejusdem generis eaedem assignandae sunt causae, quatenus fieri potest.

> And so to natural effects of the same kind are assigned the same causes, as far as they can be.

The last three words, *quatenus fieri potest* ("as far as they can be") are not to be found in E_2 but only in E_3.

Newton's manuscript shows us that he did not arrive all at once at the definitive redaction. He began by writing *assumendae*, then he crossed it out and replaced it by *assignandae*. Then he added to the formula of E_1 and E_2 the words: *Nisi quatenus diversitas ex phaenomenis patefacta sit, hae causae phaenomenis explicandis sufficiant* ("Unless their diversity be made manifest from phenomena, these causes suffice to explain the phenomena"). Then he crossed out the words *Nisi quatenus diversitas* in order to substitute for them *nisi forte diversitas aliqua* ("unless perhaps a certain diversity"); then he suppressed the entire phrase in order to replace it by *nisi diversitas aliqua ex phaenomenis patefacta sit* ("unless a certain diversity be rendered manifest by the phenomena"); after which he reduced to naught this fruit of his efforts and wrote *quatenus fieri potest* ("as far as they can be").

I have already mentioned that in E_2 the old "Hypothesis III" disappeared to give place to a "Rule," Regula III:

Qualitates corporum quae intendi et remitti nequeunt, quaeque corporibus omnis competunt in quibus experimenta instituere licet, pro qualitatibus corporum universorum habendae sunt.

The qualities of bodies which admit neither intention nor remission [of degrees], and which belong to all bodies on which one can make experiments, are to be taken as the qualities of all bodies whatsoever.

The polemic character of this rule, which opposes the empiricism of the "experimental philosophy" to the apriorism of the Continental philosophers (notably Descartes and Leibniz), is qualified by the developments which Newton adds to it:

the qualities of bodies are known to us only by experiments . . . we are certainly not to relinquish the evidence of experiments for the sake of dreams and vain fictions of our own devising; nor ought we to recede from the analogy of Nature, which is wont to be simple, and always consonant to itself.

And it is just because nature is consonant to herself that we can generalize the data of experience and attribute to *all* bodies the properties that experience shows us in those which are within our reach.

The extension, hardness, impenetrability, mobility, and inertia of the whole result from the extension, hardness, impenetrability, mobility, and inertia of the parts; hence we conclude that all the smallest parts of all bodies are also extended, and hard and impenetrable, and movable, and endowed with the force of inertia. And this is the foundation of all philosophy.

Newton is absolutely clear: extension itself – in opposition to Descartes – is declared to be an empirical datum, as are duration and impenetrability, which Descartes had not included in the "essential" properties of bodies. Furthermore, atomism – once again in opposition to Descartes (and also to Leibniz) – is proclaimed responsible for experimental philosophy and the ultimate foundation of all philosophy.

But there is even more. The end of the exposition tells us that, since all the bodies encountered in our terrestrial experience gravitate toward the earth. since the moon likewise gravitates toward the earth and our sea gravitates toward the moon, and since all planets gravitate toward one another and the comets gravitate toward the sun, it is necessary for us to hold that all bodies mutually gravitate toward one another and therefore to admit gravity as their universal property.

This is an affirmation of an incalculable scope, and one which could be understood – and was! – as including gravity among the *essential* properties of bodies. But that is something that Newton himself never did.[1] And indeed, he concludes the discussion of Rule III with the following lines:

Attamen gravitatem corporibus essentialem minime affirmo. Per vim insitam intelligo solam vim inertiae. Haec immutabilis est. Gravitas recedendo a Terra diminuitur.[2]

Not that I affirm gravity to be essential to bodies. By their *vis insita* I mean nothing but their inertia. This is immutable. Their gravity is diminished as they recede from the earth.

The empirical assertions of Rule III – it would have been easy to predict – did not convince the Continental philosophers. Quite the contrary: their opposition to the "natural philosophy" of Newton was found to be reinforced thereby. Thus in E_3 Newton returned to the charge, formulating in Regula IV the rule of conduct of empiricism, or the rule of prudence and of good sense, as follows:

In philosophia experimentali, propositiones ex phenomenis per inductionem collectae, non obstantibus contrariis hypothesibus, pro veris aut accurate, aut quam proxime, haberi debent, donec alia occurrerint phenomena, per quae aut accuratiores reddantur, aut exceptionibus obnoxiae. Hoc fieri debet ne argumentum inductionis tollatur per hypotheses.

In experimental philosophy we are to look upon propositions inferred by general induction from phenomena as accurately or very nearly true, notwithstanding any contrary hypotheses that may be imagined, till such time as other phenomena occur, by which they may either be made more accurate, or liable to exceptions. This rule we must follow, that the argument of induction may not be evaded by hypotheses.

In other words, in experimental philosophy one must stick to the facts and hold only theories duly established by, and founded on the facts, unless other facts contradict or restrict them. And if the facts are contrary to "philosophic" and abstract "hypotheses," so much the worse for the latter. As Newton concludes:

Hoc fieri debet ne argumentum inductionis tollatur per hypotheses.

---

[1] In 1717, in order to preclude any misunderstanding of his view, Newton wrote in the preface to the second English edition of his *Opticks*: "And to shew that I do not take Gravity for an essential Property of Bodies, I have added one Question concerning its Cause, chusing to propose it by way of a Question, because I am not yet satisfied about it for want of Experiments."

[2] In effect, inertia is a function of the mass of a body; gravity, on the contrary, is a function of attraction, the force of which varies with distance.

This must be done so that the argument founded on induction may not be evaded by hypotheses.

Here again the manuscripts of Newton permit us to follow step by step the elaboration of the text of Rule IV. We observe that, as in the case of Rule II, each successive redaction makes the wording stronger and tighter. Newton began with a rather long and argumentative text:

In Philosophia experimentali contra Propositiones ex Phaenomenis per Inductionem collectas[1] non sunt[2] disputandum ab Hypothesibus. Nam si argumenta ab Hypothesibus contra Inductiones[3] admitterentur, argumenta Inductionum[4] in quibus tota Philosophia experimentalis fundatur per Hypotheses contrarias semper everti possent.[5] Si Propositio aliqua per Inductionem collecta nondum sit satis accurata corrigi debet,[6] non per hypotheses, sed per phaenomena naturae fusius et accuratius observata.[7]

In experimental philosophy one is not to argue from hypotheses against propositions drawn by induction from phenomena. For if arguments from hypotheses are admitted against inductions, then the arguments of inductions on which all experimental philosophy is founded could always be overthrown by contrary hypotheses. If a certain proposition drawn by induction is not yet sufficiently precise, it must be corrected not by hypotheses but by the phenomena of nature more fully and more accurately observed.

On rereading this, Newton no doubt saw that the argumentative style was out of place in a *rule*. Furthermore, he did not have to

---

[1] Newton originally wrote *collecta*.

[2] After writing *est*, Newton wrote *sunt* above it (probably when he changed *collecta* to *collectas*) without crossing out the *est*.

[3] Newton originally wrote *ab Hypothesibus admitterentur*; and then, by means of a caret, he inserted above the line the phrase *contra Inductiones* between *Hypothesibus* and *admitterentur*.

[4] It appears that Newton originally wrote *argumenta ab Inductione*; that he then changed *ab* to *ad*; and then by crossing out *ad* and writing over the *e* in *Inductione*, made the phrase finally stand *argumenta Inductionum*.

[5] Newton originally wrote *in quibus tota Philosophia experimentalis fundatur nihil valerent, sed per Hypotheses contrarias semper everti possent*. He then changed the comma after *valerent* to a period, crossed out *sed*, and replaced it by *Nam*, which he inserted by means of a caret before *per Hypotheses*, so that the phrase read: *in quibus tota Philosophia experimentalis fundatur nihil valerent. Nam per Hypotheses contrarias semper everti possent*. Finally, he crossed out *nihil valerent. Nam*, leaving the wording as we have printed it here.

[6] Here Newton originally wrote: *Si Propositiones per Inductionem collectae nondum sint satis accuratae, corrigi debent*. He then changed *Propositiones* to *Propositio*, inserted *aliqua* after it by using a caret, and then by writing over the appropriate letters changed the text to read as it now stands (that is, changed it from the plural to the singular), perhaps because he balked at the idea of suggesting that a plural number of his own propositions might not be sufficiently precise!

[7] Originally *observanda*; written over to read *observata*.

repeat what he had already said in Rule III. He started again and wrote:

In Philosophia experimentali[1] Hypotheses[2] contra argumentum Inductionis non sunt audiendae sed Propositiones ex Phaenomenis per Inductionem collectae pro veris aut accurate aut quam proxime haberi debent[3] donec alia occurrerint Phaenomena per quae aut accuratiores reddantur, aut exceptionibus obnoxiae. Hoc fieri debet ne argumentum Inductionis per Hypotheses tollatur.

In experimental philosophy hypotheses [raised] against the argument of induction are not to be heard [i.e., taken into account] but propositions drawn from phenomena are to be taken as either accurately or very nearly true until other phenomena are produced by which either they are rendered more accurate or subject to objections. This must be done so that the argument of induction be not destroyed by hypotheses.

Thus we see the text take form. The phrases do not balance well. The interdiction of listening to (taking account of) hypotheses is out of place. Newton thus lets it drop, and transforms it into an interdiction of making use of hypotheses to correct the imperfect results of experience:

In Philosophia experimentali[4] Propositiones ex Phaenomenis per Inductionem collectae pro veris aut accurate aut quam proxime haberi debent donec alia occurrerint Phaenomena per quae aut accuratius reddantur aut exceptionibus obnoxiae. Quae nondum sunt satis accuratae, hae per hypotheses emendari non debent sed ad incudem revocari per phaenomena naturae fusius et accuratius observandia.[5] Argumenta ex Hypothesibus contra argumentum Inductionis desumenda non sunt.[6]

In experimental philosophy we are to look upon propositions inferred by general induction from phenomena as accurately or very nearly true, till such time as other phenomena occur, by which they may either be made more accurate, or liable to exceptions. Those which are not yet sufficiently precise must not be improved by hypotheses but must be revised by means

[1] Newton originally wrote *naturali*, which he then crossed out and replaced by *experimentali*.
[2] The word *Hypotheses* was originally written following *Inductiones*, but it was then crossed out and placed in its present position.
[3] Newton originally wrote: *In Philosophia experimentali, Propositiones ex Phaenomenis per Inductionem collectae pro veris aut accurate aut quam proxime haberi debent*, which, using a caret to insert some words after *collectae*, he changed to read: *In Philosophia experimentali, Propositiones ex Phaenomenis per Inductionem collectae non sunt per hypotheses corrigendae, sed hypotheses, sed pro veris* . . . Then, by crossing out the words just inserted, and inserting others after *experimentali* by means of a caret, he made the sentence read as it now stands.
[4] Newton originally began this passage with the word *Propositiones*, and then later inserted by a caret the phrase *In Philosophia experimentali*.
[5] The words *Quae . . . observanda* are crossed out in the MS.
[6] Newton originally wrote *Hypotheses contra argumentum Inductiones nil valent*, and then changed the text to the present version.

of the phenomena of nature more fully and accurately observed. Arguments from hypotheses against the argument of induction must not be chosen.

To correct the results of experiments by hypotheses . . . This is probably an allusion to the principles of conservation of Descartes, and of Leibniz. But Newton no doubt considers that this is not the place to speak of them. Furthermore, one must not "mélanger les torchons et les serviettes," that is to say, the rules of reasoning and the precepts concerning the technique of experiments. Thus he crosses it all out and starts once more, taking up again the phrase which he had rejected:

In Philosophia experimentali, Propositiones ex Phaenomenis per Inductionem collectae,[1] non obstantibus Hypothesibus,[2] pro veris aut accurate quam proxime haberi debent, donec alia occurrerint Phaenomena per quae aut accuratiores reddantur aut exceptionibus obnoxiae. Hoc fieri debet ne argumentum Inductionis tollatur per Hypotheses.[3]

And this, except for the addition of the word *contrariis*, is the version which Newton printed.

The text of E_3 contains only four rules. But the manuscripts show us that Newton, becoming more and more anti-Cartesian,[4] had projected a fifth, in which he opposed his Lockian empiricism to the innate ideas of the French philosopher. Actually, Descartes seemed to him more and more to be the chief inspiration of his Continental adversaries, who based themselves on "hypotheses" not only to reject the experimental philosophy which he was promoting but also to accuse him of being only a vulgar sensationalist and of wishing, at the same time, through his doctrine of universal gravitation, to rein-

---

[1] Newton originally wrote: *In Philosophia experimentali,* [*Hypotheses contra argumentum Inductionis non sunt audiendae, sed*] *Propositiones ex Phaenomenis per Inductionem collectae.* Then by crossing out words he arrived at the present version.

[2] Newton originally wrote: *Hypothesibus, contraijs, pro veris* . . . , but he then crossed out *contraijs.* The word *contrariis* appears in the printed version.

[3] Newton originally placed the phrase *per Hypotheses* after *Inductionis,* but he then crossed it out there and placed it at the end of the sentence. This passage has already been translated, *supra,* p. 268.

[4] The sources of Newtonian anti-Cartesianism are many and diverse; indeed, one can say that Cartesianism is opposed on all grounds: in physics, empiricism *vs.* apriorism; in religion, *Deus artifex vs. Dieu faignant.* Indeed, for Newton and the Newtonians – the preface by Cotes to the second edition of the *Principia* expresses their sentiments very clearly – the God of Descartes (and of Leibniz) is an absent God who does not intervene in the mechanistic operations of nature, a mechanism which, thanks to the law of conservation of motion (as of *vis viva*), is self-sufficient. They also accused Descartes (as Henry More had already done) of exiling God from the world. See my *From the Closed World to the Infinite Universe* (Baltimore: Johns Hopkins Press, 1955).

troduce into science action-at-a-distance (magical action), which had been properly proscribed by Cartesian mechanism.[1]

Reg. V: Pro hypothesibus habenda sunt quaecunque ex rebus ipsis vel per sensus externos, vel per sensationem cogitationum[2] internarum non derivantur. Sentio utique quod Ego cogitem, id quod fieri nequiret nisi simul sentirem quod ego sim. Sed non sentio quod Idea aliqua sit innata. Et pro Phaenomenis habeo non solum quae per sensus quinque externos nobis innotescunt, sed etiam quae in mentibus nostris[3] intuemur cogitando: Ut quod, Ego sum, ego credo, doleo, etc.[4] Et quae ex phaenomenis nec demonstrando nec per argumentum inductionis consequuntur, pro Hypothesibus habeo.

Rule V: Whatever is not derived from things themselves, whether by the external senses or by the sensation of internal thoughts, is to be taken for a hypothesis. Thus I sense that I am thinking, which could not happen unless at the same time I were to sense that I am. But I do not sense that any idea whatever may be innate. And I do not take for a phenomenon only that which is made known to us by the five external senses, but also that which we contemplate in our minds when thinking: such as, I am, I believe, I understand, I remember, I think, I wish, I am unwilling, I am thirsty, I am hungry, I rejoice, I suffer, etc. And those things which neither can be demonstrated from the phenomenon nor follow from it by the argument of induction, I hold as hypotheses.

Newton does not seem to have pursued this attempt to carry the anti-Cartesian polemic into the domain of pure philosophy. He did not even recopy the page from which I have just quoted. Did he reckon that where Locke had not succeeded he himself would have few chances of gaining the victory? Or was he afraid to provoke his adversaries and to stir up a controversy as long and as disagreeable as that which he had recently had with Leibniz? For whatever reason, he abandoned the project. Rule V has until now slept among his papers. This rule is extremely interesting, since it offers us a confession of purely *philosophical* faith on the part of Newton. It is, in fact, the only one ever permitted himself by the author of the *Philosophiae naturalis principia mathematica*.

[1] In Newton's MSS, there is a long critique of Cartesian cosmology (denial of the void) as well as of the radical separation of spirit and matter. This MS (MS 4003) has been published by A. R. Hall and Marie Boas Hall, *Unpublished Scientific Papers of Isaac Newton* (Cambridge, England: University Press, 1962), pp. 89–156, and has been studied by me in Chapter III, "Newton and Descartes."

[2] Newton originally wrote *mentis*, then crossed it out and replaced it with *cogitationum*.

[3] Newton originally wrote *reflectendo* after *nostris*, and then crossed it out.

[4] Newton originally wrote: *Ut quod, Ego sum, Ego credo, Ego doleo, ego gandeo, ego recordor, ego cogito, Ego volo, nolo, cogito, intelligo, sitio, esurio* . . . Then by crossing out words and rearranging he arrived at the present version.

VII

Attraction, Newton, and Cotes

In a well-known letter (18 February 1712/13), Roger Cotes drew Newton's attention to Leibniz's attack on him published in the *Memoirs of Literature* of May 1712, and advised him not to leave it unanswered.[1] Cotes also raised an objection to Newton's theory of attraction, or at least to the manner in which it was presented. Cotes was surely aware of Newton's frequent and numerous assertions that the term "attraction" was used by him as a perfectly neutral one, "promiscuously" with others, and could be understood as meaning pressure or whatever else, but not what it seemed to mean. Even so, Cotes found that Newtonian attraction implied the attribution of "attractive forces" to bodies, and that Newton, tacitly, made that "hypothesis," or "supposition."

In the letter I am referring to, Cotes submits to Newton's approval an outline of the Preface to the *Principia* that he had been commissioned to write. He thinks that "it will be proper, besides the account of the Book and its improvements, to add something concerning more particularly the manner of philosophising made use of and wherein it differs from that of Descartes and others," that is, to *demonstrate* from the phenomena of nature the principle it is based on (the principle of universal gravity) and not merely to *assert* it. The demonstration will be based (*a*) on the first law of motion (the law of inertia) according to which moving bodies, if no force acts upon them, move in a straight line, and (*b*) on the astronomical fact that planets do not move in this way, but describe curves. They are, therefore, acted upon by a force "which may . . . not improperly be called centripetal in respect to the revolving bodies, and attractive in respect to the central ones." But, continues Cotes,

in the first corollary of this 5th Proposition [of Book III] I meet with a difficulty, it lyes in these words [Et cum attractio omnis mutua sit]. I am persuaded they are then true when the Attraction may properly

[1] See J. Edleston, *Correspondence of Sir Isaac Newton and Professor Cotes* (London, 1850), p. 153.

be so called, otherwise they may be false.[1] You will understand my meaning by an Example. Suppose two Globes *A* & *B* placed at a distance from each other upon a Table, & that whilst ye Globe *A* remaines at rest the Globe *B* is moved towards it by an invisible Hand; a by-stander who observes this motion but not the cause of it, will say that ye Globe *B* does certainly tend to the centre of ye Globe *A*, & thereupon he may call the force of the invisible hand the centripetal force of *B* & the Attraction of *A* since the effect appears the same as if it did truly proceed from a proper & real Attraction of *A*. But then I think he cannot by virtue of this Axiom [Attractio omnis mutua est] conclude contrary to his sense & Observation that the Globe *A* does also move towards the Globe *B* & will meet it at the common centre of Gravity of both bodies. This is what stops me in the train of reasoning by which I would make out as I said in a popular way Your 7th Proposition of ye iii^d Book. I shall be glad to have Your resolution of the difficulty, for such I take it to be. If it appeares so to You also, I think it should be obviated in the last Sheet of Your Book which is not yet printed off or by an *Addendum* to be printed with ye Errata Table. For till this objection be cleared I would not undertake to answer any one who should assert that You do *Hypothesim fingere*, I think You seem tacitly to make this supposition that ye Attractive force resides in the Central Body.[2]

Cotes's objection was characterized by Edleston as "an instance of the temporary haze that may occasionally obstruct the highest intellect."[3] Even it if were so – which it is not – it would, in my opinion, be a very good instance of the facility and naturalness with which Newton's conception could be misinterpreted and misunderstood by contemporaries. Thus it seems to me to be worth while to study the case somewhat more closely.

Newton's reaction to Cotes's "difficulties" is rather interesting. He first enlightens Cotes about the meaning of the word "hypothesis"; then he tells him that universal attraction is not a "hypothesis" but a truth established by induction, and that the mutual and mutually equal attraction of bodies is a case of the third fun-

---

[1] The fifth proposition of Book III of the *Principia* (p. 410) is as follows: "That the circumjovial planets gravitate towards Jupiter; the circumsaturnal towards Saturn; the circumsolar towards the sun; and by the forces of their gravity are constantly drawn off from rectilinear motions; and retained in curvilinear orbits." The proposition itself explains that the "forces upon which those revolutions depend . . . decrease in the same proportion, and according to the same law, as the force of gravity does in receding from the earth." *Corollarium 1* reads: "There is, therefore, a power of gravity tending to all the planets: for, doubtless, Venus, Mercury, and the rest, are bodies of the same sort with Jupiter and Saturn. And since all attraction (by Law III) is mutual, Jupiter will therefore gravitate towards all his own satellites, Saturn towards his, the earth towards the moon, and the sun towards all the primary planets."

[2] *Correspondence*, pp. 152 sq.

[3] *Ibid.*, p. 152, note: "The difficulty raised by Cotes here affords an instance of the temporary haze which may occasionally obscure the brightest intellects."

damental law or axiom of motion, that of the equality of action and reaction as it is explained already in the *Principia*.

S[r]

I had yo[r] of Feb 18th, & the Difficulty you mention w[ch] lies in these words [Et cum Attractio omnis mutua sit] is removed by considering that as in Geometry the word Hypothesis is not taken in so large a sense as to include the Axiomes & Postulates, so in Experimental Philosophy it is not to be taken in so large a sense as to include the first Principles or Axiomes w[ch] I call the laws of motion. These Principles are deduced from Phaenomena & made general by Induction: w[ch] is the highest evidence that a Proposition can have in this philosophy. And the word Hypothesis is here used by me to signify only such a Proposition as is not Phaenomenon nor deduced from any Phaenomena but assumed or supposed wth out any experimental proof. Now the mutual & mutually equal attraction of bodies is a branch of the third Law of motion & how this branch is deduced from Phaenomena you may see in the end of the Corollaries of y[e] Laws of Motion, pag. 22. If a body attracts another body contiguous to it & is not mutually attracted by the other: the attracted body will drive the other before it & both will go away together wth an accelerated motion in infinitum, as it were by a self moving principle, contrary to y[e] first law of motion, whereas there is no such phaenomenon in all nature.[1]

The law of the equality of action and reaction – the so-called third law – is formulated in the *Principia* as follows:

Law III. *To every action there is always opposed an equal reaction: or, the mutual actions of two bodies upon each other are always equal, and directed to contrary parts.*

Whatever draws or presses another is as much drawn or pressed by that other. If you press a stone with your finger, the finger is also pressed by the stone. If a horse draws a stone tied to a rope, the horse (if I may say so) will be equally drawn back towards the stone; for the distended rope, by the same endeavour to relax or unbend itself, will draw the horse as much towards the stone as it does the stone towards the horse and will obstruct the progress of the one as much as it advances that of the other. If a body impinge upon another, and by its force change the motion of the other, that body also (because of the equality of mutual pressure) will undergo an equal change, in its own motion, towards the contrary part. The changes made by these actions are equal, not in the velocities, but in the motions of bodies; that is to say, if the bodies are not hindered by any other impediments. For, because the motions are equally changed, the changes of velocities made towards contrary parts are inversely proportional to the bodies.[2]

---

[1] *Correspondence*, pp. 154 sq.
[2] *Mathematical Principles of Natural Philosophy*, Motte-Cajori translation (Berkeley: University of California Press, 1946), pp. 13 sq. The Latin text of the first edition is as follows (p. 13):

And in the *Scholium* to the *Axioms or Laws* Newton says:

In attractions I briefly demonstrate the thing after this manner. Suppose an obstacle is interposed to hinder the meeting of any two bodies A, B, attracting one the other: then if either body, as A, is more attracted toward the other body B, than the other body B is towards the first body A, the obstacle will be more strongly urged by the pressure of the body A than by the pressure of the body B, and therefore will not remain in equilibrium: but the stronger pressure will prevail, and will make the system of the two bodies, together with the obstacle, to move directly towards the parts on which B lies; and in free spaces, to go forward *in infinitum* with a motion continually [perpetually] accelerated; which is absurd and contrary to the first Law. For, by the first Law the system ought to continue [persevere] in its state of rest, or of moving uniformly forwards in a right line; and therefore the bodies must equally press the obstacle, and be equally attracted one by the other. I made the experiment on the loadstone and iron. If these, placed apart in proper vessels, are made to float by one another in standing water, neither of them will propel the other; but by being equally attracted, they will sustain each other's pressure, and rest at last n an equilibrium.[1]

Newton's answer to Cotes is thus simply (*a*) a statement that Cotes misunderstood him and (*b*) a suggestion that he reread, or restudy, the relevant texts of the *Principia*.

"LEX III.

"*Actioni contrariam semper & aequalem esse reactionem: sive corporum duorum actiones in se mutuo semper esse aequales & in partes contrarias dirigi.*

"Quicquid premit vel trahit alterum, tantundem ab eo premitur vel trahitur. Si quis lapidem digito premit, premitur & hujus digitus a lapide. Si equus lapidem funi alligatum trahit, retrahetur etiam & equus (ut ita dicam) aequaliter in lapidem: nam funis utrinque distentus eodem relaxandi se conatu urgebit equum versus lapidem, ac lapidem versus equum; tantumque impediet progressum unius quantum promovet progressum alterius. Si corpus aliquod in corpus aliud impingens, motum ejus vi sua quomodocunque mutaverit, idem quoque vicissim in motu proprio eandem mutationem in partem contrariam vi alterius (ob aequalitatem pressionis mutuae) subibit. His actionibus aequales fiunt mutationes, non velocitatum, sed motuum; scilicet in corporibus non aliunde impeditis. Mutationes enim velocitatum, in contrarias itidem partes factae, quia motus aequaliter mutantur, sunt corporibus reciproce proportionales."

[1] *Ibid.*, p. 25; in Latin, first edition, pp. 23 sq.:

"In Attractionibus rem sic breviter ostendo. Corporibus duobus quibusvis A. B. se mutuo trahentibus, concipe obstaculum quodvis interponi quo congressus eorum impediatur. Si corpus alterutrum A magis trahitur versus corpus alterum B, quam illud alterum B in primum A, obstaculum magis urgebitur pressione corporis A quam pressione corporis B; proindeque non manebit in aequilibrio. Praevalebit pressio fortior, facietque ut systema corporum duorum & obstaculi moveatur in directum in partes versus B, motuque in spatiis liberis semper accelerato abeat in infinitum. Quod est absurdum & Legi primae contrarium. Nam per Legem primam debebit systema perseverare in statu suo quiescendi vel movendi uniformiter in directum, proindeque corpora aequaliter urgebunt obstaculum, & idcirco aequaliter trahentur in invicem. Tentavi hoc in Magnete & Ferro. Si haec in vasculis propriis sese contingentibus seorsim posita, in aqua stagnante juxta fluitent; neutrum propellet alterum, sed aequalitate attractionis utrinque sustinebunt conatus in se mutuos, ac tandem in aequilibrio constituta quiescent."

As a matter of fact, Newton did not stop at that, and to the text of the *Principia* to which he appealed he made some additions (it is rather strange that it is not mentioned anywhere in his *Correspondence* with Cotes): to the text of the third law he added the statement: "This law takes place also in attractions as will be proved in the next *Scholium*," and in the *Scholium* itself, after the paragraph I have just quoted, he introduced the following one, in which he explained that not only magnets and iron, but also the earth and its parts mutually attract each other in full conformity with the third law:

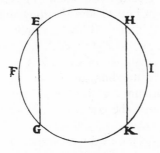

Fig. 8

So the gravitation between the Earth and its parts is mutual. Let the Earth FI [Fig. 8] be cut by any plane EG into two parts EGF and EGI and their weights one towards the other will be mutually equal. For if by another plane HK, parallel to the former EG, the greater part EGI is cut into two parts EGKH and HKI, whereof HKI is equal to the part EFG, first cut off, it is evident that the middle part EGKH will have no propension by its proper weight towards either side, but will hang as it were, and rest in an equilibrium between both. But the one extreme part HKI will with its whole weight bear upon and press the middle part towards the other extreme part EGF; and therefore the force with which EGI, the sum of the parts HKI and EGKH, tends towards the third part EGF, is equal to the weight of the part HKI, that is, to the weight of the third part EGF. And therefore the weights of the two parts EGI and EGF one towards the other are equal, as I was to prove. And indeed if those weights were not equal, the whole Earth floating in the nonresisting ether would give way to the greater weight, and, retiring from it, would be carried off *in infinitum.*[1]

[1] Motte–Cajori, p. 26; addition of the second edition (Cambridge, 1713), p. 22:
"Sic etiam gravitas inter Terram & ejus partes, mutua est. Secetur Terra F I plano quovis E G in partes duas E G F & E G I: & aequalia erunt harum pondera in se mutuo. Nam si plano allo H K quod priori E G parallelum sit, pars major E G I secetur in partes duas E G K H & H K I, quarum H K I aequalis sit parti prius abscissae E F G: manifestum est quod pars media E G K H pondere proprio in neutram partium extremarum propendebit, sed inter utramque in aequilibrio, ut ita decam, suspendetur, & quiescet. Pars autem extrema H K I toto suo pondere incumbet in partem

He also changed somewhat the wording of Prop. V[1] and added to it a corollary in which the mutual character of the attraction is once more reasserted (Cor. 3):

All the planets do gravitate towards one another by cor. 1 and 2. And hence it is that Jupiter and Saturn when near their conjunction, by their mutual attraction sensibly disturb each other's motions. So the sun disturbs the motions of the moon; and both sun and moon disturb our sea as we shall hereafter explain.[2]

Cotes did not reply to the admonition of Newton. Was he convinced? Did he recognize that he was wrong and that he had made a blunder? I do not think so. At least not quite: I think that he became convinced that he was *right*, but that, nevertheless, he made a blunder. Indeed, the reasoning of Cotes was perfectly correct (Edleston and others notwithstanding) and he was right to point out that it is only if bodies *act* upon each other – in our case if they really *attract* each other – that the law of equality of action and reaction

---

mediam, & urgebit illam in partem alteram extremam E G F; ideoque vis qua partium H K I & E G K H summa E G I tendit versus partem tertiam E G F, aequalis est ponderi partis H K I, id est ponderi partis tertiae E G F. Et propterea pondera partium duarum E G I, E G F in se mutuo sunt aequalia, uti volui ostendere. Et nisi pondera illa aequalia essent, Terra tota in libero aethere fluitans ponderi majori cederet, & ab eo fugiendo abiret in infinitum."

[1] Proposition V of Book III of the second edition (p. 365) is as follows:

"Propositio V. Theorema V

"*Planetas circumjoviales gravitare in Jovem, Circumsaturnios in Saturnum, et Circumsolares in Solem, & vi gravitatis suae retrahi semper a motibus rectilineis, & in Orbibus curvilineis retineri.*

"Nam revolutiones Planetarum Circumjovialium circa Jovem, Circumsaturniorum circa Saturnum, & Mercurii ac Veneris reliquorumque Circumsolarium circa Solem sunt Phaenomena ejusdem generis cum revolutione Lunae circa Terram; & propterea per Reg. 11 a causis ejusdem generis dependent: praesertim cum demonstratum sit quod vires, a quibus revolutiones illae dependent, respiciant centra Jovis, Saturni ac Solis, & recedendo a Jove, Saturno & Sole decrescant eadem ratione ac lege, qua vis gravitatis decrescit in recessu a Terra.

"*Corol. 1.* Gravitas igitur datur in Planetas universos. Nam Venerem, Mercurium, caeterosque esse corpora ejusdem generis cum Jove & Saturno, nemo dubitat. Et cum attractio omnis (per motus Legem tertiam) mutua sit, Jupiter in Satellites suos omnes, Saturnus in suos, Terraque in Lunam, & Sol in Planetas omnes primarios gravitabit.

"*Corol. 2.* Gravitatem, quae Planetam unumquemque respicit, esse reciproce ut quadratum distantiae locorum ab ipsius centro.

"*Corol. 3.* Graves sunt Planetae omnes in se mutuo per Corol. 1 et 2. Et hinc Jupiter & Saturnus prope conjunctionem se invicem attrahendo, sensibiliter perturbant motus mutuos, Sol perturbat motus Lunares, Sol & Luna perturbant Mare nostrum, ut in sequentibus explicabitur."

[2] *Ibid.*, p. 365; Motte–Cajori, p. 410. In his own interleaved copy of the *Principia* Newton had written, "Graves sunt Planetae omnes in se mutuo per corol. 1 et 2. Omnis enim attractio mutua est per motus legem tertiam." In the printed text the *omnis enim . . .* is left out. Indeed it only repeats what has already been stated in cor. 1.

can be applied to them.[1] He was also right in suggesting that Newton's whole reasoning is based upon this presupposition: of course, if a body "pulls" or "draws" (the Latin text says *trahit*) another it is also, and as strongly, drawn or pulled by it.[2] But if a body is only pushed toward another? The action and reaction take place between the pushing body and the pushed one, and not between this latter and the body toward which it is pushed. Their reaction is not "mutual."

That is exactly what Cotes objects to in Newton.

Let us elaborate his reasoning; let us assume, for instance, that planets are deflected from their rectilinear path and forced to move in curved lines not by a force that ties them to the sun (as a stone whirled in a sling is dragged back by the sling) but by an outside pressure, be it "a hand," or the pressure of a Cartesian, or Huygenian, vortex, or by the rush toward it of aethereal particles,[3] or by the continuous place shifting of "grosser" and more "tenuous" particles of the aether,[4] or, finally, by the action of an "elastic aether" of which the density (and therefore the pressure) increases with the distance from the sun (the "hypothesis" of Query XXI of the 2nd English edition of the *Opticks* of 1717): the planets will be pushed toward the sun; but the sun will *not* be pushed toward the planets. Thus "somebody" could, indeed, *say* that "the planets are attracted by the sun" (as Leibniz did in his *Tentamen de motuum coelestium causis*). But he would certainly be wrong to assume that this "attraction" would be "mutual." All the more so as, in the case of such – or analogous – mechanisms, we could, as Huygens has shown,[5] dispense with the sun altogether.

---

[1] The third law is somewhat tricky in its application and we must be careful not to extend it beyond its limits: dynamics (in common life *action*, and even *attraction*, are, alas, as often as not unilateral), and not forgetting that, *stricto sensu*, it implies either contiguity or immediate action at a distance. Indeed, in an action through a medium it takes place only between the contiguous parts of this medium and not between the objects (bodies) acting and acted upon.

[2] Even in this case, if the body is pushed not directly, but, say, by a stick, or pulled by a string, the application of the law is not immediate.

[3] See Newton's "Hypothesis explaining the Properties of Light, discoursed of in my several Papers" of 1675, T. Birch, *The History of the Royal Society of London* (London, 1757), III, 250 sq., reprinted in I. B. Cohen, *Isaac Newton's Papers and Letters on Natural Philosophy* (Cambridge, Massachusetts: Harvard University Press, 1958), pp. 180 sq.

[4] See the letter to Boyle of 28 February 1678/9, Cohen, *Newton's Papers and Letters*, pp. 250 sq.; *Correspondence*, II, 288 sq., and letter to Halley, 27 July 1686, *Correspondence*, II, 446 sq.

[5] See his *Discours sur la cause de la pesanteur*, published as an appendix to his *Traité de la lumière* (Leiden, 1690), *Oeuvres complètes*, vol. XXI.

Newton tells us that he had made experiments with magnets and iron, and thus demonstrated that the law of equality of action and reaction is valid in the case of magnetic attraction. From this he can rightly conclude that magnets really "act" upon iron or, in Cotes's terms, that we have here a case of attraction "properly so called." This, indeed, is extremely important: it excludes from the field of magnetism the kind of unilateral action, which was thought possible even by Gilbert and Kepler, by which the terrestrial magnet attracted iron without being attracted by it, or the sun attracted and repulsed planets without being affected itself by this action.

As a matter of fact Newton could have asserted that this "attraction" was mutual – and equal – even without having performed his experiment: we can hardly assume that a magnet "drags" a piece of iron toward itself without at the same time "tending" toward that piece of iron. On the other hand, it is just the unilateral character of this "tending" that is excluded by the subjection of magnetism to the third law.

The case of the earth alleged in the second edition of the *Principia* is already somewhat more difficult. Of course, *if* the earth holds together by "attracting" its parts, this "gravitation" will not be a unilateral action or a "tendency" of these parts toward the whole, but a mutual action: and the earth and its parts will have "gravity" or "weight" toward each other. But from the fact that the earth (*a*) does hold together and (*b*) does not run away into space with ever-increasing speed, we can hardly conclude that it is really held together by such an attraction. Could it not be pressed together by an external action?

As for the planets, their case is obviously completely different; we do not even know whether they are *really* "attracting" each other – attraction, according to Newton's repeated assertions, may be *really* pressure, or whatever else – we only know that they are subjected to centripetal forces. To assert that these forces are "mutual," because *omnis attractio* is such and obeys the third law is, obviously, to beg the question, or, even worse, to commit a *petitio principii*.

Yet we can hardly ascribe to Newton such an elementary fallacy: we have, therefore, to try to explain his reasoning in some other way. But the only way to do it – at least so it seems to me – is to admit that for Newton "attraction," all the pseudo positivistic and agnostic talk notwithstanding, was a real force (though not a mechanical and perhaps not even a "physical" one) by which bodies really *acted* upon each other (though not immediately through a void, but by means of an *immaterial* link or medium), and that this "force" was somehow located in, or connected with, these bodies and was also dependent on, or proportional to, their masses. In other words, as Cotes put it, this attraction was "properly so called."

The only error that Cotes committed was to assume that this conception was an (unconscious or tacit) "hypothesis" made by Newton in order to permit him to subject that "attraction" to the provisions of the third law, whereas for Newton – as he tells Cotes, and as he tells also in the third *Regula philosophandi* of the second edition of the *Principia*, as well as in the *Scholium generale* of the same – attraction is an experimentally or, better, empirically ascertained and demonstrated fact (of which only the cause is unknown) and by no means a hypothesis.

Cotes seems to have understood it perfectly well: he blundered in treating attraction as a "supposition." Thus he became convinced, or confirmed in his conviction, that attraction was, as a matter of fact, a property of body, and even a primordial one. Accordingly, he said so in his preface. At first he even overshot the mark and wrote that gravity (attractive power) was an *essential* property of body. This was an obvious error[1] for which he was taken to task by Clarke, to whom he submitted the draft of his preface.[2] He answered that he did not mean "essential" to be taken in the full sense of the term; he only wanted to indicate that, as we do not know what matter really is, we may ascribe to it all kinds of properties, namely, all those that, by experience, we learn it possesses:

Sir: I return you my thanks for Your corrections of the Preface, & particularly for Your advice in relation to that place where I seem'd to assert Gravity to be Essential to Bodies. I am fully of Your mind that it would have furnish'd matter for Cavilling and therefore I struck it out immediately upon Dr Cannon's mentioning Your Objection to me, & so it never was printed. My design in that passage was not to assert Gravity to be essential to Matter, but rather to assert that we are ignorant of the Essential properties of Matter & that in respect to our Knowledge Gravity may possibly lay as fair a claim to that Title as the other Propertys which

[1] It is rather clear that, as long as one remains a partisan of atomism and "mechanical philosophy," that is, as long as one considers matter to be nothing else than something that "entirely and adequately" "fills" space, it is impossible to include forces – repulsive any more than attractive – in the essence of body, which is then fully determined by extension, impenetrability, hardness, mobility, and inertia. Or, if one prefers, the only "force" that can be included in it is the (pseudo) force of inertia.

[2] Clarke's letter has not been preserved and one can only infer its contents from Cotes's answer.

I mention'd. For I understand by Essential Propertys such propertys without which no other belonging to the same substance can exist: and I would not undertake to prove that it were impossible for any of the other Propertys of Bodies to exist without even Extension (Cambridge, June 25, 1713).[1]

Whereupon he corrected his text, and, like Dr. Cheyne some years before,[2] stated that attractive power was a *primordial* property of body: *Inter primarias qualitates corporum universorum vel Gravitas habebit locum, vel Extensio, Mobilitas et Impenetrabilitas non habebit.*

[1] See Edleston, *Correspondence*, p. 158. Newton shared this view, which, by the way, was the traditional one. Thus, in the General Scholium (an addition to the second edition of the *Principia*) he wrote (p. 546 of the Motte–Cajori translation): "What the real substance of anything is we know not. In bodies we see only their figures and colours, we hear only the sounds, we touch only their curved surfaces, we smell only the smells, and taste the savours; but their inward substances are not to be known either by our senses; or by any reflex act of our minds." In the unpublished drafts of this passage he went even further; see A. R. Hall and M. B. Hall, *Unpublished Scientific Papers of Sir Isaac Newton in the Portsmouth Collection, Cambridge University Library* (Cambridge, England: Cambridge University Press, 1962), pp. 356 sq.: "Substantias rerum non cognoscimus. Nullas habemus earum ideas. Ex phenomenis colligimus earum proprietates solas & ex proprietatibus quod sint substantiae. Corpora se mutuo non penetrare colligimus ex solis phaenomenis: substantias diversi generis se mutuo non penetrare ex phaenomenis minime constat. Et quod ex phaenominis minime colligitur temere affirmari non debet.

"Ex phaenomenis cognoscimus proprietates rerum & ex proprietatibus colligimus res ipsas extare easque vocamus substantias sed ideas substantiarum non magis habemus quam caecus ideas colorum . . .

"Ideas habemus attributorum ejus sed quid sit rei alicujus substantia minime cognoscimus."

[2] Dr. George Cheyne, *Philosophical Principles of Religion: Natural and Reveal'd* (London, 1715–1716), p. 41: "*Attraction* or *Gravitation* is not *essential* to Matter but seems rather an *original Impress* which continues in it by virtue of the Omnipotent Activity, in the *Divine Nature* of which it is a *Copy* or *Image* in the low Degree suitable to a gross creature and so may be now reckon'd among the primary Qualities of Matter, without which, as it is now constituted Matter cannot be." Dr. Cheyne added (p. 42) that it could not be explained mechanically. See also J. Rohault, *System of Natural Philosophy, illustrated with Dr. Samuel Clarke's Notes; taken mostly out of Sir Isaac Newton's Philosophy* (London, 1723), II, 96 (part II, chap. XXVIII, note 12): "Gravity or the weight of Bodies is not any accidental Effect of motion or of any very subtile Matter, but an original and general Law of all Matter impressed upon it by God, and maintained in it perpetually by some efficient Power, which penetrates the solid Substance of it Wherefore we aught no more to inquire how Bodies gravitate than how Bodies began first to be moved. Hence it follows, that there is really *a Vacuum* in Nature."

Index